How the Soviet Jew Was Made

How the Soviet Jew Was Made

Sasha Senderovich

HARVARD UNIVERSITY PRESS

Cambridge, Massachusetts
London, England
2022

First printing

Library of Congress Cataloging-in-Publication Data

Names: Senderovich, Sasha, author.
Title: How the Soviet Jew was made / Sasha Senderovich.
Description: Cambridge, Massachusetts : Harvard University Press, 2022. |
    Includes bibliographical references and index.
Identifiers: LCCN 2021048963 | ISBN 9780674238190 (cloth)
Subjects: LCSH: Jews in popular culture—Soviet Union. | Jews in
    literature. | Jews in motion pictures. | Russian literature—Jewish authors—
    20th century. | Yiddish literature—Soviet Union. | Jews—Soviet Union—
    History. | Wandering Jew in literature.
Classification: LCC DS134.85 .S46 2022 | DDC 305.892/4047—dc23/eng/20220127
LC record available at https://lccn.loc.gov/2021048963

For Liora

Contents

Note on Transliteration and Translation

In transliterating Russian-language sources, I have relied primarily on Library of Congress rules; I have done the same for occasional transliterations of Hebrew. In transliterating Yiddish-language sources, I generally followed the guidelines of the YIVO Institute. When following these standards to the letter would have meant "correcting" the somewhat more idiosyncratic ways in which authors titled their own works, I stuck to the authors' idiosyncrasies (so, the work discussed in Chapter 1 is *Mides-hadin* and the work in Chapter 5 is "Shabos-nakhamu"). Occasionally I deal with Yiddish sources that were translated into Russian, and vice versa, where the names of authors don't always entirely line up across languages. I deviated somewhat from both Library of Congress and YIVO guidelines when certain words, especially personal names, have spellings that are familiar to English-language readers (for example, Bergelson is David, not Dovid, and Babel is Isaac, not Isaak).

The question of how to refer to place names in a book that contends with the legacy of the multiethnic and multilingual territory once known as the Pale of Settlement is a conundrum familiar to all scholars dealing with this part of the world. I primarily used Russified spellings, because that is how they appeared in both the Russian and the Yiddish sources I work with. On occasions when it was important to note a given place name in the official language of the political entity that ruled it at the time—including on the map, which notes state borders in the interwar period—I followed such spellings. Whenever a place name had an internationally recognized name familiar to the English-language reader, I opted for such usage: for example, Moscow, rather than Moskva (Russian) or Moskve (Yiddish), and Vilna (in the interwar period, Wilno, Poland), rather than Vil'na.

Unless otherwise noted, all translations from Russian and Yiddish are my own. All translations from Bergelson's *Judgment* in Chapter 1, unless otherwise noted, are the product of my collaborative work with Harriet Murav. Translations that are not my own are, on occasion, modified by me and are noted accordingly.

USSR with national borders as of 1922. Inset: Western borderlands of USSR, 1922–1939. Shaded area on both indicates pre-1917 Imperial Russia's Pale of Settlement.

Pale of Settlement before 1917

Railroad

USSR border (1922)

Baltic Sea

LATVIA

• Riga

• Moscow

LITHUANIA

• Kaunas

• Smorgon

Wilno
(Vilna)

• Logoisk

EAST
PRUSSIA

• Minsk

U S S R

BELORUSSIAN
SSR

• Warsaw

P O L A N D

• Chernigov

• Chernobyl

• Ostyor

• Kharkov

• Równe

Zhitomir

• Kiev

• Dubno

• Shepetovka

• Ostropol

Dnieper R.

• Lwów

• Medzhibozh

Vinnitsa

UKRAINIAN
SSR

CZECHOSLOVAKIA

Dniester R.

• Balta

HUNGARY

• Odessa

ROMANIA

CRIMEA
(RUSSIAN SFSR)

Black Sea

Sakhalin Island

Lake Baikal Chita

Amur

• Birobidzhan

• Khabarovsk

MANCHURIA

• Harbin

JAPAN

• Vladivostok

Sea of
Japan

OUTER MONGOLIA

KOREA

C H I N A

Yellow
Sea

0   500 miles

1000 km

Introduction

Dispersion of the Pale

In Isaac Babel's 1932 short story "The End of the Almshouse," set in Odessa during the period of violent unrest between 1918 and 1921 that came to be known as the Russian civil war, the Bolsheviks expel a group of old Jews from a poorhouse located on the grounds of one of the city's Jewish cemeteries. The poorhouse was a charitable institution of the sort that had made Jews in the Russian Empire a self-functioning communal entity prior to 1917, when the tsarist regime fell in February and Lenin's Bolsheviks seized power in October.[1] Now, with the dissolution of those community structures, the elderly become displaced. "The heat tormented the heap of rags that was dragging itself across the earth," the narrator notes in the story's final lines. "Their road lay along a joyless, scorched and stony highway past wattle-and-daub shanties, past fields choked by stones, past bombed-out houses, past the Plague Hill. Once upon a time in Odessa this inexpressibly melancholy road had led from the town to the cemetery."[2] Jolted out of place by the upheaval of the revolution and no longer able to live out their days in peace, the elderly Jews find themselves on the road.

This road—stretching past buildings recently ravaged by violence and alongside the century-old burial mound that contains the bodies of victims of a much earlier disaster, Odessa's 1812 plague epidemic—is said to have "once upon a time [*kogda-to*]" linked the city with the cemetery.[3] Indicating "1920–1929" as the time span of composition at the bottom of the text, Babel published "The End of the Almshouse" in 1932, more than a decade after the events described in it. In the story, the road appears suspended in time and place, as though no longer leading where it once did. Moreover, "their road [*doroga ikh*]"—or, given another meaning of the noun in Russian, "the journey

1

of theirs"—is not just a physical space, which the writer calls a "highway [*shosse*]" in the same sentence, but also the displaced Jews' trajectory to destinations unknown. As the story's language turns the group of older Jews into a "heap of rags [*grudu lokhmotiev*]," the people begin to resemble their disintegrating clothes, reminders of a faraway past that manage to persist.[4]

What happened to Babel's "heap of rags," last seen moving along a road and suspended out of time? Perplexed by the open-ended conclusion of "The End of the Almshouse," I began to follow the remnants of a once-rooted culture scattered across the landscape of Bolshevik Russia and, after its formation in 1922, the Soviet Union in the first two decades after the revolution. I traced this proverbial "heap of rags," defined by its many idiosyncrasies, as it was dispersed from its origin points in Ashkenazi Jewish communities of the Russian Empire's western borderlands and through its subsequent encounters with the USSR's stated ideological and cultural program: building the world's first multiethnic society united by the common aim of equality under communism.[5] I came to understand the "heap of rags" here not as a pejorative term but as a shorthand for the collection of habits, practices, and cultural tropes, associated with the defunct empire's Ashkenazi Jews, that were upended by the revolution but did not remain behind and die off in the old world.[6] Instead, personal characteristics, worn-out possessions, disaggregated bits of culture, and uprooted customs carried on across the landscape of the Soviet experience. Along the way, these bits of culture encountered and were modified by new ideological messages and structural pressures. The Soviet Jew—the layered, indeterminate, and fluid figure that emerged from this alchemy—remained in perpetual motion. This book outlines this figure's contours.

Between the end of the eighteenth century and the demise of the Russian monarchy in February 1917, Jews could not reside outside the Russian Empire's western borderlands, known as the Pale of Settlement.[7] Moreover, they were barred from most larger cities inside the Pale with some exceptions, which included Odessa, the Black Sea port at the Pale's southern end, and Vilna, not far from the coast of the Baltic Sea in the north. A small number of Jews in nineteenth-century Russia, because they held professional affiliations as merchants and lawyers, did qualify for a broader range of residential options outside the Pale, including in the imperial capital of Saint Petersburg and in other major cities.[8] The mobility of Jews within the Pale—and, by skirting imperial laws, beyond it—increased with the construction of railroads at the turn of the twentieth century.[9] With the outbreak of violent pogroms and the passage of anti-Jewish laws following the assassination of Tsar Alexander II in 1881, hundreds of thousands of Jews began making their way out of the Russian Empire. They formed communities in North and South America, Palestine, and other places, which could be described as diasporic in relation to the émigrés' places of origin in the Pale.[10] Even with the departure of two million Jewish migrants from Eastern Europe between the 1880s and the 1920s, more than three million Jews remained, for most of the interwar period, in those areas of the Pale that would become parts of the Soviet Union.[11] And on the eve of the Second World War, almost a million and a half Jews—nearly half of all Jews in the USSR—lived in parts of the country, primarily in major cities, that had been off-limits to them prior to 1917; the vast majority were first-generation residents there.[12]

The abolition of the Pale of Settlement in February 1917 by the Provisional Government and Lenin's subsequent seizure of power in October of that year prompted an unprecedented wave of Jewish mobility. Large numbers of Jews fled the violence of the civil war that enveloped the territories of the former Pale for Western Europe, Palestine, and North America as well as for other areas of the new Bolshevik state, including those far away from their places of origin.[13] Some of those who had earlier left Russia chose to move back. Some aspects of the Jews' movements inside the new Bolshevik state mirrored those of other populations, including Russian peasants, who also were beginning the process of becoming Soviet citizens in a rapidly modernizing and industrializing society. Jews, like members of many other groups, relocated from the provinces to larger urban centers for new professional opportunities.[14] Beginning in the late 1920s, the era of the country's industrialization, some migrated to sites of massive construction projects.[15] "Most of the Jews who stayed in revolutionary Russia did not stay at home," writes Yuri Slezkine, comparing Jews with other groups who migrated from the provinces to urban centers after 1917: "they moved to Kiev, Kharkov, Leningrad, and Moscow, and they moved up the Soviet social ladder once they got there."[16]

The figure of the Soviet Jew was a product of this broader mobility of the postrevolutionary era. Its contours were defined at the intersection of practices of Judaism both active and defunct—unique customs or their remnants that were expressed in rich folkways of Jewish life in the former Pale—and the experience and historical memory contained in and shaped by Yiddish, a Jewish language that continued to exert its linguistic pull even as Russian became the dominant tongue of the USSR's Jews. The process by which the somewhat nebulous contours of the Soviet Jew came into focus is the subject of this book. It traces multiple types of literary and cinematic protagonists whose journeys shed light on the experience of Ashkenazi Jews during the first two decades of the Soviet era. Refugees and displaced persons left the Pale of Settlement to flee the anti-Jewish violence of the Russian civil war or to answer the calls of ideology, economic need, or aspiration.[17] Most Jews who moved beyond the Pale had come from shtetls (in Yiddish, the word *shtetl* means "small city"), a unique ecosystem whose culture and customs had developed over generations.[18] Some joined Jews returning to the USSR from abroad, where they had gone to flee the tsarist regime's antisemitic violence, newly compelled by both the USSR's official dedication to fighting antisemitism and the socialist promise the Soviet state represented as the Great Depression hit the capitalist countries where they resided. Others moved about within expanding Soviet metropolises, which swallowed up Jewish enclaves as public transit networks and electric grids proliferated. Still others went much farther away, to a distant corner of Siberia that Stalin's government set aside for Jewish settlement, which was meant to transform Jews from shtetl middlemen and small-scale traders to agriculturalists.[19] Sometimes Jews didn't physically move anywhere at all but instead saw the borders of new nation-states cut violently and traumatically across the familiar lines of their lives and livelihoods in the former Pale. No single trajectory on its own characterizes the emergent figure of the Soviet Jew, and its making must be reconstructed across multiple intertwined and indeterminate vectors during the first two decades after the revolution.

The period that this book considers begins with the dissolution of the Pale of Settlement in 1917. The Russian monarchy had collapsed in February of that year due to internal pressures exacerbated by the country's involvement in the First World War; the Bolshevik Revolution and the violence of the Russian civil war soon followed.[20] This study concludes at the end of the 1930s, by which time Jews still residing in the geographic area of the former Pale faced another upheaval when the Soviet Army occupied parts of Poland and the Baltic countries of Latvia, Lithuania, and Estonia and incorporated them into the USSR. The Soviet occupation of these territories, which brought significant new

Jewish populations under Soviet control, took place in accordance with the secret protocols of the nonaggression agreement signed in August 1939 by the foreign ministers of the USSR and Nazi Germany. The Molotov-Ribbentrop Pact, which Nazi Germany would soon violate with its invasion of the USSR in June 1941, laid the groundwork for further displacement of Jews into the Soviet interior—as far as the Ural Mountains and Central Asia—and also for their extermination during the Second World War in the territories that Timothy Snyder has called the "bloodlands" of Eastern Europe.[21] Less a definitive historical type than a suggestive and sometimes contradictory cultural outline drawn both from experience and reflections on that experience, the figure of the Soviet Jew that emerged via the geographic and cultural routes of the interwar period would persist through the twentieth century and into the twenty-first, both in Soviet and post-Soviet culture and beyond.

Indeed, the figure of the "Soviet Jew" as such would become prominent only decades after its formation. During the Cold War, Jews in the United States and other Western countries rallied to the cause of "saving Soviet Jews," as the slogan at the time had it, referring to advocacy on behalf of Jews who wished to emigrate from the USSR between the 1960s and the early 1990s.[22] The term, as well as variants like "Soviet Jewish" and "Soviet Jewry," remain in use to this day as ways of referring to Jews from the former USSR who reside in states such as Russia, Ukraine, Belarus, and Lithuania, as well as in immigrant communities in the United States, Canada, Israel and the Occupied Palestinian Territories, Germany, and elsewhere. The term is also used retrospectively to refer to Jews who once resided in the USSR itself. The term "Soviet Jew" in English, however, does not correspond neatly to a single set phrase in Russian to refer to Jews in the USSR during the Soviet era. The Russian noun *evrei*, which was used, including for bureaucratic and statistical purposes, to refer to Jews as members of an ethnic group, did not carry the modifier *sovetskii*, because every ethnic group within the USSR was, by default, a Soviet one. "Soviet Jew" is thus a descriptor used historically by those looking in from the outside, whether spatially or temporally.

Because I write this book in English, I use the term mindful of both its history and its subsequent resonances for readers in the English-speaking world. The Soviet Jew—a figure who would be cast in a geopolitical play involving the superpowers after the Second World War—in fact came into existence some decades earlier, at the dawn of the Soviet era. To put it another way, this book offers a kind of cultural prehistory of the Soviet Jew as a figure that would become familiar to the English-language reader as one of the central rallying causes of the more recent Jewish experience, particularly in North America in the second half of the twentieth century.[23] The Soviet Jew that I'm interested in preceded the figure of the Soviet Jew of the Western imagination, which came to be defined by its ambivalence toward traditional Jewish religious and cultural practices and was constituted by what the political scientist Zvi Y. Gitelman has referred to, dismissively, as "thin culture."[24] This book is about the Soviet Jew imagined within Soviet culture *before* it became a figure that needed to be "saved" and reunited with expressions of Jewish identity legible to Jews in the West.[25]

The figure of the Soviet Jew I explore in this book was consistently depicted as male. Though there are female protagonists and many things to say—as I will—about questions pertaining to gender in the texts under consideration in this book, the characters who embody the tropes associated with the emergent Soviet Jew are universally male. The figuring of the iconic Jew as male dates to the earliest Israelite and Jewish texts, which reflected assumptions about gender and group representation shared across traditions. The equation between Jew and male is most prominently reflected in the conception of male circumcision—a topic I discuss in this book—as *the* marker of Jewishness, leading the biblical scholar Shaye J. D. Cohen to ask, provocatively, whether and to what extent women can be considered Jews.[26] In Christian Europe, both Catholic and Orthodox, circumcision became another marker of the Jew's refusal to accept Christ, a primordial act that destined him to wander for eternity; the Wandering Jew—a mythic figure of the European imagination that I discuss as well—is a wandering male Jew.[27] Not surprisingly, as circumcision became increasingly uncommon in the latter half of the Soviet period, its absence figured prominently in Western and Israeli Jews' expressions of doubt about the very Jewishness of men from the USSR—and of the Soviet Jew.

The image of the Soviet Jew drew on these symbolic Christian prototypes, but in the context of a discourse, by then well developed, about Jews' capacity for inclusion as minority citizens in emerging nation-states. Russia granted Jews equal citizenship in 1917 after the February Revolution, and the Bolsheviks subsequently maintained these rights. By the time Russia enfranchised its Jewish population, multiple other European empires and states had grappled with the question of Jewish fitness for inclusion, both before and after formally emancipating them. These discourses, characteristic of the Berlin Haskalah—the Hebrew term "Haskalah" is commonly translated as "the Jewish Enlightenment"—and then its later counterparts in the Austro-Hungarian territory of Galicia and in the Pale of Settlement, understood fitness not only spiritually or psychologically but also physically and conceived of it always in terms that were gendered male. Such a trend drew on the emphasis on the symbol of the young virile man by multiple national movements, including imperial nationalisms in newly centralized states. In Berlin, the eighteenth-century biblical scholar Johann David Michaelis questioned whether the Jew, imagined as a Jewish man, was physically suited for military service given his stereotypically short stature. In Austria, Joseph II emancipated Jews in 1782 on the condition that they be encouraged to engage in productive labor and display their masculine fortitude in agriculture rather than in the rabbinic study hall.[28] In the large Jewish German-speaking and German-reading sphere, which extended eastward beyond the German lands, Jewish proponents of modernization (*maskilim*) expressed growing anxiety about the association of Jews (again, Jewish men) with physical weakness, femininity, and homosexuality. Jewish modernization movements of multiple political orientations—from Socialist to Zionist to Liberal—put physical fitness and the remasculinizing of Jewish men at the top of their organizational priorities.[29]

The Zionist leader and social critic Max Nordau's 1892 treatise on Jewish degeneration became the clarion call for Zionists to create a new type of "muscular Judaism" that would prove the Jews' national fitness to the doubting, implicitly non-Jewish public.[30] The poorer, more religious populations of the Pale of Settlement were the implicit targets of these Western and Central European campaigns, even as their reach remained limited to more educated, urban Jewish communities. By the time of the Bolshevik Revolution, then, the Pale had already been configured as a degenerate space, and Jewish thinkers had already articulated a desire to reform it through a process of masculinization. When the Bolsheviks, building on the aesthetics of manliness prevalent both within a range of Russian modernist movements and in Bolshevik mythology, constructed their own variant of the masculine national figure in the guise of the New Soviet Man, they were adapting an older European discourse and, implicitly, casting the male Jew from the Pale as one of its opposites and, on occasion, its foil.[31]

The Soviet Jew I trace in novels, short stories, literary sketches, and films, and through the larger historical and cultural contexts in which they were produced and circulated, is a deeply ambivalent figure. Protagonists who embody and thus shape it run headlong into, but also evade, the ideological expectations of what a Jew in the USSR was supposed to become, especially as these expectations were articulated in a string of official pronouncements during the first two decades after the revolution. The figure of the Soviet Jew is shaped and reshaped by these encounters with various aspects of Sovietness—itself a category in the making that shaped different groups of people according to its evolving logics and rules. A figure in the process of formation, the Soviet Jew speaks to a deeper reality of cultural and political ambivalence during and regarding the early years of the Soviet project. Just as the trajectory of Isaac Babel's fictional old Jews remained indeterminate, so too did the trajectory of the revolution: the Soviet Jew is thus a figure of indeterminacy that emerged from within the Soviet project, was defined by it, and, on occasion, defined it in turn.

* * *

The conflict that resulted in the expulsion of the elderly Jews from the poorhouse in Babel's "The End of the Almshouse" was, broadly speaking, a showdown between the old and the new. Such seemingly Manichean oppositions characterized many depictions of the revolutionary era's social, economic, and intellectual upheavals and the resultant cultural and generational shifts. On one side of the Jewish instantiation of this larger conflict were Jews whose traditional life and ritual practices did not befit the revolutionary age. These Jews had traditional-appearing lifestyles and practices that could be attacked or dismissed by a militantly atheistic new regime that saw all religious practice as backward.[32] On the other side of this conflict were Jews of a purportedly new type who had participated in the making of the revolution or were buoyed by it.

In "The End of the Almshouse," one of several stories in which Babel invented the literary myth of his native Odessa, the writer plays up an apparent conflict of this kind.[33] During this time of economic devastation, material deprivation, and famine, the Jewish elderly from the poorhouse at the cemetery had taken possession of a coffin. They survive on proceeds from leasing the coffin to bereaved families of modest means. In free-thinking Odessa, the story's narrator relates, the upwardly mobile Jews had taken up the non-Jews' practices of burying the dead in coffins, but a timber shortage made it difficult to maintain this practice. Sensing an opportunity, the Jews from the poorhouse appointed themselves as self-righteous guardians of the traditional—but already forgotten—Jewish custom of using only burial shrouds.[34] "The rented coffin did not stand idle," the narrator comments. "The deceased lay in the oak box at home and at the service; he was lowered into the grave in nothing but a shroud. This was done according to a forgotten Jewish law."[35] Babel's elderly Jews are guided by an overwhelming concern with their own survival rather than by their desire to uphold Judaism's ritual laws: they pass themselves off as traditional Jews to enable their ongoing enterprise with the coffin. But when a group of Bolsheviks bury a fallen Jewish comrade, the elderly Jews are forced to entomb the man inside the priceless casket. They are told that the deceased's bravery and his long-term membership in the Party had earned him the privilege not to be, as the Bolsheviks see it, simply dumped in the ground. The Bolsheviks are unimpressed by traditions upheld by people who are their fallen comrade's ethnocultural—but not ideological—brethren. The Jewish elderly thus lose access to their livelihood.

The elderly Jews then turn to Broydin, the cemetery's Jewish director, requesting that he supply them with wood for a new coffin, but he refuses: "'There are people,' Broydin thundered, hearing nothing, 'who are worse off than you, and there are thousands upon thousands of people who are worse off than the ones who are worse off than you.'"[36] Broydin—a former tailor elevated to his position by the new regime and openly grateful to it—places what he sees as his duty as a Bolshevik over the needs of the Jewish elderly. In denying their pleas, he assesses their request against the more dire needs of other people elsewhere in the country. In a sense, Babel's old folk evoke some of the antisemitic caricatures of deceitful Jews from Russian literary history. Works by classic authors like Gogol, Dostoevsky, and Chekhov are steeped in antisemitic stereotypes rooted both in Western cultural sources and in Russian Orthodox liturgy.[37] In "The End of the Almshouse," Babel playfully engages such tropes but also calls them into question by locating the old Jews' grotesquely self-serving behavior within the dire threat to their physical survival. In contrast, the Bolshevik hero who is honorably buried in the old Jews' prized coffin serves as a kind of model—or, given Babel's penchant for satire, a caricature of a model—for what Jews should have aspired to become after the revolution. The cemetery's director—a Jew in whom the revolution has vested its authority—puts the older Jews in their ideologically determined place by denying them special privileges based on a shared ethno-cultural heritage and instead elevates Bolshevism itself to an article of faith. The old Jews, who make their living from an ancient rite retooled to meet their pressing needs of survival, now appear as decrepit figures desperately grasping onto antiquated customs.

From the outlines of Isaac Babel's short story, four implications arise for the study of the figure of the Soviet Jew. First, the emergent Soviet Jew is neither the ideologically laden New Soviet Man nor the Jewish Bolshevik. Scholars of literary texts that focused, in whole or in part, on Jews after the revolution have commented on the subgroup of Jews buoyed by Soviet power and on the figure of the heroic Jewish Bolshevik as a distinct type.[38] In the years immediately following the revolution, a minor but noticeable procession of fictionalized Jewish Bolsheviks emerged in literary works; as Soviet culture moved into the Stalin era, this type became but one variant of the extensively studied figure of the New Soviet Man.[39] The Jewish Bolshevik as a cultural phenomenon reflected an historical fact: Jews participated in notable ways in revolutionary movements and, subsequently, in Soviet military, government, and civil service. Broydin, the cemetery director in "The End of the Almshouse," is representative of countless administrators within the Soviet bureaucracy who happened to be Jews. By the same token, the figure of the Jewish Bolshevik—with Leon Trotsky, who founded the Red Army, as its most famous exemplar—was also a source of antisemitic propaganda that contributed to the persistent myth of Judeo-Bolshevism. A set of conspiracy theories, Judeo-Bolshevism made revolutionary agendas synonymous with the purported dangers of global domination by nefarious Jewish interests. It was deployed by a range of anti-Bolshevik forces during the Russian civil war and in interwar Europe, and then through the rise to power of the Nazi and other fascist governments.[40] The Jewishness of these protagonists was notable precisely because of the Bolsheviks' commitment to internationalism and their official opposition to antisemitism, which they viewed as a remnant of the unenlightened *ancién regime*.[41] But although some Jews sought and found positions of influence within the Soviet government, military, civil service, and culture, most did not. My interest is not in the USSR's Jews as figures of ideological integration into Bolshevism or as "Mercurians" whom the revolution propelled out of the old world of the Pale into what Yuri Slezkine has termed "the Jewish century."[42] The figure of the Soviet Jew is not a composite of historical individuals defined by facts of biography and ethnic origin but rather a cultural type whose distinctive markings are more elusive and harder to track. These features, which unfold across this book's chapters, are visible through issues of translation, displacement, memory, and language within novels, literary sketches, and films.

Second, the Soviet Jew carries and continuously reinterprets traces of the Pale of Settlement without either "preserving" the "authentic" culture of the Pale or "abandoning" it in search of Bolshevik integration. In "The End of the Almshouse," the Jewish Bolshevik laid to rest by a posse of his Jewish and non-Jewish comrades is not Isaac Babel's main protagonist. Rather, the writer focuses on the elderly Jews who conduct the fallen man's burial. My interest centers on what happens to them when they lose their shelter and are shuttled toward the Soviet project, which may not welcome them and which they may be able to join only partially. Pitted against the Jewish Bolshevik and the Jewish bureaucrat elevated by the revolution, the figure of the old Jew has proven significant in the field of literary studies. Scholars have commented on echoes of the prerevolutionary Jewish world in the imagination of Soviet-era authors and, as Alice Nakhimovsky has put it, in "literature written in Russian by writers of Jewish origin [that] reflects on the changing problems of the Russian-Jewish identity."[43] Writers, usually referred to in English-language criticism as Russian-Jewish, have been studied with an emphasis on how they felt torn between revulsion at and nostalgia for what had long been left behind in the world associated with the Pale.[44] The figure of the old Jew and his "Judaic chaos [*khaos iudeiskii*]," as the poet Osip Mandelshtam famously wrote—together with his dusty prayer books and religious folios—sparked a good deal of reflection among Jewish writers who had left that cultural environment behind.[45] Scholars have studied the unceasing gravitational pull of the intricacies of the old world on the identities of and the literary characters created by some of the notable writers, poets, photographers, and filmmakers who came to be identified as exponents of Russian-Jewish culture during the Soviet era.[46] This gravitational pull, however, did not exist merely along the binary of revulsion and nostalgia—rather, it inflected and transformed those under its sway and the figure of the Soviet Jew itself.

Third, while tracing the figure of the Soviet Jew across the first two decades of the Soviet period, this book departs from the work of scholars who have focused either on the Jewish identities of creators of literary works, their protagonists, or on the process of identity formation as such. In her now-classic monograph on Russian-Jewish literature, Alice Nakhimovsky defined the subject of her research as "any Russian-language writer of Jewish origin for whom the question of Jewish identity is, on some level, compelling."[47] Central to this definition is the category of identity and the assumed opposition between "Russian" as a linguistic medium and literary tradition and "Jewish" as an enduring ethnoreligious identity category. Thus framed, Russian-Jewish literature is always involved in a kind of complicated balancing act. On the other hand, some literary criticism has focused on identity formation as a process by which authors or their protagonists uneasily blend "Russianness" and "Jewishness." Some scholars have seen their role as highlighting, as Maxim D. Shrayer has put it, "how much of the Judaic heritage is captured and preserved in [their] pages," even and especially when an initial reading of texts "published in the literary [i.e. Russian] mainstream reveals only superficially Jewish references."[48] This formulation reifies the "Jewish" content of Russian-Jewish cultural output as a fixed and limited set of markers submerged (but findable) within a text. Such a focus on "Judaic heritage" means that Jewish religious tradition, even when no longer practiced, remains the central point of reference in discussions of "Jewishness." This formulation can be misleading because it can obscure—or lead a critic to overlook—Jewish experiences that are neither motivated by "Judaic heritage" nor defined in relation to religious observance. A focus on identity that prioritizes "Judaic heritage" is also hard to square with the fact that a good deal of prerevolutionary Jewish creative expression, including much of the modern Yiddish literary project that had begun to develop in the Russian Empire, had been channeled through a "secular" idiom that formed its own point of reference for subsequent cultural production. "Judaic heritage," although seemingly an obvious measuring stick for determining what might be considered a work of Jewish literary expression, proves limiting when the object of interest is the Soviet Jew as a cultural figure.

I follow in the footsteps of scholars who have suggested shifting our focus from the Jewish identities of writers and their protagonists toward questions that arise from the literary qualities of texts and the intertextual relations between different works of culture. Alliteration, prosody, sentence structure, and, in the case of films, gesture and sound—in other words, the nuts and bolts of what makes creative works what they are—can point to rich palimpsests of cultural memory. Harriet Murav has noted that framing the question of identity around the search for markers of ethnoreligious distinction is tantamount to approaching the subject "with a fixed template of what Jews and Jewishness are," which, in turn "precludes the discovery of anything new." "Assumptions about Jewishness." she argues, "must be suspended in order to discover the meanings and associations of this term,"—particularly in the context of the Soviet experiment, in which the meaning of Jewishness was redefined more than once.[49]

Amelia Glaser has written on the works of interwar Communist Party-aligned Yiddish poets, in the Soviet Union and elsewhere, who were devoted to the struggles of non-Jewish ethnic groups, including Black people in the United States and Ukrainians in the USSR. Glaser identifies this body of work as an important chapter in Jewish literary history that had been overlooked precisely because its subject matter could not be easily identified as dealing directly or specifically with Jewish issues. However, writes Glaser, such poetic works gave their authors access to the experiences of marginalized groups around the world and "established a precedent for translating Jewish trauma into empathy."[50] Some of the curvatures in the outline of the Soviet Jew were drawn through similarly unexpected discoveries. Following the uncertain pathways of this cultural figure, I stumbled upon texts that did not appear to be, as Shrayer classified the selection criteria for his anthology of the literature of Russian Jews, concerned with a Jewish topic, theme, or motif. On a few occasions, empathetic descriptions of the plights of other ethnic groups inside the USSR make Jews conspicuously *absent.* In places in literary texts where the reader might have expected to see him described, the Soviet Jew becomes legible through omission.

Fourth, the texts this book employs to locate the figure of the Soviet Jew are not limited to works in the Russian language: Yiddish and Russian get an approximately equal amount of attention. Though Isaac Babel—the most famous and most frequently studied exemplar of the phenomenon of Russian-Jewish literature—wrote in Russian, the elderly Jews who would have been the prototypes for the characters in "The End of the Almshouse" would not have spoken that language to each other. A focus on Jewish writers' works in Russian has been central to the foundational scholarship on Russian-Jewish literature. Russian, however, was not the native language—or, sometimes, not the only native language—of most Jews who had grown up prior to the Bolshevik Revolution in the Pale of Settlement. Around the time of the revolution, Yiddish was the dominant mother tongue and the vernacular of Ashkenazi Jews with a centuries-old history in Central and Eastern Europe.[51] Some Russian-Jewish authors writing in Russian came from assimilated families and never learned Yiddish as children; others were conversant in Yiddish in childhood and let traces of the language and its cultural referents seep into their Russian-language works. By the interwar period, the Yiddish language itself, together with Russian, was central to the cultural output by Jewish writers and intellectuals in the Soviet Union. Modern Yiddish literature, which traced its origins to the Haskalah in Eastern Europe around the middle of the nineteenth century and subsequently came of age in the century's latter half, was in full bloom.[52] One of modern Yiddish literature's most notable figures, Sh. Y. Abramovitch, was buried, in 1917, at the same Jewish cemetery in Odessa where "The End of the Almshouse" was set. Given both the vibrant nature of modern Yiddish literature at the turn of the century and the Soviet government's policy to promote socialist cultures in vernacular national languages, Yiddish enjoyed state-level support in the years after the Bolshevik Revolution—and, with it, a proliferation of periodicals, newspapers, and literary and cultural institutions producing both high-brow and popular culture.[53]

The Yiddish-language texts I discuss were created through interactions with Russian-language Soviet literary paradigms and emergent Soviet literary politics; some of their authors were also translators between the two languages. Conversely, the Russian-language texts under consideration were created at points of encounter with the Yiddish language and with Yiddish-linked vernacular cultural expressions that manifested even beyond the use of Yiddish itself and occasionally hinted at the existence of an implied Yiddish original below the surface of the Russian-language text.

To a great extent, Yiddish enjoyed official support at the expense of Hebrew—the language of the Bible, Jewish prayer, and scholarship that was then being revived as a modern spoken tongue by Zionists in British-ruled Palestine. In official Bolshevik rhetoric, Hebrew was associated with both religious "clericalism" and, increasingly, bourgeois nationalism.[54] However, early Soviet Yiddish poetry, fiction, journalism, and theater did not straightforwardly reflect or perform the Stalin-era vision that cultural output in minority languages should be "national in form, socialist in content." In Western criticism during the Cold War, this dictum has been used to dismiss a good deal of Yiddish creativity in the USSR as little more than a Jewish language severed from its rich Jewish roots in service of the Soviet state. Exemplifying this dismissive trend in literary scholarship, Ruth R. Wisse has written that "Jewish writers and intellectuals were able to publish, conduct research, and teach in Yiddish as long as they were solidifying the *Communist* future, not the future of the Jews."[55] Yet, as scholars of USSR's Yiddish culture have demonstrated in recent years, Soviet Yiddish literature—including explicitly Marxist works that broadened the scope of what Jewish culture could look like and aim to accomplish—was richly intricate, creative, and experimental in its attempts to represent the Jewish experience after the Bolshevik Revolution.[56]

The figure of the Soviet Jew that emerged as a result of geographic and cultural displacements after the revolution existed at a point of Russian-Yiddish linguistic interaction. Harriet Murav, who treats Russian-Jewish and Soviet Yiddish literatures side by side, has noted, "The wall that has been erected in critical literature separating Yiddish from Russian obscures the rich interplay between the two languages and literary traditions."[57] Borrowing from Todd Presner's exploration of "German / Jewish modernity," in which both German and German-Jewish cultures are seen as "always already German / Jewish," I approach my sources for the figure of the Soviet Jew neither as separately Russian nor as separately Yiddish but instead, as always already Russian / Yiddish.[58] The Yiddish component of this nexus, moreover, did not represent—in opposition to the Russian one—a provincial tradition. In the interwar period, Yiddish had become a diasporic language with several active centers of literary and cultural production around the world, not only in Minsk, Kiev, and Moscow, which figure in this book, but also in Warsaw, Berlin, and New York, where the works I discuss were reviewed and analyzed at the time. The circulation of Yiddish-language works during this period meant that the Soviet Jew evolved, at least in part, in the context of a global literary discourse, some of which—through the circulation of Yiddish materials across borders—was available to Jews in the USSR.

* * *

In English-language criticism and Cold War-era Western cultural memory, Jewishness in the USSR was determined by and marked in the notorious "fifth line" of the Soviet passport. *Piataia grafa* in Russian—sometimes translated as "point five," "the fifth paragraph," or "line five"—identified the document bearer's "nationality" (*natsional'nost'*), a term referring to a given Soviet citizen's ethnonational background. In writing about Russian-Jewish authors, Alice Nakhimovsky made the decision to "exclude by definition writers whose passport nationalities leave no trace in their work."[59] Efraim Sicher has similarly noted that "[t]he majority of Jews who wrote in Russian were 'point five' Jews, Jews only by definition of their Soviet passports" and thus not truly producers of "Jewish" texts.[60] Nakhimovsky and Sicher reference the bureaucratic definition of Jewishness in the USSR even while pointing out that not all writers who had the word "Jew" noted in their passports contributed meaningfully to Russian-Jewish literature and that, conversely, literature these scholars deem "Jewish" was not limited in its range of concerns by the state's official definition of who was and was not a Jew. Soviet citizens who were children of mixed marriages could choose the official nationality of either parent for their passport's "fifth line"—something that enabled numerous Jews in the Soviet Union to hide their Jewishness during periods of state-sponsored antisemitism and pass as Russians, Ukrainians, Belarusians, or members of other ethnic groups. Referring to this history, Shrayer notes "a popular Soviet adage" that "[t]hey hit you not on the passport but on the face.'" In other words, there were periods when discrimination against Jews in the USSR had to do less with official nationality and more with what Shrayer calls "phenotypic or visible linguistic and cultural markers of one's Jewish origin."[61] A given writer's passport is not necessarily the right place to look for evidence of their life trajectory or for experiences that would clarify their contributions, or lack thereof, to a specifically Jewish literary discourse. Be that as it may, the word "Jew" in its bearer's passport has come to stand metonymically for the experience of Jews in the USSR, an experience widely understood to have been primarily defined by discrimination.[62]

Any discussion of the "passport nationalities" of Jews in the Soviet Union is anachronistic, however, when it comes to the first two decades after the revolution—the time period within the scope of this book. How to comprehensively define and count members of ethnic groups in the multiethnic Soviet state was a subject of ongoing debate throughout the 1920s and the 1930s.[63] Prior to the collapse of the Russian monarchy in February 1917, Jews carried a notation of their ethnoreligious origins in their internal passports, which determined where they could and couldn't reside within and beyond the Pale of Settlement.[64] In the USSR, however, internal passports were introduced only in 1932 as part of Stalin's agricultural collectivization program. Even then, they were issued only to residents of cities so that peasants forced to join collective farms could not legally leave them to settle in urban centers.[65] It wasn't until 1938 that the NKVD—the USSR's state security agency—issued a directive that required a new level of compliance with the passport law, under which every passport holder had to declare a "nationality" corresponding with the ethnonational origins of one of their parents. This decision, too, was not focused on Jews: the NKVD was primarily concerned with tracking citizens of the USSR who were ethnic Germans and Poles, amidst fears of a Nazi or Polish attack on the Soviet Union.[66]

Contrary to what has become a commonplace understanding of the Soviet Jewish experience, then, the initial intent of the Soviet passport's "fifth line" had little to do with the state's concerns about Jews. Not until after the Second World War did it come to be associated with state-level antisemitism and anti-Jewish discrimination. Moreover, given its limited purpose before 1938, the Soviet passport played no role in marking and defining Jews during the years covered in this book. It is worthwhile, then, to conceptualize the bookends of the story I tell here in terms of the ebbs and flows of bureaucracy. The indeterminacy of the Soviet Jew I identify emerged during the period between the end of the Russian Empire's internal passport system in 1917 and the beginning of the enforcement of the nationality notation in the Soviet internal passport at the end of the 1930s. The figure of the Soviet Jew in its formative years was not tethered, either officially or symbolically, to the categories of USSR citizens' identification papers. Rather, it developed in a dynamic encounter between the fragmented cultural world of the Pale and aspects of the Soviet Union's official culture, which was then still in the making.

The discussion about the Soviet passport, moreover, reminds us that the figure of the Soviet Jew would have been defined by both the limits and the possibilities of Soviet culture as it evolved through the 1920s and the 1930s. Each of the five chapters of this book considers the iconic features of the emergent Soviet Jew in a different setting—geographic, thematic, or both. Each begins with or is structured around a single text, event, or issue that links to other texts and contexts. In Chapter 1, with the help of David Bergelson's Yiddish-language novel *Judgment* (*Mides-hadin*), I explore the lasting trauma of pogrom violence as a definitional aspect of the figure of the Soviet Jew. Jews who had just narrowly survived the pogroms of the Russian civil war in the former Pale of Settlement—and especially, as in Bergelson's novel, in Ukraine—now faced Bolshevik accusations of economic crimes and anti-revolutionary sabotage. Despite the Bolsheviks' official denunciations of antisemitism and their claims to be the saviors of the Jews, these accusations drew on older antisemitic tropes about Jews and capitalism.

Chapter 2 takes us to the city of Minsk in Soviet Belorussia and considers ethnographic discourses about Jews from the former Pale produced by the USSR's research institutions. Our guide is Moyshe Kulbak's *The Zelmenyaners* (*Zelmenyaner*). This satirical Yiddish-language family novel employs the scholarly and political tropes of salvage ethnography, which was being cast at the time as a tool to preserve the cultural heritage of Jews precisely as they were being reimagined as productive Soviet citizens and their heritage was being officially sublimated into that goal.

Chapter 3 undertakes a journey to the Soviet Far East (and a textual detour to Palestine during the British Mandate) to think about Jews from the former Pale who were expected to settle in Birobidzhan, a new territory designated for colonization, and to assume the new role of muscular Jewish agricultural workers. It focuses on texts created around a 1929 expedition to Birobidzhan conducted by international observers and members of the Soviet press. Texts by two of the expedition's participants—the Russian-language writer Semyon Gekht's novel *A Ship Sails to Jaffa and Back* (*Parokhod idët v Iaffu i obratno*) and the journalist Viktor Fink's book of literary sketches, *Jews in the Taiga* (*Evrei v taige*), struggled to describe the Jewish settlement in the Far East. In the process, I argue, they traced the contours of the Soviet Jew through this figure's absence.

Chapter 4 shuttles between Palestine, Poland, and the United States as it follows Jews who had emigrated from the Russian Empire but subsequently returned to the Soviet Union in the 1930s during the economic depression in their new capitalist homelands. It centers on the film *The Return of Neitan Bekker* (*Vozvrashchenie Neitana Bekkera*)—alongside several other contemporary motion pictures including *Seekers of Happiness* (*Iskateli schast'ia*), *The Border* (*Granitsa*), and *Gorizont*—in which the Soviet Jew becomes a figure associated with a return from abroad.

Finally, Chapter 5 revisits the entire two-decade period of the 1920s and 1930s as it tracks the journey of a trickster protagonist from Ashkenazi folklore, Hershele Ostropoler, through the work of Isaac Babel. Hershele surfaces in texts written during—and against the grain of—three ideologically charged moments: the Bolshevik-Polish War of 1920, when the Red Army made a failed attempt to take the revolution beyond the borders of the Bolshevik state; the collectivization of agriculture between the late 1920s and the mid-1930s; and the antireligious campaigns that took place, in different forms, throughout this period. I suggest that Babel's implicit cycle of stories about Hershele Ostropoler presents the folkloric trickster as a cipher for the Soviet Jew.

I approach each of the texts or sets of texts under consideration with the help of other contemporary literary, cinematic, or journalistic texts from the corpus of the Soviet experience, as well as both contemporary and retrospective literary criticism. The Soviet Jew, on the move in the first two decades after the revolution, comes into existence in spaces of encounter between the cultural attributes ascribed to the Pale of Settlement and the inchoate cultural space of Sovietness in the making.

* * *

In Isaac Babel's "The End of the Almshouse," the indigent elderly Jews are uprooted from a poorhouse located, of all places, on the grounds of a cemetery and then cast out on a journey. They are thus physically and symbolically extracted from the anticipated and speedy extinction that would have otherwise been their lot had they simply been left in peace. The figure of the Soviet Jew begins to emerge on that "melancholy" road of indeterminate length and unclear direction—a space characterized by trauma and survival but also by a jolt into unexpected longevity.

1

Haunted by Pogroms

David Bergelson's *Judgment*

In David Bergelson's novel *Judgment* (*Mides-hadin*), written in Yiddish in Berlin in the mid-1920s and set at the beginning of the decade, counterrevolutionaries readying an uprising against the nascent Bolshevik rule smuggle a non-Jew named Ushak across the Polish border into Ukraine. Ukraine was then a territory being contested by an assortment of forces, including the Bolsheviks, their many opponents, and local warlords aligned with multiple sides in the bloody conflict commonly known as the Russian civil war.[1] Ushak is brought in to help plan an attack on the Bolsheviks' Cheka outpost located inside a ruined monastery in a fictional place called Kamino-Balke. Established by Lenin's decree mere weeks after the Bolsheviks seized power in 1917, the Cheka's mandate was to prevent and punish cross-border smuggling and sabotage.[2] Ushak's precise role in the emerging plot against the Cheka base is never made clear. However, in this novel about aspiring escapees from the Bolshevik regime, contrabandists, and counterrevolutionary agitators, his arrival in Ukraine toward the end of winter of 1920 is an eagerly anticipated event.[3] Ushak's hosts belong to the local cell of Socialist Revolutionaries, known as the SRs. This political party supported the overthrow of the tsar but was banned by the new regime after some of its members broke with Lenin's Bolsheviks.[4] In *Judgment*, set in and around the fictional shtetl of Golikhovke, the local SR cell, like the larger SR Party at the time, includes both Jewish and non-Jewish members.[5] Ushak poses an especially pernicious danger for the area's Jews, who were then caught up, like many Jews throughout the former Pale of Settlement, in recurring cycles of deadly antisemitic violence. Pokras, one of the local Jewish SR members, contemplates the addition of Ushak to his counterrevolutionary group: "He didn't feel all that good about it: after all, he was a Jew, while Ushak had been mixed up in pogroms—a lot of pogroms, the worst and bloodiest in the region."[6]

The Bolsheviks, against whom the SRs are conspiring, would have taken control of the region a short while earlier, after dislodging one or several anti-Bolshevik forces, including those of the Ukrainian People's Republic headed by Symon Petliura. This would not have been the first time that power had changed hands between the Bolsheviks and their opponents during an extended period of multiparty violence. Between 1917 and the Bolsheviks' eventual consolidation of power in 1921, tens of thousands of Jews perished in assaults by a succession of warring armies, paramilitary formations, and marauding bands vying for control of a patchwork of territories in the former Russian Empire's western borderlands.[7] In the scope of their brutality, these pogroms eclipsed even the historical trauma and vernacular memory of anti-Jewish violence during the Cossack uprisings led by Bohdan Khmelnytsky almost three centuries earlier.[8] When the SRs tell Ushak that they wish to proceed with planning their revolt "in an orderly fashion," he inadvertently confirms his association with Petliura, who was widely associated with the worst of the then-recent pogroms: "Nice words! [. . .] That's how you get yourself finished—even if you're Petliura!"[9] Ushak, we learn, had "had to flee to the other side of the border several months earlier" when Petliura's forces would have been first driven out by the Bolsheviks. His gang, now reassembled on the Polish side, "was armed and always at the ready" to return to Ukraine and fight the Reds.[10] The implications for the area's Jews were dire.

The notorious pogromist thus returns to a place where he had left a trail of Jewish blood. "It's not necessarily a good thing that he carried out pogroms—but, in any case, it's worth hearing him out to see what kind of plan he has," Pokras's SR cell concludes about Ushak.[11] The SRs' challenge to the Bolsheviks' hold on power in the area, where shtetl Jews involved in cross-border trade saw their livelihoods threatened by the Cheka's crackdown on smuggling, is a common cause that brings local Jews and non-Jews together.[12] However, the counterrevolutionaries' strategy of aligning with a known pogromist against the Bolsheviks puts Pokras—a Jew cognizant of Ushak's reputation—on edge.

Pokras's concern is hardly surprising: by the late winter of 1920, when the events described in Bergelson's novel took place, many of the worst pogroms had already occurred. This violence was perpetrated, in most cases, by a range of anti-Bolshevik forces. The Bolsheviks themselves, meanwhile, punished known pogromists.[13] At the same time, the Red Army, whose recruits from among peasants and workers could not be easily reeducated in the Bolsheviks' ethos of internationalism and opposition to antisemitism, carried out some pogroms as well.[14] Given the scale of the destruction of Jewish life in the former Pale, which followed on the heels of an already destructive experience for Jewish communities during the First World War, by 1920 the wave of anti-Jewish violence was referred to, in Yiddish, as *khurbn*. The word, which originated in the Hebrew Bible as a reference to the destruction (*hurban*) of both the First and the Second Temples in ancient Jerusalem, had also been used to identify large-scale tragedies that befell the Jewish people through the centuries; it would reemerge two decades later to refer to the Holocaust.[15]

In the midst of the *khurbn*, Ushak had Jewish blood on his hands. Bergelson introduces Ushak into the plot of *Judgment* when the Bolsheviks' opponents in the novel return him to the vicinity of the shtetl. Here, the novel makes palpable the anxiety and fear that Jews in parts of the former Pale would have felt at the time about the recurrence of pogrom violence, which appeared to have ended only a short while earlier. As the reality of War Communism— the set of economic policies intended to support the new regime's tenuous conquests through the nationalization of all industries and strict control of foreign trade—was settling in, along with the attendant regime of Red Terror,[16] the Bolsheviks were threatened by counterrevolutionaries, some of whom, as in *Judgment,* were willing to align with pogromists or were pogromists themselves. A seemingly vanquished past—traumatically marked by the pogroms of yore—now appeared as a revanchist force suddenly encroaching on the present. This was the stuff of Gothic literature that Bergelson could draw on while writing a novel about the aftermath of the revolution in the former Pale of Settlement—itself a relic of the recent past that seemed not to have fully vanished.

A little more than a decade after the French Revolution, the Marquis de Sade speculated about the popularity of Gothic literature on the opposite side of the English Channel. Seeing the appeal of this genre after 1789 as "the necessary offspring of the revolutionary upheaval which affected the whole of Europe," de Sade speculated on the emergence, in England, of works like Anne Radcliffe's *The Mysteries of Udolpho* (1794) and Matthew Lewis's *The Monk* (1796).[17] In these novels, with their haunted castles, ruined monasteries, colorful villains and frightening monsters, the postrevolutionary terror in France served as a screen onto which the British projected anxieties about their own earlier political upheavals, civic strife, and regicide—together with their fear that the violence and terror unfolding in France would return to England.

Gothic literature has been associated with unwanted and feared returns of threatening specters from the past. Drawing on psychoanalysis, Dale Peterson has noted that the "core intrigue at the center of any Gothic narrative is some contemporary enactment of the mental trauma Freud denominated as 'the return of the repressed.'" Vestiges of the past seep into the present, and a "sudden immersion in an antiquated environment is found to awaken the most anachronistic feelings and experiences in 'innocent' protagonists, who think of themselves as belonging to some later, more enlightened age."[18] A number of early Soviet works manifested fears about the return of bourgeois habits after the stringent economic regime of War Communism was relaxed starting in 1922.[19] In *Judgment,* however, the repressed that threatened to return, with the outcome of the Russian civil war still uncertain, was the violence of pogroms. "Your hands are covered in blood, brother," one of the SR conspirators thinks to himself as he looks at Ushak, newly returned to Ukraine: "it seems that a little too much blood is on your hands even for this civil war." The potential for the return of violence is high now that Ushak, the embodiment of such violence in the novel, has himself returned: his appearance reminds one of his handlers "of a criminal—from long, long ago [*gor fun amolike tsaytn*]."[20] Emerging from what Bergelson refers to in Yiddish as a very distant past, Ushak is one of the "remnants that ought to be defunct," stealing his way across a poorly guarded border back into the area now held by a new power trying to establish authority over a population still traumatized by recent violence.[21]

Valeria Sobol has argued for expanding the list of literary works that should be read as Gothic beyond the classic examples that informed de Sade's comment at the turn of the nineteenth century; she suggests that list include novels characterized by "a deployment of recognizably Gothic tropes and narrative techniques in connection to the dominant Gothic themes of irrationality, transgression, and past history haunting the present."[22] Mikhail Bakhtin has noted that the chronotope of the castle, which appears as a setting in many classic Gothic texts, "is saturated throughout and through with a time that is historical in the narrow sense of the word, that is, the time of the historical past."[23] Moreover, notes Bakhtin, "legends and traditions animate every corner of the castle and its environs through their constant reminders of past events."[24] Castles—but also monasteries, another setting typical of the Gothic novel—are among the tropes that extend to literary works that do not, on the surface, appear to be Gothic fictions but are nonetheless written in "the Gothic mode."[25] Into a given work's narrative present, Gothic tropes introduce a sense of the antiquated and the long gone, which floats to the surface anew after being seemingly pushed out of consciousness.

Bergelson's route toward the Gothic mode—to which *Judgment*, with its fear of the past's return, belongs—likely passed through Berlin, where he lived between 1921 and 1934. Expressionism—interwar Germany's central contribution to the Gothic mode—dominated the artistic scene of the Weimar Republic, especially in cinema. Films like Robert Wiene's *The Cabinet of Dr. Caligari* (1920), F. M. Murnau's *Nosferatu* (1922), and Carl Boese's and Paul Wegener's *Golem* (1920)—the last of these based on a sixteenth-century Jewish legend—would have left an imprint on Bergelson's imagination with their distorted, angular sets, shifts in narrative perspective, and haunting shadows of monsters and evildoers.[26] Bergelson's description of the ruined monastery near the Polish border, its "[a]bandoned buildings peer[ing] out of all the dark corners" and the "wrinkled tip of a [guard's] nose and [. . .] icy lips" protruding from a heart-shaped peephole at the gate, recall the jagged angles and uneven surfaces of German Expressionism.[27] Those entering Kamino-Balke are judged by Filipov, the head of the Cheka outpost and a frightening man whose past is shrouded in mystery and whose neck is disfigured by illness. With his voice "sour, hoarse, and mean" from the boils on his neck and "fear emanating from [his] towering figure," he cuts a monstrous silhouette not unlike Wegener's portrayal of the Golem of Prague.[28] Local denizens are afraid not only of Filipov's ghastly appearance but also of his lack of concern for his own health—a harbinger, it is thought, of his ruthlessness toward those under his rule: "This was a person who was his own worst enemy, how would he treat people who fell into his clutches?"[29] Frightening in his looks and with his power over others seemingly unchecked, the non-Jewish Filipov has emerged from a mysterious past to haunt the as-yet unclear present.

At the same time, neither the monstrous appearance of the stern enforcer of Bolshevik law nor the frightening physical edifice that houses the Cheka branch under his control can hide the weakness of the power they represent.

This weakness has resulted from the ruins of the old that the Cheka and Filipov attempt to occupy. As the new regime inhabits—and manifests the features of—a classic Gothic edifice, the bygone threatens to encroach on the present in the guise of the pogromist Ushak, who slips past the frightening but, in the end, porous border outpost.

The pogromist's appearance on the Bolshevik-held side of the border does not, at first, seem to amount to much in *Judgment:* Ushak drinks himself into a stupor, and the SRs at whose invitation he had returned to Ukraine eventually give up on enlisting him as a co-conspirator. However, when he is last seen in the novel, Ushak speaks with brutish, raging defiance. "Wait, you just wait! I'll show you yet, sons of bitches!" he yells after the SRs when he discovers that they had left him behind at a safehouse.[30] His threat of violence hangs in the air, suspended as an ever-present and never-distant possibility. The novel ends and we never see Ushak involved in another pogrom, but neither do we see him returning to the Polish side of the border: the threat of anti-Jewish violence lingers. Filled with such anxiety, *Judgment* focuses on the moment of in-betweenness when some of the most destructive pogroms of the Russian civil war had already ended but fear of their possible reignition persists as counterrevolutionary forces fight against the shaky Bolshevik rule. This period of time, marked by the lingering threat of the return of violence, profoundly shaped the figure of the Soviet Jew, the emerging contours of which become visible in Bergelson's novel.

* * *

David Bergelson was born in 1884 in the shtetl of Okhrimovo in Ukraine. After stints of varying lengths in Warsaw, where he launched his career in Yiddish literature in 1909; Kiev, where he founded the avant-garde Yiddish literary and artistic organization Kultur-lige (the Culture League) just after the revolution[31]; and, briefly, Moscow, he moved to Berlin in 1921. Except for a six-month stay in New York in 1929, Bergelson remained in Berlin with his wife and young son until Hitler's rise to power (figure 1.1). In 1934, after a brief sojourn in Copenhagen, he resettled with his family in Soviet Moscow.[32]

At the beginning of the 1920s, the massive wave of pogroms was fresh in Jewish collective memory, and testimonies about it were already being collected and published. Berlin—home to thousands of Jewish refugees from the former Pale of Settlement who fled the violence of the Russian civil war,

Figure I.I. David Bergelson with his son Lev in Berlin, 1922. Reproduced with the kind permission of Lubov Bergelson.

numerous cultural figures like Bergelson among them—became a major publishing center for such accounts in the 1920s. These included Elias Tcherikower's collection of testimonies and his foundational volume on the pogroms, which was published with an introduction by Simon Dubnow, the dean of Russian Jewish history who then also lived in Berlin.[33] Some of Bergelson's texts confronted head-on the experience and legacy of the pogroms: in his stories "Among Refugees" and "Two Murderers," written and set in Berlin in the mid-1920s, he dwelt on the lingering trauma felt by Jewish survivors then living in close proximity to the perpetrators of violence, as Ukrainian nationalists, the Whites (monarchists), and other counterrevolutionaries also found refuge from the Bolsheviks in Berlin.[34] However, Bergelson was far from the only writer at the time attempting to write about this trauma. In many other texts of the period, the recent pogroms were a barely articulated yet urgent trace. These works drew faintly visible connecting lines between pogrom violence, the Jews' displacement from the shtetl, and the effects of these phenomena on the emerging figure of the Soviet Jew.

In 1927 the Russian-language writer Semyon Gekht published a novella titled *The Man Who Forgot His Life* (*Chelovek, kotoryi zabyl svoiu zhizn'*); parts of the novel were republished in 1931 under the title *The Shoemaker's Son* (*Syn sapozhnika*). Set in Ierusalimka (literally, "Little Jerusalem"), a largely Jewish district of the Ukrainian city of Vinnitsa, the novella recounts the murder of Nakhman, the only son of the Jewish shoemaker Isaac Zelts. A voracious reader of Russian adventure tales, the young teen befriends Katya, the daughter of an antisemitic policeman. The boy becomes a regular at Katya's and her sisters' house when the girls' father isn't home. The year 1917 arrives; Katya's father, who had served the now-deposed tsar, flees, abandoning his family. After the ensuing interregnum during the final months of the First World War, when Austrian and German troops briefly occupied Vinnitsa, Petliura's Ukrainian National Army takes over, with a man named Zaremba, referred to as "Ataman" (chief) now in charge. Nakhman feels he needs to show Katya his bravery and support for the Ukrainian nationalist cause.

This turns out to be a tall order. "It's not your fault [. . .] all Jews are cowardly," Katya tells Nakhman. Seeking to prove her wrong, he attempts to enlist in Petliura's army but gets arrested at the Ataman's headquarters.[35] After Zaremba promises to release his son, Zelts is subjected to a series of humiliations: he is forced to eat pork, make the sign of the cross, and denounce Judaism—all in front of a large crowd of the town's Jews, whom the occupying army had ordered to assemble (figure 1.2). Out of desperation, Zelts, like some Jews during the historical experience of the pogroms of the time, effectively converts to Christianity.[36] However, unbeknownst to Zelts, Nakhman has already been shot. In the city held captive by Zaremba's forces, Nakhman's death carries the symbolic weight of a pogrom. Spurned by the town's Jews for his public "apostasy" and grieving his son's death, Zelts loses his mind and flees Vinnitsa with a roaming band of Roma (figure 1.3).

Thus displaced, Zelts resembles the mythic figure of the Wandering Jew. Several years later, he is spotted on a Moscow tram, where he identifies himself as "Ahasuerus"—one of the monikers, mistakenly picked up from the name of the Persian king in the Book of Esther, referring to the Wandering Jew in medieval European legends since as early as the thirteenth century.[37] A specter of the antisemitic imagination, the Wandering Jew was said to have been a Jewish cobbler from Jerusalem who was condemned to eternal displacement after failing to acknowledge the divinity of Christ.[38] A Gothic

Figure I.2. Isaac Zelts visits Ataman Zaremba's headquarters, pleading for his son's release. Illustration by Mendel Gorshman in Semyon Gekht's *The Shoemaker's Son* (Moscow 1931). Courtesy of the National Library of Russia.

Figure I.3. Zelts flees his hometown, Vinnitsa, after his son's killing. Illustration by Mendel Gorshman in Semyon Gekht's *The Shoemaker's Son* (Moscow 1931). Courtesy of the National Library of Russia.

figure from the distant past, the Wandering Jew was conjured up as a grotesque, haunting "other" against whom European Christians could construct
narratives of historical progress.[39] Far from his native town and years after
the anti-Jewish violence that had transpired there, Zelts is haunted by a
tragedy that affected him but that he cannot narrate. After being forced to
renounce Judaism—an act that would have figured as the acceptance of Christ
in the denouement of the medieval legend—Zelts nonetheless becomes a caricature from the antisemitic imaginary. In Gekht's take on the legend of the
Wandering Jew, Zelts has internalized the violence of the pogroms he has experienced and turned it outward, becoming an aggressor against Jews.
Claiming that he is not a Jew, he yells out, "I'll be cutting up Jews until the
last drop of blood" to fellow passengers on a Moscow tram, dismayed that
too many Jews had flooded into the capital city.[40]

In moving to Moscow, Zelts follows an itinerary common for many pogrom survivors fleeing shtetls for bigger cities in the 1920s.[41] Through this
journey away from the former Pale of Settlement, Gekht's protagonist charts
a feature of the emergent figure of the Soviet Jew: the embedded trauma of
antisemitic violence. Zelts is a Gothic specter of violence of the sort that
Karen Grumberg has called "evidence of a restless past that intrudes on the
present."[42] He cannot coherently narrate what had transpired yet brings
distorted fragments of this fractured, traumatic history into the vibrant
political and cultural center of Soviet life after the Russian civil war—and
into the figure of the Soviet Jew—long after and far from the acts of violence
themselves.

The killing of Jews during the Russian civil war of 1918–1921 was closely
intertwined with physical destruction in the former Pale. Commenting on
Peretz Markish's 1920 Yiddish poem "The Mound" (Di kupe), Amelia Glaser
has pointed to the work's central topos—the marketplace—as a synecdoche
for the destroyed shtetl, where the previously vibrant commercial, linguistic,
and cultural exchange between Jews and Slavs has given way to a "violent
interchange."[43] A mound of corpses in the middle of the marketplace speaks in
the first person:

No, tallowed sky, don't lick my clotted beards,
Brown streams of pine-tar ooze from my mouths;
Oh brown leaven of blood and sawdust,

No, don't touch this gash on the earth's black thigh.
Get away from me, I stink. Frogs are crawling over me.[44]

Rotting bodies of pogrom victims fill the devastated landscape as though re-populating it—but this repopulation "depends on the memory of a normal market landscape, where goods are assigned value, and where items are often broken and sold piecemeal."[45] In the aftermath of violence, the shtetl is re-duced to its broken remains and itself becomes a heap of spectral shards, which refuse to be consigned to the past.

The Bolsheviks aimed to replace the social and cultural structures of the shtetl with markers of their new political and economic regime. Literary attempts to describe the violence of this process, however, confronted the limits of language and opted for opacity instead. Markish's poem "Brothers" (Brider), written nearly a decade after "The Mound," centers a new type of revolutionary hero, the Jewish Bolshevik, who is the revolution's engaged, en-thusiastic participant. Harriet Murav has argued that this figure overflows its seeming contours, the apparent embrace of the new ideology, through intertextual allusions both to "The Mound" and to the devastation of the shtetl during the pogroms. Because the losses to life "could not be mourned openly," they became visible instead "in the vast, messy corpus of the text, whose words appear as the swollen traces of unacknowledged wounds."[46] Rot-ting remnants of a once-living culture both offer immediate evidence of the shtetl's destruction and haunt the project of revolutionary renewal unfolding in its place.

The lingering effects of the pogroms of the Russian civil war were felt even in early Soviet-era works that did not primarily address the condition of Jews. In Alexander Tarasov-Rodionov's 1922 novel *Chocolate* (*Shokolad*)—a foun-dational text in the canon of works about the Cheka—Abram Katsman, a se-cret police agent with an identifiably Jewish name, is murdered while on assignment. Immediately after the news of the murder spreads, someone at the local Cheka, referring to Katsman by his name and patronymic, eulogizes the fallen comrade: "Look, they offed Abram Moiseich! What a pity, the poor thing! He was such a good and honest man! He kept dreaming about moving his family here from Orsha. And what amazing work he did!"[47] Katsman's reportedly well-known wish to relocate his family from Orsha, in Belorussia, into the Russian interior, where the novel is set, implies—without stating explicitly—that the Chekist was eager to rescue his kin from the pogroms then unfolding in the lands of the former Pale. Katsman dies during an operation to apprehend some Socialist Revolutionaries in the area—a detail of the plot that posits, as in Bergelson's *Judgment,* a connection between the anti-Bolshevik SRs and the killing of Jews.[48]

The new world launched by the Bolshevik Revolution was haunted by spectral remnants of a past that had never fully receded. These traumatic vestiges hid in plain sight in widely celebrated Soviet literary works that, on the surface, appeared to tout the achievements of the revolution—including those that largely benefited Jews. Iosif Utkin's multipart 1925 poem, "The Tale of Red-Headed Motele, Mr. Inspector, Rabbi Isaiah, and Commissar Blokh," focused on the eponymous Motele's journey from working as a tailor's apprentice to enlisting in the Red Army. Anatoly Lunacharsky, then the Commissar of the Enlightenment in the Bolshevik government, praised the poem as a significant achievement of "our young poetry."[49] Motele fights in the Russian civil war and, by the poem's end, is a celebrated hero. As a tailor's apprentice during his boyhood, Motele would affix "ten patches / onto a single vest [*on stavil desiat' zaplatok / na odin zhilet*]" for impoverished Jewish clients unable to afford new garments. By contrast, the revolution propels Motele, through the fields of battle, toward the collectivist task of "mending our holes [*Motele budet shtopat' / nashi prorekhi*]"—patching up the fissures in the social fabric of a community that comes to proudly claim him as one of their own.[50]

Utkin's tailor-cum-Bolshevik had been scarred by pogroms. Referring to the 1903 and 1905 pogroms in Kishinev—the first of which would shape the perception and impact of subsequent pogroms during the Russian civil war[51]—the poem emphasizes, with its pathos punctuated by ellipses, how "just . . . / two . . . / pogroms . . . / and Motele became / an orphan [*vsego . . . / dva . . . / pogroma . . . / i Motele stal / sirota*]."[52] As Brendan McGeever has noted, personal experiences of tragedy during tsarist-era waves of pogroms motivated individuals long active in and committed to Jewish socialist politics to compel and ultimately shape the new Bolshevik government's response to the wave of anti-Jewish violence that rolled across the former Pale during the Russian civil war.[53] Motele, orphaned in a pogrom when he was a child, could, as a Bolshevik later in life, "mend" communal ruptures (*prorekhi*). Some of these fissures, as Utkin's poem hints, may have resulted

Figure I.4. A scene of violence directed by pogromists at the Jews of Vinnitsa. Illustration by Mendel Gorshman in Semyon Gekht's *The Shoemaker's Son* (Moscow 1931). Courtesy of the National Library of Russia.

from Jews' experience of violence. Without being fully acknowledged or mourned, the tragedy of these pogroms is incorporated into the psyche of the Jewish Bolshevik. The scant evidence in Utkin's long poem acknowledging its hero's traumatic past is one among many such spectral remains in the literature of the time. Pogroms, this corpus of works hints, marked the emergent Soviet Jew with barely articulable traces of personal and historical trauma, which would remain inscribed on this figure well into the Soviet period (figure 1.4).

* * *

The narrator of Bergelson's *Judgment* describes the world brought forth by the Bolshevik Revolution as a "strange [*modne*], new, harsher world."[54] Such strangeness manifested in literary texts through narrative inconsistencies. Harriet Murav has noted such inconsistencies in Itsik Kipnis's modernist 1926 Yiddish novel, *Months and Days* (*Khadoshim un teg*), about a pogrom in the Ukrainian shtetl of Slovechne in 1919. She has pointed to the author's awareness of his "strange" (*modne*) task of having to make sense of violence and to note in his novel the details that "make these events strange, unpredictable, and lacking in rationale" to those who were involved in pogroms as perpetrators, bystanders, and victims.[55] In novels, poems, and stories haunted by what is barely mentioned or remains entirely unsaid, "strange" details—including omissions, evasions, and repetitions—become important tools for close reading and noticing nuanced meanings beneath the surfaces of texts.

One of the "strange" aspects of literary texts about pogroms is their frequent conflation of military forces that had entirely different goals. Gekht's young protagonist in *The Man Who Forgot His Life* is held in a cellar along with forty-eight other prisoners; another story by Gekht (which I discuss in Chapter 3) repeats exactly the details about the cellar and the number of prisoners—but whereas in the former the prison guards are Petliura's nationalists, in the latter the protagonist is held by White monarchists. The repetition of these strangely identical details across texts appears to equate Petliura's men with the Whites despite their irreconcilable goals—one seeking Ukraine's independence, and the other the restoration of Russia's imperial power. However, because both directed violence at Jews, the two armies became interchangeable in the Jewish collective imagination. Given its relative success in preventing attacks on Jews by such anti-Bolshevik forces, the Red Army was depicted as a liberating force in a number of literary texts, including Leyb Kvitko's *1919*, a book of poetry that was published, like Bergelson's novel, in Berlin, and Kipnis's *Months and Days*.[56] Different armed formations seemed interchangeable to Jews, who were subjected to pogroms by successive regimes in the former Pale.

Other literary works from the time focused both on a widespread contemporary perception that Jews were synonymous with the Bolshevik regime and on the anti-Jewish violence that resulted from this popularly held view. In Ilya Ehrenburg's 1928 Russian-language short story "A Ship Fare" (Shifs-Karta), the son of the watchmaker Girsh Ikhenson emigrates to the United States and promises to send his father a steerage ticket to make the transatlantic journey in due course. Ikhenson's daughter and son-in-law had been brutally murdered in what the narrative obliquely implies was a pogrom, at some point during the wave of anti-Jewish violence between 1903 and 1906: "His daughter married a fiddler from Balta," notes the narrator. "They called on him to come inside the army headquarters; toward morning, they smashed his violin, stripped the fiddler naked and, having kept him for an hour inside a barrel of sour beer, rolled him in the snow as though it were flour. He caught a cold. Stopped creaking. After him—his wife." About the orphaned child of Girsh's daughter and son-in-law, the narrator relates: "The granddaughter remained with Girsh. She became like a daughter to him. Called him 'father.'"[57]

The lines about Girsh's daughter and son-in-law's demise are as brief as they are elusive. The son-in-law appears to have fallen ill while being brutalized; he died when he ceased "creaking [*otskripel*]." The allusion is likely to a cough the man contracted while inside a barrel filled with cold liquid in subfreezing temperatures; his wife—Girsh's daughter—is said to have met a grim end as well. The lack of precision in this narrative appears deliberate, a hint at a horror so hard to fathom that it cannot be described precisely.

This nearly inaudible articulation of tragedy reverberates through Girsh's life. His granddaughter, who was a baby when her parents perished in the pogrom, remains the watchmaker's only link to his deceased daughter: in her relation to Girsh, the girl takes the symbolic place of her murdered mother. However, another wave of pogroms sweeps through Girsh's shtetl a decade and a half later, during the Russian civil war. In the corner of Girsh's watch repair shop sits the old man's granddaughter: "thin [. . .] frightened Leah. [They] frightened [her] in the first year of the war [*V pervyi god voiny ispugali*]. She was fifteen."[58] The language here is strikingly imprecise: the sentence notes that something was done to Leah "in the first year of the war" by men who "frightened" her, but neither the act nor its perpetrators are named. Instead, Ehrenburg uses a past-tense verb form consistent with the third-person plural subject, *ispugali*—literally, "[they] frightened [her]": the connotation here is that Leah was raped when she was fifteen. The timing of the event, as indicated by Leah's age, suggests that the assault—possibly, a gang rape as would have been consistent with accounts of gendered violence at the time—would likely have happened around 1919, the year of the most severe pogroms in the former Pale.[59]

The experience of rape traumatized Leah. Any attempts to converse with her elicit only fearful, nonverbal responses: "Just say one word to her—she would get startled, yell out weakly, hide in the corner with all the stuff and mice [*zab'etsia v ugol, gde skarb i myshi*]"; the word *skarb*—a generic term for household items—itself evokes the state of disarray after a pogrom.[60] Girsh also remains almost entirely silent, uttering not much more than the words "Shifs-Karta," which, on the surface, refer to the ship fare once promised by his son. During yet another violent outbreak, words that had originally indicated Girsh's desire to go to America are gradually severed from their referent and transformed into a near-messianic hope for redemption. When he greets the pogromist who ultimately kills him, Girsh proclaims, "You have arrived, Shifs-Karta!"[61] Like his granddaughter's frightened appearance, like the oblique language used to tell the story of his daughter and son-in-law's deaths, Girsh's final utterance briefly breaks through the silence before he perishes himself.

Omissions and inconclusive phrases also convey how victims and survivors of pogroms might have understood the causes of the violence that they had experienced. Gekht's repetitions suggest that different military forces became interchangeable in the Jewish imagination given the similar violence that each had perpetrated. The pogrom that kills Girsh in Ehrenburg's "A Ship Fare" takes place right after the Bolsheviks—who had only recently taken control of his shtetl—were pushed out by yet another anti-Bolshevik force. A change in power is afoot as the guns of the advancing anti-Bolshevik unit resound in the distance: "There's worry in town. Already cannons—not just guns. [. . .] And finally—thunder—thump! All the fussing around. Train station. The Jewish Section atop the train cars."[62] Some of the Jewish Bolsheviks fleeing Girsh's shtetl are affiliated with the Jewish Section (Evsektsiia)—card-carrying Party members tasked with bringing the revolution's message to the Jewish masses.[63] Their flight in the face of arriving anti-Bolshevik forces presages a new round of violence for the shtetl Jews who had stayed behind.

Both Petliura's troops and the Whites fought the Bolsheviks' Red Army; both also conflated Bolsheviks and Jews as their enemy. The presence of some Jews in the new regime's high-profile positions was instrumental to the emergence of the myth of Judeo-Bolshevism, which held that nefarious Jewish interests dictated revolutionary activity. There was no better target for Judeo-Bolshevism than the Red Army's founder, Leon Trotsky, who was Jewish. Antisemitic caricatures of Trotsky as the devil, drawing "on a long tradition of representing Jews as demons and Jewish designs as evil" or as a gigantic red beast "straddl[ing] the walls of the Kremlin, a Star of David around his body," graced some anti-Bolshevik propaganda materials.[64] The myth of Judeo-Bolshevism, in turn, led to the use of antisemitic tropes in anticommunist propaganda, and, ultimately, to the violence against Jews perpetrated by anti-Bolshevik forces.[65]

Despite the Bolsheviks' stated opposition to antisemitism, however, the Red Army also perpetrated anti-Jewish violence on the heels of violence perpetrated by other forces. In Isaac Babel's diary of the Bolshevik-Polish war in 1920, when he was embedded with the Red Army's Cossack regiment, he describes acts of brutality that the Red Army committed against Jews: "The Zhitomir pogrom, organized by the Poles, was continued, of course, by the Cossacks."[66] The Red Army prosecuted some of the perpetrators of pogroms in its own ranks but, in so doing, reinforced the antisemitic canard of Judeo-Bolshevism: that the Bolsheviks protected Jews because the revolution itself was fundamentally guided by Jewish interests. Because the Bolsheviks were viewed by the Whites and by Petliura's forces as sympathetic to Jews and because, in several cases, some Jews were involved in communist activity and in aiding the Red Army, anti-Bolshevik groups used these alliances, both real and imagined, to rationalize their attacks on Jews in the former Pale.[67]

In Ehrenburg's "A Ship Fare," Girsh is murdered during one such antisemitic attack. While the Red Army flees the arriving counterrevolutionary forces, the shtetl's residents, with nowhere to go, quickly prepare for the arrival of a new military and political force. The main protagonist of Vasily Grossman's 1934 short story "In the Town of Berdichev" (V gorode Berdicheve) describes such transitional periods during the Russian civil war as "the best time of all for [the] townsfolk. One ruling power [*vlast'*] has left—and the next is yet to arrive. No requisitions, [. . .] no pogroms."[68] In Ehrenburg's story, Jews use such a respite to destroy all traces of association with the Bolsheviks that they have or are believed to have acquired while the Reds held power. These include identity documents, as well as household items. Blankets, because of their color, suggest an association with the Bolsheviks and turn their owners into easier targets. As these items are burned, the narrative describes "puffs of smoke from the chimney, leaflets, newspapers, passports getting burnt. Thump, thump. Already so close! Sarah, throw out the red blanket! Better not to excite them."[69] With an anti-Bolshevik unit—and the threat of pogroms—approaching, Jews in Girsh's shtetl try but ultimately fail to mitigate the severity of the ensuing disaster.

In "A Ship Fare," the Bolsheviks' takeover of the shtetl is not a fait accompli. Rather, it is merely a phase—one of several and certainly not the last—in the messy and prolonged struggle for power that unfolded across the territories of the former Pale after the revolution. In their attempted acts of survival, Jewish residents try to avoid being associated with the Bolsheviks as they anticipate the return of anti-Red forces. Ehrenburg's story focuses not on the pogrom itself but on the fear local Jews experience long before the new wave of antisemitic violence even takes place. This fear, captured in a literary text, was well justified given the then-recent history of civil war violence. For example, a chain of tragic events in the town of Tetiiv in March 1920, when Bergelson's novel was likely set, began with the temporary departure of a Bolshevik leader who had been protective of local Jews. The momentary power vacuum led to a peasant uprising against Bolshevik rule, the Bolsheviks' subsequent withdrawal from the town, and a pogrom directed at Jews who were seen as being under the Bolsheviks' protection.[70] The period of Bolshevik rule that precedes the return of anti-Bolshevik forces is a vanishingly short and uncertain moment, during which the victory of the revolution is by no means assured.

The ambiguity and liminality of this stage of the Russian civil war inform my reading of Bergelson's *Judgment.* Although this novel has been generally understood as a text about the entrenchment of Bolshevik rule in the former Pale, shtetl Jews in *Judgment* doubt whether the Bolsheviks have actually secured their hold on power. One of the novel's protagonists—a dentist—expresses his certainty about the limited staying power of the Bolsheviks in an exaggerated way: "Every time he put a piece of gauze in a patient's mouth, he would run to the window to check whether the current regime had been abolished."[71] The Bolsheviks, thought Golikhovke's Jews, were not going to last long; associating with them might prove imprudent when the inevitable regime change occurred yet again.

Mikhail Krutikov has noted the peculiarities of narration in the parts of *Judgment* that describe the shtetl in the present tense. These narrative moments, he writes, allow Bergelson to create "an impressionistic effect of uncertainty and fragmentation as opposed to the logical clarity of the revolutionary world-view." Though the events described in the novel have already taken place, they are told as though they were still unfolding, foreclosing "a standpoint located safely in the future, when the revolution has already triumphed."[72] However, for the characters in the novel, the Bolsheviks have not yet triumphed—the lives of Golikhovke's Jews hinge on their actions in a conflict that is still unfolding. *Judgment* is suffused with the fear of punishment for allegedly misbegotten alliances that might befall the shtetl's Jews as soon as power changes hands and with anxiety that such a power shift would be imminent. This fear and anxiety accompany and shape the Soviet Jew at this figure's very moment of inception.

* * *

Judgment's suspenseful storyline and multiple parallel narrative threads represent a departure from Bergelson's earlier works, which had earned the writer fame in Yiddish literature. Bergelson's novella *At the Depot* (*Arum vokzal*, 1909) and novels, *The End of Everything* (*Nokh alemen*, 1913) and *Descent* (*Opgang*, 1920), were richly laden with ruminations on the inner lives of characters but featured few events.[73] During the 1920s, however, Bergelson would have frequented the movie palaces of Weimar Berlin and, like many of his contemporaries, would have been exposed to the techniques of parallel editing and montage in the emerging art of cinema.[74] *Judgment* extends the modernist complexity of the writer's by-then published fiction while matching aspects of his style with the literary devices and emplotment techniques necessary for depicting characters in a fast-paced narrative. In addition to the indecisive and self-doubting characters familiar from Bergelson's earlier prose, *Judgment* contains active scenes of pursuits and shootouts. "He fired off a couple of shots, making the sign of the cross with his bullets," the narrator relates about a man on horseback trying to halt a group of horse-drawn wagons in a style reminiscent of the Hollywood Westerns popular with cinemagoers in Berlin and other urban centers in the interwar years.[75]

Judgment opens in the fictional Kamino-Balke, amidst "abandoned churches [. . .] from the monastery that had been destroyed."[76] The Cheka had established its regional outpost inside a ruined structure of the kind that, in Gothic literature, "frequently becomes personified within the narrative framework, contributing to the action no less than human actors."[77] The local Cheka is headed, as of two weeks prior to the start of the novel's events, by a man identified by his *nom de guerre,* Filipov. Filipov is rumored to have acquired his revolutionary alias while working in a coal mine. The Cheka becomes a space defined by "the cold fires of judgment" over which Filipov "presided." These are the fires of a "strange, new, harsher world"—the Bolsheviks' universe.[78] This world is also Gothic in that it carries within itself traces of a bygone past imprinted in the literal architecture of power. By locating its offices inside a ruined monastery, Filipov's regime, although associated with revolutionary change, is contaminated with "the archaic [. . .] that which was prior to, or was opposed to, or resisted the establishment of [. . .] civilized values and a well-regulated society."[79]

Filipov becomes head of the Cheka at Kamino-Balke when he replaces an agent who had been reported to the authorities, by a character called Comrade Sasha, for unspecified "negligence [*nakhlozikayt*]."[80] To carry out his orders, Filipov relies on agents Igumenko, Andreyev, and Zubok, who constantly bicker with each other and also snipe at Filipov, frequently out of his earshot. Despite the power they hold in the hierarchy of the Bolshevik secret police, this trio of enforcers of the law appear as bumbling figures. This occasional comedy is leavened by a touch of cruelty that bespeaks the broader ruthlessness expected of them in their positions. Igumenko, fuming at Filipov, once "punched [his] horse hard on the head between its ears" as a substitute for one of the "crazy stunts that he would have enjoyed playing on the new boss."[81] None of the men in Filipov's retinue is Jewish, nor is the "boss" himself. When Bergelson renders their implicitly Russian-language conversations in Yiddish, he occasionally disrupts the flow of language with words transliterated directly from Russian to remind readers that these characters would not have been speaking a Jewish language. One particular Russian phrase, whose hissing Slavic sibilants sound both frightening and sarcastic to the novel's other protagonists through its numerous repetitions, marks Filipov's speech: "What are you, joking? [*Chto vy, shutite?*]"[82]

Like many novels written in the Gothic mode, *Judgment* is a story about uncertain inheritance and succession: Filipov, for all his apparent power, suffers from a debilitating ailment, and none of his deputies is well positioned to succeed him. In classic Gothic novels such as Horace Walpole's *The Castle of Otranto* (1764), disruptions in genealogical lines lead to family disputes over private property. This kind of disruption and subsequent strife was especially common after the French Revolution, when economic power was redistributed from feudal elites to the bourgeoisie. In Gothic works, fictional castles became haunted by the ghosts of would-be claimants who had been denied their apparent rights. Underlying the question of inheritance in Gothic literature was a more general sense of anxiety about the return of the old world order.

Similar anxiety pervaded the institutions of the fledgling Soviet state in the years right after the Russian civil war. It swirled around the fate of the working class, whose members had not yet gained the revolutionary consciousness thought necessary for them to govern themselves in an appropriate revolutionary manner. The period of War Communism, which was implemented by the Bolsheviks during the Russian civil war and which led to famine and large-scale hardship, gave way to the New Economic Policy (NEP): starting in 1922, a limited return of private enterprise was allowed to facilitate the speedier restoration of the country's economy. Some Bolshevik leaders, together with the rank and file, feared that bygone bourgeois habits, which the revolution had sought to root out, would resurface during NEP. Eric Naiman has termed the resulting literary and journalistic discourses "NEP Gothic."[83] Unlike in classic Gothic novels with their concerns about the disputed ownership of haunted castles, in *Judgment,* questions about succession pertain not to the inheritance of private property but rather to the inheritance and transmission of revolutionary ideals and Bolshevik legitimacy.

As agents of the Cheka, Filipov and his retinue pursue, arrest, and try those found to be in violation of the new Bolshevik laws; the condemned are either sent to concentration camps, part of the state's nascent carceral system, or executed right on the premises of the former monastery.[84] Kamino-Balke casts a long shadow over the area as the Cheka surveils the goings-on in the vicinity. The nearby shtetl of Golikhovke, caught in the Cheka's crosshairs, "lay[s] waiting without any light and with bated breath" for Filipov's wrath even as it experiences an acute economic crisis.[85] Golikhovke's decline has been several years in the making: several times in the novel the narrator uses dark humor to describe an unnamed shtetl Jew "with blue-tinted glasses and [the] smell of smoked fish, although there was no smoked fish to be had since before the war."[86] Golikhovke's unfolding economic devastation resulted, in part, from the shtetl's separation from its economic network as new post–First World War state borders divided parts of the former Pale from one another. After the concessions-filled peace treaties signed by the Bolsheviks in 1918, Golikhovke—a fictionalized treatment of many actual shtetls—ended up on the Ukrainian side of the border with a newly independent Poland.[87] Commercial exchanges that would previously have been unremarkable had become illegal.

As new state borders fragmented the formerly contiguous commercial space of the Pale of Settlement and the adjacent areas of what had been formerly known as Congress Poland (a part of the Russian Empire prior to 1917), whole categories of people became suspect under the Bolsheviks' new economic system. In *Judgment*, many end up in the prison run by Filipov's Cheka. One group of prisoners had been owners of factories, managers of estates, and tradesmen who had either become reliant on smugglers or turned into smugglers themselves. One of these is Aaron Lemberger, the wealthy proprietor of a tannery, who concealed his inventory to avoid paying new taxes and smuggled some of his leather merchandise to Poland. Another is a clockmaker—a man whose name, as is the case with many characters in the novel, is never disclosed—who forged passports for contrabandists. Another group of prisoners had been forced willy-nilly into illicit commerce because of Golikhovke's location at the border. Among them, Shmuel Voltsis, who had been employed at a sawmill, ended up renting rooms to lodgers who passed through the shtetl as they fled the new regime to Poland. "Suddenly the world had become good to him, a pox on it, and begun to shower him with easy money," Voltsis explains during his arrest, for sheltering a fugitive. "What'd he know? [. . .] He saw that everyone was doing it and did the same . . ."[88] This fugitive, Voltsis's first and only tenant, is known simply as *di blonde*—the blonde. She is later revealed to be the wife of a White general organizing against the Bolsheviks from across the border in Poland. With a crucifix dangling prominently between her breasts, she carries on a sexual liaison with Yokhelzon, a double agent who smuggles propaganda materials to Poland on behalf of the Bolsheviks and brings contraband goods back to Golikhovke. With wry humor, the novel's narrator notes how Voltsis's wife looks through a keyhole into the blonde's room and observes that "a misfortune was taking place there—for Yokhelzon's wife," as the blonde deploys her sexual powers in exchange for the double agent's knowledge about safe routes across the border.[89] Eventually, Filipov—some weeks after his deputies, tricked by the blonde's charms as the novel's *femme fatale*, failed to detain her when she had first attempted to cross the border and allowed her to return to her lodgings at Shmuel Voltsis's—arrests her himself.

Everyone in the novel who is involved in cross-border smuggling of people and goods relies on the services of other shtetl Jews, many of whom have of necessity become landlords. Others, including Bunem the Red and Hatzkl Shpak, get hired as coachmen who could be observed, on occasion, "look[ing] like sleepy fiddlers after a night of performing at a wedding—and [taking] their advance payments almost unwillingly."[90] These new fields of occupation for Golikhovke's Jews arose from the area's redefined economic landscape: "At dawn, a new group of people would arrive in the shtetl, a whole mob of smugglers, and also ordinary folk, who hated the revolution and wanted to escape it—places had to be readied for this crowd."[91] As the web of commercial, conspiratorial, and political liaisons, determined by Golikhovke's location near the new border, becomes ever more intricate, Filipov keeps watch over the area from the Cheka's headquarters in the ruined monastery in Kamino-Balke.

Bergelson communicates the uncertain, ever-shifting atmosphere of a border town in transition with the help of free indirect discourse, a variant of third-person narration that stays close to the minds of individual characters without the use of dialogue to identify speech as the character's own. Free indirect discourse, which the author perfected in his earlier novels, muddles the boundary between a character's inner thoughts and a seemingly objective reality.[92] In *Judgment,* the elderly physician Babitsky provides Bergelson with a steady opportunity to deploy this technique. Babitsky was once involved in socialist and anti-tsarist political movements and served a sentence in internal exile in Siberia. Nonetheless, after "the revolution took the wrong turn" with the Bolsheviks' rise to power, he found himself on the sidelines.[93] On one occasion, Babitsky, whose mind is swirling with thoughts of death, material deprivation, and the suffering associated with Filipov's ruthless enforcement of new Bolshevik laws, perceives the sound of leaves over his head as the wailing of a patient in need of medical attention. The narrative moves seamlessly from the disturbing images of nature to the doctor's thoughts motivated by what he sees and hears:

> In the deep darkness naked branches clattered. A hoarse cry of pain broke from the disheveled trees. The events hidden in the nooks and crannies of the countryside seemed to be rifling through their leaves. It sounded as if the rustling was causing someone pain.
>
> If they were to come, these events, they would engulf the entire area like a fire, and would spare only his house, the doctor's house with its dilapidated fence and broken gate, because he was a man on the sidelines.[94]

Earlier in his life, if the cries for help had come from someone who had been hurt, the doctor would have intervened to alleviate the pain. But now Babitsky has an opposite response: he convinces himself to feign indifference so as not to attract Filipov's attention—and, with it, his ire.

Babitsky lives with someone rumored to be his illegitimate son, an intellectually disabled man whom the novel identifies as a "deaf-mute." Three years earlier, "in the first festive weeks of the revolution"—a reference to February 1917—Babitsky taught his son to say "revolution," which, in his son's rendition, came out as "Rrrrree . . . vv . . . vv . . . vo . . . o . . . o . . . lluu . . . shshsh . . . un!!!" The more democratic Socialist Revolutionary project, which Babitsky had supported, abruptly gave way to the Bolshevik coup that was seen by many—including Babitsky—as the revolution's hijacking. Now, in the novel's narrative present, the word "grated in [Babitsky's] ears" and "was claptrap and dangerous besides," but it stuck because "taking the word away from the deaf-mute was a lot harder than giving it to him."[95] The word "revolution," now firmly associated with the Bolsheviks, seems dangerous to Babitsky as he and other SRs find themselves in opposition to the new regime. As a result, Babitsky has become an aloof elderly man who is no longer involved in politics.

Nonetheless, at the request of Sofia Pokrovskaya, the head of the local SR cell, Babitsky helps hide political leaflets. Pokrovskaya, a priest's daughter from the nearby village of Yanovo and a longtime acquaintance of Babitsky's, coordinates anti-Bolshevik, social democratic activities against Filipov's regime. The group's other members include the Pokras brothers, two Jewish veterans of the First World War. Babitsky once sees them sleeping, their "every snore [serving] as a reminder that they had sacrificed themselves for the 'work' Sofia Pokrovskaya was carrying out in the region and that, like her, they wanted to save the peasants nearby, to save life itself all over the country."[96] Muli Spivak, another SR, runs the shtetl's pharmacy; every mention of the pharmacy includes the fact that it had been recently nationalized—a detail that occurs in another novel about the Cheka, Yuri Libedinskii's *A Week* (*Nedelia*). Published in 1923, *A Week* has a character who sours on the new regime after the Bolsheviks requisition his privately owned pharmacy.[97] Pokrovskaya sends Muli's brother Yuzi, an aloof intellectual with little actual contact with Russian workers and peasants whose cause the SRs champion, on some of the most dangerous missions. As the counterrevolutionary group plots its uprising together with their comrades-in-arms on the Polish side of the border, Yuzi Spivak comes to play a major role in the Socialist Revolutionaries' plans.

Sofia Pokrovskaya and Yuzi Spivak are eventually apprehended by the Cheka. Pokrovskaya is executed on Filipov's orders. For Spivak, however, the imprisonment sets off a lengthy process of self-discovery. Upon his arrival at Kamino-Balke, Spivak shares a prison cell with Pinke Vayl, a Red Army soldier whose family roped him into smuggling and whose accounts of his Jewish childhood remind Yuzi of his own. As he becomes close with Pinke, who felt liberated by the revolution despite being imprisoned by its enforcers, Spivak undergoes a kind of conversion to the Bolshevik cause. *Judgment* appears to end with a decisive Bolshevik victory. With their political opponents defeated and the shtetl intelligentsia—represented by Spivak—on their side, the Bolsheviks seem to be in complete control of the area. However, the submerged but faintly visible pogrom violence against Golikhovke's Jews haunts not only the Jewish protagonists of *Judgment* but also the figure of the Soviet Jew emerging in the pages of Bergelson's novel.

* * *

Judgment contains noticeable instances of imprecision that reflect Bergelson's attempts to square the new Bolshevik reality with the characters' uncertainty about the nature of the new regime. One textual slippage pertains to the nomenclature Bergelson uses to refer to Filipov and his crew at the Cheka. When the narrator names the Cheka in the opening sentence, he employs a direct Yiddish translation of the full bureaucratic term used by the new Bolshevik regime. *Chrezvychainaia komissiia,* shortened to "Cheka," is rendered in Yiddish as *bazunder opteylung,* which literally reflects the Russian meaning, "the Extraordinary Commission." Like other early Soviet texts, *Judgment* attempts, via linguistic calque, to assimilate new Bolshevik terms into the literary language. But the translated term in Yiddish lacks the specificity of the Russian "Cheka," which had become a recognizable abbreviation by the time Bergelson started working on his novel. The narrator of *Judgment* stops referring to the local Cheka as *bazunder opteylung* after its first mention. Instead, the Cheka's location, Kamino-Balke, rather than its formal name, becomes the referent for the secret police and border patrol headquartered there. Likewise, although two of the men serving under Filipov are referred to by their last names and titles, Agent (*agent*) Zubok and Investigator (*sledovatel'*) Andreyev, both Filipov and his predecessor at Kamino-Balke are referred to informally as simply "boss" (*nachal'nik*).

All the titles that Bergelson uses are in Russian, transliterated in Yiddish. *Nachal'nik,* when used to refer to Filipov and his predecessor at the local Cheka, stands out both because it is a Russian word and because it is not a correct contemporary term for Filipov's position. Given the range of Filipov's duties at the Cheka, his title would have been "chairman" (*predsedatel'*) as, for example, in the contemporary abbreviation *predgubcheka,* which denotes the chairman of the regional Cheka. By using the imprecise word *nachal'nik* to describe Filipov as a generic "boss," the novel's narrator betrays his uncertainty about the exact nature of the new regime. This uncertainty, in turn, matches the lack of clarity in some characters' minds about the new system of rule. The new regime's "bosses" just didn't seem to last, and the expected duration of the Bolsheviks' reign appeared unclear as well. Filipov, like his predecessor, seems frightening and powerful, but the local population has already seen how quickly such men could fall.

Not unlike the narrator of Fyodor Dostoevsky's *Demons*, Bergelson's anonymous first-person narrator is situated in the provinces, facing the challenge of telling a story in an information vacuum. Many of the novel's characters fail to understand the ideological meaning of events unfolding around them and rely on hearsay and outright rumors. One topic of especially robust rumors is the departure of the previous *nachal'nik* and Filipov's subsequent appearance in Kamino-Balke. The downfall of Cheka agents was a commonplace of contemporary fiction about the early Bolshevik years. Tarasov-Rodionov's *Chocolate* (1923) culminated in the arrest and execution of a Cheka chairman who had been accused of patronage and taking bribes, including in the form of the eponymous contraband confection. Bergelson might have read *Chocolate* along with *Life and Death of Nikolai Kurbov*—Ilya Ehrenburg's contribution the same year to the literary fiction about the rapid ascent and similarly rapid demise of Cheka agents.[98] The rumor that Filipov's predecessor was turned in by his own comrades circulated in the context of a larger, vague sense that, as fearsome as they may have seemed, such men were replaceable cogs in the same Bolshevik machinery they had created.

The incorrect term *nachal'nik* is a reminder that the narrator and Golikhovke's Jews had already seen the demise of Kamino-Balke's previous head by the time Filipov came along. Locals would not have had much time to learn these men's titles—each of them was simply a "boss" who wouldn't last. Opponents of the Bolshevik rule would have seen in the first *nachal'nik*'s departure an opportunity for overthrowing the apparently vulnerable regime led by a new appointee. The demise of one "boss" and the perceived weakness of another would also have presaged to Golikhovke's Jews the return of the pogroms that had been perpetrated prior to the arrival of the Bolsheviks, and that the Bolsheviks were supposed to prevent.

Another set of rumors that made Filipov's staying power as the local "boss" seem less likely, pertained to his background: "No one knew where he came from or how he used to make his living. From the beginning there were rumors that he had been a magnate who had his own mines and lived in a palace."[99] If indeed Filipov had been a "former magnate," as the gossip suggested, some in Golikhovke would have also seen him as one of the "former people" (in Russian, *byvshie liudi*)—a legal category in the Bolshevik law applied to members of the prerevolutionary upper classes who were viewed with suspicion by the new regime and stripped of their civil and individual rights.[100] Such rumors amplified many local Jews' fears that they, too, might fall into the category of the newly disenfranchised.

The narrator continues with yet another rumor, this one about Filipov's illness: "Then the story about his former wealth was abruptly abandoned, although the connection to the mines was retained. He had been a worker in the mines all his life, people said, and the toxic gases underground [*unter der erd*] had caused his illness and the infection of his bandaged neck."[101] Whether he was a magnate who used to live in a palace or a coal miner who fell ill because of the harsh subterranean work conditions, Filipov appears in *Judgment* as a monster who emerges from either the depths of the earth or the secluded castle, both common Gothic tropes.

Filipov's illness seems severe enough that both those close to him and townsfolk in Golikhovke consider him to be either near death or as good as dead. At the start of the novel, Igumenko refers to Filipov as "that carcass [*ot a neveyle*]."[102] The term comes from Hebrew. Within Judaism's dietary laws governing the preparation of kosher meat, *neveyle* refers to an animal that wasn't properly slaughtered but, instead, died of old age or disease; such meat is deemed unfit for consumption. Placed in charge of a small posse of Cheka men, Filipov appears to them as carrion, a dead hunk of putrefying flesh. Igumenko's ongoing insubordination points to his doubts about the local Cheka head's authority and to wider questions about the future of Bolshevik rule in Ukraine.

To those in Golikhovke, who likely were survivors of recent pogroms, the signs of the Chekist's weakness are ominous. When Filipov first arrives in the shtetl to confront those involved in cross-border smuggling, he cuts a "huge, mighty figure of a man [. . .] riding [a] nag" who "could be recognized only by the bandage on his neck, his peasant coat, and sheepskin hat pulled over his ears."[103] Filipov sets himself up inside an abandoned shop where he prepares to interrogate the coachmen. Sitting with his back to the door, "he kept on frowning" before, "grimacing in pain, he unwrapped the bandage from his neck and throat." Bunem the Red, one of the Jewish coachmen, has already been let into the room, but instead of turning to face his interlocutor, Filipov "picked up a small mirror from the policeman's desk and, looking into its scratched surface, gingerly poked at the hard, swollen bumps on his neck."[104] Earlier, when rumors about Filipov had only begun swirling in Golikhovke, Bunem noted that his fellow shtetl dwellers were scared of the person "in the peasant cap, who hangs around Kamino-Balke . . . It's probably the new executioner, the boss himself."[105] At the end of their encounter, Filipov threatens Bunem with execution if the coachman continues taking people to the border.

Bunem observes Filipov's poor state of health up close and, as a coachman who interacts with the many people he drives around the area, he is uniquely positioned to circulate rumors. The rumors about the gravity of Filipov's condition also spread by another route familiar in Golikhovke: the movements of Doctor Babitsky. "If they asked for Babitsky, it meant that the patient was on his last legs," the novel's narrator notes. "In those cases, Babitsky came quickly and his visit itself was a sign that the sick person would die."[106] When, several days after Filipov's visit to town, a wagon from Kamino-Balke that everyone knew by sight and "feared like a hearse" was seen "rush[ing]" to pick up Babitsky, it offered ample evidence that Filipov's health may have declined and that the rumors of his proximate demise may well have been true.[107] If the new *nachal'nik* were going to be as vulnerable as the previous one, then Golikhovke's Jews, concerned about their economic and physical survival, would have had little reason to side with his regime.

Filipov was not the only man with a serious illness placed in the position of a Bolshevik literary hero. Similarly afflicted protagonists populated Soviet culture from its early days and throughout the Stalin era, betraying that the Bolsheviks' hold on power was more tenuous than official discourses suggested.[108] In fact, Filipov appears as a bricolage of protagonists from earlier novels about the Cheka, already in wide circulation by the mid-1920s. Zudin from Tarasov-Rodionov's *Chocolate,* whose last name contains the Russian root for "itch," suffers from chronic exhaustion and dies by the revolver-wielding hand of his Cheka comrades after quickly convincing himself that facing the firing squad would help secure the revolution's future—a logic that appears to be tinged with suicidal intent.[109] Srubov, in Vladimir Zazubrin's "Shchepka"—a protagonist whose last name comes from the Russian root for "to cut down"—begins hallucinating after witnessing daily mass executions in the basement of the local Cheka that he heads; he commits suicide by drowning, imagining that "he was swimming again along a river of blood."[110] Robeiko, the Chekist in Libedinskii's *A Week*—his last name comes from the Russian root for "to be fearful"—suffers from tuberculosis of the throat, which makes every word he speaks feel like a "sharp shard of glass [that] rose to his larynx and ripped it apart."[111] Robeiko's symptoms are closest to Filipov's; his dedication to his work despite his illness is also similar to Filipov's in that— as with Zudin and Srubov—it borders on suicidal. In *A Week*, Robeiko is killed by anti-Bolshevik forces; in *Judgment*, Filipov knows full well that he would die if he decided to confront the opponents of the new regime. The same forces also threaten Golikhovke's Jews with the return of pogroms that the Bolsheviks had promised to thwart.

The threat of pogroms is personified in the figure of Ushak. The notorious pogromist crosses the border with the help of SRs, who want his assistance in a planned uprising against the Cheka outpost at Kamino-Balke. Even though the SRs leave Ushak behind after he drinks himself into a stupor, he still exerts his violent influence on the area through his entourage:

They [the SRs] traveled through the forest, their heavy wagons screeching. When darkness fell, somewhere deep in the middle of the forest a string of gunshots rang out—one after another, continuing for a long time, as if submerged in thought. In the wagons, they discussed the gunfire:
"Maybe it's Ushak's gang? They are bent on protecting him."
"Oh, yes, he is precious to them . . ."
"Whenever he travels across the border, two or three others follow him—that's the rumor, anyway . . ."[112]

Distant sounds of gunshots point to the carnage that Ushak is feared to have brought with him to Ukraine. Soon enough, Filipov falls victim to these lurking forces, and a rumor begins to spread that Filipov had been killed by Ushak's presumed companions: "In Tatarovke only the villagers whose houses bordered on the [. . .] forest heard the shots—in the middle of the night, some later reported, or, according to others, by the gray light of dawn."[113] Witnesses confirm that Ushak never traveled alone and that his gang was larger than the SRs had suspected: "Early in the morning, several of Ushak's men rode into the village requesting fresh towels to use for bandaging [. . .] From this, the villagers concluded that a couple of Ushak's men were wounded."[114] The narrative remains imprecise about the size of Ushak's retinue: there are "several" of them—a number larger than the previous SR estimate of "two or three [who] follow him." And they have claimed their biggest prize: "Last night we took down the big shot himself!" the gang members boast, confirming that they killed Filipov.

As Babitsky, doctor only to those who cannot be saved, prepares to be taken to Filipov's sickbed at Kamino-Balke—not long before Filipov's final mission and during one of the regular flareups of the disease affecting the *nachal'nik*'s throat—he contemplates the nature of the Chekist's illness:

> It seemed to the doctor that Filipov was sick with a strange illness that nobody had ever heard of. This was an illness that could infect only a man like Filipov. When he ordered someone's death, when he gave the command, "Shoot!"—there was no wisdom that could dissuade him because it wasn't Filipov who was giving the orders. It was History. Just as quickly, however, Babitsky's thought turns into an unuttered joke evident in his facial expression: "And who has fallen ill, hmm? . . . The ambassador of History!"[115]

How could a man perceived to be "the ambassador of History" complete his mission if he is already all but dead, Babitsky wonders? Why should Babitsky—or any other Jew from Golikhovke—trust that the Bolshevik regime, which had promised to protect Jews, would last any longer than its local enforcer? Filipov chooses to die at the hands of Ushak and his gang. Already perceived by others as ineffective in his role, he sees greater utility in being violently killed for the cause, than in dying of his illness: he imagines himself being "brought [. . .] back to Kamino-Balke, a dead man, murdered by criminals." A martyr, Filipov foresees himself being capable of inspiring both his Cheka colleagues and local civilians to unite and defeat the revolution's enemies.[116]

Filipov's death from illness is expected from the beginning of *Judgment*. When he does die, however, he does so while on a suicide mission—his final charge against the foes of the revolution. Though Bergelson appears to follow the by-then commonplace blueprint for the creation of a Bolshevik hero, the continuous rumors about Filipov's inevitable demise also turn the Chekist's seemingly heroic end into something entirely unsurprising. To the untrained eye—or, perhaps, to the eye glazing over after reading too many novels about the Cheka in the 1920s—Filipov may look like the revolution's selfless hero; however, the misalignment between the novel's seemingly sudden ending and the certainty about Filipov's eventual death written into many of its earlier pages warrants a closer look. Bergelson's concern in *Judgment* may not have been with the fate of the novel's apparent protagonist at all but, instead, with the fate of the shtetl dwellers who were justly served neither by Filipov's reign nor by the seemingly heroic nature of his demise.

* * *

David Bergelson, who had spent the immediate years after the revolution mostly in Kiev—then a major center of cultural life in Yiddish—began serializing *Judgment* in 1926, five years after his move to Berlin, which by then had become a haven for Russian, Hebrew, and Yiddish writers. He published the first six chapters in the short-lived journal *In Harness* (*In shpan*), which he edited. After *In Harness* folded, Bergelson continued to serialize sections of the novel in Yiddish periodicals in Poland, the United States, and the Soviet Union. The completed novel came out in book form in 1929 in two separate editions: in the USSR as a standalone volume published by the Kultur-lige (Culture League) and in Vilna (then, Wilno, Poland) as the seventh volume of Bergelson's collected works put out by the Kletskin publishing house (figures 1.5 and 1.6). Disseminated across geographic boundaries by the sprawling network of periodicals and publishers that comprised the interwar Yiddish republic of letters, *Mides-hadin* was discussed and debated by literary critics near and far.

Bergelson's novel was all the more notable because its publication coincided with the author's announcement that he was preparing to return to the USSR.[117] For this reason, *Judgment* has been commonly understood as a

דוד בערגעלסאָן

מ י ד ת - ה ד י ן

ווילנע – 1929
ווילנער פארלאג פון ב. קלעצקין

Figure I.5. Title page of David Bergelson's
Judgment (*Mides-hadin*), published as the
seventh volume of his collected works in
Vilna (then in Poland) in 1929. For the
novel's title, Bergelson borrows from
the Jewish religious tradition and uses the
Hebrew-language concept denoting the
measure or quality of divine judgment.
Courtesy of the Yiddish Book Center.

ד. בערגעלסאָן

מידאס-האדין

קאָאָפּעראַטיווער פאַרלאַג „קולטור - ליגע"
קיעוו – 1929

Figure I.6. Title page of David Bergelson's
Judgment (*Mides-hadin*) published
in Kiev, USSR, in 1929. The spelling of
the novel's title follows the orthographic
conventions of Soviet Yiddish, which
require phonetic renderings of Hebrew-
origin words. Courtesy of the Yiddish
Book Center.

literary expression of Bergelson's apparent endorsement of the Bolshevik regime, a kind of application for an entry visa to the USSR. In the issue of *In Harness* that included the novel's first installment, Bergelson published an essay arguing that the USSR, with its state-level funding for cultural activities of ethnic and linguistic minorities, presented the best set of opportunities for the future of Yiddish literature.[118] However, Bergelson was neither in a hurry to move to the Soviet Union when he first signaled his cultural allegiances to it in 1926, nor did he necessarily intend for *Judgment* to guarantee his admission to the USSR. After he first announced his intention to move to the Soviet Union, he headed to the United States, where he stayed for six months from the end of 1928 until the late spring of 1929.[119] He ultimately made it to the USSR in 1934, via a stopover in Denmark, where he had moved after the Nazis' rise to power compelled his family to leave Germany and where he also contemplated staying.[120]

At the time of the novel's publication, some Soviet critics doubted whether Bergelson's apparent endorsement of the Bolshevik Revolution was genuine; those who did give him the benefit of the doubt felt it was half-hearted.[121] The doctrinaire critic Yasha Bronshteyn saw *Judgment* as a misguided imitation rather than a properly ideological text.[122] He maintained that Bergelson simply situated his usual prose about the decline of the shtetl amidst theatrical props that looked like the revolution ("*rekvizit-revolutsie*") to frame this radically new subject in a fresh ideological perspective.[123] Instead of answering the revolution's call with a new style befitting the political changes afoot, the author of *Judgment*, Bronshteyn quipped, "bergelsonified [*farbergelsonevet*]" the revolution instead.[124]

Bronshteyn's criticism of the author's "bergelsonification" of the revolution all but disappeared in subsequent literary criticism on *Judgment*. Instead, scholars have viewed the novel as a text, which was uniquely focused on its protagonist, the Chekist Filipov, as the embodiment of Bergelson's earnest attempt to represent Bolshevism. Susan Slotnick has called Filipov the novel's "messenger of the revolution,"[125] whereas Mikhail Krutikov has seen him as the embodiment of the book's title: the "mystical concept of *mides-hadin,* literally 'measure of judgment,' which in the Jewish tradition is associated with the rigor of divine justice."[126] For Marc Caplan, the "pseudonymous and mysterious Filipov [. . .] functions by default as the novel's protagonist."[127] When scholars take the novel as Bergelson's own effort to understand the Bolshevik Revolution as a force of history, they see Filipov as the incarnation of this force, which Bergelson was domesticating for Yiddish readers with the help of the traditional Jewish concept of divine justice.

Assuming that Bergelson had signaled his pro-Bolshevik allegiances through his protagonist Filipov, some critics have speculated that he must have written *Judgment* to please his supposed Soviet handlers.[128] The poet Rokhl Korn, writing from her adopted home in Montreal on the tenth anniversary of Bergelson's 1952 execution on Stalin's orders as a member of the Jewish Anti-Fascist Committee, called the writer a "collaborator of Commissar Filipov."[129] Filipov is not, in fact, a commissar—the Bolshevik term for a Party official embedded with an organization or a military unit and tasked with the ideological education of its members. But Korn reaches for a recognizable moniker synonymous with "Bolshevik" in the Cold War–era popular imagination to convey her ideological impression of Bergelson. The works Bergelson wrote after his 1926 announcement about returning to the USSR, Korn suggests, do not merit the same attention bestowed on his earlier prose. A decade and a half after Korn, in 1977, Irving Howe and Eliezer Greenberg included English translations of some of Bergelson's work in their collection *Ashes out of Hope*. The editors rationalized their choice not to include anything that Bergelson wrote after the mid-1920s by explaining that the kind of literary texts that "Yiddish writers had to compose during the worst years of the Stalinist period—these should be familiar enough to anyone who has read equivalents in other languages."[130] In other words, they suggested, these works were not much more than Soviet boilerplate and not, as such, of literary interest. Similarly, in 1977, an English translator of one of Bergelson's earlier novels dismissed Bergelson's later writing as work that clearly showed the emergence of "a political ideologue, a revolutionary propagandist."[131]

But just as they presume Bergelson's professed fealty to the Bolsheviks in his portrayal of Filipov, critics have also stressed the protagonist's lack of character depth. According to Mikhail Krutikov, Filipov possesses none of "that opaque psychological complexity that was hallmark of Bergelson's pre-revolution characters."[132] Harriet Murav and I have argued, in contrast, that Filipov does share notable characteristics with the protagonists of Bergelson's earlier works and that, moreover, some doctrinaire Soviet critics compared *Judgment*'s Bolshevik hero, unflatteringly, to those moody and indecisive literary creations.[133] One way or another, measuring Filipov by the yardstick of a "Bolshevik hero" may be misleading; it has prompted scholars to conclude that the novel lacks the literary complexity of Bergelson's earlier fiction, that it was penned merely for instrumental reasons, and that it is an inferior work within Bergelson's otherwise praiseworthy oeuvre.

Joseph Sherman has suggested that, for Bergelson, Filipov represented the Bolshevik ideal of a triumphant and heroic figure who undertook an act of self-sacrifice for the cause: "the uncompromisingly moral Chekist Filipov embodies the 'truth' of the revolution and sacrifices himself for it." "All who oppose him," Sherman comments on the aftermath of Filipov's death at the novel's end, "from common criminals to religiously observant Jews, are in different ways brought to concede his inevitable triumph."[134] This "triumph" results from Filipov's solitary charge against a band of enemies—a suicidal attack of the kind that had by then already been described in Soviet literature. "His heroic death," concurs Krutikov, "enables him to fulfill his messianic mission to the very end, because his sacrifice helps to mobilize those demoralized forces of the revolution that were on the brink of moral and physical collapse."[135]

The immediate aftermath of Filipov's death, however, does not match the heroism of an archetypal revolutionary martyr. A brief final chapter—the novel's shortest—emphasizes the symbolism of Filipov's demise but offers little indication of how the narrative might progress from this point. "Filipov was laid out on a couch in the office and was covered with a red cloth," the narrator comments; "the walls were also decked out in red—they gathered up whatever banners they could find in Kamino-Balke, even though there weren't enough." Pinke Vayl, then alone in the room with Filipov's body, fixates on the funereal décor: "this wasn't the proper way to honor Filipov—whole swaths of wall remained white." As mourners arrive, a decision is made to attack a gathering of counterrevolutionaries in a neighboring village "before nightfall." The noted pogromist Ushak, who had been smuggled in by Filipov's enemies, is rumored to be there. The decision to attack is made "in the name of Comrade Filipov," with the intent to transform Filipov's symbolic sacrifice into a Bolshevik military victory.[136]

To accomplish this task, the slain Filipov's Jewish protégé Yuzi Spivak, who underwent a kind of conversion to Bolshevism while imprisoned at Kamino-Balke, heads off to "the far-flung shtetls to recruit workers willing to join the effort," while Pinke Vayl heads to Golikhovke to recruit "eight or nine young workers" in preparation for an offensive. Spivak and Vayl, two Jews newly turned to Bolshevism, are hoping to recruit other shtetl Jews, traumatized by recent pogroms and disenfranchised by the Bolsheviks' laws, to join the Bolshevik cause. The novel's concluding scene takes place in Golikhovke where Pinke Vayl had gone in search of recruits: "His comrades assembled outside, Pinke gave a speech—for the first time in his life; he wanted to explain what Filipov had given his life and blood for." However, Vayl's words remain inaudible to his audience: "It didn't bother him that his voice was so hoarse. Chills running down their spines, his comrades saw the blood flowing to his face from straining to speak with all his might; they saw his lips moving without hearing a single word—the wind outside was too strong—but, in any case, there were no words to describe what Filipov had given his life for, and maybe it was actually for the best that Pinke's voice was so hoarse while he spoke."[137] Vayl strains to achieve what some scholars and critics of the novel have wrongly understood to be a fait accompli: turning the symbolism of Filipov's self-sacrifice into a meaningful leap toward the revolution's victory. Despite Vayl's effort, no discernible words reach their intended audience. The narrator offers varied excuses for their inaudibility: Vayl's ineffectiveness as a first-time public speaker, his hoarse voice, the strength of the wind. Finally, he rationalizes, in a roundabout way, that there had been no use in giving the speech in the first place. Aware of his failure to make a rousing appeal, Vayl suddenly stops trying to recruit new men. He remembers "that there were patches of exposed white wall in the office where Filipov's body was laid out—not honoring him properly." Facing the workers whom he had tried to recruit, Vayl yells at them twice, with the second time serving as the novel's concluding sentence: "Surrender all your banners, all of them, for him—to put on the walls!!!"[138] Having come to the shtetl to find men for a military effort, Vayl instead gathers up their banners to amplify the symbolic appeal of Filipov's sacrifice for the cause of the revolution.

In this abrupt ending, Bergelson performs a sleight of hand, making a show of turning his protagonist's death into a revolutionary hero's feat. However, the novel's reader—like the intended audience of new potential recruits—observes in the final scene only the effort, not its result. As red banners are gathered to decorate the room where Filipov lies in state, we do not see new men joining the Bolshevik cause under those banners. Neither does Bergelson show us any military advance—let alone a successful one—against the counterrevolutionaries who threaten the Bolsheviks' hold on power amidst the unfolding internecine conflict. Vayl's attempt to recruit shtetl Jews to the Bolshevik cause fails when he uses Filipov's martyrdom as a rallying cry—rather than what would have been a more resonant cry: to avenge the deaths of fellow Jews at the hands of pogromists who also happen to be the same thugs who murdered Filipov.

Bergelson was not the only writer to focus on a revolutionary hero's self-sacrifice and its trumpeted—but unrealized—potential to lead to a Bolshevik military advance. "Squadron Commander Trunov," Isaac Babel's story about a Red Army man who died in a suicidal artillery attack, begins by describing the eponymous hero's mutilated body: "At noon we brought to Sokal the bullet-riddled body of Trunov [. . .] He had been killed this morning in action against enemy aircraft. All the bullets had hit Trunov in the face, his cheeks were covered with wounds, his tongue torn away."[139] Similarly, in *Judgment,* Pinke Vayl observes the body of Filipov who, like Trunov, was killed in a suicidal charge against the revolution's enemies: "Filipov was shot multiple times—perhaps five or six bullets. Besides that, there was a deep, bloody slash on his face reaching all the way to his forehead."[140] Babel's short story was based on an article he published in a Red Army newspaper during the war between the Bolsheviks and Poland in 1920, the same year that Bergelson's fictional Filipov was killed. *The Red Cavalryman* article, full of propagandistic clichés typical of Babel's work as an army correspondent, celebrated the fallen hero's "proletarian heart shattered so that it could color the red banners of the revolution with its blood."[141] By the time Babel reworked his article into a short story, first published in February 1925 in the preeminent literary journal *Red Virgin Soil* (*Krasnaia nov'*), red banners rhetorically displacing mutilated bodies had become an established trope.

"Squadron Commander Trunov" was part of *Red Cavalry*—Babel's cycle of short stories about a military campaign that the Bolsheviks did not, in fact, win. Published to great acclaim and immediately translated into several languages, *Red Cavalry* immortalized both a new pantheon of civil war heroes and one of the conflict's campaigns in which the Bolsheviks failed. When Bergelson ended his novel with Vayl's thwarted attempt to rally potential Red

Army recruits around the spectacle of Filipov's mutilated corpse, he called attention to the fact that *Judgment* concluded in medias res, in the midst of an ongoing conflict that the Bolsheviks were not certain to win. The heavy-handed symbolism of the final chapter far from settles the question of whether Filipov's successors could retain control of the area. Beneath Vayl's overstated demand for red banners, emphasized by three exclamation marks, anxiety about whether the Bolsheviks would hang on to power—and what their failure to do so could mean for local Jews—remains palpable.

* * *

Such anxiety about Filipov's regime, the likely demise of which is prefaced by the account of the Chekist's death, betrays an additional fear experienced by Golikhovke's Jews: that the Bolsheviks' rule—though it touted itself as a bulwark against pogroms—was not free of antisemitism in the first place. Indeed, the Bolshevik law imposed on Golikhovke centered on prohibiting and criminalizing the kind of economic activity that was, in practice, identified with Jews. The Bolsheviks may have, in their stated policy, opposed antisemitism, but the mechanisms of Filipov's rule, de facto, hurt them. Embracing Filipov's regime would not have felt all that straightforward: in fact, doing so might have meant, for Golikhovke's Jews, casting their lot with someone not altogether different from the pogromists whose reign he had supposedly ended.

In its August 1925 issue, the journal *30 Days* (*30 dnei*) ran "By the Border Post," a travel sketch about the involvement of Jews in cross-border smuggling. The article focused on Shepetovka, a small town of "Gogolian houses—dead, sleepy, with closed window shutters," located in western Ukraine near the Soviet-Polish border—not far from Rovno (Równe), which was then in Poland—but separated from it by a vast, densely forested expanse. The Red Army in Shepetovka, assisted by the special forces of the Bolshevik secret police, kept watch over smugglers and contrabandists. Jews were involved in those illegal movements: Jewish coachmen (whom the article identified by the Hebrew-origin Yiddish word *balagole,* which had become domesticated into Russian as *balagola*) ferried merchandise across the border.[142] The Soviet border guards were said to have already won significant victories in bloody battles in the dark forest, but the fighting was far from over. At the time of the article's publication, the struggle of the nascent Bolshevik state against the illicit border economy was still ongoing.

A premier Soviet literary journal, *30 Days* circulated widely in the 1920s and the 1930s and published some of the most notable authors of the day. The article about Shepetovka came out a half-year before the first installment of *Judgment.* Cross-border smuggling—driven by economic policies and supply and demand on both the Soviet and Polish sides of the border—continued to be an issue into the 1920s, several years after the end of military conflicts.[143] In *30 Days,* Shepetovka's sleepiness is similar to that of Bergelson's fictional Golikhovke, where "[d]uring the day the window curtains slept" and "[t]he streets slept" and "the church was dead, absolutely dead."[144] Inside a grocery store, the article's author relates, one could observe "an old Jew drinking tea with blackberry jam—drinking it slowly, lazily, winking his half-blind eyes." Shepetovka appeared as an unmistakable remnant of a bygone time and of a disappeared but still eerily present place: the former Pale of Settlement.[145]

With the dissolution of the Pale of Settlement, both Shepetovka and Bergelson's Golikhovke were transformed from quiet towns into major thoroughfares for smuggling and contraband. Although the abolition of the Pale offered Jews the freedom of movement they had not enjoyed under the tsars, it also created shape-shifting borders that separated Jewish communities from one another within what had previously been a contiguous economic space. The new borders thwarted the exchange of goods, limited the movement of people, and upended cultural-political networks and sources of livelihood. With commercial activity newly illegal, the shtetl and its environs felt deadened, empty. Bergelson evocatively describes the area next to the border as "a cavernous hole. Once busy roads had rushed to it, crisscrossing at that spot. Now the snow raged there as if to lay waste and destroy everything around."[146] At the same time, this gash in the landscape, in attracting both smugglers and the vigilant border guards who try to thwart them, offers a stage for confrontations that had not existed before and that generate the novel's plot. Earlier works of Yiddish literature, published shortly before Bergelson's, had focused on the changing social and economic ecosystems of shtetls in new border regions. Oyzer Varshavsky's 1920 novel *Smugglers* (*Shmuglares*), described the colorful criminal underworld that operated in a Polish shtetl at the time of the German occupation during the First World War. The Russian translation of *Smugglers* was published by the USSR in 1924 and reissued in 1927.[147] In *Judgment,* new borders generate the novel's narratives about smugglers who turn into economic criminals when they run headlong into new Bolshevik laws.

Speculation—in Russian, *spekuliatsiia*—was a criminal charge to which Jews were especially vulnerable during War Communism and, subsequently, the New Economic Policy. Campaigns against speculation, Andrew Sloin has written, "delineated a system of economic practices purportedly bound to pre- or counterrevolutionary vestiges within the Jewish community." Furthermore, "if ethnicity is understood to be a system of group identity constituted, in part, through shared cultural traits and practices," rhetorical attacks on the newly defined economic crimes "simultaneously articulated a need for Jews to wean themselves from dubious 'ethnic' practices for the sake of national renewal and the full integration into Soviet society."[148] Because Jews were so heavily involved in trade—an activity newly criminalized as smuggling—criminality came to be seen as a de facto aspect of Jewishness. This equation between ethnonational identity and economic practice meant, Brendan McGeever has argued, that Bolshevik rhetoric was marked by antisemitism and that the newly implemented penal code ended up targeting Jews living in the borderlands of the former Pale.[149] The conflation of the Jews of the former Pale with economic criminality continued into the mid-1920s and can be easily seen in the article about Shepetovka in *30 Days. Judgment,* which is set a few years earlier, displays an awareness of this nuance. Given their mandate to safeguard the tenuous borders of the new Bolshevik state, Filipov and his retinue at the Cheka enforce policies that target shtetl Jews with unique severity.

The first encounter between Filipov and Golikhovke's Jews occurs when he visits the shtetl. Filipov has not yet been identified by name when he arrives, and he is described, from the perspective of the narrator in Golikhovke, as a "huge, mighty figure of a man [*a rizik kreftike figur*]" riding a "bedraggled horse." Recognized "only by the bandage on his neck, his peasant coat, and a sheepskin hat pulled over his ears," the person fitting Filipov's rumored description appears in Golikhovke shortly after he was said to have single-handedly arrested several coachmen on their way to escort escapees from the Bolshevik regime across the border.[150] These arrests, which affected numerous Golikhovke households, proved to the shtetl that all the hearsay about the new Cheka boss's severity was true. No one had been able to move for days preceding the arrival of the large man in a peasant hat: "The houses in Golikhovke were full to bursting with smugglers trying to escape misfortune. The houses were swollen like the piles of snow in front of their windows."[151] The sense of "fear emanating from the towering figure" sends rumors swirling that, as someone on the street puts it, eventually confirming the identity of the man astride a horse, "Filipov is in town."[152] Filipov's reputation precedes his arrival in the shtetl; in turn, to Filipov, the Jews of Golikhovke are an abstract class enemy.

Filipov orders Golikhovke's denizens to assemble outside the town's new makeshift police station. Multiple voices convey his order as it spreads through the shtetl: "He sent for all the coachmen," "And the innkeepers, too." As confusion sets in about who exactly must show up, one of the townsfolk yells out, "Drag out the rabbi, too. It's clear he keeps guests. There are lodgers in his house, too."[153] Filipov has come into town to announce his crackdown on smuggling, the root cause of economic crimes that he has a mandate to eradicate, but Golikhovke's coachmen and innkeepers immediately understand that the wrath communicated by his order is directed at them, collectively, as Jews—and at Golikhovke as a shtetl full of Jews. Even the shtetl's communal leaders are on the wrong side of the law, newly considered criminals because of their attempts to simply ensure their physical survival. With the entire community thus redefined, Filipov's appearance in Golikhovke presages the collapse of the shtetl's communal structure: "Everyone has to go with us," say the coachmen spreading word of Filipov's order to assemble. "Everyone. Around here every household has paying guests."[154]

Golikhovke is a weak link in the Bolsheviks' attempts to seal the border, but the shtetl's Jews understand Filipov's crackdown as hostility not toward certain types of economic agents but toward themselves as vulnerable Jews. "Outside the [. . .] police station, coachmen's sheepskin jackets [*balagolishe 'polushubkes'*] and the fine, sensitive faces of ordinary Jews huddled together," notes the narrator, separating the outfits of Golikhovke's denizens, denoted by a Russian word in the Yiddish plural form, from their persons.[155] Disaggregating the body, as Harriet Murav has observed, is one of Bergelson's favorite textual strategies.[156] Here, the writer uses it to emphasize that his characters' economic functions, targeted for elimination by the Bolsheviks, can be rhetorically separated from the individual persons—simple Jews—who embody them. However, the sentence is also self-conscious about the ethical limitations of such rhetorical disaggregation: the economic criminals out-fitted in sheepskin jackets *are* actual Jews who will be punished because they found themselves living in precarious economic circumstances and tried to survive. Filipov sees and addresses the sheepskin coats, while the flesh-and-blood Jews of Golikhovke suffer from his application of the law.

When, after making them wait in the cold for a long time, Filipov finally addresses the assembled group, the narrative does not convey his words directly; instead, Bergelson relays the impressions his address made on Golik-hovke's Jews. Such indirectness emphasizes both that Filipov's menacing utterances mean little outside their shocking effect on their intended audi-ence and that the novel's narrative interest lies in conveying that effect rather than the message itself. When Filipov "unexpectedly turned to the people in front of him and began addressing them," an old innkeeper (*an altitshker bal-akhsonye*) standing in the back of the crowd, who "was hard of hearing and didn't understand much," asks a man in front of him about what Filipov is saying:

> The old man got his answer: "He says that he has the authority [*polnomotsh*]."
> The old man scowled. "What is that, then?"
> "From the revolution . . . he says he has the authority from the revo-lution to reduce everyone here to ashes, and all of Golikhovke, too."
> "For what? Huh?"
> "Because people are smuggling every damn thing across the border."[157]

This scene of encounter infuriated the Soviet critic Yasha Bronshteyn when he reviewed Bergelson's novel in 1929. Bronshteyn faulted the writer for squan-dering an opportunity to show the rhetorical effect of Filipov's speech on a population in need of political instruction. Instead, Bergelson's transmis-sion of Filipov's message through the compromised faculties of a hard-of-hearing participant had the effect of "cutting off the revolution's tongue [*oysgerisn di tsung bay der revolutsie*]."[158] An anonymous Jew from Golikh-ovke rephrases and immediately passes on the words that had been unreli-ably heard from the head of the local Cheka. Filipov's message, as conveyed in this fashion, is that "everyone here"—all the coachmen and the innkeepers whom Filipov had summoned because of their involvement in smuggling—

would be reduced to ashes along with "all of Golikhovke." When Filipov claims the "authority" to punish both the economic criminals and the entire shtetl, Bergelson uses the word *polnomotsh*, a garbled Yiddish version of the bureaucratic Russian word *polnomochie*: the old innkeeper, who already can't hear very well, finds the term incomprehensible. Uncertain about Filipov's "authority," Golikhovke's Jews don't see it as merely an economic matter but, instead, as an issue of anti-Jewish aggression.

Other aspects of Filipov's language display hostility toward Jews. While applying a compress to the boils on his neck and avoiding eye contact with his interlocutor, Filipov tells one of the coachmen that the revolution is "a sack": "We keep on patching it up [*mir shtopn im un shtopn*], and you here at the border are like mice [*ir zayt do ba der grenetz, vi di mayz*], nibbling away. You [plural] are eating out a hole at the edge of the sack and everything is going to spill out."[159] In the post-Holocaust world, the association of Jews with vermin is mainly understood as an invention of the Nazis; however, the analogy preceded Hitler by decades. Wilhelm Marr, the "father" of modern political antisemitism, used such imagery in the early 1880s.[160] Filipov makes it clear, using similarly derogatory terms, that he sees Jews as the Bolshevik regime's collective enemy. The Bolsheviks may have tried to appeal to internationalism as a rhetorical antidote to antisemitism, but the mark of economic criminality could not be separated from the people the regime associated with it. Like the Gothic images that created "a monstrous Jew against which Christian Europe [. . .] define[d] itself" in the Middle Ages and beyond, Filipov's references to Jews as vermin reintroduces the menacing specter of Jew-hatred to shtetl dwellers now living under Bolshevik rule.[161]

Among the novel's examples of the antisemitic rhetoric implicit in the Bolshevik discourse and laws about economic crimes, the story of one prisoner at Kamino-Balke, the tannery owner Aaron Lemberger, is particularly far-reaching. Lemberger is first mentioned at a meeting of the tribunal at which Filipov sentences the Cheka's prisoners. The narrator interrupts the novel's familiar flow to quote from Lemberger's arrest file, written in a kind of bureaucratic language:

Following the decree requiring all factory owners to indicate the quantity of finished goods they had, he reported only thirty percent. He shipped the remaining seventy percent to the other side [*iber der grenetz*], for which he received payment in foreign currency [*valyute*]. He therefore speculated [*shpekulirt*] on the seventy percent of the goods with the purpose of personal enrichment—now, of all times, during this period, etc. etc.[162]

Lemberger's engagement in speculation is an economic crime according to the new set of laws and is thus the stated legal basis for his arrest.[163] After hearing the summary of the charges, Filipov is said to be as "cold and indifferent toward himself as he was cold and indifferent toward the destiny of the being referred to as 'Aaron-Yisroel Yosifovich Lemberger,' who was preoccupied with personal enrichment now of all times, during this period of etc. etc."[164] To see himself as an arbiter of revolutionary justice, Filipov must be shown to lack any compassion for those he judges. The legalese from Lemberger's file—including the bureaucratic tediousness of the charges that make it unimportant to reference them in full—seamlessly slips into his own thoughts, precluding any possibility of his understanding the man's fate outside those terms.

However, Bergelson grants Lemberger a far more generous amount of narrative space than he gives to Filipov's ruminations about the tannery owner's alleged crimes. Lemberger is a stocky, strong elderly man. In a kind of inverse homage to Isaac Babel's description of spectators staring at "the withered, curly manhood of the emaciated Semite" in one *Red Cavalry* story published in 1924, *Judgment*'s narrator dwells on the impressive size of Lemberger's genitalia protruding through his pants.[165] With the same self-confidence that he used to establish his authority among the new prisoners in Kamino-Balke's general holding cell, Lemberger refuses to see Filipov as the ultimate arbiter of his fate or to accept a Bolshevik frame of reference to understand his punishment: "So what? Let it be Filipov! As far as I'm concerned, he's no more than a messenger"—a messenger, in Lemberger's mind, of judgment determined not by Filipov but by God.[166] Later, while hosting his cellmates for a meal to mark the end of the Sabbath, Lemberger explains,

> Here, down on earth, a man wouldn't even be able to hurt his own finger if it weren't deemed appropriate in heaven above, as it is written, "There are four means of punishment: fire, stoning, decapitation, and strangu-

lation." In the Talmud, Rabbi Shimon says: "By fire, by stoning, by strangulation, by decapitation" because decapitation is the easiest way to die. And "they"—the Bolsheviks—are no more than messengers. I have no complaints—it's quite likely that I deserved this.[167]

Lemberger is quoting from and offering an interpretation of passages about punishment from the Mishnah Sanhedrin, an early Rabbinic text that deals with criminal and civil proceedings. In accepting his fate within the context of Jewish law without any need to contend with the law represented by Filipov, Lemberger strips the Bolsheviks of the power they claim to possess.

Bronshteyn, the critic quick to point out the slightest deviation from the Party line, condemned Bergelson for the writer's portrayal of Lemberger. Before being taken away for execution, Lemberger tells a former servant where he had hidden some of his money and asks the young man to convey that information to his family. Bronshteyn faults Bergelson for not emphasizing these lines, which he sees as tantamount to Lemberger's admission of guilt for the crime of speculation. Bronshteyn wishes that Lemberger—whom he refers to as "the speculator [*der spekuliant*]"—had directly acknowledged his violation of the Bolshevik law and accepted his punishment by the authorities. Instead of doing so, writes Bronshteyn, "the leather factory owner Aaron Lemberger dies 'for the sanctification of God's name' [*alkidesh hashem*] just as his great-grandfathers did, with a feeling of security [*bitokhn*] and calmness."[168] Bronshteyn, in other words, protests the fact that Bergelson has Lemberger apprehend his own death through a specifically Jewish lens, rather than within the economic logic of Bolshevik law.

To Bronshteyn, Lemberger dies the death of a pious Jew who accepts God's will, not a death that can be understood in Bolshevik terms. The implied heresy, to use the word ironically, is grave: Lemberger's specifically Jewish martyrdom is an instance of the "sanctification of God's name" (in Hebrew, *kiddush ha-shem*), traditionally defined as the willingness to sacrifice one's life and assert one's commitment to God rather than worship false idols. In refusing to understand his punishment in the context of Bolshevik law, Lemberger in effect labels the Bolsheviks false idols, wielders of illegitimate justice. Bergelson understood the antisemitic appearance of the Bolsheviks' economic policies, which disproportionately affected Jews. But he also knew that shtetl Jews, like Lemberger, could mount a kind of ideological resistance that stripped the Bolsheviks of their symbolic power.

The evidence against Lemberger that Filipov hears at the tribunal is based on numbers: all factory owners were obligated to report their assets, but Lemberger had reported only a fraction of his. But when Lemberger incorporates numeric references while ruminating on his proximate execution, the numbers come not from Bolshevik law but from Jewish law: "Four paces away from the place where he is to be stoned," Lemberger recites from a Talmudic passage, "remove the criminal's clothing." "Know-nothings," he continues, addressing the other prisoners in his cell and imploring them to see their confinement at Kamino-Balke as an act of divine justice, "what we're seeing here is exactly as it is written."[169] Filipov understands Lemberger within the parameters of the legal code he enforces as a loyal soldier of the revolution; his own feelings about the individual man are decidedly irrelevant to him because he serves a function predetermined by history. Lemberger understands what is happening to him within a different paradigm that subsumes his punishment and his individuality within a divine plan, discernible from Judaism's legal texts. Lemberger is a bit player in a larger drama—a Bolshevik drama for Filipov and an eternal Jewish one for Lemberger. But whereas Filipov sees himself as a lead protagonist, for Lemberger, Filipov is just a minor actor who ultimately doesn't matter at all.

Lemberger's understanding of Filipov as a mere messenger of divine judgment puts him at odds with some of the novel's other protagonists. Babitsky, for one, sees Filipov as "the ambassador of History." Comrade Sasha, when she summons the aged doctor to Filipov's bedside, emphasizes that the latter "is dear to us." Yuzi Spivak, while in jail, begins to understand that his desire to fight for the working people requires him to shift his allegiances from the Socialist Revolutionaries to the Bolsheviks; he comes to this realization through the power of Filipov's presence. If Filipov embodies the revolutionary force that Babitsky and Spivak, each in his own way, see in him, then Filipov is unique; when Comrade Sasha says that Filipov "is dear to us," she communicates her fear that Filipov cannot be replaced. Spivak's conversion to the Bolshevik cause under Filipov's influence appears to signal that other Jews in Golikhovke ought to find safety in following Yuzi's example. But Lemberger's dismissal of Filipov's unique role ultimately emphasizes the Chekist's insignificance. Jews in Golikhovke, already traumatized by pogroms, hear a tinge of antisemitism in Filipov's speech and perceive it in his actions. Even if they could be convinced that Filipov sided with those who wished to punish rather than empower Jew-haters, they must first be persuaded that Filipov and the law he represents are there to stay. At a time when power kept changing hands between the Bolsheviks and different pogromist forces, that conclusion was by no means self-evident.

* * *

In the opening pages of *Judgment,* Cheka agents and office staff make merry at a party inside their outpost at the abandoned monastery when, suddenly, they hear a "series of dull, hard thuds." These thuds "sounded distant at first, as if they came from deep inside the earth," but "the longer they continued, the more persistently they struck the wall and the more clearly everyone understood their origin."[170] Filipov, when he knocks on the wall from his bed in an adjacent room, interrupts the party and thus makes his entrance into the novel. The sound from the other side of the wall is the way that Filipov's spectral presence becomes apparent. The signal that the border patrol's nightly mission must commence emanates from a kind of otherworldly space as though from inside a deep grave.

At the sound of the thuds, Marfusha, the cleaning lady, fixes her eyes "on the wall, as if it were a holy icon."[171] The narrator repeatedly refers to Marfusha by the Yiddish word for a non-Jewish woman, *shiksa,* and her gaze turns Filipov into a sacred presence that can inspire without being seen. Through Marfusha's vision, shaped by beliefs about the miraculous properties of Russian Orthodox icons and relics, Bergelson calls attention to the capacity of a Christian person's imagination to transform a Bolshevik into a saintly figure. The same properties also turn Filipov into something akin to "ghostly remnants, or revenants, which can return without being anticipated," tropes associated with the Gothic mode.[172] Before taking his revolutionary name, as was common practice among Bolsheviks including Lenin (né Ulyanov) and Stalin (né Dzhugashvili), Filipov had been known by his family name, Anastasiev—a name originating in the Greek word *anastas,* resurrection. "It's the third night in a row," notes Marfusha when she hears Filipov, alluding to his persistent, debilitating pain.[173] As the novel begins, on the third night after

Filipov took to bed, he is "risen" Christ-like, his spectral presence leading his followers to act on his wordless directives without seeing him in the flesh.

Bergelson also speaks in the language of Christian idiom when he describes Yuzi Spivak's transformation from a Socialist Revolutionary into a Bolshevik. Spivak observes the diseased body of Filipov, naked from the waist up: "Muscles on his shoulders tensed and quivered as if from cold, but his head and face, suffused with blood, bent deeper and deeper over [a] bowl, and then drop after drop of pus started to drip into the bowl from a couple of swollen wounds on his neck." Filipov refers to the dripping pus as bits of "oozing rot just like the bourgeoisie" and asks Spivak to help apply fresh bandages to his neck: "Yuzi washed his hands, squeezed the swollen wounds, bandaged Filipov's neck, and washed his hands again." After coming in direct physical contact with Filipov's disfigured body, Spivak reflects, "A certain feeling grew in his breast—compassion for a worker from the mines, who had become the boss of Kamino-Balke, and who thought the bourgeoisie was like [the] pus in his wounds."[174] Spivak has an epiphany, becoming, in the words of one of the novel's contemporary reviewers, a "member of the intelligentsia who rediscovered the true faith [bal-tshuve—inteligent]."[175] In Judaism, a bal-tshuve (in Hebrew, ba'al teshuva) is a person who returns to ritual practice after a period of apostasy or lapse in observance. In Spivak's case, the true faith is embodied, literally, in the working-class man's ailing body, which, by the novel's end, will lie on display. Writing about Holbein's painting "The Dead Body of Christ in the Tomb," in which Christ's wounded body is depicted in grotesquely physical detail, Julia Kristeva wonders whether the artist "invite[s] us to change the Christly tomb into a living tomb, to participate in the painted death and thus include it in our own life, in order to live with it and make it live?"[176] For Spivak, the encounter with Filipov's mortal body marks the beginning of his conversion to the Bolshevik faith. This new faith supersedes Spivak's earlier Socialist Revolutionary allegiances and puts him in the line of succession to Filipov.

Through Marfusha's gaze, fixed on Filipov's spectral appearance, the novel's opening allows Bergelson to frame the story of the Bolshevik Revolution in Christological terms, with the figure of Filipov—not unlike the figure at the head of the revolutionary procession in Alexander Blok's famous 1918 poem "The Twelve"—as Christ.[177] At the end of the novel, Vayl and Spivak seek to endow Filipov with similarly symbolic powers to lead others even after his physical demise. The two Jewish Bolsheviks' attempted speeches serve as the culmination of a succession struggle that has simmered throughout the novel as multiple characters assume that Filipov is close to death. Unlike in classic Gothic novels, the issue of disputed inheritance in *Judgment* focuses not on the unsettled ownership of a castle but rather on claims as to who can lead the revolution forward.[178] In this, *Judgment* reflects its historical moment: the struggle over the revolution's future following Lenin's death was in full swing as Bergelson worked on the novel.

In the inaudible speeches that Vayl and Spivak try to deliver to other shtetl Jews, Filipov's would-be successors embrace the pseudo-Christological framework in which their deceased *nachal'nik*'s mission endures after his death. However, the Christological understanding of the revolution and of its Bolshevik avatars also binds Vayl and Spivak to the undercurrent of anti-semitic thought in Christianity itself. This kind of thinking opens the door for the return of pogroms.

The blond woman who tries to flee to Poland and ends up as a prisoner at Kamino-Balke represents the antisemitic underbelly of the novel's Christo-logical idiom. Seeking information about the best route across the border, she starts sleeping with the double agent Yokhelzon, a Jewish man in Golikhovke who knows the terrain well. Yokhelzon breaks up with the blonde after Filipov threatens him with arrest. Consequently, the blonde "spen[ds] the whole night crying—her eyes were swollen and red from regret that she had given her body to a Jew."[179] In a village closer to her planned path of escape, she hires a "religious God-fearing peasant" to guide her across the border. "Hastily unbut-toning her blouse, she showed him the crucifix on her chest: let him see that she was a real Christian who had nothing to do with these kikes [*zi hot gornisht tsu ton mit di arumike zhides*]," the narrator comments on the blonde's eroticized attempt to build trust with her new guide.[180] Her performance of piousness grows in proportion to the antisemitism that undergirds it: "She—a devout Christian—had let her body be defiled by a dirty Jew without rhyme or reason. She crossed herself and pleaded with God to forgive her."[181] Yokhelzon—whom the blonde had imagined as a savior set to lead her across the border—is re-placed by the peasant guide and meanwhile turns in her mind into a filthy Jew.

Filipov arrests the blonde as she attempts to cross the border. At Kamino-Balke, she shares a jail cell with Sofia Pokrovskaya, the SR leader locked up for organizing an uprising against Filipov. The two women couldn't be more different from one another, thinks Pokrovskaya, who, the narrator notes, "picked a fight with the officials" about why they put her, the principled political activist, "in the same cell with smugglers and prostitutes." Treating this scene with a kind of wry humor, the narrator notes that Pokrovskaya's "mattress distanced itself by what seemed like miles from the blonde's mattress in the opposite corner of the cell." The SR activist wants nothing to do with the blonde, as a voice in her head tells her, "Why do you even have to look in her direction?"[182]

In placing Pokrovskaya and the blonde in the same confined space, Bergelson points to a convergence of their stories. In their shared cell, both women hear the news that a mysterious peasant—referred to in Yiddish as "the goy"—has also been arrested. Each woman begins projecting her own wishful thinking on this man. Pokrovskaya first thinks that the peasant is an SR activist and that his arrest signals that her long-planned uprising against the Cheka has finally begun. Then she begins to think of the peasant in terms that resemble her cellmate's performative piety: "She was drawn toward 'him' as if he were a saint. [. . .] He came from the people—someone completely unlike her, someone from the depths of the village; it was in his name and in the name of his fellow villagers that the SRs had spent several decades risking their necks on too many gallows."[183] Pokrovskaya's wishful thinking about the peasant resembles Yuzi Spivak's epiphany about Filipov's suffering: the nameless "goy" and Filipov represent, respectively, the peasants and the workers, on whose behalf the two Socialist Revolutionaries have fought without ever interacting with members of these underclasses. The blonde, in turn, "was certain that the peasant was sent here by her 'Whites'; she felt no less certain about that than Pokrovskaya herself, who was certain that 'he' was sent here by her SRs."[184] The blonde briefly rejoices when she hears the news of Filipov's murder, proclaims that her faith in the mysterious peasant had saved her, and insists to Pokrovskaya that the peasant is "a holy man . . . Put your faith in him . . . He will save you, too."[185]

Instead, the blonde is executed on charges of espionage outlined in an order Filipov had signed several hours before his death. Filipov's thumping on the wall at the beginning of the novel—an act understood by Marfusha as a miracle comparable to the workings of a holy icon—had dispatched a team of Cheka agents on the nighttime border patrol that first prevented the blonde from crossing the border. At the end of the novel, the blonde's execution order, enforced just hours after Filipov's death by the same people who first tried to stop her at the border, hints at Filipov's similarly spectral presence. The mysterious peasant, whom the blonde, with her suddenly pious fervor, had begun to imagine as a Christian saint, is a false idol. In contrast, Filipov—his word outlasting his mortal body—plays the ultimate role in the blonde's fate.

Noting her own Socialist Revolutionary credentials and the blonde's involvement with the Whites shortly before her execution, Pokrovskaya tells the blonde, "I am what I am, but I am not in the Black Hundreds like you!"[186] Referring to the ultranationalist, violently antisemitic movement supportive of autocracy in Russia, Pokrovskaya makes a distinction between her counterrevolutionary movement and the Bolshevik regime's other enemies, represented in her jail cell by the blonde, by drawing attention specifically to the anti-Jewish violence they committed. However, Pokrovskaya fails to recognize that her political group, the SRs, are responsible for the return to the region of a notorious pogromist, Ushak, whose record of antisemitic violence now threatens Golikhovke's Jews anew.

While Pokrovskaya languishes in jail, Ushak wreaks havoc in Golikhovke. The narrator reports that a Ushak-affiliated gang has broken into the house of Haykel Berezovsky, a rich man: "Berezovsky's daughter began talking to them (the daughter who got stuck there, whose husband had married her for her beauty, and to this day was a rich man living somewhere else)—and they took one look at her . . ." The narrator picks up the interrupted account, citing another witness: "It's better not to remember how they looked at her . . . But then they noticed there was cherry brandy on the sideboard, in bottles, well, and then they had a wild time all night long!"[187] The evasive phrasing suggests that the pogromists, drunk on alcohol, raped Berezovsky's daughter during the night. The following morning, in the shtetl's marketplace, "all kinds of hidden troubles got raked up [hot tsunoyfgeshart . . . ale umglikn]," as the implications about what might have befallen at least one of the shtetl's women are augmented by testimony that the pogromists had ransacked many other houses in Golikhovke and killed a man.[188]

The description of this new pogrom in Golikhovke is shaped by the novel's prevailing Gothic mode and its invocation of the "power of the past to command a repeat performance."[189] The troubles that get "raked up" on a scale reminiscent of earlier pogroms are not unexpected. Golikhovke, caught between rapidly shifting regimes, exists in precarious circumstances rife with violence against Jews, regardless of who happens to be in control at any given moment. Ushak's gang carries out the kind of anti-Jewish violence most associated with monarchists and nationalists, but it is the Socialist Revolutionaries who bring Ushak back and enable the return of pogroms. Although Filipov, before he was killed, gave orders to punish both types of opponents, his spectral presence points to his own culpability in the new anti-Jewish flare-up. Filipov had branded Jews economic enemies, paving the way for the Bolsheviks to expropriate Berezovsky's house and turn it into a club for Communist youth after Ushak's anti-Bolshevik forces attacked it. Filipov's insufficiently diligent control of the local Cheka allowed Ushak to slip through the border in the first place: in a novel ostensibly about securing the Bolshevik state's new frontier, the return of the notorious pogromist to Ukraine is the only instance of smuggling that Filipov did not manage to prevent.

* * *

In a lyrical essay published in *Pomegranate* (*Milgroym*), the richly illustrated literary and art journal he coedited in Berlin in 1922, Bergelson wrote about pogroms that had recently occurred in Ukraine, describing an unnamed shtetl that stood in the path of impending violence:

> From the large Jewish shopkeepers' quarter right across the entire area around this locality an acrid old world lingers, a God-forsaken world, exposed to the chill of winter, to the wind that might gust down from the north, and to the trouble that had yet to erupt and sweep down from very far away, from a God-forsaken town in the furthest distance where it had already erupted and come to pass: a massive slaughter [*a groyse shkhite*] had taken place there.[190]

In this long, breathtaking sentence, Bergelson describes a place experiencing a moment of quiet while anticipating a catastrophe, a brief period of calm before the ongoing storm that has already hit another distant shtetl. The certainty about what is coming is unmistakable: "a massive slaughter has taken place" in the other shtetl, and it "had yet to erupt" in the town not named in the essay. Pogroms were happening all around: some had already taken place nearby, and others were sure to follow.

The essay's title, "The Beginning of Kislev 5679" (Onheyb kislev tar'at), refers to the Hebrew month and year corresponding to November 1918. The pogrom is expected both within the eschatological "nightmares of two thousand years" of Jewish life in the diaspora and in the context of the more recent anti-Jewish violence in the area—Bergelson references a 1768 massacre in the shtetl of Uman a century and a half earlier.[191] Remnants of the past, both ancient and more recent, haunt the present—or, as Harriet Murav has put it in reference to this essay, "the calamity that has already occurred reflects the calamity that is about to come, and these calamities are a link in a chain of calamities that extend into the entirety of Jewish history."[192] The unnamed shtetl in "The Beginning of Kislev 5679" prefigures Bergelson's portrait of Golikhovke in *Judgment,* which the author would write a few years later and set in the year 1920. It is a space where one catastrophe follows another after the Bolshevik Revolution but before the Bolsheviks' final solidification of power. This indeterminacy of outcomes, the ambiguous relationship to power, and the lingering shadow of historic violence would all become features of the ascendant figure of the Soviet Jew as the twentieth century unfolded.

2

Salvaged Fragments

Moyshe Kulbak's *The Zelmenyaners*

The opening paragraphs of Moyshe Kulbak's Yiddish-language novel *The Zelmenyaners* (*Zelmenyaner*), set during the USSR's cultural and industrial revolution at the beginning of Stalin's reign, present the reader with a distinct, but endangered, East European Jewish space (figure 2.1). "This is Reb Zelmele's courtyard [*hoyf*]," the novel opens, establishing as its subject a group of houses clustered around a common area where inhabitants mingle, garments dry on a clothesline, and the sounds of bickering residents fly from one open window to the next for all to hear.[1] Reb Zelmele—"Reb" in Yiddish is an honorific akin to "Mr."—had built the family's home, and consequently everyone calls it "Reb Zelmele's courtyard." For the sake of brevity and by way of satirizing the Soviet manner of creating many a new acronym, the appellation shortens, on occasion, to "RebZe courtyard." There reside the progeny of the late patriarch, the eponymous Zelmenyaners, until, in the final pages of the novel set several years later, their *hoyf* is demolished to make way for a new factory.

A few paragraphs into the novel, perhaps in anticipation of the courtyard's eventual demise, the narrative briefly shifts to a setting quintessentially associated with modernity, mobility, and displacement: a train car. There, we encounter one of Reb Zelmele's descendants:

> It's been known to happen that, in a railroad car packed with Jews all yawning at a frosty morning, someone opens his eyes and asks a passenger:
>
> "Excuse me. You wouldn't happen to come from N_____, would you?"

"As a matter of fact, I would."

"You're not a grandson of Reb Zelmele's!"

"To tell you the truth, I am."[2]

Although Reb Zelmele, in his will, had implored his progeny to remain in their domicile in perpetuity, they pick up and begin to disperse far and wide. But even as they leave their place of origin, the courtyard and those who once lived there remain identifiable: "over time, Zelmenyaners [had] developed their own smell."[3] This smell is how a passenger picks out Reb Zelmele's descendant on the crowded train. Although the family may have scattered around the new Soviet Union, their characteristics—presented as essential and immutable—persist.

By the time of this reported encounter on the train, Reb Zelmele's courtyard, once defined as a territorial unit, has been transformed into a mobile set of unique characteristics that scatter to new locations. The train and the railroad are liminal spaces: the train with passengers aboard has left its point of origin but not yet reached its destination. Reb Zelmele's descendant

Figure 2.1. A residential courtyard in Minsk (1926). Reproduced with permission of the Belarusian State Archive of Films, Photographs, and Sound Recordings (BGAKFFD).

is no longer in his ancestral home, but he is still, somehow organically, a Zelmenyaner—and the meaning of his geographic displacement is not yet clear. By the end of the novel, the courtyard may be gone, but there is no certainty that its disappearance has spelled the family's demise. Kulbak's novel centers on Jews from the former Pale of Settlement who are becoming Soviet—a process presented as ongoing, its outcome deferred. Reb Zelmele's descendants are an embodiment of the evolving figure of the Soviet Jew.

The fictional courtyard in Kulbak's novel is located in Minsk, a city so central to Jewish life before the revolution that it continued to be identified with the former Pale of Settlement even after the Pale had been abolished. In contrast to Jewish communities in cities like Moscow, which swelled with new members as earlier residential restrictions were canceled after 1917, the Jews of Minsk, as Elissa Bemporad has written, "remained, so to speak, in the shtetl, among Jews, in a historic Jewish center."[4]

Minsk, strictly speaking, was a moderately sized city rather than a shtetl, the Yiddish term for the market towns with sizable Jewish populations that dotted the map of the former Pale. Nonetheless, it is useful to see Reb Zelmele's courtyard as a microcosm of the shtetl, which at the time was the subject of ethnographic, sociocultural, and economic debate among both Jews and non-Jews, many of whom took it as a symbol of Jewish backwardness before the revolution.[5] The cultural and technological innovations of Soviet modernity, they felt, could improve the conditions of Jews from the former Pale only if they left the old shtetl and its ways behind.

The plot of *The Zelmenyaners,* it would seem, tells the story about precisely the kind of space that Jews were supposed to abandon to become Soviet. At the beginning of the novel, the courtyard is defined by distinct, familiar characteristics coded as Jewish; by its end, a Soviet factory rises in its place and some of the *hoyf*'s residents are resettled in newly built modern Soviet apartments. This paradigm was replicated in contemporary works such as Alexander Fadeev's *The Last of the Udege.* Published beginning in 1930, this novel showed how a space associated with a particular ethnic culture changed, modernized, and became Soviet. The plot of *The Zelmenyaners,* too, seems to be about the shtetl becoming a factory and the Jew from the Pale becoming the New Soviet Man. The sighting of Reb Zelmele's descendant on a moving train far away from the courtyard appears as evidence that Jews did, in fact, depart from the shtetl en masse. However, the passenger's lingering smell, a metonymy for cultural practices deemed retrograde, raises a question: Did the Zelmenyaners, whom the novel turns into stereotyped Jews from the former Pale, become Soviet—or had they evolved into a new, and as-yet unidentified cultural type befitting the mobile, indeterminate setting of the train where we meet one of them?

Social programs intended to dislodge hereditary Jewish tendencies circulated widely in the Soviet public sphere at the time, buoyed by the French zoologist Jean-Baptiste Lamarck's popular, if pseudoscientific, theories of evolution. The belief that a Jew could, in theory, become a Soviet person was seemingly affirmed by the emergence of deracinated, highly educated, and mobile Jews, whom Yuri Slezkine has described as the most successful product (and producer) of the Soviet system.[6] But this small cadre of ethnically Jewish elites, many of whom ascended to the highest echelons of the Bolshevik state, were vastly outnumbered by the much broader and more diverse population of *proste yidn,* simple Jews like Kulbak's Zelmenyaners who, collectively and individually, constitute the figure of the Soviet Jew. The new cultural constellation of the Soviet Jew, as distinct from Jewish elites in the Soviet system, was born from a much more ambivalent engagement with revolutionary changes.

Kulbak's novel bears a complex relationship to the Soviet promise and expectation of Jewish integration. On the surface, the plot tracks major developments in the USSR at the time and appears to describe just such a transformation: the illiterate among the Zelmenyaners learn to read and write during the state's literacy campaigns; older family members make the transition from working as independent tradesmen to working in factories; and some in the younger generation give their children new revolutionary names. However, critics at the time attacked the novel as a parody of the Soviet transformation narrative rather than an exemplar of it. The doctrinaire had reasons to be worried. Written by an author who had spent the 1920s in Berlin and Vilna before settling in Minsk in 1928, and who was familiar with modernist trends in European art after the First World War, the novel dwells in discontinuity rather than coherence (figure 2.2).[7] Using narrative techniques that resemble cinematic montage, it juxtaposes conflicting elements that do not end up harmoniously resolved but, instead, create something new. Ilya Kukulin has suggested that montage, particularly in modernism, destabilizes the relationship of art to represented "reality." "Meant broadly," he writes,

Figure 2.2. Moyshe Kulbak in the 1920s.
Reproduced with permission of the Belarusian
State Archive of Films, Photographs, and
Sound Recordings (BGAKFFD).

arguing for an understanding of montage beyond the cinematic method most associated with the films of Sergei Eisenstein, "montage assumes that the world is as if cut up into fragments, and then re-organized in a new order; this 'redone-ness' [*peredelannost'*] is not merely something that the reader, viewer, or listener notices—it also becomes the constitutive principle of the work." Montage becomes a "new type of mimesis" that reveals the "hidden meanings" of artistic processes rather than their external manifestations.[8] This interaction does not produce a mimetic replica of the Soviet state's ideal—in the case of Kulbak's novel, a Jew imbibing Soviet ideology and shedding retrograde traits, practices, and characteristics—but instead a collection of clashing parts, the meaning of which the novel leaves provocatively unclear.

Like the courtyard it depicts, the text of *The Zelmenyaners* is a kind of cultural space out of which the figure of the Soviet Jew—as distinct from the Jew as a version of the New Soviet Man—emerges. Written and published both serially in the periodical press and in book form between 1929 and 1935, the novel is inseparable from the context of Soviet Minsk—and of the USSR as a whole—during the period bracketed by the First Five-Year Plan and the beginning of the purges, which, in 1937, would claim the life of the author himself.[9] Conscious of the events outside the novel, *The Zelmenyaners* reflects

Mikhail Bakhtin's idea that the word in the novel "lives, as it were, on the boundary between its own context and another, alien, context."[10] The world of *The Zelmenyaners* is shaped by the context in which it is placed and, in turn, re-creates that context in the guise of literary fiction.

In Reb Zelmele's courtyard the hereditary, seemingly immutable traits of a Jewish family mix and clash with central civilizing aspects of Soviet modernity. In depicting this interaction, Kulbak's novel bursts at the seams with ideologically weighted protagonists, some of whom appear comically enthusiastic about the Soviet project and others comically antagonistic toward it. It is tempting to read the novel as a battle between those characters hell-bent on fully Sovietizing the *hoyf* and the seemingly retrograde resisters who attempt to preserve something "authentic" that the process of modernization threatens to crush. But the seemingly clear dichotomies between the different factions are much more muddled. One contemporary critic referred to Reb Zelmele's progeny as "the generation of the desert [*dor ha-midber*]."[11] He was referencing the biblical phrase used to describe the generation of Israelites who wandered for forty years in the desert after the exodus from Egypt but did not enter the Promised Land, thus highlighting the Zelmenyaners' position in the midst of an incomplete transition from the Pale of Settlement to new Soviet life. This comparison was intended negatively: the critic wanted to see the younger Zelmenyaners direct their parents toward the new way of life rather than wander in the proverbial desert alongside them. The critic's frustration highlighted the fact that the apparently clear distinctions among the ideologically opposed Zelmenyaners collapse into unexpected similarities that mark them as a cohesive unit.

The Zelmenyaners is itself a site of the emergence of a figure of the Soviet Jew characterized by both modernizing and preservationist tendencies. In what follows, I examine how the aspects of the novel that deal with modernization and industrialization—such as the new electric grid, urban rail, and cinema in Minsk—collide with the experience of the Jewish family described in terms of ethnography and heredity. In correlating much of the fictional plot with historical events in Minsk during the second decade after the revolution, Kulbak foregrounds the question of whether heredity, which in the novel becomes synonymous with various attributes of Jewishness, is tied to a specific space, such that the dissolution of that space under the influence of Soviet power could also transform those who used to live within it. The novel's answer is ambivalent. The Soviet Jew who emerges in these circumstances is a distinctly new cultural type, but one marked both by transformation and by the inability to transform: this new figure is akin to Reb Zelmele's grandson who is identified by his unique smell on a crowded train while he journeys across the landscape of the USSR. A novel that on the surface describes the disappearance of a fictional family's habitat—a microcosm of the dismantled Pale of Settlement—in the early Soviet period, in fact charts the process of that space being reconstituted in new and as-yet unclear circumstances. By the end of the novel, the Jewish courtyard itself may be gone, swallowed up by the larger Soviet city, but its newly scattered and still-scattering denizens—marked by the experience of displacement—remain a breed unto themselves.

* * *

In the fall of 1929, Minsk, the capital of Soviet Belorussia, launched its first electric tramway line. A provincial backwater, Minsk was catching up with the industrial innovations of the time. The city's daily *The Worker* (*Rabochii*) wrote triumphantly that Belorussia, which had been known as "the land of swamps, [was] turning into the land of electricity and the tram."[12] On October 15, the newspaper chronicled the tram's maiden voyage through the streets of Minsk: "A ringing and cautioning warble of the bells—unexpected and new in the evening silence—was heard by numerous passersby who experienced uniform feelings of triumph."[13] Three weeks later, on the eve of the twelfth anniversary of the revolution, *The Worker*, like newspapers around the USSR, carried a speech by Joseph Stalin that celebrated the radical restructuring of Soviet economy and industry and called 1929—the first full year of the First Five-Year Plan—"the year of the great breakthrough."[14] The celebration of a tramway launch in a regional capital aligned perfectly with the newly touted successes of the Soviet state writ large (figure 2.3).

Kulbak's novel, its plot tracking contemporary events in the city, records the tram's first appearance near the Zelmenyaner courtyard, now linked both to the urban center and to the grid of Soviet power: "The tramway line was inaugurated. It was a sight for sore eyes. Starting from the central station, the tram sped through the streets. Its cars were brand-new, its windows [. . .] were crowded with passengers. It raced uphill and down all the way to the out-

Figure 2.3. A street scene in Minsk, with the tram in the background (1931). Reproduced with permission of the Belarusian State Archive of Films, Photographs, and Sound Recordings (BGAKFFD).

skirts of town." The subsequent passage brings the fictional Zelmenyaners into contact with the tram: "The day began with the Zelmenyaners hearing an unfamiliar bell ring near the courtyard. The first to run was Uncle Itshe, who loved novelties. He returned home late at night, and was so embarrassed to tell Aunt Malkaleh where he had been that he said it was at a friend's house."[15]

Uncle Itshe, one of Reb Zelmele's sons, is a tailor and one of the four brothers who serve as the protagonists of *The Zelmenyaners*—the others are Uncle Yuda, the carpenter and amateur violinist; Uncle Zishe, the watchmaker; and Uncle Folye, the tanner. By the time the novel opens, Reb Zelmele has already died. His widow, Grandma Bashe, has survived him into an uncertain age of revolutionary fervor and social and cultural transformation; she dies at the end of the novel's first half without ever understanding the incipient changes. Each of the novel's "uncles" has a wife, referred to as an "aunt": Itshe's wife, Aunt Malkaleh; Zishe's wife, Aunt Gita; Yuda's wife, Aunt Hesya; and Folye's wife, whose name nobody in the family seems to know, in a kind of humorous display of how strong-headed the Zelmenyaners are when

Figure 2.4. Emblem of the Belorussian Soviet Socialist Republic (BSSR) used between 1927 and 1937, with the slogan "Workers of the world, unite!" (literally, "Proletarians of all the countries, unite!") in BSSR's four official languages at the time: Belorussian, Russian, Yiddish, and Polish. Reproduced with permission of the Belarusian State Archive of Films, Photographs, and Sound Recordings (BGAKFFD).

they dislike one of their own. Each couple has several children, although their precise number is also comically unknown. Most of the children, whose names the novel's narrator does reveal, are in their twenties and thirties, and some are beginning to have offspring of their own.[16]

Kulbak published his novel in serial installments in the Minsk-based Yiddish monthly *The Star* (*Shtern*) intermittently between 1929 and 1935.[17] Yiddish at the time was one of four official languages of Soviet Belorussia along with Russian, Belorussian, and Polish (figure 2.4).[18] The novel was also published in book form, the first part in 1931 and the second in 1935. The plot's episodic structure focuses on numerous manifestations of Soviet modernity and its encroachment on the traditional family space of the courtyard. In addition to the tram, other innovations including electrification, literacy campaigns, and the cinema were appearing in Minsk when both the narrative of the novel and its serialization began in 1929. When Uncle Itshe climbs onto the roof of one of the houses while helping his son install a radio antenna, he is cognizant of how technological changes have altered his environment: he "found it hard to believe that the hundreds of buildings and scaffolds glimpsed through the dull bronze of the autumn trees belonged to the same city" where he had lived since birth.[19] Collectivization, industrialization, and propagandistic campaigns against religious observance would follow the Zelmenyaners into the mid-1930s, giving Kulbak contemporary material to rework within the serial installments of his novel's fictional universe.

Specific protagonists, identified by their views on the revolutionary changes afoot, propel the novel's plot, which effectively clothes ideological disagreements in terms of intrafamilial conflicts. Among the generation of Reb Zelmele's grandchildren, Bereh, Uncle Itshe's son, is most closely associated with the technological innovations that arrive during the First Five-Year Plan as part of the Soviet state's emphasis on industrialization. Bereh's apparent opponent in the quest for technological modernity is Tsalke (short for Tsalel), Uncle Yuda's son. Tsalke, who functions as the courtyard's amateur ethnographer and collector of family lore, resembles other protagonists in early Soviet literature in Russian, which Kulbak read and spoke. Such characters reluctant to embrace revolutionary change include Nikolai Kavalerov from Yuri Olesha's 1927 novel *Envy;* Tsalke, who wears "glasses on his nose [*mit briln afn noz*],"[20] looks like the sensitive Jewish intellectual famously described, using the same words about eyeglasses, in Isaac Babel's *Odessa Tales* and *Red Cavalry* published in the 1920s. Tonke, a daughter of Uncle Zishe, is posed as the novel's—and the family's—doctrinaire Marxist. Seemingly more knowledgeable than Bereh about ideology, she articulates the reasons for carrying out the revolutionary agenda. Like Bereh, she is pitted against Tsalke: through a plot of unrequited love, she challenges Tsalke's allegedly retrograde tendencies.

In addition to these conflicts between cousins, the novel's comic plot also emerges from intergenerational struggles between Uncle Itshe, his brothers, and their wives—who had grown up before the revolution—and their children, who matured in the early Soviet years. In setting up these dynamics, Kulbak borrows from Yiddish literature's classic text, Sholem Aleichem's cycle of stories about the stalwart dairyman Tevye, completed a decade and a half before Kulbak began working on *The Zelmenyaners*. Tevye's daughters—living amidst political and social ferment before, during, and after the revolution of 1905—force their traditional father to grapple with ongoing and ever more challenging societal changes. In replicating this literary structure, Kulbak seemingly reflects a Marxist view of history: each generation is in conflict with the previous one and this conflict drives historical progress.

But *The Zelmenyaners* is not as much a typical family saga as a comic inversion of one. Several generations exist simultaneously, and their lives are explored within a short time span rather than over the course of decades.[21] Despite apparent conflicts between characters from different generations, the older Zelmenyaners respond to the changes caused by Soviet modernization in ways that resemble the motivations that lead their children to introduce these changes in the first place: ideological approaches vary broadly, but the style of arguments both for and against a range of Soviet innovations is similar, regardless of which member of the family makes them. Similarly, although conflicts within Bereh, Tonke, and Tsalke's generation might, at first glance, align Tsalke with his older relatives, a nuanced reading of the novel offers a more complex picture in which a set of traits visible in all Zelmenyaners blurs generational and ideological lines. The arrival of the tramway in Minsk in 1929, while it appears to presage the Zelmenyaners' unequivocal and rapid transformation into urbanized Soviet citizens, also highlights the liminal nature and the uncertain outcome of such a transition.

* * *

The similarity—as opposed to the seeming opposition—between the different Zelmenyaners' reactions to Soviet modernization is particularly visible in the showdown between Bereh and Uncle Folye over bringing electricity to Reb Zelmele's courtyard. Because extending the country's electrical grid was a key aspect of the USSR's industrialization effort, articles about the countrywide electrification campaign frequently appeared in the Minsk press at this time, as they did in newspapers all over the USSR. As he finishes reading the newspaper one time, Bereh considers an old kerosene lamp hanging from the ceiling: "I am sitting and thinking how one would go about electrifying the courtyard [*vi azoy me ken do elektrifitsirn dem hoyf*]."[22] The old kerosene lamp becomes a source of nostalgia for older family members after the age of electricity arrives: Uncle Yuda continues to read by the kerosene lamp, "pushing his glasses up on his nose to let everyone know that electric light was worthless"[23]; on her deathbed, Grandma Basha asks for the electric light to be turned off because "she couldn't die in all that glare."[24] The elder Zelmenyaners would long for the shadows that had disappeared under the bright glow of "Lenin's little light bulbs" (*lampochki Il'icha*), named after the Soviet leader who saw electrification as a key aspect of revolutionary modernity.[25] When electricity finally arrives in the Zelmenyaners' courtyard, "thousands of little shadows that had clung to the corners for generations [*doyres lang*] were dislodged as though by a broom. The rooms looked more spacious and freer."[26] Kulbak puns on the visual vocabulary of the electrification era—images of brooms sweeping the old order aside—and so this turn of phrase offers both a seemingly clear ideological interpretation of electricity's transformative role and a commentary on the sudden qualitative change it marks in the Zelmenyaners' lifestyle.

The Zelmenyaners express strong reactions to electricity's arrival but are slow to understand its ideological importance. Folye, who is supposedly in the reactionary camp by virtue of being a member of the older generation, initially takes a liking to the new electric reality for an idiosyncratic reason: "believing [it] to be a Bolshevik initiative, he was happy that someone had cut the Zelmenyaners down to size."[27] Having nursed a grudge against the rest of his family since childhood, he aligns himself with "the Bolsheviks"—he understands the term as referring to those who are not his relatives—as a means of getting back at the other Zelmenyaners. "Go tell the courtyard that Folye's become a Bolshevik," he instructs his wife, assuming that this pronouncement would force his relatives to respect him; they laugh at him instead.[28] Folye's proclamation, which sounds like a statement of ideological alliance with the Bolsheviks, serves instead as a way to express larger and longer-lasting rivalries within the family: "Zelmenyaners don't like Zelmenyaners," the novel notes at the outset.[29] After Folye learns that Bereh—not "the Bolsheviks"—is responsible for the electrification, he "climb[s] a ladder propped against his window and [begins] cutting the electric wires."[30]

Soon after, Bereh and Folye have a fistfight in the middle of the courtyard, after which Folye tells Bereh: "That's the last electricity you install around here, you son of a bitch."[31] Bereh didn't explain the meaning and origin of electricity when he decided—on a whim—that the courtyard needed to be connected to the grid. The older Zelmenyaners perceive electricity negatively, leading Folye—who acts as impulsively in reaction to electricity's arrival as Bereh did when deciding to connect the courtyard to the grid—to associate the latest Soviet innovation with what feels like Bereh's oppositional stance toward the family. The two generations, although they appear to be against one another act out of similar impulses, even as a member of one facilitates electricity's arrival and a member of another, its dismantling.

Some of the reviews of the novel at the time of its publication picked up on this generational divide.[32] One reviewer in Warsaw's *The Moment* (*Der moment*) saw the first published chapters as a progressive commentary on the rapid separation of the petit-bourgeois older generation from a new generation excited to promote socialist construction.[33] Another critic first praised the book as a realistic work—a welcome change, according to him, from the impenetrable mysticism of Kulbak's earlier prose. However, the reviewer went on to criticize the novel's episodic comedy about the introduction of revolutionary innovations to the courtyard; he claimed it would undermine the book's realism by making it difficult for the reader to recall any specific details.[34]

To this latter critic, the novel appeared overly episodic because much of its plot is driven by conflicts over and comic reactions to a rapid succession of innovations brought to the courtyard. For example, when a literacy campaign activist arrives to teach Aunt Malkaleh how to read and write, she is "so discombobulated that she crawl[s] into bed with her coat, boots, and shopping basket."[35] Electricity brings with it bright lights, which upset the older men who find they have been deprived of the convenience of urinating in peace in the formerly dark corners of Reb Zelmele's courtyard.[36] The radio, cinema, and Bolshevik public festivals all provoke similarly comic responses; for instance, Uncle Itshe, while at a demonstration, leads other men in singing revolutionary songs "with a cantorial quiver [*mit a khazonishn kvetch*]."[37] The episodic structure of this part of this serialized novel was so effective in capturing the comedy of the intergenerational experience of Stalin's cultural revolution that it was adapted for the stage as part of a revue show presented in Warsaw in 1933.[38]

Yet, the episodic structure and absence of central protagonists in the first part of *The Zelmenyaners* also reflect Maxim Gorky's observation that the literature of the Stalin era's First Five-Year Plan was about "little men" who were more valuable as parts of the larger social machinery than as individuals.[39] The first part of the novel is consistent with the period's "profusion of subplots in search of a central plot or, worse still, the absence of any plot at all."[40] But whereas the "little men" of the era's literature were involved in efforts to industrialize the country, Kulbak's characters participate in a parody of this process, a joke-filled commentary on the modernization unfolding in Minsk.

The novel deploys both the uncles and their children in its large cast of "little men," but even though the two groups seem to be locked in an ideological struggle over the merits of socialism, the similarity between the generations bothered its critics. Reflecting on the entire book, Nakhmen Mayzel, who was based in Warsaw, criticized Kulbak's use of the same set of techniques to portray both the older protagonists and the younger Zelmenyaners, whom the critic wanted to see depicted as exemplars of a changing world.[41] When the novel's first half was published in 1931, Mayzel reviewed it enthusiastically; his critique only emerged in 1937, two years after the publication of the entire novel.[42] By then, priorities on the Soviet literary scene had shifted in favor of protagonists who were bigger and more exemplary than the "little heroes" of the First Five-Year Plan—and better suited as potential role models than the kinds of characters who dominated the earlier chapters of Kulbak's novel. Extending the story and its publication into the mid-1930s meant subjecting *The Zelmenyaners* to new literary pressures.

In a 1934 article—published midway through the serialization of part two of the novel—the doctrinaire Minsk-based critic Yasha Bronshteyn noted that much of Kulbak's poetry and prose, preceding but also including *The Zelmenyaners,* contains a particular type of "stormy-raw [*stikhiesh-royer*]" and "biologically stripped [*biologish-antbloyzter*]" protagonist, whose behavior was driven almost entirely by hereditary, primitive motivations.[43] Bronshteyn calls this type a *shiluye*—a rascal or whippersnapper—a word Kulbak himself uses as an epithet for some of the younger family members. When Bronshteyn appropriates the term, he makes it more inclusive, applying it not only to the family's younger generation but also to the generation of the four uncles and their wives, whom he also sees as impulsive "rascals."

The term *shiluye,* which for Bronshteyn had a wholly negative connotation, refers to protagonists driven more by gut feelings than by consciousness. This category includes both people who support the revolution and those who oppose it. What unites both groups, according to Bronshteyn, is their reliance on biological instincts rather than on higher-order thinking. Here, Bronshteyn operates within the parameters of Soviet criticism, taking his cue from Lenin's influential 1902 treatise, "What Is to Be Done?" Fearing that the largely illiterate and poorly educated Russian working class and peasantry would not be able to organize themselves into a revolutionary force, Lenin proposed relying on a vanguard of the proletariat that would provide a consciously derived method of implementing revolutionary ideals. Literary scholar Katerina Clark has located the spontaneity-consciousness dialectic articulated by Lenin at the foundation of both Soviet state ideology and the ideology of the Soviet novel.[44] Spontaneity—a quality Bronshteyn identified in Kulbak's "rascals"—came to be seen, in the context of the Soviet novel in the 1930s, as an anarchic quality that needed to be tamed through appropriate ideological discipline. Eventually, the literary landscape shifted from privileging numerous protagonists, none of whom were decisively dominant, to putting greater emphasis on positive heroes guided by the state's reigning ideology.[45]

For Bronshteyn, the Zelmenyaners were ill-fitting protagonists of a Soviet novel because they exemplified a move toward spontaneity and away from consciousness. He asserted that the "call of blood [*di shtim fun blut*]" and the Zelmenyaners' own "version of world history [*nusekh fun velt-geshikhte*]" were regrettably stronger than the effects of Soviet ideology or the positive changes that the younger generation of the family could enable.[46] The self-described rascals themselves—even the most ideologically progressive—are, first and foremost, typical Zelmenyaners. Bronshteyn pointed out that the younger Zelmenyaners, even those who appear ideologically reliable, are described according to their typical Zelmenyaner traits and spontaneous decisions, rather than—as would befit proper Soviet heroes—evolving from spontaneity to consciousness. The novel's chapter about electrification helped Bronshteyn illustrate his argument. He noted that the idea of extending electricity to the courtyard occurs to Bereh spontaneously—an unacceptable development, according to the critic, because electricity should have been presented as a proper ideological matter and should not have been portrayed in a way that elided the leading role of the Party and a protagonist demonstrating a "conscious" approach to this enterprise.[47]

Bronshteyn's critique of *The Zelmenyaners* was published at the beginning of 1934, before the serialization of the novel's second half was completed later in 1934 and in 1935.[48] Its unfinished serialization turned this novel about characters in transition into a kind of liminal site itself. The author even had an opportunity to respond to his critics from within the work's later pages—

something not uncommon in the history of serialized literature—including in novels like Leo Tolstoy's *Anna Karenina,* in which the author could allow the characters to engage with historical developments that had not yet occurred when the serialization of the novel first started.[49] Aware of developments in literary politics, Kulbak might have tried to adjust the direction of the narrative by introducing a new type of positive hero into the text. This protagonist, engaged in a process of evolution from spontaneity to consciousness, tries to set himself apart from his older relatives as a member of a distinctly new Soviet generation.

* * *

On March 17, 1936, the Belorussian State Publishing Company's in-house Communist Party committee (*partkom*)—which, like other such outfits attached to specific organizations, was responsible for keeping an eye on ideological compliance—convened for one of its periodic meetings. The minutes of the discussion, preserved in the National Archive of Belarus, record that an editor had been given an angry talking-to after being found ideologically at fault over a matter concerning literary translation. "Frequently," the minutes reported, "translations are assigned to unqualified, untested, and even [ideologically] alien [*chuzhdym*] individuals; [. . .] all this leads to distortions of the meaning in the translation and, in several places, to political distortions." The editor in question here, Livshits, had erred by appointing "the Trotskyite and bourgeois nationalist Kh[atskl] Dunets" to translate Nikolai Ostrovsky's Russian-language novel *How the Steel Was Tempered* into Yiddish.[50] Livshits was duly censured.

Ten days later, Livshits appealed his censure. Following the contemporary fashion of self-criticism, he admitted his fault: "Of course, I made a mistake when I assigned the book, written by the Bolshevik Ostrovsky and demonstrating a Bolshevik's path of struggle, to the Trotskyite Dunets."[51] At the end of the meeting, the committee lifted Livshits's censure. Dunets would be executed a year later—one of many in Minsk's Yiddish circles to perish during the purges.[52] When Ostrovsky's novel, one of the foundational texts of Stalin-era literature, came out in Yiddish translation a year later, Dunets's name did not appear on the title page. It was, instead, replaced by the name of a new translator credited with having "literarily edited" (*literarish baarbet*)

Dunets's work, which was now suspect for having been ideologically tainted.[53] This new translator and literary editor was Moyshe Kulbak.[54]

Kulbak's qualifications for the task were obvious: by the mid-1930s, he was at work on the Yiddish translation of Nikolai Gogol's *The Inspector General,* a Russian literary classic.[55] Kulbak was also on record amplifying the role of translation in building a multilingual Soviet literary corpus. In 1934, he attended the First All-Union Congress of Soviet Writers in Moscow. This was the gathering where Socialist Realism—an ideology that called on Soviet literature to represent "reality in its revolutionary development"—was codified as the new state's regnant literary dogma. On returning to Minsk, Kulbak published a brief Russian-language article in *The Worker* about the need to translate Yiddish literature into other languages of the USSR.[56] His article, in Yiddish, about the work of the Belorussian poet Jakub Kolas in the October 1936 issue of *Shtern,*[57] appeared right after an article by the critic A. Damesek that publicly denounced the very same "Trotskyite" Dunets whose translation of Ostrovsky had been reassigned to Kulbak earlier that year.[58] Both on his own initiative and willy-nilly, by the mid-1930s Kulbak had become involved in the work of introducing Russian literature, Soviet literature, and Soviet Belorussian literature to the Yiddish reader.

Kulbak had already published the completed second part of *The Zelmenyaners* by the time he began editing Dunets's translation of *How the Steel Was Tempered.* However, he would have been aware of Ostrovsky's novel in Russian, which was published in two parts in 1932 and 1934 and was widely discussed while he was still at work on his novel about Reb Zelmele's courtyard. *How the Steel Was Tempered* focuses on an ordinary worker named Pavel (Pavka) Korchagin and his involvement in the Russian civil war; the novel mentions the anti-Jewish pogroms of the era as well. Despite Pavka's undisciplined and boisterous attitude through much of the novel, his service in the postrevolutionary military conflict allows him to be elevated into the pantheon of heroes of Socialist Realist literature. As Katerina Clark has noted, Ostrovsky's novel symbolically bridges the Stalinist 1930s and the earlier period of the Russian civil war by equating the later era's heroic project—to tame nature through socialist construction—with the heroism displayed by Red Army soldiers immediately following the revolution.[59]

Likely tempted by the opportunity to include emerging state rhetoric about the civil war into his own novel-in-progress, Kulbak appears to have reworked his treatment of it between the two parts of the book. In part one, he describes some Zelmenyaners after the war: "The Zelmenyaners returned from the front in stiff army greatcoats and tattered fur hats. At first they prowled the yard like wolves, gulping down whatever came to hand. Slowly they were lured back into their homes and gently talked to until they reverted to their former selves."[60] Bronshteyn had focused on this passage to criticize Kulbak. Instead of seizing the opportunity to describe veterans as newly emergent Soviet heroes, he thought that Kulbak had portrayed the Zelmenyaners as people overtaken by the complacency that was always part of their nature. Bronshteyn noted that the Zelmenyaners had through utter inertia, returned to being their regular selves again, as if the massive social upheaval that accompanied the revolution had never happened.[61] Before long, the military coats that could have clad new, Bolshevik-inspired heroes are instead hung on the doors of their homes as insulation.[62] The army coats, thus repurposed, blend into the background of Reb Zelmele's courtyard and fail to distinguish the war veterans from their family members.

As Kulbak wrote the second part of the novel, he was aware not only of Bronshteyn's critique and the ideological winds that had brought it about but also of the evolving place of the Russian civil war in Soviet fiction. The novel's serialization schedule suggests that Kulbak attempted to retrofit the earlier chapters into the requirements enshrined by Socialist Realism, which was itself a major development in Soviet literary history between the publications of the two parts of the novel. Kulbak's attempt to rewrite the plotline of his novel in this later part focused on returning to the liminal space of the road, revisiting the story of Bereh's travels during the war, and seeking a new storyline that would allow him to recast Bereh in the novel's central role.

Having already begun the serialization of part two with a prologue about Bereh in the March 1933 issue of *Shtern*,[63] Kulbak seized on the new literary directive that required a central protagonist in the process of evolution from spontaneity to consciousness. A Socialist Realist hero could not evolve by himself; he needed the help of a mentor channeling the wisdom of the Party. Because *The Zelmenyaners* did not have a central protagonist, mentored or otherwise, as critics had made very clear, Kulbak appears to have tried to invent one—and a mentor for him—after most of the novel had already been written and serially published.

In the prologue to the second part of the novel, published a year and half before the 1934 All-Union Congress of Soviet Writers, Bereh is dispatched to the front, where he presumably could have earned a military distinction.

There, an officer named Porshnyev befriends him and becomes, in effect, his mentor. After the 1934 writers' congress, however, Kulbak must have judged this early chapter insufficient to establish Bereh's credentials as the novel's central hero. In January 1935—after several chapters of the novel had already been serialized in *Shtern* in 1933 and 1934—Kulbak published an additional chapter about Bereh's wartime experience.[64] Modifying the utterly unheroic Bereh of the already published prologue, this new chapter presents him as something of a hero. Returning to earlier events, it recounts how Bereh declined a marriage proposal that would have made him a family man and instead embarked on decidedly picaresque adventures, during which he acquired more wartime experiences that could help recast him as the main hero of a Soviet novel.

When the second half of *The Zelmenyaners* came out as a book in 1935, this later chapter was included, but now in a different place in the narrative: as the sequential chapters 3 and 4 of part two, immediately following the initial 1933 prologue, which became chapters 1 and 2. Bereh's newly embellished biography—the kernel of his subsequent evolution from spontaneity to consciousness—thus appeared as though it had been conceived that way from the start. Kulbak introduces new material that clarifies his attempts to reroute his novel into the strictures of Socialist Realism: he adds an autobiography written by Bereh as part of his application for a job at the police station. Such autobiographies were common for Soviet citizens seeking Communist Party membership and employment at a time when anyone without a suitable class background would have had trouble getting a position.[65] By narrating his own adventures during the war, Bereh presents his youthful exploits as a biography befitting a hero in a Soviet novel.[66]

The recasting of Bereh as a positive hero makes an impression on his family: his civil war biography, which plays no role in the novel's first half, now draws the Zelmenyaners' attention. In the initial chapters of part two, Bereh emerges as a kind of messenger from the "promised land" of the revolution—someone who could both turn the family's fortunes around and influence their ideological evolution. This kind of messenger has its roots in classic Yiddish prose. Sh. Y. Abramovitch's satirical novel *The Brief Adventures of Benjamin the Third* (1878) includes an episode in which a visitor arrives in the shtetl of Tuneyadevka (which translates, roughly, as Lazy Town) bearing a date from a date palm. The entire town gathers to look at the exotic fruit: "A Bible was brought to prove that the very same little fruit grew in the Holy Land. The harder the Tuneyadevkans stared at it, the more clearly they saw before their eyes the River Jordan, the Cave of the Patriarchs, the tomb of Mother Rachel, the Wailing Wall."[67] Kulbak references this scene when, during Bereh's adventures at the frontlines, someone delivers to the Zelmenyaners an apple rumored to have come from Bereh himself:

> The apple lay for a few days on a plate on the table. [. . .] Everyone touched its cool peel and lifted it by the stem while thinking of Bereh and his exploits on the battlefield.
> For those few days, the whole yard dreamed of him. Suddenly he was seen as the rising star of the family, which had seemed to be falling.[68]

Abramovitch's episode about the date is a harsh critique both of the shtetl and of the messianic imagination that makes life only more difficult for impractical Jewish dreamers. Like the denizens of Tuneyadevka, the residents of Reb Zelmele's courtyard mistake the mysterious fruit for a definitive promise of a redemptive future instead of understanding it as the symbol of liminality and indeterminacy that it really is. The Zelmenyaners, seeing in Bereh's apple the promise of their own feats under the new regime, fail to envision the trials they would undergo in the hands of Bereh as its new enforcer. Bereh, meanwhile, uses his family to alter his status in Soviet society.

As the protagonist of a Soviet novel, Bereh needs to actively distinguish himself from members of the older generation and to earn the trust of the political mentor who assists him in his ideological evolution. In this context, Kulbak stages a do-over of Bereh's biography by revisiting his earlier conflict with Folye over electrification. In this developing intrafamily conflict, Folye's opposition to the innovations that Bereh represents is elevated to the status of a crime, while Bereh's fight with his uncle becomes an expression of attaining ideological maturity.

Kulbak first published the chapter "Bereh and Uncle Folye Fight for the New Man" in *Shtern* in September 1934. Much of the rest of the journal's issue was filled with speeches and reports from Moscow's First All-Union Congress of Soviet Writers, whose agenda, a month earlier, centered on ways of describing "the New Man" in Soviet literature. In the context of this publication, it is hard not to see Kulbak's chapter from the novel as a programmatic piece of writing.[69] Fired from his work at the police station on charges of "khvostism," Bereh finds work at a newly mechanized leather factory, where his uncle Folye works and where Bereh can try again to retool himself for the Soviet age. "Khvostism," a common accusation at the time, was aimed at people found to be at the tail end (in Russian, *khvost*) of revolutionary work or a specific industrial production effort. Kulbak's turns the term into a clever pun: in the novel, Khvost is the Zelmenyaners' actual surname, so Bereh's specific case of "khvostism" can also be construed as the transgression of his being insufficiently *unlike* his kin. To disprove this literal charge of "khvostism," Bereh needs to both move from the tail end of revolutionary efforts to their vanguard and to demonstrate his distance from his family. Bereh and Folye fight (*shlogn zikh*) over kinship relations as much as over ideology in this tellingly named chapter of the novel.

Bereh's new industrial job is described in explicitly ideological terms: "Porshnyev had agreed to Bereh's working in the factory in the hope that there, on the assembly line, shoulder to shoulder with his old mates from the tannery, he would grow with them and the work."[70] In addition to getting reeducated as a self-aware member of the laboring class, Bereh is singled out for a leadership role in ideological work: "To the factory's Party committee, he confided that he was looking for a 'serious social challenge.'" Kulbak's Yiddish phrase for Bereh's "serious social challenge" (*groyse gezelshaftlikhe onlodung*) is a calque of the Russian-language *obshchestvennaia nagruzka,* which designated a public service obligation that a worker takes on in addition to his or her immediate job responsibilities.[71]

Bereh has an opportunity to prove himself when his fellow factory workers meet to discuss the case of a certain Shimshe and his proprietary hold on a liquid deemed essential in manufacturing glue from the tannery's waste products. Sensing that it would be sufficient to confiscate Shimshe's flask and analyze its contents, Bereh is too timid to make such a proposal. At the same time, he knows not to carry out his plan on his own initiative without first articulating a rationale for it. When he finally approaches the podium, he offers a seamless string of ideological boilerplate that he might have encountered in the daily press:

Comrades! You are attending a meeting called by the Bolshevik Party to consider how best to build socialism for all the workers. Today, in the

capitalist countries, there are sixty million unemployed. They go around
with no work, rummaging in garbage pails, though everyone knows they
have sweated for the bourgeoisie and had their blood sucked, not just
by heavy industry, but by the banks and stock markets, too . . . [72]

After enunciating what is, essentially, a parody of widespread contemporary
discourses, Bereh confiscates Shimshe's flask to analyze its contents—it turns
out to be a "concoction of glycerin, molasses, and cherry brandy" that is in-
consequential to the tanning process—and exposes him as a fraud.[73] Such
an action is not dissimilar from Bereh's earlier electrification of the courtyard; indeed, Kulbak implies that Bereh is motivated to do both actions by
what he would have read in newspapers. The crucial difference between these
two events lies in Bereh's newfound ability not only to undertake specific
tasks, as he had done before, but also to articulate the ideological underpin-
ning of his actions and show the Party's role in inspiring them.

Having shown his know-how by exposing Shimshe's ruse, Bereh turns his
attention to Uncle Folye, who has stolen a hide from the factory where they
both work. The factory itself, which had been a tannery, has employed Folye
from the time he was a boy. After being nationalized, it grew into a large
leather goods factory where—despite consistent protests by Folye and his
fellow elderly coworkers—much of the labor was mechanized. Folye's theft
is presented as a logical continuation of his resistance to the factory's industrial upgrades and his insistence on continuing to use traditional methods
in his work: "An unmechanized holdout, he stood on his board with his
scraping knife, the same Folye as always."[74] Folye's attitude places him on a
slippery slope that leads from simple resistance to crime: Folye might have
gained access to animal hides by circumventing the inventory process in the
newly mechanized factory. As Folye makes his way home with a heavy sack
on his back, Bereh pursues his uncle.

In trailing Folye and subsequently reporting on his "reactionary" uncle,
Bereh sees a way to earn a second chance with the authorities after he is caught
sleeping on the job while working for the police: "The rumor that Bereh had
been fired from the police for turning a blind eye to a thief was, it seems, un-
warranted. He had, in fact, been keeping an eye on his cunning uncle for
some time."[75] Bereh's awareness of Folye's retrograde, iconoclastic tendencies led him to spy on his uncle. Bereh had not ideologically matured enough

to display such vigilance in the electrification incident described in the first part of the novel.

Folye's downfall evokes his early years at the tannery while also contrasting his inability to change with Bereh's apparent evolution. As a child, Folye once foraged for animal bones, hid them at home, and was punished by Reb Zelmele when the source of the ensuing stench was discovered. Reb Zelmele interpreted his son's behavior as a manifestation of his destiny to work with animal parts and thus directed Folye to the tannery. The new hidden sack—this time filled with animal hides instead of bones but otherwise similar—suggests that Folye is unable to overcome what is presented as an innate trait. A victim of his unchangeable nature—"flayed horses were his destiny," as the text later states about the matter—Folye is a fitting target for Bereh, who needs an opportunity to try to show his ideological evolution.[76]

When Bereh catches his uncle red-handed, Kulbak restages their earlier fistfight over the electrification of the courtyard. In the first part of the novel, after Folye smashed the newly installed electrical transmitters, Bereh's brother Falke calls Folye a "wrecker [*vreditel'*]," a commonly used term for those suspected of sabotaging Stalin's industrialization plan for the country.[77] At the time, the accusation was not audible to anyone outside the courtyard. Now, however, Folye's transgression receives a public airing. Indeed, the theft of state property from a factory falls squarely under the definition of "wrecking" (*vreditel'stvo*), and Folye, like many at the time, is put on trial for this industrialization-era crime. Folye's downfall and his ensuing trial become a proxy for the downfall and public exposure of Reb Zelmele's courtyard itself.

Reminiscent of the era's show trials, Folye's prosecution unfolds at the Workers Club with all "seven hundred employees of the factory [. . .] in attendance."[78] Bereh's mentor Porshnyev is among the judges, standing before the astonished Zelmenyaners, who had regarded him as a figment of their imagination.[79] Though he expresses his fondness for his mentee, Porshnyev makes clear that the real purpose of his mentorship of Bereh was to expose the backwardness of the RebZe courtyard. Folye's accusers don't blame him alone for his actions; rather, they locate the source of his guilt in the very nature of the Zelmenyaners' domicile. The trial of one family member becomes the trial of all Zelmenyaners.

In the proceedings, Folye's niece Tonke delivers a fierce, cruel accusation that equates Folye's crime with the Zelmenyaners' way of life: the courtyard, she notes, "even when it doesn't steal, is potentially stealing all the time."[80] To bolster her case that the courtyard represents a threat to society, Tonke describes the family's material possessions and daily and ritual practices as ideologically nefarious baggage that keeps the Zelmenyaners apart from others:

> For generations, the Zelmenyaners have collected bits of this and that and built their world from it. The courtyard [. . .] is in fact composed of nothing but bits. The Zelmenyaners own no banks or grand estates but they do have eighteen trash bins, twelve copper ladles, a chamber pot, a fur muff, and plenty more. [. . .] The courtyard subsists on leavings and scrapings, on the remnants of superstition and religion, on naively distorted scraps of scientific knowledge.[81]

For Tonke, Folye's loot is part of the larger clutter of Rev Zelmele's courtyard. Made up of both physical items and what she identifies as disparate scraps of anachronistic beliefs, these scattered bits serve as building blocks of the family's defiant idiosyncrasy. Tonke's take on such evidence is reminiscent of the novel's previous descriptions of generations-old Zelmenyaner traits. Calling her a "Jew hater," Tonke's relatives banish her from the family for this testimony. By perceiving an antisemitic streak in Tonke's attack, the Zelmenyaners identify their peculiar family traits and scattered odds and ends as attributes of Jewishness. In this equation, Reb Zelmele's courtyard becomes a proxy for Soviet Jewishness in transition.

What rubs Tonke the wrong way—even more than the similarity between Folye's crime and the larger shortcomings of the courtyard—is the family's attempt to elevate their odds and ends to the level of a culture in need of cataloging and preservation. She proclaims, "That's Reb Zelmele's courtyard—and yet there are those who make it an ideal, a philosophy, even a science. Ah, our Zelmenyaner intellectuals, who would prove that the courtyard has its own distinct culture, the culture of bits!"[82] Tonke takes a derisive tone when she defines her family's "culture of bits" as retrograde; however, by mentioning these "bits" in the first place, she brings them into the narrative in such a way that other protagonists can interpret these fragments in alternative ways. Tonke's speech at the trial is not the only place in the novel where the Zelmenyaners' disparate possessions become a proxy for their uniqueness. These "bits," like the family members' hereditary traits, define the Zelmenyaners; the discussion about their meaning—always contested and unclear—takes center stage not only during Folye's trial but also in the amateur ethnographic work of Tonke's cousin Tsalke.

* * *

When Folye's brother Itshe went to the movies for the first time, he was as enthusiastic about the experience as he had been earlier about the tram. Minsk's city planners had envisioned a connection between the tramway and the cinema: the day before the launch of the tram, the head of the city's light rail system wrote about the cultural benefits that public transit could bring to residents of peripheral city districts (figure 2.5). A quick ride on the tram and the "cultural possibilities of the center—cinema, theater, libraries, lectures, etc.—will now be available to residents of the outskirts [okrain]," the article proclaimed.[83] Itshe wants to see the film again but his wife does not want to make the trip so the tailor "had to make do with once again recalling the Arctic seas with their polar bears that had flashed before his eyes on that magical night in the cinema. [. . .] At night, while stitching a pair of quilted pants, he thought wistfully of the snow-white bears and those wanderers on the frozen ice for whom quilted pants would have been just the thing."[84]

Kulbak does not identify the film that Itshe saw, but the details of his imaginings match a film that was reviewed on October 17, 1929. "The picture," the reviewer for *The Worker* noted, "was made in the Arctic North and all that we see on the screen is real life [. . .] During snowstorms the movie camera captured the hard labor of the Eskimos. Without persistent, hard labor, life beyond the Arctic Circle is impossible." The reviewer noted that the film, which had opened at one of Minsk's cinema theaters the same week as the urban transit system that helped turn Itshe and his kin into moviegoers, "should be shown to the wide masses of viewers."[85]

The reviewer was recommending that Minsk audiences, which now included the fictional Zelmenyaners, see *Nanook of the North*—a film about the Inuit in the Canadian arctic, which was shown in Minsk seven years after

Figure 2.5. The "Red Star" movie theater on Minsk's Soviet Street (1932). Decorations honoring the fifteenth anniversary of the Bolshevik Revolution are on the building's facade; the tramway tracks are in front. Reproduced with permission of the Belarusian State Archive of Films, Photographs, and Sound Recordings (BGAKFFD).

Figure 2.6. Cinema and theater listings in Minsk's daily newspaper. The listing for *Nanook* is second from the bottom; the listing for David Bergelson's play *Glukhoi* (*The Deaf Man*) is at the top. Reproduced from *Rabochii*, October 17, 1929.

its release in the United States (figure 2.6). The same issue of *The Worker* that carried the review of *Nanook* also printed the listings of films on offer around the city that day: in addition to *Nanook*, Sergei Eisenstein's film about collectivization, *The Old and the New*, had just opened—as did *Chang*, a U.S. production about a poor farmer and his daily struggle for survival in the jungles of Thailand. Printed just above the movie listings was an advertisement for a play by David Bergelson, *The Deaf Man* (*Der toyber* or, as it was advertised in Russian, *Glukhoi*), premiering that day at the Belorussian State Yiddish Theater, located in a building that had formerly been a synagogue (figure 2.7).

Nanook of the North, which was directed by Robert Flaherty, has entered the history of cinema as the first commercially successful feature-length

Figure 2.7. Belorussian State Yiddish Theater—formerly a synagogue—in Minsk, decorated with slogans in Yiddish and Belorussian in honor of the fifteenth anniversary of the Bolshevik Revolution (1932). Reproduced with permission of the Belarusian State Archive of Films, Photographs, and Sound Recordings (BGAKFFD).

documentary. The Inuit family that was the subject of *Nanook* may seem very distant from Kulbak's Zelmenyaners, but the novel's Uncle Itshe likely empathizes with the film's central protagonist because he sees in him a kind of uncanny relation: someone whose traditional way of life is being undermined through the varied processes of modernization. A conveyor belt at the clothing factory would soon replace Itshe's job as an independent tailor, just as Folye's manual labor as a tanner was falling into obsolescence at the leather factory. At the same time, above the Arctic Circle, the white man's new gadgets and civilizing mission were eroding Nanook's way of life. As the technologies of modernity, including cinema, appeared in Minsk, Kulbak's simple Jews became self-conscious liminal figures in a kind of unfolding drama that bore similarities to what *Nanook* depicted.

Flaherty claimed that he was able to film *Nanook* simply by observing the Inuit[86]; *The Worker*'s reviewer, too, focused on the film's apparent fidelity to the life it represented. More recently, the film's many nondocumentary elements have come to light. Flaherty wanted the Inuit to appear "authentic," so he made them stage and perform their already anachronistic practices for the camera. Flaherty's method has come to be known as "salvage ethnography"—a practice now criticized for a taxidermy-like depiction of people that calcifies them in their "primitive" state.[87]

Salvage ethnography was motivated by researchers' perception that the cultures they were observing were under threat and facing extinction. Ethnographers would arrive at a "primitive" location only to discover that processes of modernization, buoyed by the introduction of contemporary technology, had already began to displace the "authentic" lifestyle they had come to find. In *Nanook,* Flaherty found his subject already hunting with a rifle, so he asked the Inuit man to use the more traditional harpoon so that the filmmaker could preserve the vanishing customs of his people on celluloid. The Zelmenyaners' trip to see a film about a "primitive" culture threatened by modernity hints at Kulbak's awareness that similar questions were being asked about Jews in the USSR. *The Zelmenyaners* itself is a two-pronged work of salvage ethnography. First, it is based on one of the character's efforts to salvage the Zelmenyaners' odds and ends, condemned at the show trial in the novel's final scenes. Second, the novel can be seen as a work of salvage by its author—salvage not merely of the scattered "bits" but also of the process of the family's transition to becoming Soviet Jews.

The Zelmenyaners, like *Nanook*, is set in a space undergoing a significant transformation. The family's encounter with Flaherty's film occurs outside the boundaries of the courtyard, in a movie theater made accessible by the same process of urban development that will ultimately displace them from their homes. In describing the courtyard, Kulbak uses techniques of salvage ethnography similar to those that Flaherty used in *Nanook;* in contrast to Flaherty, however, Kulbak calls attention to this process. The ethnographer in Flaherty's film stays invisible behind the camera, and his work staging the "authentic" experiences of the Inuit becomes apparent only when the film's documentary claims are suspended. In contrast, the cast of characters in *The Zelmenyaners* includes someone who embodies and makes legible the ethnographic inclinations of Kulbak's novel. He acts as a kind of local informant who is visible in the text and whose research provides the basis for Kulbak's novel itself. This protagonist is Tsalke—the hapless and amateur intellectual subjected to Tonke's attack at Folye's trial.

Tonke attacks Tsalke's work more than Tsalke himself. She detests his "The Zelmeniad [*Zelmenyade*]," which the novel presents as a found text containing notes for a study of the courtyard. Framed as a "scholarly investigation," the text is "compiled and edited [*baarbet*] from the notes of the research associate [*visnshaftlikhn tuer*] Tsalel [Tsalke] Khvost, himself the courtyard's native."[88] Tsalke's notes are implicitly revised by another research associate—Kulbak, whose actual job title at the time matched Tsalke's fictional occupation in "The Zelmeniad." Between 1930 and his arrest in 1937, Kulbak was employed as a *nauchnyi sotrudnik* (the Russian term for "research associate" that the Yiddish calques) at the Belorussian Academy of Sciences. Specifically, he worked as a stylistic editor on the ethnographic projects of the Jewish Sector.[89]

The Jewish Sector of the Belorussian Academy of Sciences underwent several structural changes after its founding in 1924 as the Jewish Department of the Institute of Belorussian Culture, or *Inbelkult*.[90] It became a "sector" in 1927–1928 and was transformed into the Institute of Jewish Proletarian Culture after the *Inbelkult* itself was restructured as part of the Belorussian Academy of Sciences.[91] The tasks, roles, and methods of the Jewish Sector's locally focused commissions resembled those of the YIVO Institute, founded in Vilna in 1925.[92] In his job in Minsk, Kulbak, familiar with YIVO from the time he lived in Vilna, would have processed and edited Yiddish-language texts for publication. The pseudoscientific language of Tsalke's study is thus "edited" by an implied author who is himself an associate at a major Soviet research organization with an entire department invested in the ethnographic study of Jews.

Referred to as "one of the newly educated [*er iz der, vos fun di naye gelernte*]," Tsalke has a good ear for the speech of others. On hearing something of interest, he "always ask[s] you to repeat what you've said so that he can write it down in a notebook."[93] Kulbak's widow Zelda recalled that Kulbak himself acted similarly: "He loved to speak with workers and simple people. He used to say to his students: 'One must listen to the language of the people, to idioms and sayings, to folklore.' Together with other students he would go on excursions to the market. They would eavesdrop on and record the words of merchants and customers."[94] "The Zelmeniad," Tsalke's exercise in mock ethnography, is the fictional, parodic version of the kind of ethnographic work with which Kulbak was familiar in his position at the Belorussian Academy of Sciences.[95]

In his 1922 essay, the Russian formalist critic Yuri Tynianov, a contemporary of Kulbak, saw parody as the process by which a new text dialectically engages with earlier texts and argued that it was an essential tool in the dynamic process of literary evolution. By shifting the initial intentions of an "original," parody creates a new text with a different stylistic and generic orientation. "If the parody of tragedy is a comedy, then the parody of a comedy might very well be a tragedy," Tynianov noted, insisting that, despite generic refashioning, the process of parody always retains a remnant of the parodied text in the new work.[96] "The Zelmeniad" shifts the expressed intentions of Soviet ethnography while preserving its parodied traces. In claiming to have "edited" Tsalke's ethnographic "study," Kulbak relies on Tsalke's catalog of the Zelmenyaners' comic traits, language, and customs to turn this fictional family into a paradigmatic example, not of the Jew as the intended subject of Soviet ethnographic research but of the Soviet Jew as a product of a process that parodied that same state research agenda.

Indeed, "The Zelmeniad" follows but parodies the conventions of ethnographic research. Like Kulbak's novel, it opens with the story of Reb Zelmele's founding of the courtyard and presents this space as a subject of ethnographic research: "Set apart from their neighbors, the Zelmenyaners forged a distinctive lifestyle of their own."[97] The subsequent chapters describe specific customs and practices: "The Technology of Reb Zelmele's Courtyard," "Medicine in the Courtyard," "Zelmenyaner Geography," "Zelmenyaner Zoology," "Zelmenyaner Botany," and "Zelmenyaner Philology."[98] These chapters consist of folkways, linguistic coinages, and whimsical lists of items in the family's possession and their intended uses. These lists of odds and ends look similar to those that Tonke discusses at the show trial, but Tsalke's "Zelmeniad" presents these items in a different context.

Assessed in this fashion, Reb Zelmele's courtyard is a microcosm of the shtetl, the larger unit of Jewish habitation subjected to ethnographic investigation and debates at the time. Authorities urged that the shtetl's economy be shifted away from professions that were no longer relevant in—or were actively harmful to—the Bolshevik state's centrally planned economy.[99] Ethnographic research on the shtetl promised to help the government set appropriate policies to modernize Jews in the former Pale of Settlement and move them into "productive" professions, in effect turning them into Soviet citizens.

Ethnographic studies of the shtetl were part of a broader set of policy initiatives through which the government produced knowledge about the USSR's population. A crucial instrument of state building, ethnographic research enabled the regime to use data about different ethnic groups in developing economic and social policies.[100] As policy makers endeavored to manage a geographically and culturally diverse country, social scientists received the political license and financial support to conduct their research. A collaboration between two sets of interests, ethnography was defined as a social science field in the service of the state. The use of ethnographic knowledge was part of a Lamarckian project of "state-sponsored evolutionism" that aimed to usher "the entire population [of the USSR] through the Marxist timeline of historical development."[101] This project targeted different ethnic groups' supposedly backward and anachronistic traits and practices, seen as malleable to the Soviet state's modernizing ethos. When it came to Jews, the shtetl was for Soviet ethnographers the kind of space that, instead of disappearing, persisted as "a site of unregulated commercial exchange that could easily become a conduit of counter-revolutionary ideology" and therefore needed to be studied so as to be changed.[102]

In his influential 1928 pamphlet, *Research Your Shtetl!* the historian and literary scholar Hillel Aleksandrov called on amateur ethnographers like the fictional Tsalke to undertake the study of their hometowns, and he even specified their research topics: "the geographic position and appearance of the shtetl," "the history of the shtetl," "population," "the economic system of the shtetl," "education in the shtetl," "facilities and sanitary conditions," and "practices and culture."[103] *Research Your Shtetl!* was published in Minsk the same year Kulbak settled in the city and by the very same institution that would employ him two years later—the Jewish Sector of what would become the Belorussian Academy of Sciences.[104] The structure of the fictional "The Zelmeniad" appears as a response to Aleksandrov's agenda and follows its research categories. At the same time, it parodies the very premise of the enterprise when it applies the kinds of research categories outlined by Aleksandrov to the study of Reb Zelmele's courtyard.

Some critics, however, read "The Zelmeniad" as a straight-up ethnographic text. In his 1936 review of the novel, A. Damesek opens with the question, "What is Zelmenyanovism? [*Vos iz di zelmenyanovshine?*]"[105] The formulation evokes the nineteenth-century Russian critic Nikolai Dobroliubov's question, "What is Oblomovism?" Writing in response to Ivan Goncharov's 1859 novel *Oblomov,* Dobroliubov sought to define a phenomenon—which he named after the novel's protagonist—characterized by the social malaise of Russia's landed gentry. Following Russia's "utilitarian" critical tradition that treated fiction as a platform for promoting a social agenda,[106] Damesek questions whether Kulbak had sufficiently critiqued the complex phenomenon of "Zelmenyanovism," which Damesek presents as a generalized social type (*tipazh*).[107] On the surface, Damesek notes, the novel seemed to tell a story of a backward petit-bourgeois family forced to modernize during Stalin's cultural and industrial revolution and of its members who were "born anew [*ibergeboyrene*]" as reformed Soviet citizens.[108] But despite seemingly following this narrative trajectory, Damesek continues, the novel didn't actually support this reading. In fact, he goes on, it was extremely difficult to conclude whether the Zelmenyaner "type" reflects the possibility of change or instead its impossibility: the Zelmenyaners' very uniqueness impedes their path toward transformation. As an example, Damesek quotes the anecdote from the beginning of the novel (cited at the start of this chapter), in which a train passenger recognizes Reb Zelmele's grandchild by his smell. Damesek's reference shows that the Zelmenyaners' hereditary traits made them unable to internalize the Soviet worldview and be transformed by it.[109]

In commenting on the possibility or impossibility of proper Soviet transformation, Damesek seems to have drawn from Lamarckian theories of
evolution, popular at the time within the Soviet scientific establishment. In
the Lamarckian formulation popularized in the work of agronomist Timofey
Lysenko starting in the late 1920s, characteristics acquired during the lifetime of a given organism could be inherited by its descendants. Moreover,
Lysenko claimed, the evolutionary influence of present circumstances was
stronger than Darwinian natural selection.[110] Nonetheless, notes Damesek,
the Zelmenyaners' hereditary and "spontaneous" traits prove stronger than
the transformative power of new social circumstances; the persistence of
such hereditary determinism produces characters who can't be changed by
their environment because they are insufficiently "conscious" of it.

Damesek thus operates within two paradigms: the consciousness-
spontaneity dialectic embedded in Socialist Realism and the Lamarckian
paradigm of evolution that privileges the effects of current—and, for Damesek,
revolutionary—conditions over the Darwinian play of hereditary traits. In
doing so, Damesek singles out Tsalke for opprobrium. He notes that Tsalke
possesses only the sort of consciousness that is antithetical to the aims of a
Soviet novel. Damesek describes Tsalke's collection of ethnographic tidbits
as "an actively hostile force [*an aktive fayntlikhe kraft*] that manifests itself
all the more because it senses its own proximate and absolute demise."[111] This
formulation—ethnographic preservation in the face of proximate demise—
resembles the language of salvage ethnography. But Tsalke's method of recording the family culture seems to Damesek to deliberately undermine the
larger social project that Soviet ethnography was intended to serve. Tsalke's
consciousness, which according to the critic should have been aimed at modernizing his family in the spirit of the present moment, instead drives him
to record and preserve their undesirable heritable traits. Tsalke's activity, then,
becomes for the critic a motivated and, as such, doubly dangerous counter-
reaction to the Soviet project: at a time when technological innovation driven
by Soviet ideology is in the process of transforming the courtyard, Tsalke
salvages what should be allowed to vanish.

The critic Damesek—like the fictional Tonke in Kulbak's novel—condemns
Kulbak's writing about Tsalke's intentional work of cultural salvage. Tsalke's
"The Zelmeniad," writes Damesek, "occupies itself with the specificity of
Jewishness with the purpose not just of preventing it from becoming part of

a museum display, but of transforming it into a folk tradition, an exalted national form."[112] Here, the critic makes a distinction between the multiethnic Soviet project's encouragement of cultural differences that could show the advances of the revolution to be, as in Stalin's famous quip, "national in form, socialist in content,"[113] and the kind of doubling down on the national form without any socialist content that he sees in Tsalke's work in *The Zelmenyaners*. Joining other critics of the novel who chastised Kulbak for his insufficient use of satire,[114] Damesek fears that Kulbak has created Tsalke not to ridicule the Zelmenyaners' anachronistic traits, as would have been ideologically appropriate, but rather to perpetuate folksiness and idiosyncrasies that should have been exposed instead. Kulbak does so, in part, by presenting "The Zelmeniad" as a parodic inversion of the kind of ethnographic text about Jews in the Soviet Union that the authorities and doctrinaire critics actually wished to see.

Tonke's attack on Tsalke at Folye's trial occurs shortly after Tsalke kills himself—coming on the heels of so many prior attempts that his string of unsuccessful suicides became a kind of running joke in the novel. Tonke, whom the novel consistently presents as acting in a particularly heartless manner toward Tsalke and her other family members, attributes Tsalke's demise to his interest in collecting and preserving the anachronistic culture of the RebZe courtyard: "Tsalke, an educated young native of the courtyard, spent so long investigating its uniqueness that he hanged himself out of sheer spiritual poverty."[115] However, both the critic Damesek and the fictional character Tonke fail to see the nuance in Kulbak's work. Tsalke's "The Zelmeniad"—like Kulbak's *The Zelmenyaners*—does not seek to preserve an unadulterated version of an anachronistic "Zelmenyanovism." Instead, these texts capture the denizens of Reb Zelmele's courtyard in the moment of their transformation and depict the process by which all Zelmenyaners, Tonke included, were becoming Soviet Jews.

* * *

Tsalke's pursuit of Tonke and the couple's tortured relationship punctuate much of the novel. Whereas Tsalke imagines that the two would live in a house by the sea, Tonke considers this petit-bourgeois vision antithetical to her revolutionary ideals. Rather than marry Tsalke, Tonke goes to Vladivostok on a Party assignment at the end of the first part of the novel only to return home, in part two, with a baby in tow. As Tsalke continues to seek her attention through much of part one, Tonke does not educate him—as a person with revolutionary consciousness would be expected to. Instead, she taunts him. Thus, even though Tonke resists the bourgeois marriage plot, she fails to be a mentor figure in the Socialist Realist mold and instead becomes party to a different, conventionally bourgeois plot: a story of unrequited love.

Tsalke's suicide poses a further complication. In the USSR in the 1930s, suicide was viewed as a societal concern. At a time when social progress was said to have bettered the lot of individuals, suicide could be "construed as the product of one's [negative] attitude toward the regime [and thus] everyone involved in the drama of self-destruction was potentially at fault."[116] Any case of suicide could reflect badly on the deceased individual's social environment, which was understood to include those who had led the victim to this self-destructive act and were thus accessories to his or her counterrevolutionary crime. Accordingly, those attempting suicide often left notes either absolving or blaming others for their demise.[117]

Tonke gestures toward such an assumption of collective responsibility when she blames Reb Zelmele's courtyard for Tsalke's death. At the same time, she fails to consider herself part of the larger social context that she faults. Here, Kulbak makes a connection that Tonke as a character in the novel does not: he playfully inserts Tonke in the middle of the first of Tsalke's failed suicide attempts, linking her, by implication, also to his last—successful—one.

Kulbak's description of Tsalke's first recorded attempt to take his own life combines the character's interest in Tonke with his interest in ethnographic inquiry and introduces Tonke's name into what is ostensibly his suicide note. Aunt Malkaleh, who had just learned how to read thanks to a literacy campaign activist, retrieves the note from Tsalke's body. The note proves rather befuddling to the family:

Ume—liver (butcher's language)

Gudegarde (?)

Serkhele—scent; it smells, exudes odor (stinks)

Fidldemone - pennies, money (in different jargons)

Tchevekhtch (?)

To like, to love—there is a nuance.

What would be better to say: "I like Tonke" or "I love Tonke"?

Tonke, Ton-ke.[118]

The genre of a suicide note might seem incompatible with that of an etymological inquiry. However, in this document Kulbak brings together Tsalke's practice of salvage ethnography and his attraction to Tonke, who would go on to condemn his ethnographic project. Ripped from his fieldwork notebook, the text is a list of linguistic entries in Yiddish, some of which he has not yet defined, traces within an ongoing study. Tonke—nominally an item on the list—becomes one of the "entries" that require a definition, a subject of an ethnographic inquiry in her own right. Her presence in Tsalke's notebook suggests that his research is devoted not only to the world of the past but also to understanding the new phenomena of the Soviet era, including Tonke herself.

Tsalke's note, like his suicide attempt, turns up in the novel following a comically failed rendezvous with Tonke. During that encounter, Tsalke excitedly tells Tonke about the previous night's scholarly achievement: he was able to correctly identify a seventeenth-century book without a title page.[119] Tonke is not impressed and questions the usefulness of such a discovery to the project of "socialist construction [*sotsboyung*]," to which she has devoted herself.[120] Tonke and Tsalke appear to inhabit completely different worlds.

Kulbak has Tsalke inadvertently comment on the process of socialist construction right after Tonke dismisses his research skills as useless for this task. Yet Tsalke's ethnographic observations and linguistic acuity appear to be quite fitting for the new Soviet world that both cousins are trying to figure out, each in their own way. Kulbak describes the landscape they see:

> The road stretched to the piney horizon. Between the low shadows of the potato fields, the burning wheat rippled in big, rectangular brass beds. [. . .]
>
> Far off on the horizon rose a spiral of smoke. A tractor chugged beneath it, creeping slowly along the edge of the earth without vanishing.
>
> Tsalke said:
>
> "BlessedartThouOLordourGodKingoftheUniverseWhobringeth forthbreadfromtheearth!"[121]

Sizing up a natural landscape altered by new technology, Tsalke recites, in one breath (which Kulbak denotes by not using any spaces between words in the sentence), the Hebrew blessing over bread traditionally pronounced at the beginning of a meal. Viewed simplistically, Tsalke's utterance sounds like an anachronistic religious custom. However, when the words of Tsalke's verbal outburst are taken literally, a different interpretation emerges. The traditional blessing praises God who "brings forth bread from the earth." In pronouncing the same words upon seeing a tractor chugging through a field of wheat, Tsalke implicitly reassigns the praise to the new industrial machine that, quite literally, brings forth bread from the earth. Tsalke's interest in salvaging the odds and ends of practices that are both Zelmenyanish and Jewish is directed here toward what, in Tonke's parlance, could actually be understood as socially useful *sotsboyung*—socialist construction. Both Tonke, the ostensible socialist, and Tsalke, the ostensible reactionary, are building identities for themselves at the intersection of the disintegrating Pale's old customs and the new Soviet reality.

When Tonke and Tsalke pass a crew laying rails for the tram, the sight of the workers' muscles, which "rippled like living creatures in a wave that ran down the street as though in a strange brown sea," reminds Tonke of a poem she attributes to "the Zelmenyaner poet Moyshe Kulbak."[122] She recites it, ventriloquizing Kulbak's curious bit of self-citation: "And bronzed youths / were then filled / with a will / to still / the rage / of years / that had been lost."[123] The lines are from Kulbak's long poem "The City" (Di shtot), parts of which were first published in 1919 and which is animated by the poet's revolutionary zeal. Ruth R. Wisse concludes that because Tonke turns out to be the villain of *The Zelmenyaners* for betraying her family, Kulbak's insertion of his earlier verse into this protagonist's mouth "seems less an advertisement than an apology for his youthful zealotry."[124] Here, Wisse reads Kulbak as a writer who wished to recant his earlier revolutionary poetry in the face of what had become Soviet reality. However, Kulbak's assessment of the Soviet condition—and the Soviet Jew being made in that period—is far more complex.

Yasha Bronshteyn's contemporary critique of Kulbak's self-quotation in *The Zelmenyaners* questions the premise that the poem was ever straightforwardly revolutionary. Though the poet claims in "The City" to have heard the call of the working class and decided to prod others to revolutionary struggle through his work, Bronshteyn believes that Kulbak fails to show the "bronzed youths" marching consciously under the revolution's banner. Instead, the critic writes, Kulbak portrays them as a passive herd capable only of issuing an inarticulate "silent cry [*a shtumer geshrey*]."[125] This silence extends to *The Zelmenyaners* as well. Tonke observes the workers before launching into her recitation of the poem, and the narrator draws attention to the silent nature of the scene of labor the cousins observe: "They worked in incandescent silence."[126] Tonke is inspired not by what she sees in front of her but by the "silent cry" of the poet Kulbak, whose work she suddenly remembers. Kulbak's self-quotation is not an apology for a bygone period of revolutionary zeal but instead a suggestion that his words from 1919, ambiguous when written, could be adapted and used to complicate narratives of socialist construction during the First Five-Year Plan.

Yet Kulbak doesn't have Tonke merely recite his poem; instead, he has her identify with his own earlier incarnation as a revolutionary poet. Both Kulbak the young poet and Tonke, that poet's later protagonist, share the very "zealotry" that Wisse finds alarming. More akin to spontaneity than to consciousness in Socialist Realist terms, this "zealotry" is a kind of revolutionary romanticism that does not pay adequate attention to the directives of the revolutionary elites. As such, it is similar to the Zelmenyaners' quality of being "rascals," which Bronshteyn singles out for critique. When Tonke identifies Kulbak as a "Zelmenyaner poet" while reciting his verse, she is suggesting that she is like him and that he, like her, is "a Zelmenyaner through and through."[127] Tonke may be the novel's chief doctrinaire character, but her impulsiveness betrays a complicated form of revolutionary consciousness that makes her similar to every other member of the Zelmenyaner kin: they all collectively possess the traits of the figure of the Soviet Jew, of which the poet Kulbak is implicitly a variant.

Though it seems improbable that Kulbak would identify parts of his authorial persona with a character who condemns her own family member, having Tonke identify with him in his novel does serve a purpose: it allows the author to claim a passable revolutionary credential for his work within an otherwise ambiguous text. The scene of Tonke's recitation of Kulbak's poem follows the process by which something akin to a cinematic montage image is formed. Tonke first sees the workers laying rails for the tramway line and then recites Kulbak's poem as a commentary on the scene: from these two elements, the newly observed achievement in Minsk's industrialization during the First Five-Year Plan appears to have been anticipated by the poet's earlier verse. Though the hostile critic Bronshteyn saw "The City" as insufficiently engaged with the revolutionary present, Tonke rehabilitates Kulbak's poem as a commentary on a clear instance of "socialist construction" actually underway and observable in Minsk at the time Kulbak's novel was set.

Tonke comments on socialist construction, with the help of Kulbak's early verse, in the presence of Tsalke. This occurs just after Tsalke, mouthing the words of the Hebrew blessing, had reassigned the divinity's role in "bringing forth bread from the earth" to the tractor, an exemplar of Stalin-era industrialization. Tsalke's voice disappears at the end of the novel because he kills himself at the very time that the dismantling of the courtyard begins. However, the two texts attributed to him in the novel—"The Zelmeniad" and the suicide note—preserve his ethnographic research and depict the RebZe courtyard in its moment of transition. As mentioned, the first reader of Tsalke's suicide note is Aunt Malkaleh—a stand-in for the newly educated Soviet reader who learned to read thanks to the USSR's literacy campaign, which was described, with a comic flair, in the novel's early chapters. In turn, "The Zelmeniad," although it is compiled by Tsalke, is "edited [*baarbet*]" by the novel's implied author, Kulbak—who was then an editor of Soviet ethnographies of Jews and whom Tonke identified as, in spirit even if not literally, part of the Zelmenyaners' clan.

Kulbak suggests that *The Zelmenyaners* should be read with Tsalke's ethnographic approach in mind. Like the courtyard it describes, *The Zelmenyaners* is a textual space and a cultural site. By focusing on the mechanism of its own construction, the novel turns itself into a kind of compilation of research and interpretation—one that does not simply preserve the old world or, conversely, document its displacement by the new Soviet reality. Rather, it is a text that captures the creation of the Soviet Jew as a cultural type composed of both these strands.

* * *

Two separate and seemingly irreconcilable notions of mobility define the space of Reb Zelmele's courtyard during its time of transformation. The first is a distinctly modern and industrial mobility that captures the Zelmenyaners in the process of becoming Soviet persons; the second is the timeworn mobility of migration, displacement, and ritual cycles that the novel codes as distinctly Jewish. Like the constitutive elements of montage in the Soviet cinema of the time, the two notions of mobility in the novel are in conflict and strive for a resolution that can be created only in the mind of the reader. As Reb Zelmele's courtyard becomes a microcosm for the changes experienced by Jews in the USSR writ large during the era of industrialization, the textual space of Kulbak's novel becomes a cultural site where the composite figure of the Soviet Jew emerges as diffuse elements, seen as Jewish, encounter aspects of the ascendant Soviet modernity.

Kulbak highlights new industrial modes of mobility when he compares Reb Zelmele's courtyard to a train station. While looking at the outdated lighting fixtures in one of the houses, Bereh—who, as a soldier during the war, would have moved about, including by train—sits quietly "as, once upon a time, someone would sit [vi es zitst amol . . .] at a train station, waiting for his train to finally arrive."[128] Bereh turns to electrification, widely promoted as part of the industrialization effort, as a means of transforming his family's old stomping grounds into a well-lit terminal of progress. When the courtyard is fully electrified, the text likens it to that initial symbol of advancement with which Bereh's quest began: unlike the surrounding houses still using kerosene lamps, the courtyard "was suddenly [. . .] shining like a train station [vi a vokzal]."[129] The industrial simile links the courtyard to progress and mobility that augur the family's dispersal.

But a second notion of mobility, presented in terms that are culturally Jewish, rings truer for Zelmenyaners who don't share Bereh's experience of modern travel but do have access to a traditional vocabulary of displacement. Not everyone in the family is opposed to the electrical revolution; some, in their enthusiasm, "scaled moldy walls and roofs to bang in nails and hang wires as if they were building—pardon the comparison [lehavdil]—a holiday sukkah."[130] The sukkah, a temporary booth-like structure erected during the autumn harvest festival of Sukkot, has its origins in the preindustrial world in which human activity was tied to seasonal cycles. In its mythic origins, the sukkah—in which Jews are expected to dwell for the duration of the weeklong holiday—is also a reminder of the temporary shelter that accommodated ancient Israelites during their desert wanderings after the exodus from Egypt. Through the merging of an agricultural tradition with the story of the Exodus, the sukkah is reinterpreted in the Jewish tradition as a site of a distinctly Jewish national memory.[131] Because Kulbak negates the comparison of the electrified courtyard to the sukkah, he appears to highlight the difference between the modern possibilities of electricity—for example, the courtyard as a train station—and the religious custom of building the sukkah.

Kulbak uses the word *lehavdil,* "pardon the comparison," to highlight the apparent distinction between the illuminated modern courtyard that looks like a train station and the traditional sukkah—the two different metaphors of mobility. The term, clearly used in a tongue-in-cheek fashion, shares its Hebraic root with the Havdalah ceremony that separates the Sabbath from the rest of the week and demarcates the boundary between the sacred and the profane. The sukkah is, in its mythic origins, a structure of the desert. One of the novel's critics called the Zelmenyaners "a generation of the desert." The structure linked in Jewish memory to the liminality of the Israelites in the desert, the death of a whole generation of slaves, and the emergence of a generation that knew no slavery appears as a simile for the electrified courtyard. Kulbak's use of the word *lehavdil* calls attention to this linkage. The train station and the sukkah become related and overlapping spaces as Soviet modernity stretches over—but doesn't completely blot out—traditional ways of dealing with the memory of displacement in Jewish culture. Reb Zelmele's courtyard is a kind of composite, montage image, a structure that is both a train station and a sukkah: it is a new kind of mobile, liminal space for the new figure of the Soviet Jew.

Both Tonke and Tsalke are interested in the proverbial and actual baggage of a family about to be displaced: Tonke in her preoccupation with the Zelmenyaners' odds and ends and Tsalke in his focus on collecting the same material and linguistic artifacts that Tonke condemns. Kulbak identifies partially with both characters, given his pedigree as a famed poet of the revolution and his knowledge of the Soviet social sciences. The textual space of the resulting novel contains both of Kulbak's impulses and, as such, allows the Soviet Jew to emerge at the point of overlap between the dialectical poles that appear to be represented by the two characters. *The Zelmenyaners* is a textual and cultural site that resembles the seemingly unchanging space of the courtyard that, in fact, is destabilized by forces of mobility and is captured in its process of transformation.

On the one hand, it appears that Tonke's prosecutorial lineup of the Zelmenyaners' odds and ends has an edge over the amateur juxtaposition of the same items in Tsalke's notebooks. On the last page of the novel the court-yard is destroyed to make way for a new factory—which occurs at least in part because of Tonke's damning testimony at Folye's trial decrying the family's traits, habits, and possessions. On the other hand, Tsalke's approach to the same odds and ends colors that same scene of destruction: the sur-viving family members forage through the remains of what had been their home, salvaging household items that could be taken to the new apartments where they are being resettled. They pick up pots, pans, shoes, and inkwells. Someone takes down a mezuzah—a ritual object containing a piece of parch-ment with verses from Deuteronomy—from its traditional place on the door-post, perhaps planning to install it at the entrance to a new apartment.[132] To follow the critic Yasha Bronshteyn's—and also Tonke's—logic, this salvaging effort could be seen as one last case of the family's heredity trumping all social circumstances. Even when the courtyard is gone, the Zelmenyaners carry, and carry on with, their old baggage, allowing its disassembled and scattered pieces to continue to define them. The Zelmenyaners' apparent inability to become Soviet even after relocating is on full display.

However, the logic of the novel suggests a different way of reading this ending. Tsalke's death occurs simultaneously with the courtyard's dissolu-tion into a pile of disparate objects. These objects acquire a transitional status: no longer parts of what Tsalke had seen as a unified space, they must now, with Tsalke's perspective newly unavailable, be viewed separately from the larger system of which they had formerly been a part. Tonke's condemna-tion of these items, although it brought about the end of the courtyard, did not spell the obliteration of the objects themselves. No longer a concrete phys-ical space, the courtyard continues to exist in and through these very ob-jects. Their meaning deferred, the Zelmenyaners' odds and ends persist, awaiting an uncertain reinterpretation in still unknown destinations.

The tension between stasis and mobility may have been a key aspect of the courtyard's hereditary and cultural makeup from its creation. Reb Zelmele is said to have arrived in Minsk from "deep Russia [*tif rasey*],"[133] a mythic location in the family lore and, as "The Zelmeniad" has it, "a blessed place in which it is always summer."[134] The genesis of the courtyard lies in the patri-arch's relocation from a place of origin that sounds Edenic and his subsequent founding of a household on a new site. The demise of the courtyard reactivates this process—but in reverse. Now, members of a unified household become displaced as each presumably wanders off to a different location, carrying physical objects and other nonmaterial tidbits—some marked as hereditary traits—salvaged from the courtyard.

The courtyard's founder Reb Zelmele actually writes the process of displacement into his progeny's inheritance. In dating his last will and testament, the family's patriarch hints that the courtyard might end up as both a place of residence and an origin point for his kin's eventual dispersal. The date on the will, which instructs the Zelmenyaners to live in the courtyard, is given not according to the secular calendar but to the traditional Hebrew one, which specifies the portion of the Torah to be read during each week's Sabbath services. Reb Zelmele's will is dated to the week of the portion called "B'shalakh."[135] Corresponding to Exodus 13:17–17:16, this Torah portion, whose title refers to its opening words, "when the Pharaoh let the people go," narrates the beginning of the mythic wanderings of the Israelites after their crossing of the Red Sea, implicitly pointing to Reb Zelmele's own originary peregrinations and to both the emplacement and displacement of his progeny.

As a site that encompasses aspects of both stasis and mobility, Reb Zelmele's courtyard resembles another mobile structure—the Tabernacle (*mishkan*)—also described in the Book of Exodus. Kulbak implies Tsalke's connection to the story of the Tabernacle in his very name. Tsalke is the informal nickname for Tsalel, which is itself short for Bezalel; in the biblical narrative, Bezalel is the artist appointed by Moses to oversee the Tabernacle's construction. Exodus 31:1–11 describes Bezalel's work in precise and pedantic detail. First, Bezalel collects jewelry, precious metals, and other materials from fellow wanderers—the Israelites in the desert—after their departure from Egypt. Then, the artist uses his skills to literally recast these items as part of the structure of the *mishkan* based on his interpretation of God's instructions. The Tabernacle that Bezalel creates is a temporary mobile structure that enables a wandering people to communicate with the divine. A replica of this structure would later be incorporated in the Temple in Jerusalem after the Israelites established their new domicile there—a memory of a people's mobility en route to the Promised Land concretized, upon the end of their journey, in a permanent physical space. Later, the memory of the ruined Temple, with the Tabernacle's replica inside it, would become the *axis mundi* for the Jewish diasporic imagination following Jerusalem's destruction and the Jews' subsequent dispersal and further mobility.

Tsalke's ethnographic collection of his family's curiosities evokes the biblical Bezalel's process of gathering materials for the Tabernacle. Like Bezalel, Tsalke responds to a call—here, by the USSR's social science establishment rather than by God—to collect disparate items and compile them into a new edifice that reconfigures the meaning of its constituent pieces. In Bezalel's work described in the Book of Exodus, pieces of precious metals and jewelry lose their individual value when they are melted down to become material for the construction of the mobile structure that enables communication with the divine. Tsalke's "The Zelmeniad" in Kulbak's novel undertakes a similar collection: in following the standard structure for a work of Soviet ethnography, it supposedly makes Reb Zelmele's courtyard legible to the authorities.

We must recall, however, that Soviet social science at the time was concerned with documenting the shtetl in the era of revolutionary change precisely because it saw the demise of the shtetl as a necessary condition for Sovietizing the Jews of the former Pale. By this measure, Tsalke's "The Zelmeniad" is hardly the same kind of text as those written by professional social scientists. Rather, it is a parody of the genre Kulbak knew intimately as an editor of Soviet ethnographic texts at the Belorussian Academy of Sciences. Given Tsalke's ultimate disappearance from the novel, Kulbak—the implied editor of "The Zelmeniad"—transfers Tsalke's fieldwork inside the RebZe courtyard to the novel he authors. Where once Tsalke collected fragments, now the novel becomes a repository of phenomena related to the Zelmenyaners as they go through a period of transition. The novel itself turns into a kind of Tabernacle, a site that preserves a culture in a liminal moment: in this case, Jewish culture as it becomes the culture of the Soviet Jew.

Kulbak presents this transitory space in his ambiguous portrayal of Bereh. By turning Bereh into a positive hero, Kulbak appears to redirect the second part of his novel through a kind of Socialist Realist funnel. On closer examination, however, there is evidence that Kulbak uses Tsalke's ethnographic method to undermine this apparent attempt: the novel turns out to be a parody of what a Socialist Realist text might have looked like. Tsalke, who inserts Tonke's name into one of his ethnographic compendia, subjects Bereh to a similar treatment, poring over his cousin's wartime autobiography—a text crucial to establishing Bereh's status as a Socialist Realist hero—"night after night."[136] After finding inconsistencies in the lists of names and places that Bereh claims to have visited during the war, Tsalke's concludes that "[f]urther research suggested that the entire document was unreliable"— that is, that the normative Bolshevik exploits it mentions were not true to what Bereh had actually experienced and, implicitly, that Bereh's transformation into a heroic character was a result of his cousin's fabrication of his life's narrative.[137]

Bereh's autobiography is one of several items in Tsalke's collection that make their way into the novel by Kulbak, the implied editor of Tsalke's amateur work. Tsalke does Kulbak's bidding, but Kulbak is the one who creates *The Zelmenyaners* and turns the novel into a site where the new cultural figure of the Soviet Jew emerges. Tsalke is a version of the biblical Bezalel insofar as he follows the process of collecting materials for the making of the Tabernacle. Building a mobile edifice from these materials, however, requires commentary on the processes of collection and remolding. Kulbak, a skilled artist, is the master craftsman of *The Zelmenyaners* as a mobile textual space and a kind of literary Tabernacle.

When *The Zelmenyaners* is viewed as a liminal cultural site rather than simply as a novel with a beginning and a conclusion, the dismantling of Reb Zelmele's courtyard does not spell the clan's end, even though it appears synonymous with the family's demise. The language in the novel deftly sums up items and practices that no longer exist while preserving them inside the textual space of the novel itself. For instance, when the Yiddish text makes a comparison between the courtyard's electrification and the construction of the sukkah, it doesn't mention the sukkah directly but instead refers to hammering sounds that resemble those that "once upon a time occurred on the eve of Sukkot [*vi amol erev sukes*]."[138] There is no longer a sufficient level of religious observance in the courtyard for the family to put up the traditional holiday structure, but noises connected to the erection of electricity poles resemble those once made when a sukkah would have been built. Similarly, when Uncle Yuda prepares for the wedding of his daughter Khayeleh to Bereh, he picks up his violin and begins playing a tune that for him—in the absence of traditional wedding musicians—represents the "Klezmer musicians playing at Khayaleh's wedding."[139] For Yuda, the music commemorates his late wife, "who had departed before her time, before she could stand by her daughter's side under the wedding canopy [*bay der tokhter tsu der khupe*]."[140] There is no *khupe*—no traditional wedding canopy (in Hebrew, *huppah*)—at Bereh and Khayele's wedding because Bereh, then trying to become a proper Bolshevik, considers Jewish ritual anachronistic. The ritual object representative of the Jewish wedding does, however, exist in the textual space that is Moyshe Kulbak's novel.

We see the most striking evidence of the courtyard's persistence in the appearance, at the beginning of the novel, of one of Reb Zelmele's descendants on the train. The implied location of this encounter is outside the courtyard; the scene presumably takes place in the aftermath of the courtyard's physical destruction. This encounter reverses the chronological order of the novel's plot, implicitly placing its conclusion—the taking apart of the courtyard—at the beginning. The end of Reb Zelmele's courtyard may be the culmination of the plot of the novel called *The Zelmenyaners*, but *The Zelmenyaners* as a cultural site—a kind of textual Tabernacle—is a narrative space for the courtyard's continued and ongoing transformation in as-yet unknown ways.

The unnamed representative of the Zelmenyaner clan traveling by train is a Soviet person living during the USSR's era of rapid and dramatic industrialization—on his way, perhaps, to one of the massive construction sites of the Stalin era or maybe relocating to a bigger city. His unique smell of "hay mixed with something else" gives him away as a Zelmenyaner. This organic smell presents the family as a unique breed whose hereditary makeup is synonymous with the kind of Jewishness that developed in the courtyard. But it would be wrong to suggest that the courtyard is an image of stasis, of the nostalgic preservation of some essential Jewishness. Rather, as Kulbak mixes industry and nature, Sovietness and Jewishness, the courtyard resembles both a train station and a sukkah. In turn, the same forces shape Reb Zelmele's descendant on the train, with his typical Zelmenyaner smell. In mixing traditional and idiosyncratic traits with elements of Soviet modernity, he becomes a Soviet Jew, a figure who destabilizes both the Soviet rhetoric about transformation and nostalgic rhetoric, including in some more contemporary scholarship and popular writing on Jews in the USSR, around the preservation (or not) of traditional Jewish markers.

The choice of an organic marker as the passenger's identifying trait is consistent with Kulbak's poetics in this novel and in his other work. Through processes of transformation, the natural environment of the courtyard becomes a part of the industrialized Soviet city: "In early morning, as a gray dawn broke, the stars ceased their singing. In Reb Zelmele's courtyard, a polyphony of [factory] sirens took their place."[141] The metaphoric song of the silent night transitions into industrial noise—two strikingly different images, one visual and one aural, linked together in a montage. Similarly, Tsalke's traditional Jewish blessing during his outing with Tonke implicitly reassigns the agency for "bringing forth bread from the earth" from God to the machine, creating new possibilities for a remapping of "Jewish" phenomena as also and at the same time "Soviet."

Concerns with industry's effect on nature underline Kulbak's larger poetics. Like the "bronzed youths" of his 1919 poem "The City," who turn up in *The Zelmenyaners* by way of Tonke's quotation, the smell of hay as an identifying trait can be traced to Kulbak's other work that preceded his novel— his 1922 poem "Belorussia" (Raysn). On the one hand, Tonke's quotation of Kulbak's revolutionary verse updates his poetry for the industrial age, turning the romantic "bronzed youth" of the revolution into the builders of a new Soviet city. On the other hand, the fact that the "smell of hay" evokes Kulbak's earlier poetry speaks to the persistence of "natural" and organic metaphors long into the age of industrial progress. Moreover, the recurrence of this image demonstrates continuity in Kulbak's authorial strategies of commenting on Jewishness that undergoes a constant process of redefinition.

In "Belorussia," Kulbak describes a family of Jewish peasants headed by a patriarch who works the land ("A farmer with a horse and with an ax and with a sheepskin") and a matriarch who gives birth to one son after another to produce the narrator's sixteen uncles. These sixteen uncles—mighty in number and strength ("Hauling logs out of the forest; driving rafts upon the river")—are the literary precursors of the family in *The Zelmenyaners*.[142] The uncles of "Belorussia" are close to the soil—they exemplify Kulbak's poetic craft, which is credited with enriching literary Yiddish with many original organic locutions and metaphors drawn from local nature.[143]

The poem's description of the uncles in "Belorussia" suggests a relationship between these protagonists and the Zelmenyaners of Kulbak's later novel: "They eat their supper from a single plate; / And fall into their beds like bales of hay [*vi di snopes*]."[144] Immediately after, the poem notes that the men's work consists of "scything hay [*me kosyet hey*]," so the comparison of the uncles to the bales of hay is also olfactory insofar as it suggests that they absorb the smell from their work in the fields.[145] The origin of this smell in *The Zelmenyaners* is unclear, but if we see Reb Zelmele's progeny as literary relations of the mythic uncles of "Belorussia," the smell of hay originates in Kulbak's own oeuvre, in an organic metaphor for a kind of idiosyncratic Jewishness rooted in the land.

Modeled on its protagonist Tsalke's practice of salvage ethnography, Moyshe Kulbak's *The Zelmenyaners* goes a step further than simply preserving the disappearing odds and ends of a Jewish family and its shtetl-like courtyard. The novel, constructed as a kind of mobile textual edifice, preserves the very process of a Jewish family's transition to Soviet modernity and offers a parody of the process by which it itself becomes a Soviet literary text. Kulbak's whimsical Zelmenyaners appear to become new Soviet persons who lose their domicile and end up leaving their traditional habitat in the Pale of Settlement. However, through his deployment of complicated montage-like images that contain references to biology and society, heredity and social change, nature and industry, Jewishness and Sovietness, Kulbak imagines the Zelmenyaners as characters of a new sort who are destined for places yet unknown. The courtyard in the novel is meant to become an abandoned space. Instead, it becomes a space whose fragments diffuse along with its former denizens as elements of an indestructible heredity. Reb Zelmele's courtyard, as a metonymy for Jewish spaces of residence in the Pale of Settlement, continues on as a disaggregated sum of its parts now encoded in the new mobile, liminal figure of the Soviet Jew.

3

The Edge of the World

Narratives of Non-Arrival in Birobidzhan

More than one hundred pages into *Jews in the Taiga* (*Evrei v taige*), a 1930 collection of literary sketches about a Far Eastern region that the USSR had designated for Jewish settlement two years earlier, the writer Viktor Fink acknowledges that he had displaced the ostensibly central subject of his work—Jews who had moved there. "The reader expected a book about Jews," writes Fink, but "he got through all these many pages already and he is still reading about some Cossacks, hunters, local primitives, about poachers who shoot deer, and almost nothing about the Jews in the taiga. Why?"[1] Answering his own question, Fink suggests that his sketches about the region's non-Jewish inhabitants help the reader understand the context in which Jewish settlers lived. However, while he describes the newly resettled Jews in dry prose laden with statistics, the old-timers appear in colorful, vivid vignettes. This contrast illuminates both the near-absence of Jews in Fink's text and their overall near-invisibility in Birobidzhan, as the region, which took its name from the local rivers Bira and Bidzhan, became informally known. A town by the same name was established in 1931 as the administrative center of the region on the site of an earlier stop on the Trans-Siberian railroad.

Fink's book compiled impressions he had accumulated during a trip to Birobidzhan in the summer of 1929, when he accompanied a group from the United States on a weeks-long expedition to the largely undeveloped territory. The delegation, led by the Brigham Young University president Frankin S. Harris, included agronomists, sociologists, and specialists in other fields who traveled to the distant border region separated from Manchuria by the Amur River. The group had come to conduct a study commissioned by the Organization for Jewish Colonization in Russia, formed in New York in 1924 and known by its Yiddish acronym, IKOR. IKOR's 1930 report, published the same year as Fink's book, was filled with optimistic statistics about climate, crop cultivation, and Jewish demographic projections for the region. However, it lacked specific descriptions of existing Jewish settlements. The scarcity of observable detail, both in Fink's literary sketches and in IKOR's report, reflected what the Soviet government did not readily acknowledge: by 1929, a year after Jewish migrants began arriving in Birobidzhan, successes were few and far between. Matters were made all the worse that year by an epidemic that felled the settlers' cattle and by torrential rains that destroyed much of their crops.[2]

Birobidzhan was touted as a solution to Jewish economic degeneracy that stemmed from the Jews' employment as small-scale traders and artisans and which persisted after livelihoods based on these established Jewish occupations were upended by the demise of the Pale of Settlement and recast by the world's first state of workers and peasants.[3] After the failure of earlier attempts to establish Jewish agricultural colonies in Ukraine, Belorussia, and Crimea, the Soviet government set its sights on the Far East.[4] The Soviet government presented the area, sparsely populated by, among others, ethnic Koreans and Chinese, as a kind of new "promised land" for Jews—doing so with full awareness of the similar rhetorical tropes and historical connotations connected to the Land of Israel.

Birobidzhan's designation as a region for Jewish settlement hinged on the government's expectations for Jews in the Soviet Union, which were rooted in its nationalities policy. The state's approach to "nationalities"—in the Soviet context, a term roughly equivalent to "ethnic groups"—centered on the premise that population groups residing across the USSR were historically, culturally, and linguistically linked to defined geographic areas.[5] The state hoped to slot Jews into a population category similar to Tatars and Bashkirs, among others, but faced the unique complication that Jews, unlike many other ethnocultural groups in the USSR, had no "national" territory of their own.[6] Although largely concentrated in the territory of the former Pale, Jews could not lay claims to the country's western borderlands because they didn't form ethnic majorities there. Birobidzhan was set up, in part, to make Jews in the USSR more akin to other territorially grounded groups—albeit thousands of miles away from established Jewish population centers in Eastern

Europe. Given the apparent incongruity of assigning Jews a territory so far from places identified with their cultural rootedness, the aim of the IKOR expedition was to assess the feasibility of a Jewish homeland in Birobidzhan and the role that financial and political support from North America might play in its success.[7]

The U.S. delegation's report conveyed the transformative potential of the Birobidzhan settlement. The document summarized the history of legal restrictions on Jewish residence in the Pale; the adverse economic conditions of many Jews employed as middlemen, property leaseholders, and shopkeepers; and the extent to which Jews had emigrated en masse from Imperial Russia at the turn of the century and from the territories of the former Pale during and after the pogroms of the Russian civil war.[8] The survival of Jews as a national group in the USSR, according to Mikhail Kalinin, the nominal head of the Soviet state, depended on their transformation into "an economically stable, agriculturally compact group" located in their specific "place in the Soviet Union."[9] Given the lack of available land close to sites of historically significant Jewish presence in Eastern Europe, the relocation of Jews to the Far East for the purposes of the region's agricultural colonization was deemed necessary—despite the fact, as the report noted, that Jews had little prior experience of land cultivation.[10] The report, disseminated in Russian and English, presented IKOR's findings regarding the outlook for rice cultivation, beekeeping, and mining of precious metals and other natural resources. Chiefly, it endorsed the Soviet government's agenda to encourage Jewish settlement in Birobidzhan.

On arriving in Birobidzhan, the shtetl Jew was to undergo a transformation into a variant of the New Soviet Man. The anticipated emergence of this figure, trumpeted in official iconography as a tiller of the soil and a productive member of society,[11] was inextricably linked to the unidirectional nature of Jewish mobility—from the Pale to the Far East—that government proposals envisioned. Unlike official pronouncements, however, literary and artistic representations of the territory abounded with gaps, absences, and a kind of fluid multidirectionality. In them, Jews who set out to move to Birobidzhan didn't always arrive there either physically—because they never made it or left soon after first setting foot there—or metaphorically, as subjects of literary texts that failed to describe their new lives. Ideologically intended as a program that would yield a Soviet Jewish home, Birobidzhan instead contributed to shaping the figure of the Soviet Jew through narratives of non-arrival.

This chapter explores this textual fluidity in writings about Birobidzhan. Viktor Fink (1888–1973), with his literary sketches, was one of two writers who accompanied the American delegation to the region in 1929. The other was Semyon Gekht (1900–1963).[12] Both grew up and came of age in Odessa and moved to Moscow in the 1920s. Both spent much of the decade after IKOR's expedition to Birobidzhan writing about the region in a variety of genres, including fiction, drama, literary sketches, and children's literature. Although their writing shared traits with other literary work on Birobidzhan well into the 1930s, Gekht's and Fink's contributions across several literary genres were uniquely rooted in their on-the-ground reporting in 1929. The IKOR expedition, because it affirmed the Soviet government's public pronouncements about the region, furnished these writers with a kind of cover to probe and covertly challenge these intentions while propagating them at the same time. The expedition also helped them bring to light the incongruities between the objective of making Birobidzhan a Jewish territory and the emerging literary and cultural figure of the Soviet Jew, which was far more ambivalent than the official script intended to be used for its creation.

Even Gekht's and Fink's journalistic work written not long after the 1929 expedition exposes tensions between Birobidzhan as an observable place and Birobidzhan as a regnant but potentially unachievable metaphor for the end to Jewish wanderings. In an article published in the popular weekly *Ogonëk* soon after the trip, Gekht noted a sharp distinction between the former Pale's "impoverished and decrepit shtetls" and the place of abundance that Birobidzhan was seen as becoming, "if not today and not tomorrow then certainly in a future that is not far off." In an ambiguous phrase, Gekht described one aspect of this bright future in the promise that the site held for gold mining: "*stanet zdes' dragotsennaia draga.*" This phrase can be translated as "here there will be a dredge for precious metals" or, somewhat more loosely, as "this place is going to be a gold mine."[13] This latter metaphorical reading imagines a complete transformation of the region. A journalist and a writer of fiction, Gekht offered this statement not only to comment on gold mining in the typical language of a fact-finding mission but also to offer a literary metaphor for a place that could spark grandiose visions without needing to rely on any specific future achievement.

In 1934, five years after Gekht's essay, Viktor Fink published an article in *Ogonëk* as well. Citing statistical data on the numbers of schools established and factory output measured in tons, Fink remarked that the Jewish settlement project could be considered a success. However, like Gekht, whose observation about gold was both concrete and metaphorical, Fink offered an ambiguous statement, this one more ominous, about another detail of the Far Eastern landscape: the taiga. Fink began his article by describing the old-timers' fears that the noisy agricultural equipment brought to the region by Jewish colonists would cause the animals that the locals had customarily hunted for food to "vanish into the taiga." Having noted the Jewish settlers' purportedly successful taming of the land, Fink suggested that they were "building socialism in the wilds of the taiga [*v dikoi taige*]."[14] The wilderness, it seems, had not been tamed, despite the passage of half a decade—the same period that had elapsed since Fink had traveled to Birobidzhan. Despite the passage of time, the taiga remained not only a feature of the local geography but also a persistent trope in texts about the region, a reminder of its resistance to the Jews called on to relocate there from other parts of the country.

Because Birobidzhan was a less desirable destination for prospective migrants than the Soviet state had intended, propagandistic writing about its settlement focused on lists of planned, measurable accomplishments. In Gekht's and Fink's articles, such lists also stood rhetorically for the project's purported success. At the same time, a close reading of some of the details in the two writers' journalistic works—such as about the gold and the taiga— suggests that these texts stage both the supposed progress of the Jews' settling of Birobidzhan and its undoing. Gekht and Fink introduced rhetorical figures that were central to the ideological creation of Birobidzhan, but did not yet exist, in relation to people, places, and objects that did. They did so through the substitution of metaphors. In the absence of concrete accomplishments, gold as a metaphor for the richness of the region replaces gold as an extractable precious metal while appearing to suggest that gold had in fact been found. Similarly, the word "taiga," a metaphor for the difficulty of human settlement in the region, replaces the notion of a real wild space that newly muscular Jewish settlers could tame and, instead, signifies an unconquerable landscape. While ostensibly describing the new domicile of Jews in the USSR, these texts produced narratives about the region's nonviability as a Jewish home. The place meant to be transformed by the USSR's Jews—who were themselves to be transformed by moving there—appears, instead, as a space where the Soviet Jew perpetually fails to arrive.

Gekht's and Fink's use of rhetorical substitution to suggest the nonviability of Jewish settlement in Birobidzhan also characterizes their other work on this topic. In the years after the IKOR expedition, both authors produced literary texts informed by their experience in Birobidzhan: Fink's *Jews in the Taiga*, a book of literary sketches published in two editions in the early 1930s[15] that served as the basis for his play *The New Homeland* (1933), and Gekht's novel *A Ship Sails to Jaffa and Back* (1936) and children's book *The Budler Family's Resettlement* (1930). Both writers, while continually relying on the kind of ideological commonplaces they had deployed in their respective *Ogonëk* articles, cast doubt on the feasibility of these very commonplaces and on the project of settling Jews in the Far East. They do so by avoiding detailed discussion of either Birobidzhan's transformation into a Jewish territory or of the shtetl Jew's transformation into a new type of muscular Jew.

Instead, Gekht and Fink substitute the main trope of the Birobidzhan discourse—the new Jew coming into his own in the new Soviet "Zion"—with seemingly unrelated details that take up large portions of each of their respective texts. These details highlight inconsistencies between the figure of the Jew in the USSR as a variety of the New Soviet Man and his rather tenuous claims on Birobidzhan, his newly touted domicile. Instead of directly tracing the evolution of Jews in Birobidzhan, one text focuses on the difficulties faced by the region's non-Jewish population in a way that casts doubt on the outlook for local Jews. Another text, instead of describing Birobidzhan, offers an extensive treatment of Zionist settlement in Palestine—the product of the competing contemporary ideology, which envisioned Jews returning to and establishing political autonomy in their storied ancestral homeland. One other book—a children's story—seemingly focuses its narrative on a Jewish family's relocation from their shtetl in the former Pale to the Far East but skillfully exploits the possibilities of its genre and becomes a tale of the family's non-arrival. The works explored here make such surprising substitutions because, in the absence of sufficient observable, reportable detail in Birobidzhan, these rhetorical replacements allow their authors to make claims about the faraway territory through analogies. Such analogies cast doubt on the future of the Jewish homeland in the USSR and, instead, continue to map out the contours of the Soviet Jew whose defining feature in relation to this territory is the act of non-arrival.

* * *

At the time of IKOR's 1929 expedition, the tiny population of Jews in Biro-bidzhan and the accompanying dearth of details about their lives led the authors of the delegation's report to contrast the lachrymose Jewish past in the Russian Empire with the bright future of Jews in the Soviet Union—all at the expense of focusing on the observable present. Viktor Fink followed this blue-print in those parts of his book where he did write about Jews. In failing to offer a coherent and lively portrait of Birobidzhan's Jewish "now," both the IKOR delegation's report and Fink's book resembled other writing about the Jewish settlement in the Soviet Far East, including official pronouncements, journalism, and pamphlets, as well as literary fiction and essays.

The Russian-born, New York-based Yiddish literary critic Shmuel Niger picked up on the propensity of texts about Birobidzhan to focus dispropor-tionately on the future and to elide the narrative present. "The home that they [Jewish settlers] intend to construct for themselves, they are only preparing to build," Niger writes. "Everything either was or relates to the future. But what about the present?" he asks, before promptly answering his own question: "The present is a narrow band, like a board by which one crosses an unexplored stream from one bank to the other."[16] Similar avoidance of the present characterized much contemporary cultural production in the Soviet Union. Socialist Realism, which would be codified by the middle of the 1930s, famously emphasized the depiction of "socialist reality in its revolutionary development"—a kind of imagined present continuously elided by the ever-proximate future that never arrives.

Even though texts about Birobidzhan continued to evoke the Jewish past in the Pale as a negative point of comparison, by the 1930s, as Katerina Clark has observed, the USSR had largely shifted from repudiating Russia's pre-1917 legacy and toward focusing on active nation building as a way of justifying its transformational revolutionary experiment. Socialist Realism played a key role in these efforts in part because "the realization of the new society [it-self] still proved elusive."[17] Depictions of Birobidzhan reflected this broader phenomenon: literary representations of the Soviet society of the near future replaced depictions of tangible achievements in the present. Evgeny Dob-renko has gone as far as arguing that socialism in the USSR did not exist outside the cultural artifacts of Socialist Realism: "If we remove Socialist Realism—novels about enthusiasm in industry, poems about the joy of labor, films about the happy life, songs and pictures about the wealth of the land of the Soviets, and so on—from our mental image of 'socialism,' we would be left with nothing that could properly be called socialism." Instead of focusing on Socialist Realist output in Soviet culture as an idealized representation—but a representation nonetheless—of the country's experience, Dobrenko sug-gests that it is possible to "conclude that Socialist Realism produced social-ism's symbolic values by de-realizing everydayness."[18] Socialist Realism deemphasized reality as such: the everyday and the present existed primarily as ideological constructs.

When it came to Birobidzhan, not only was the "now" absent as a subject of textual representation but also representation itself was not necessarily the goal of the writing about the region. The present ended up suspended some-where between the retrograde Jewish past in the Pale—referenced to empha-size the appearance of a revolutionary narrative—and the promised bright future. Both Semyon Gekht and Viktor Fink take up the literary paradigm of Socialist Realism in their treatment of the meager present reality of Jewish settlement in the Far East, while calling attention to the strategies of occlu-sion they are compelled to use in writing about this difficult subject.

Gekht's novel *A Ship Sails to Jaffa and Back* tells the story of Alexander Gordon's circuitous journey from prerevolutionary Odessa to Birobidzhan. The protagonist's experience includes a twenty-year sojourn as a Zionist in the Yishuv—a network of Jewish agricultural and urban settlements in Pal-estine under the British Mandate. Gordon considers returning to his native country, which by then had become the USSR, after receiving a letter about Birobidzhan from the novel's other major protagonist, James Brown. Gekht's Brown is a lightly fictionalized version of a real-life American—Benjamin Brown, who, in 1929, took part in the same IKOR expedition as Gekht. In Gekht's novel, Brown had met Jewish colonists in Palestine before travelling to Birobidzhan and wrote to them following his Birobidzhan visit. Although the text of Brown's letter is not in the novel, Gekht's narrator relays that Brown wrote "in detail about the findings of the American IKOR's expedition, in which he participated."[19] Like the IKOR report, which concluded that "there is no reason why this region cannot be developed into a rich and populated territory," Brown's letter in Gekht's novel encourages Jewish immigrants in Palestine—Alexander Gordon among them—to consider resettling in Birobidzhan.[20]

Gekht calls attention to the letter's age: Gordon "was shown Brown's yellowed letter. He spent a long time staring intensely at the lines penned by the American, at the envelope and the postage stamp, and his heart beat even faster with dreams and sadness."[21] Elsewhere, the novel references the influx of Jewish refugees fleeing Nazi Germany to Palestine: by the time Gordon would have read Brown's 1929 letter, the narrative present has shifted to 1933–1934 or even later. The novel's "now" is closer to the publication date of Gekht's book (1936) than to the time of Gekht's (and the fictional Brown's) 1929 visit to Birobidzhan with IKOR.[22] In calling attention to the age of the "yellowed" letter, the novel emphasizes the delay between Brown's sending the missive and Gordon's receiving it. Gekht's protagonist gets inspired to move to Birobidzhan by a letter several years out of date that mapped out the region as it was expected to appear in the future.

Like Gekht, Fink also fiddles with the time frame in *Jews in the Taiga*. The book is a collection of literary sketches—a popular genre in the USSR in the 1920s, in which Fink and Gekht published consistently throughout their careers. The sketch (in Russian, *ocherk*) was an intermediate genre between journalism and creative fiction; it was popular both in Yiddish literature and in Soviet literature more generally[23] and, as Maxim Gorky, the doyen of Soviet literature, put it, stood "somewhere between a researched report and a short story."[24] In the introduction to the second edition of *Jews in the Taiga*, Fink recalls bringing the first edition of the book, which was based on the 1929 expedition, with him on his return trip to Birobidzhan a year later, in 1930. Fink writes that though he may have fought "with his pen for a better Birobidzhan" when he criticized the project's lack of planning during his first journey there, by 1930 his sketches had become dated or, as he put it, "had become historical in nature [*moi ocherki poluchili kharakter istoricheskii*]." Fink claims to have revised his earlier writing because the problems he identified in his book's first edition were supposedly fixed.[25] In other words, new developments Fink claims to have observed between 1929 and 1930 appear to have prompted him to issue a new version of the book that more diligently reflected the successes of Birobidzhan's Jewish settlement.

In making changes between the two editions, Fink was responding to criticism of the book's initial iteration. He alleged that the "worldwide bourgeois Jewish press" had seized on his earlier negative statements about Birobidzhan to prove that Jewish settlement in the USSR had failed.[26] Given its stated objective, however, the second edition of *Jews in the Taiga* appears to have been fixed rather sloppily. The revised book still contains criticisms of the lack of planning in Birobidzhan—with the occasional addition of footnotes that indicate how a few select problems had been resolved. Not fully incorporated into the text, these footnotes stand out as a kind of rough stitching. They draw attention to the way Fink's presumably outdated book was marshaled into promoting his supposedly updated positive impression of Birobidzhan.

Fink and Gekht write about Birobidzhan as though the vision for it had already been realized—without getting into the particulars of such an accomplishment. In the process of negotiating between ideology and practice, both writers flesh out a vision of a certain Jewish subject: not the new Jew as a version of the New Soviet Man propagated in official ideology about Birobidzhan but, instead, a Soviet Jew defined by rootlessness, migration, and an unsteady discursive location both inside and beyond Soviet ideology. Socialist Realist depictions of the future, Katerina Clark has written, were part of the state's larger mission of "sacralizing space"—a process by which the distant time that is yet to come becomes "higher-order space" mediated through architecture, in the case of physical spaces like reimagined cityscapes, or through construction metaphors in other artistic genres.[27] The planned construction of buildings such as the Palace of the Soviets in Moscow "sacralized" the city as the seat of Bolshevik power by encoding the vision of the aspirational new society in a physical structure that was imagined on the grandest of scales but wasn't actually built.[28] Such architecture embodied, in Vladimir Paperny's words, "the future [that] was postponed indefinitely."[29]

To be caught between past and future was typical for Soviet authors writing about the state's revolutionary aspirations, which were allegedly being realized all around them. Evgeny Dobrenko has noted that cultural artifacts such as stamps and atlases, nominally tethered to geographic spaces, facilitated the "art of social navigation" around the vast, developing country and helped constitute "the world of utopia." Importantly, this utopia "cannot be presented in any other way than by means of specific 'substitutes'—architectural plans, motion pictures, novels, 'parks of culture and recreation,' postage stamps and postcards—which stand for various kinds of descriptions. [. . .] The mythology of space is good in every way—except that it does not work for life."[30]

Dobrenko's concept of the "mythology of space," produced by substituting idealized and aestheticized depictions of spaces for their less impressive realities, echoes Clark's notion of the role of Socialist Realism in "sacralizing" space. Substitution swaps the imaginative vision of something still unfinished or nonexistent for something that is apparently "real." The very notion of "reality" in Socialist Realism was not "that which is merely present (observable, subject to direct experience)" but rather "that which makes present," that which "calls to life new phenomena, new realities of life."[31] The achievements of socialism and Soviet spaces did not manifest as matters of fact but rather as results of imaginative projection. In relation to Birobidzhan, the objective of literary and cultural production was not to reflect the already completed creation of the new Jewish homeland and of the Jew as a New Soviet Man evolving there but instead to participate in its production. Fink and Gekht participate in this larger project, but because they are attached to the notion of observable facts gleaned from their 1929 expedition to Birobidzhan, they also call attention to the discrepancy between the vision of reality and its absent "realness." This discrepancy, in turn, is the chasm in which the figure of the Soviet Jew comes into focus—identified in Fink's and Gekht's works by non-arrival in the place meant to be his new homeland.

* * *

In their work on Birobidzhan, Viktor Fink and Semyon Gekht substituted something still merely anticipated with something else that could be portrayed as already completed. By doing so they drew attention to the constructed nature of "reality" at the center of their literary enterprise. Specifically, they mined the past for negative examples to which Birobidzhan could be compared and inserted this material in place of detailed discussions about the present. This erasure of the present followed the contours of state doctrine that "sacralized" the newly established Soviet Jewish homeland as an embodiment of a socialist—and Socialist Realist—vision for the New Soviet Man who happened to be Jewish.

Unlike some other authors who could avoid writing about Birobidzhan in detail, Gekht and Fink were not satisfied with the future-oriented project that was to be described in supposedly realist terms. The writer David Bergelson, who visited Birobidzhan while being encouraged by the government to relocate there, once described a character stunned by the sun's glare on the bright whiteness of the snow—a scene of both natural beauty and a blindness-inducing impediment to a vision of Birobidzhan itself.[32] Having participated in a fact-finding expedition, however, Fink and Gekht were tethered, at least to a certain extent, to observable facts. But unlike other participants in the 1929 trip, the two writers had a toolbox of literary tricks at their disposal that offered them workarounds for their inability to represent that which they needed to describe but could not. Chief among these was the strategy of substitution.

Alexander Gordon's journey from Palestine to Birobidzhan in *A Ship Sails to Jaffa and Back* provides a premise befitting the era's ideological priorities. The USSR's political discourses in the 1920s–1930s depicted Palestine, then under British rule, as a bourgeois, nationalist, and imperialist alternative to the nascent socialist Jewish homeland in the Far East.[33] Gekht's novel, however, describes Palestine in far greater detail than Birobidzhan, even though he never visited Palestine either under Ottoman rule or during the British Mandate; instead, he likely drew on existing Russian-language literary works about it to supply details and locutions for his novel.[34] Gordon makes his gradual ideological journey to Birobidzhan while moving extensively—and often on foot—around Palestine. The literary and rhetorical tropes of Zionist settlement in the Middle East provide Gekht with the type of topographic, agricultural, and labor imagery that Birobidzhan still lacked.[35] In arguing for the return of Jews to the Land of Israel, Zionists appropriated traditional Jewish messianic discourses about the centrality of the "promised land." Given this discursive parallel, substituting Palestine for Birobidzhan offers Gekht a pathway to "sacralize" the Jewish territory in the USSR without having to represent it directly.

In Gekht's novel, Jews in the USSR could understand moving to Birobidzhan—a place where they had no ethnocultural roots—the way Jews might have thought about moving to the Land of Israel. The socialist vision, like the Zionist vision, resided in a kind of future that resembled Judaism's messianic time. However, while seemingly showcasing the Soviet state's program of Jewish mobility, Fink and Gekht in fact challenge its top-down vision of where and how Jews were supposed to move. In effect, the two writers substitute idiosyncratic wandering, rooted in their own experiences, for the ideologically touted one-way route of resettlement.

The historians Lewis Siegelbaum and Leslie Page Moch distinguish "repertoires" of mobility—the heterogeneous perspectives, experiences, and itineraries of individual migrants—from prescriptive "regimes" of migration, such as the official map of "national" territories in the USSR that were set aside as places of residence for specific titular ethnic groups.[36] These two modalities enter into a conflictual relationship in writings about Birobidzhan. On the one hand, the Jewish territory was the rhetorical product of migration regimes tethered to the projected future of a settled, prosperous Birobidzhan. On the other hand, the region was constituted in practice through multiple repertoires of mobility based on the subjective experiences of migrants and sojourners who were actually on the move and who could, deliberately or unintentionally, contradict or undermine ideologically weighted regimes of movement. The works by Fink and Gekht were positioned somewhere between Birobidzhan's migration regimes and its repertoires of mobility. Some of the two writers' protagonists and narrators mouth Party rhetoric and affirm the state's prescriptive migration regime for the relocation of Jews to the Far East yet the narratives of wandering at the center of these works highlight their protagonists' and narrators' mobility on the ground. In so doing, they call attention to the inability of Socialist Realism to describe spaces that, though products of an ideological vision, were also actual locations that the writers themselves could visit and explore in situ via their own mobility repertoires.

In noting the physical and rhetorical routes by which each writer navigates the larger place, these texts question the same optimistic conclusions about the Birobidzhan project that they appear, on the surface, to promote. The figure of the Soviet Jew emerges through these repertoires of mobility, as distinct from the figure of the Jew as a New Soviet Man that the state sought to create through its regime of migration.

* * *

In 1858, three-quarters of a century before the USSR designated Birobidzhan as a homeland for Jews, Russia acquired the sparsely populated area in a treaty with China's Qing Dynasty, which ruled Manchuria just across the Amur

River.[37] Soon after, Russia's imperial government forcibly relocated Cossacks who belonged to the Trans-Baikal Cossack Host, headquartered in Chita, to the newly annexed territory, about a thousand miles eastward. Despite this population transfer, the strategic region subsequently fell under Japan's influence when it gained dominance over Manchuria after the 1904–1905 Russo-Japanese War. The border along the Amur remained unstable well into the Soviet years.[38] Meanwhile, the Russian Empire's migration regime led to the destruction of the Trans-Baikal Cossacks' cultural and ancestral habitat: the group was even renamed the Amur Cossacks after their migration. Stories of a torturous journey to the stretch of land, at the confluence of the rivers Bira and Bidzhan and buffeted to the south by the Amur, entered the displaced Cossacks' personal and collective memory narratives.

In the late 1920s the Soviet government presented its plan to move Jews to the same territory in the Far East, albeit in a new political context: the Jews would be settled in their own new Soviet homeland and so would become like members of any other territorially anchored ethnic group in the USSR.[39] As with the Russian Empire's relocation of the Trans-Baikal Cossacks in the 1850s, Soviet-era plans for Birobidzhan were guided, in part, by the USSR's interests in safeguarding the country's borders.[40] In the 1920s, threats emanating from Manchuria's side of the Amur came from, among other sources, counterrevolutionary White detachments that had crossed the new Soviet border to regroup and carry out military attacks on the underpopulated Soviet side of the river.[41]

Thus, the Soviet regime planned to kill two proverbial birds with one stone. First, the territory would be the place where shtetl Jews would become more like other land-settled ethnocultural groups in the USSR. Second, by moving to Birobidzhan, Jews would increase the population in the contested region, further securing the country's borders—not unlike the Amur Cossacks had done decades earlier. But lingering stories of the Cossacks' ill-fated resettlement to the Far East haunted those writers tasked with conveying the Soviet regime's program to relocate Jews. In Viktor Fink's *Jews in the Taiga,* the example of three generations of Amur Cossack experiences in the Far East offered narrative possibilities for writing obliquely and critically about what awaited Jews in the region—without referring directly to Jews all that much or even at all.

Fink's *Jews in the Taiga* is filled with Fink's conversations with local inhabitants, American members of IKOR's expedition, and various Soviet officials. His interest in the region's Cossack population is especially noticeable as he recounts his travel experiences in 1929. He writes at length of the warm relations between Cossack old-timers and the newly arrived Jewish settlers. In one vignette, an old Cossack gets a ride in an automobile brought by one of the Jewish colonists and marvels at the new technology. Now that he's been in a car, the Cossack opines in what Fink renders in a kind of colloquially substandard Russian, he could "die in peace [*Teperia, odnako, ia slobodno i pomeret' mogu*]."[42] Another elderly Cossack comes along for a short ride in an airplane—another technological wonder central to Soviet representations of their mastery of landscapes.[43] Subsequently, he tells a priest that, after he had traveled through the sky, he was able to say conclusively that God didn't exist: "God doesn't exist, there's just science and technology [*netu boga, odna nauka i tekhnika*]."[44] Fink reports that the locals have come to see Jewish colonists as "transmitters of culture [*iavliaiutsia kul'turtregerami*]" because along "with the new colonists, new tractors appeared along with road construction machinery and excavators—some of them are Soviet-made, some had been sent by [the Soviet Jews'] friends from America."[45] Exploring—on the granular level of local reporting—the place where Jews were expected to move, Fink coveys some of the major talking points about Birobidzhan's purported global significance.

At the end of the book, Fink writes about Jews and Cossacks joyously dancing together. The very placement of "Cossacks" and "Jews" in a single sentence was sensational given the frightening image of Cossacks in Jewish culture. That stereotype was a byproduct of the devastating effects of Bohdan Khmelnytsky's uprising on the Jewish communities of Ukraine and Poland in the seventeenth century.[46] At the same time, comparisons rather than contrasts between Cossacks and Jews were also part of the larger collective imagination in the 1920s. Isaac Babel's *Red Cavalry* cycle, published between 1923 and 1926, contains stories not only about Cossack violence toward Jews but also of the empathy the Jewish narrator develops for the Cossacks' way of life and their idiosyncratic sense of justice and morality. Some Zionist settlers in Palestine, meanwhile, had begun to appeal to the image of the Cossack as a model of strength and masculinity to project against Arab natives.[47] Amur (formerly Trans-Baikal) Cossacks, unlike the Cossacks in the Russian

Empire's western borderlands, had a history unmarked by any animosity toward Jews. The scene of Jewish-Cossack dancing that Fink describes would become a kind of commonplace in cultural production about Birobidzhan, propagating the "brotherhood of peoples" narrative that would eventually be enshrined in Soviet culture as "the friendship of peoples [*druzhba narodov*]."[48] When Fink and others wrote about Birobidzhan, one way to demonstrate the friendship of peoples was through narratives about Jews leading members of other ethnic groups into the age of technological and industrial progress.

In addition to noting the Cossacks' positive attitude toward Jews, Fink emphasizes the Cossacks' experience of being forcibly resettled in the Far East three-quarters of a century earlier. Ostensibly, Fink blames the Cossacks' failure to adapt to their new domicile on Imperial Russia's colonialist practices and presents the Soviet-era resettlement of Jews as a kind of corrective, a chance to compensate for one failed migration regime by orchestrating a new, more successful one. Russia's nineteenth-century history, used discursively to create a negative contrast with the USSR's plan, held the potential to showcase the new migration regime in a positive light. At the same time, the captivating personal stories that Cossacks relayed to Fink, combined with the absence of *ocherk*-worthy stories about the resettlement of Jews, produce a counternarrative that becomes a thinly veiled warning about the noticeable similarities between Amur Cossacks in the past and the figure of the Soviet Jew in the present.

The promising government data about Birobidzhan promulgated by Fink in his sketches conflict with the more subversive interpretive strategies suggested by these texts' literary structure. Seemingly undermining the apparent meaning of his own work, Fink manages to capture the evolving figure of the Soviet Jew, which differs from the officially sanctioned blueprints for transforming Jews in Birobidzhan into a new kind of Soviet people. Fink was not the only writer who produced these kinds of conflicted texts about the Soviet Jew at the time: reading Gekht's 1923 sketch about a decaying shtetl, Harriet Murav points out that Gekht "performs a strange double gesture, at once bringing into the Soviet and Russian-language cultural space the figure of the old Jew of the past and at the same time marking him as doomed."[49] These sketches from the early 1920s about the collapse of the Pale of Settlement[50]— which describe Jews who were meant to be transformed by the revolution— produce the shtetl Jew as a "figure of the past [that] haunts the project of the future."[51] In a similar vein, Fink supplants his "researched" portrayal of the Jewish settler, built on the basis of statistics and publicly disseminated lists of accomplishments, with other meanings that haunt the pages of his book. He does this by emphasizing the insufficient presence of Jews and replacing them with descriptions of and narratives about Cossacks.

The title of Fink's book, *Jews in the Taiga*, announces its ideologically relevant topic: the new Jew in the Soviet Far East, who is created by a Soviet migration "regime" aimed at the resettlement of former shtetl dwellers. Throughout much of the book, however, Fink tiptoes around his stated subject as he meanders around the region and describes his wanderings. Fink acknowledges halfway through the book, in a section titled "A Foreword in the Middle of the Text," that he has written very little about Jews.[52] In this part of the book, which appears almost twenty pages after he asks rhetorically why he had written more about Cossacks than about Jews, Fink reproduces boilerplate language about Jewish settlement in Birobidzhan from speeches by various Soviet officials. Returning to his original question at the foreword's end, Fink points out the mistakes that Russia's prerevolutionary government had made in planning the Cossacks' nineteenth-century resettlement in the Far East. His book includes material that is not about Jews, Fink claims, because "the dramatis personae of the initial chapters" could highlight mistakes that Birobidzhan's new Jewish settlers ought not repeat.[53] However, rather than situating Jews as the successful counterexample to their unlucky Cossack predecessors, Fink forebodingly implies an historical analogy between the resettlement of Cossacks and the relocation of Jews. Fink's sketches about Cossack community elders, who still remember the traumatic migration from near the shores of Lake Baikal to the banks of the Amur, make for some of the most compelling prose in Fink's book.

In one sketch titled "Grandpa Onisim" (Ded Onisim), Fink recounts a conversation with an old Cossack who had arrived in the region as a young child. Building on Onisim's narrative and supplementing it with historical details about the Cossacks' relocation in the 1850s, Fink conveys the personal and communal trauma that resulted from this displacement. "All of us Amur Cossacks [. . .]," Onisim says, "were forcibly driven here out of the Trans-Baikal Cossacks [*iz zabaikal'skikh kazakov siuda prignany*] in 1858."[54] One way to interpret Fink's report of his conversation with Onisim is to note that the sentence contains an implied switch between past and present identities: the

Cossacks in Birobidzhan *are* Amur Cossacks but they also know that they *were* Trans-Baikal Cossacks once upon a time. At the same time, given the syntax of the sentence in Russian, Onisim's words suggest a fracturing and a forced separation from ancestral lands: out of one people, another group splits off. Onisim's words imply that although he and his kin and brethren have taken on a moniker assigned to them by the Russian Empire's migration regime, traces of their past identity continue to linger.

To further flesh out the raw coexistence of past and present among a group of people still marked by a decades-old experience, Fink reports on an oral tradition Onisim shared with him: "We even have a song about it," said Onisim of his family's displacement. In 1858, the song begins, "being ordered to the Amur we were [*naznachali na Amur e-nas*]." The song contains riveting details about the long and treacherous journey down the river, an account of boats frequently running aground, and the recollection of the many times the Cossacks had cursed their fate.[55] Triggered by his performance of this song and claiming that he can't remember any other ones, Onisim is forced to confront memories he appears not to have shared with outsiders until the moment Fink showed up and asked him about his life.

Next, Onisim performs a second song about how the migrants left their ancestral homes laden with possessions and arrived in the Far East with their eyes full of tears ("*priplyvali s gor'kimi slezami*").[56] Onisim speaks for his people when he acknowledges that they became Amur Cossacks only because the migration regime had commanded them to undergo this transformation. The lingering oral tradition, haunted by the trauma of the move, calls into question the group's new moniker: Amur Cossacks had never fully ceased to be Trans-Baikal Cossacks.

Fink asks Onisim to clarify who was responsible for forcibly transporting the Trans-Baikal Cossacks to the banks of the Amur; in response, Onisim offers additional traumatic recollections. The responsible figure, he said, was General Nikolai Muravyov, who also expelled ethnic Koreans and Chinese from the territory when it was annexed to Russia. The expulsion of native residents resulted "in the region [becoming] a complete wasteland." The Trans-Baikal Cossacks, in turn, were ordered to relocate to the banks of the Amur and so populate Russia's newly acquired and violently cleared territory. Those who refused these military orders, Onisim tells Fink, were threatened with having their horses expropriated—a harsh punishment for the community because Trans-Baikal Cossacks had had mounted regiments for generations.[57]

Trying to prompt the old man to admit that his fellow Cossacks' lives have improved since their arrival in the Far East, Fink interjects to ask him a leading question about the "bountiful [*blagodatnyi*]" conditions of Birobidzhan. Although Onisim initially confirms that the region is, indeed, quite bountiful, he also protests that "abundance alone is not enough [*Da it' odnoi blagodati malo*]."[58] Noting that Onisim has rejected the opportunity to describe his life in positive terms, Fink proceeds by describing the visible manifestations of trauma on the old man's face: "But here, suddenly, recollections about what he had seen seventy years earlier rushed before him—and a shadow of suffering was upon his face" as he remembered widespread incidents of cannibalism. These, he explained, were induced by famine at the time of the 1858 migration and subsequent resettlement: "We ate the flesh of the dead [*mertvechinu eli*]."[59] Fink expects Onisim to confirm for him that Birobidzhan is a good place to live. His vaguely worded question, however, gives the old Cossack an opening to recount the concrete suffering his community endured when they were forcibly moved from their ancestral lands.

When he encounters Jewish settlers, Fink asks similarly leading questions with the goal of eliciting positive answers. In one instance, he sets out to hunt deer with a local Cossack but gets sidetracked when he meets a Jewish man. Fink promptly aborts the hunt because he "did not want to miss a chance to converse" with a local Jew: a local Jew available for conversation is a sight as rare as—if not rarer than—elusive game.[60] Fink proceeds to ask his subject the same kind of leading question he asked Onisim: "Are the conditions here livable? [*zhit' mozhno?*]" In contrast to Onisim's rejection of the invitation to supply positive clichés about Birobidzhan, the Jewish man's response is strikingly propagandistic. Echoing the language of the IKOR expedition's report and any number of propagandistic pamphlets about the region, the Jewish colonist recounts the moment he got wind of Birobidzhan while still in the Pale and then happily left the miseries of the shtetl behind.[61] Fink seems to wish that Onisim's story could illustrate the failures of Russia's imperial-era colonialism, while the story of the Jewish settler would supply the requisite Soviet-era corrective. However, the Jewish colonist's clichéd answers, in merely regurgitating state language, fail to provide the kind of compelling story that Fink receives from Onisim, who refuses to engage in a scripted conversation.

Onisim, articulating a trauma that is both personal and communal, appears in the pages of Fink's book as a character with depth and complexity; the Jewish colonist, by contrast, is nothing but a kind of two-dimensional figure posited as the ideal representation of the new Jew that the Soviet regime expected to emerge in Birobidzhan.

One commentator at the time criticized the excessively literary quality of Fink's sketches and their lack of sufficient engagement with the political questions at the core of Jewish settlement in Birobidzhan. This, the critic posited, constituted a major ideological shortcoming.[62] Fink's descriptions of his encounters with the Cossacks are, indeed, particularly literary—but contrary to the critic's perception that the writing's literary quality displaces politics, the sketches hint at an unsanctioned politics that implicitly runs counter to the state's vision of Jewish resettlement.

Onisim's heart-wrenching stories of his people's forced migration help sharpen a theme woven through much of the rest of *Jews in the Taiga*: an intergenerational trauma haunts not only those Cossacks who were themselves resettled in the 1850s but also their Soviet-era descendants. Fink identifies Onisim as part of the generation of "grandfathers [*dedy*]," whose inability to adjust to new circumstances in the Far East led the entire community to become lazy and unproductive. Younger Cossacks justify their inability to construct sheds for their farm animals and horses, to build outhouses, or to get rid of mud inside their homes by saying that they avoid all improvements to their lives, including some easy fixes, because they want to live as their elders had after moving to the region. When one younger Cossack dismisses Fink's suggestion that a shed should be built for his cows and horses, he says, "Well, oh well! . . . We're just like our grandfathers [*Da uzh my kak dedy*] . . . Our grandfathers used to do things this way, and so do we."[63] Fink notes that the intergenerational transmission of knowledge was disrupted by the forcible relocation of the Trans-Baikal Cossacks from their ancestral lands. By including Onisim's story about his people's displacement from their traditional environment in his book about Jews in the Far East, Fink implies that a similar displacement—one of Jews from the former Pale—might produce equally traumatic and deleterious consequences.

Another unsigned contemporary review suggested that Fink's book began by describing the backwardness of the Amur Cossacks to draw a sharp contrast between the figure of the backward Cossack, a product of Imperial Russia's colonialism, and the heroic figure of the Jew as a New Soviet Man.[64] Fink does contrast the well-planned Soviet policies with the Russian Empire's flawed policies of yore.[65] However, despite this editorializing, Fink's emphasis lies elsewhere. Because, at the time of Fink's trip, the resettlement's effect on Jews could only be stated in terms of rosy ideological platitudes, the writer substitutes Cossacks for Jews in his narratives of encounters with Birobidzhan's local informants. Despite Fink's outward claims to the contrary, the result of such substitution is an emotionally wrought story of how a community can be substantively diminished—if not spiritually annihilated—as a result of migrating to Birobidzhan. The diminished presence of Jews in a book ostensibly devoted to them is particularly glaring when it becomes clear that Fink has replaced Birobidzhan's Jewish story with the stories of Cossacks, whose decline as a community might serve as a thinly veiled warning to Birobidzhan's Jewish settlers.

* * *

Whereas Fink, after his reporting trip to Birobidzhan, substitutes the figure of the Amur Cossack for that of the Jewish colonist, Semyon Gekht, a participant in the same 1929 expedition, replaces Birobidzhan with Palestine and Zionist settlement there. Both writers deploy similar rhetorical strategies focused on showcasing the failures of regimes elsewhere or at other times in history to boost the claims of the Soviet-era project. Fink's *Jews in the Taiga* emphasizes the tsarist government's failure to effectively accommodate the Trans-Baikal Cossacks. Gekht's novel, *A Ship Sails to Jaffa and Back,* juxtaposes the apparent successes of the Jewish settlement in Birobidzhan with Zionist efforts to establish a Jewish national home in Palestine.

A Ship Sails to Jaffa and Back presents Jews in Palestine during the post—World War I British Mandate-era as agents of European colonialism—a view that aligned with the USSR's assessment of Zionism. In 1929, when anti-British and anti-Zionist Arab riots shook Palestine, the Soviet government saw the uprisings as a sign of a brewing anti-imperialist revolt by the region's indigenous, long-term inhabitants.[66] As in Fink's case, however, Gekht's attempt to juxtapose the Birobidzhan settlement and the Zionist project in Palestine is more complex than the novel's plot allows on the surface. As with the Cossacks in Fink's work, the Zionist settlement in Palestine comes to substitute for—rather than provide the intended negative referent to—descriptions of its contemporary ideological opposite, the Jewish settlement in the USSR's Far East.

A Ship Sails to Jaffa and Back contains two narrative strands: a Palestine plotline and a Birobidzhan plotline. Although they are discrete and traceable to distinct origin points in the author's career, these strands are interwoven such that their separate attributes and constitutive elements can be substituted for one another. The Birobidzhan plot most likely dates to a short article Gekht published in 1929 in a mass-circulation periodical; the Palestine thread developed out of a short story he published four years after that, in 1933, in a different broad-readership magazine.

The Birobidzhan plot in *A Ship Sails to Jaffa and Back* likely emerged from a one-page sketch, "Americans in Birobidzhan," which Gekht published in *Ogonëk* at the conclusion of the 1929 IKOR expedition (figure 3.1). The sketch identifies some of the expedition's participants, including Benjamin Brown ("the soul of the expedition") and Brigham Young University president Franklin S. Harris, an expert in rice cultivation.[67] The participants in the IKOR expedition also turn up in a number of contemporary journalistic accounts other than Gekht's. *Tribuna,* a periodical publication of the OZET (Society for the Settlement of Toiling Jews on the Land), published impressions of some of the members of the expedition, including Harris and Brown, in an article titled "Birobidzhan—Land with a Great Future."[68] These historical figures show up as characters in *A Ship Sails to Jaffa and Back,* published seven years later. This fictionalization turns Gekht's one-page 1929 sketch into a novel that, even though it appears to make a full-fledged effort to go beyond the immediate context of the IKOR expedition and Gekht's *Ogonëk* article, never in fact does so. Although the novel does go forward in time from the 1929 expedition at its core, the later period of the novel's narrative present is noticeably thin on details. Like other works on Birobidzhan, the "now" is barely perceptible beyond some faint contours. However, what distinguishes Gekht's novel is the way it calls attention to the impossibility of representing the Jew as a New Soviet Man. Gekht moves away from efforts to write about Birobidzhan; instead, he substitutes Birobidzhan in the Far East with a plot centered on the Jews settling in the Middle East.

Issued in a print run of ten thousand copies in 1936, two years after Socialist Realism had officially become the doctrine of Soviet literary produc-

tion, Gekht's novel had the formulaic structure characteristic of this genre. The novel's narrative arc recalls several other novels and films from the same decade, which will be discussed in Chapter 4 and in which Jewish protagonists who had immigrated to Palestine or America before the 1917 revolution return to the USSR, compelled by the promise of building a new socialist society.

The novel's protagonist, Alexander Gordon, is, like Gekht, a native of Odessa. A Zionist, he is enthralled by the idea of Jewish national self-determination and by Zionism's insistence on agricultural labor as a path toward the Jews' productive self-reform after generations of oppression in the Pale. In line with the Soviet view, the Zionist settlement in the novel is an outpost of British imperialism: the British announced their support for the creation of a Jewish national home in 1917, just before capturing Palestine from the Ottoman Empire during the First World War. The novel traces how corrupt city values persist in Palestine—values identified with the kinds of "unproductive" professions in trade and commerce that Jews were meant to cast aside when they left the Pale. Young people derisively refer to living in Jerusalem as "living in that kugel fleabag [*zhit' v etom kugel'nom klopovnike*]"; the reference to kugel, a traditional East European dish, associates the disappointing, insect-infested environment with the Jews' shtetl past.[69]

Jerusalem's storied but staid meaning in Jewish culture is an affront to Gordon's youthfulness and romantic entanglements. Eventually, Gordon begins to feel emotionally, socially, and politically moribund: "It seemed to him that nothing more in life could possibly happen any longer and that he needed to somehow last until it [was] time to go to his grave."[70]

At the end of the novel, the ship that first brought Gordon, from Odessa and via the Bosporus, to the Mediterranean port of Jaffa carries him back to Odessa. By then, Gordon's native city is no longer part of the Russian Empire he had left before 1917 but is instead in the USSR. From Odessa, Gordon is said to travel to Birobidzhan: the Soviet "Zion" and the purported true homeland for Jews.[71] The novel's shifting geography—indicated in its title by the ship that sails to and from Jaffa—bookends its protagonist's apparent ideological evolution.

The narrative begins in Birobidzhan in 1929 with a conversation that takes place outdoors on a particularly dark night. An unnamed first-person narrator who, like Gekht, came to the Far East with the IKOR expedition is speaking with James Brown, an Odessa-born Jewish American who is part of the IKOR group. According to the implied timeline of the narrative, Brown had visited Palestine earlier; while there, he met new Jewish arrivals from the Pale. After his subsequent visit to Birobidzhan, Brown—a figure of global mobility linking different political and geographic contexts—began to correspond with his acquaintances among the Zionist colonists. Through this correspondence, Brown's positive impressions of the newly proclaimed Jewish homeland in the USSR reach the Jewish settlers in Mandate Palestine.

Having heard of Brown's travels in Palestine, the novel's narrator inquires about his childhood friend, Alexander Gordon, who had left Odessa before the Bolshevik Revolution as part of a wave of ideological agricultural settlers in Palestine. Brown replies that he hadn't heard of Gordon, so the narrator spends the better part of the book sharing what he had learned about Gordon's travels from Gordon's letters and secondhand from other acquaintances over the years. The novel's main storyline about the Birobidzhan expedition gets effectively edged out by the plot focusing on Gordon's wanderings. Framed by Brown's and the narrator's conversation during this single night in Birobidzhan, Gordon's "repertoire" of displacements from Odessa to Palestine and then to Birobidzhan ultimately calls into question the resettlement "regime" of the Soviet state.

The narrator's conversation with Brown about Gordon—and the story of Gordon's wanderings as such—thus takes the spotlight. Critics, however, have largely overlooked the fact that this conversation occurs in the Far East and have tended to focus instead on the subplot that unfolds in Palestine. Some have evaluated the novel based exclusively on what it does and does not show about Zionism with little reference to Birobidzhan. On the surface, such treatment seems justified: Gekht's novel devotes many more pages to Palestine than to Birobidzhan. A Russian-language edition of Gekht's selected works, edited by Mikhail Vainshtein, was published in 1983 in a series of books aimed at Israel's newly arriving Soviet Jewish immigrants, as well as at Jews in the Soviet Union who wished to emigrate. This edition excerpted only the chapters set in Palestine and omitted the novel's frame narrative entirely. These 1983 excerpts—not the full 1936 text—shaped the subsequent, misleading impression that Gekht's novel was exclusively about Jews in Palestine / the Land of Israel. However, the intersection of two stories, one in Palestine and one in Birobidzhan, produces much of the novel's idiosyncratic approach to its subject. Gekht, who never traveled to the Middle East, developed his Palestine-based narrative as a substitute for the discussion of Birobidzhan— the place that he did visit and that his novel is ostensibly about.

Vainshtein, in his introduction to the 1983 abridged edition of Gekht's work, flatly dismisses the notion that the Birobidzhan sections of *A Ship Sails to Jaffa and Back* might have any literary worth. He suggests that even if he had included the pages that he had omitted from publication, the readers would have been "forced to skip them, hastily moving on to the succulent descriptions of the Jewish Yishuv [settlement] in Palestine, the colorful pictures of Jerusalem."[72] Vainshtein's characterization of the novel's chapters that center on the Land of Israel is misleading, however. Their depictions of Jerusalem are far from "colorful"; instead, these are narratives of decay that resemble the descriptions of shtetls in Gekht's earlier sketches about the Pale.[73] By republishing only the excerpts set in Palestine in the 1983 edition—until 2016 the only republication of the novel since the book's first Soviet printing in the mid-1930s[74]—Vainshtein presents Gekht's text as a kind of covert exercise in Zionism. Vainshtein, it seems, was marshaling the novel on behalf of his own 1980s literary project of national recovery.

Literary scholar Zsuzsa Hetényi bases her analysis of Gekht's novel on Vainshtein's abridged 1983 edition; she also sees *A Ship Sails to Jaffa and Back* as Gekht's covert attempt to discuss Zionism within the constraints of the Soviet 1930s. At the same time, Hetényi chastises Gekht for having his novel's first-person narrator make statements that, "in line with the ideological requirement of the thirties, are meant to neutralize this Zionist tendency."[75] For Hetényi the novel would qualify as a kind of nationalist and Zionist narrative were it not for the fact that Gekht supplemented his discussions of Zionism with what she took to be Soviet boilerplate about Zionism's shortcomings and wrongdoings.

Alyona Yavorskaya, a scholar of Gekht's life and oeuvre, devotes a solitary sentence to *A Ship Sails to Jaffa and Back* in an otherwise comprehensive biographical note in her edited collection of the writer's work. She notes the novel's "exotic title" and, like Vainshtein and Hetényi, characterizes it as a text that deals with "the description of the colonists in Palestine—a rare occurrence for Soviet literature of that period."[76] However, the subject suggested by Gekht's title was far from exotic given the discursive prominence of Zionism in Soviet anti-imperialist discourse beginning in the late 1920s. Gekht would have likely picked up some of the historical and geographic detail for his novel from texts about Zionism and Palestine that were widely available in the 1930s. In 1935, a year before Gekht's novel was published, the Moscow State Yiddish Theater (GOSET) put on *The Wailing Wall* (*Stena placha*), an anti-Zionist play set in Palestine.[77] In addition, a number of books and pamphlets invoked Zionists in Palestine as part of Birobidzhan-related polemics. In these texts, the Jewish return to the Land of Israel is presented as a negative ideological counterweight to the resettlement of Jews in the Far East.[78] In fact, Iavorskaia's claim of "exoticism" in the depiction of Zionism in 1930s Soviet literature, deemphasizes Birobidzhan as the novel's subject. Even though Iavorskaia read the novel in its unabridged form, she echoes the claims of scholars who were familiar only with its excerpted version. All these critics have consistently overlooked the narrative pull made clear in the novel's framing: although it spends many of its pages on descriptions of the Jewish community in Palestine, Gekht's novel centers on the migration of its main protagonist to Soviet Birobidzhan.

Maxim D. Shrayer, despite his editorial decision to exclude Gekht's works from his two-volume *Anthology of Jewish-Russian Literature,* devotes two sentences to *A Ship Sails to Jaffa and Back* in his introduction to a different text, an excerpt from Mark Egart's 1930s novel about Zionist colonies in Palestine,

Scorched Earth (*Opalënnaia zemlia*). To praise Egart, Shrayer treats Gekht as the negative counterexample: Gekht's novel is a "schematic, simplistic treatment of the subject" of Zionism where "the protagonist reache[s] Palestine *only* to return to the Soviet Union."[79] The relationship between Egart's and Gekht's novels is not adequately addressed in this assessment that one novel is "more Zionist" than the other. *Scorched Earth,* based on Egart's experience of living in Palestine and subsequently returning to the USSR, was published before Gekht's novel. It is more than likely that Gekht drew on Egart's lengthy two-part opus—as well as on an established Russian literary tradition of writing about the Holy Land—to learn about a place he had not visited.[80] It is also plausible that Gekht may have even "cannibalized" a fair amount of what he had learned from Egart's work. This would, indeed, explain Shrayer's perception that, if viewed as a novel about Zionism, Gekht's was a derivative work. But Gekht would have had other reasons to write *A Ship Sails to Jaffa and Back:* he was writing about Palestine, in however derivative a fashion, to emphasize the dearth of details about Birobidzhan—the primary setting of his novel's narrative present.

Curiously, Vainshtein, Hetényi, Iavorskaia, and Shrayer reproduce some of the criticism of *A Ship Sails to Jaffa and Back* that appeared in the Soviet press in the 1930s. One long review in 1936 lambasts Gekht for the novel's alleged Zionist ethos, pointing to places in the text where Gekht did not sufficiently show, as the Party line demanded, that Zionism was an offshoot of British colonialism.[81] By attacking Gekht for expressing supposedly pro-Zionist views (and by attacking a different review article[82] for failing to highlight such views in Gekht's novel[83]), the reviewer places Zionism at the book's center. Gekht's subsequent interpreters, in effect, concur with the doctrinaire Soviet-era critic that the novel is a Zionist text smuggled into Soviet literature despite the regime's opposition to Zionism. Operating on one side or the other of a perceived ideological binary, none of these critics entertain the possibility that Gekht's novel could have been sympathetic to aspects of both Zionism and Soviet ideology, that it could have been ambivalent toward or critical of both, or that both ideologies offered similar and interchangeable aesthetic tools for depicting places and ideological positions. Working within the interstices of a perceived ideological binary, rather than squarely on either of its two sides, Gekht plays seemingly dueling ideologies and narratives off each other. *A Ship Sails to Jaffa and Back,* relying on the Zionist

intertext as a replacement for the expected description of the Jewish settlement in the USSR's Far East, is a text both about Birobidzhan and about the
limits of using Socialist Realist strategies to describe it. In the gaps between
seemingly opposite interpretations of Gekht's novel, the contours of the ambivalent figure of the Soviet Jew begin to come into sharper focus.

At the beginning of the novel, the two interlocutors ascend a small hill
near the Tikhon'kaya settlement, which up until then existed merely as a
small train station on the Trans-Siberian railroad. Tikhon'kaya—which
can be translated as "Little, Quiet One," or, as Masha Gessen has quipped,
"someone's polite way of saying 'godforsaken'"—was the site of what would,
in 1931, become the town of Birobidzhan.[84] At the top of the hill, James Brown
turns to the novel's first-person narrator and says:

> "Let's look down [. . .] Let's, in one take, comprehend our new
> homeland."
>
> "But there is nothing to be seen. It's pitch black," I objected.
>
> "What do you mean!" exclaimed Brown. "Why should it be that I, an
> average American, must teach a Soviet revolutionary? Here we have,"
> he pointed into the darkness [on tknul v temnotu], "the Tikhon'kaya
> settlement. It's illuminated by floodlights, the hearts of the wood-
> processing factories are beating, paved highways stretch out towards the
> taiga. There I see wheat fields, gardens, apiaries, windmills, schools,
> rice-growing collective farms . . ."
>
> I laughed.
>
> "You speak," I said, "as if you weren't a traveling American but rather
> a Soviet."[85]

Gekht sets this conversation between Gordon and Brown in 1929, during
the IKOR expedition. Their exchange continues in narrative flashbacks
through much of the rest of the novel. Its schematic outline—a list of Five-
Year Plan commonplaces applied to Birobidzhan—could easily pass for a
future-oriented description of the region in 1929 when it was only in the beginning stages of Jewish settlement. Gekht presents Brown's vision of what
Birobidzhan would look like in the future. However, when Gekht published
the novel in the mid-1930s, there was already supposedly something to describe. The German-Jewish writer Leon Feuchtwanger wrote in 1937 that "in

Birobidzhan there is now a real city—full of schools, hospitals, government buildings, theater; a direct express train brings you there straight from Moscow."[86] What Brown imagines in 1929 in the novel is the same as what Feuchtwanger claims to have witnessed in 1937; both texts are marked by the absence of substantially descriptive detail. Harriet Murav has made a similar observation in her analysis of David Bergelson's story "Uphill" (Bargaruf) that was published at the same time as Gekht's novel. Even though this 1936 story seems like a straightforward Socialist Realist narrative about the Jewish Autonomous Region, she concludes that "the all-important material inscription of the Jews on the land is illegible, and the meaning of Birobidzhan as a solution to the Jewish problem remains completely opaque."[87] Brown's description of Birobidzhan in words cast blindly into the darkness of the night similarly repeats clichés instead of committing to actual descriptions of the place in question.

As mentioned, Gekht's 1929 sketch published in *Ogonëk* is the origin point of the novel's Birobidzhan narrative, but the Land of Israel plot has a different source. In 1933, in *30 Days* (*30 dnei*), Gekht published "Life after Death," a short story about Akiva, an elderly man sensing his impending death. Akiva moves from Odessa to the Land of Israel, as many Jews from the Diaspora had done in their old age. Once in Jerusalem, however, Akiva manages to start a new life and marries a fifteen-year-old. The girl, in turn, happens to be the love interest of Alexander Gordon, formerly Akiva's student in Odessa. Like Akiva, Gordon had moved to Palestine, but unlike his teacher, he did so for Zionist rather than religious reasons. Gordon the protagonist of the 1933 short story is the same Gordon who reappears in Gekht's 1936 novel. In fact, Gekht recycles the short story from *30 Days* verbatim in its entirety as part of *A Ship Sails to Jaffa and Back*.[88] In other words, Gekht uses a short story written in 1933 and set in Palestine to fill out the frame narrative based on his 1929 *Ogonëk* report about the IKOR expedition to Birobidzhan.

Gekht was able to credibly substitute Birobidzhan with Palestine because of a structural similarity between the two places and their attendant ideological underpinnings. Some newer immigrants to Palestine, like Gordon, were ideologically committed to becoming muscular Jews who would live off the land and shed their stereotypical urbanity and diasporic physical weakness.[89] Such idealistic Zionists saw the pre-Zionist urban community of Palestine, made up of Jews like Akiva living in Judaism's holy cities, as a reflection of the shtetl, which had been, since the nineteenth century, the subject of opprobrium by proponents of the Jewish Enlightenment. Starting in the 1890s, they began to use the terms "Old Yishuv" and "New Yishuv" to signal the difference between non-Zionist and Zionist communities of Jews in Palestine. The inhabitants of the Old Yishuv were referred to as "children of the *halukah*," charity from diasporic Jewish communities that helped sustain a population wishing to devote their time to Torah study. The Old Yishuv, in Zionist discourse, was deemed to be a continuation of the Jewish exile (in Hebrew, *galut*), a ghetto, and a community incapable of independent action. Parts of the Old Yishuv maintained the structures that largely resembled the autonomous communal institutions typical of the East European shtetl: ritual bathhouses, kosher butchers, and housing for the elderly and the indigent, among others.[90] In contrast, members of the New Yishuv, exemplified by (if not exclusively constituted of) farmers, seemed to be living a life of vitality and creativity. The Old Yishuv and the shtetl were not one and the same, but to observers inclined to criticize both, they resembled each other in important ways: Jerusalem seemed to be a close relation of the shtetl they despised.

Gekht was working on his novel in the 1930s as these discourses unfolded in Palestine. In the novel's Jerusalem chapters, Akiva appears as an unreformed shtetl Jew. In both Zionist discourse about the New Yishuv and Soviet discourse about Birobidzhan, the shtetl Jew as a type could only become a productive citizen by engaging in and being reformed by manual labor and farm work. Zionist derision of the shtetl-like Old Yishuv resembled derision of the shtetl by Soviet proponents of Jewish resettlement to the Far East. Birobidzhan and the Zionist Yishuv could thus be discursively swapped as destinations: whether relocating to one or the other, a literary protagonist could find himself moving through ideological terrains that looked so alike as to be interchangeable.

But Palestine was different from Birobidzhan in one important way that made it ripe for appropriation and inversion by Soviet discourse: traditional Jews actually considered it their ancestral homeland. Birobidzhan, which had no such usable past, could be made to appear as the logical location for another "promised land" with the help of tropes borrowed from descriptions of Palestine, which Jews had historically come to think of as their only homeland.

While discrediting and rejecting Zionist claims about the promise of Jewish self-determination in Palestine, the Soviet regime simultaneously coopted the Zionist movement's numerous Holy Land tropes, which, in turn, had been borrowed from centuries-old Jewish discourse about the Land of Israel.[91] Tropes with positive associations in traditional Jewish communities thus got reassigned to the otherwise rhetorically barren landscape of the Soviet Far East. Although he attacked Zionist evocations of the biblical land of "milk and honey," the author of one anti-Zionist pamphlet drew attention to honey production in Birobidzhan, praising the region's meadows as conducive to beekeeping.[92] Images of Birobidzhan's apiaries and Jewish beekeepers stood out in the photographic record that circulated in the 1930s.[93] The imagery surrounding honey—and, with it, the metaphoric promise of abundance and fecundity—was symbolically reassigned from the Land of Israel to Birobidzhan, the purported new Jewish homeland.

These similarities emerged not only through borrowing but also as a consequence of the common origins of both groups of Jewish settlers. The negative Soviet rhetoric associated with Zionism obscured the fact that Zionism's dominant ideological current in the 1930s, Labor Zionism, was led by Jews who had originally come from Russia, supported socialism, and employed many of socialism's iconic cultural and ideological formulations. The iconography of Labor Zionism in the 1930s was virtually indistinguishable from that of the USSR's Socialist Realism. Making the soil ready for farming and "taming" parts of the natural terrain that had been resistant to expanded habitation were parts of all settler projects, including those in the USSR and Palestine. Just as Zionist settlers in Palestine emphasized draining swamps to make the soil suitable for agriculture and the air free of mosquitoes, literature about Birobidzhan emphasized the work of draining swamps and combating the disruptive Far Eastern mosquito (in Russian, *gnus*).

It is also not surprising that the Socialist Realist discourse associated with Birobidzhan resembled the socialist-inspired Hebrew literature that was then developing in Palestine. Texts in both literatures tended to elide the present and focus on an imagined future.[94] Hebrew fiction and poetry after the Second World War were even more directly influenced by the Soviets' doctrinaire approaches to literature.[95] Writing about the Zionist project, Jean-Christophe Attias and Esther Benbassa note that "literature, cinema, songs, posters, history, geography, archeology, and textbooks—everything conspired in this ideational reconquest of the land," arguing that "born of the Book [the Bible], Zionist patriotism in turn fabricated other books, produced other readings in order to both support the primal myth of the land and to signpost the territory when it was still only at the planning stage."[96] Like Socialist Realist literature about Birobidzhan, which used ideologically driven prose to conjure up a land that wasn't really there, a good deal of Zionist art and literature at the time relied on similar representational strategies. These strategies blurred the boundary between observable reality and an as-yet unrealized vision of the future.

Photos of Birobidzhan from the 1930s drew on attributes of Zionist iconography, including the biblical tropes therein, when they portrayed Jews reforming themselves through labor after generations of "unproductive" life in the Pale.[97] These types of images pervaded Soviet rhetoric more generally, but their particularly Jewish forms gave them a kind of inverted Zionist inflection. The aesthetic similarity between otherwise different places allowed Gekht to swap descriptions of Palestine—idealistic but rooted in a more tangible reality—for details of Birobidzhan that Gekht found hard to come by during his only trip there in 1929. Gekht's work, in effect, undermines official claims about Birobidzhan. At the same time, it questions the claims of uniqueness central to both Soviet socialism and Zionism: both ideological regimes map out idealized realities that do not correspond to the individual repertoires of the settlers themselves.

Commenting on Semyon Fridlyand's 1936 aerial photograph of a collective farm in Birobidzhan, David Shneer cites a 1930s critic who had praised aerial shots in Soviet photography more generally because they "demonstrated how the photographers have captured the work it takes to build the five-year plan."[98] To portray the purported achievements of the USSR's centrally planned economy, it was advantageous to align the observer's perspective with an all-encompassing view from above: the privileged, all-seeing perspective linked with the power of the state. The film *Seekers of Happiness*—released in 1936, the same year as Gekht's novel—contains several sequences of Birobidzhan shot from above. These bird's-eye shots play no role in the film's narrative; instead, they look like shots from propagandistic newsreels—expansive tableaus that pick out few details. The aerial photograph and all other views from above obscure the uneven and not fully assimilable facts on the ground and advance the totalizing goals envisioned at the top.[99]

Gekht, too, follows the convention of associating the bird's-eye view with the position of power. At the same time, his novel ends up undermining this elevated perspective. He sets the hilltop conversation between his novel's narrator and James Brown in the dead of night. A vantage point that should have offered the interlocutors a commanding view of the would-be city instead provides them no view at all. Throughout the novel, as the narrative keeps circling back to this conversation, the narrator comments on the length and the darkness of that night. Once the night has ended, Birobidzhan is shrouded in dense fog that further obstructs the narrator's and Brown's vision.[100] At precisely the moment when the fog lifts and the sun rises—when Birobidzhan could have finally been observed from the hilltop—Brown asks the narrator to stop speaking so he can "greet the sun in complete silence."[101] Gekht repeatedly calls attention to the fact that Birobidzhan cannot be observed directly and that ideological commonplaces further obstruct—rather than sharpen—the gaze. Because his vision, too, is impeded, Gekht navigates the region through descriptions of the Zionist Yishuv in Palestine. His commentary about his inability to describe Birobidzhan highlights the inability of any top-down ideological regime to fully steer the reader away from noticing that the unrealized aspirations of the present showcase a future vision as current reality.

The short last chapter of *A Ship Sails to Jaffa and Back* reads like a rushed apology for the narrator's failure to describe Birobidzhan. Written in the second person, it points to the supposed evidence by which the reader could verify the chapter's claims. "Every one of you who visits Birobidzhan can stop by the collective farm 'Our Truth,'" the chapter opens. There, the visitor would be informed, in the stock phrases characteristic of the time, that "the affairs of the collective farm are in good shape." The following sentence, however, briefly slips from the assertive to the speculative in its description of Gordon, who is said to have finally made his way to Birobidzhan: "they say [*govoriat*]" that he married a local Cossack woman; "they say" that the wedding was a merry occasion and that even the old folks in attendance danced both gentile and Jewish dances interchangeably ("*dazhe stariki otpliasyvali to komarinskuiu, to freylekhs*"). The narrator continues, "The collective farm's chairman has some photographs [of the event]. You can take a look at them."[102] These photographs were, presumably, taken on the ground rather than from the air. These details are rhetorical commonplaces: there is no reason to trust a narrator who has so extensively drawn attention to his inability to describe the places he had visited. As mentioned, Fink's *Jews in the Taiga* also ends with a scene in which representatives of the two peoples—Jews and Cossacks—dance together.[103] Reading such endings in light of Fink's substitution of Amur Cossacks for the Jews, however, suggests an uncomfortable similarity between the migration regimes that moved both to the Far East.

The final paragraph of *A Ship Sails to Jaffa and Back* is the only passage in the novel that offers a glimpse of Birobidzhan after Gordon's return in the mid-1930s, the novel's narrative present:

> And Birobidzhan has gone a long way from what it was when I saw it in 1929. In this taiga settlement the lights are shining, factories are productive, highways have been built through the taiga. . . . Finally, there is Jewish Theater in Birobidzhan. If you like its wonderful stage sets, don't be surprised and fooled: Alexander Gordon works there as a set designer. But of Alexander Gordon's second life I will tell in my next book.[104]

The narrator acknowledges in this passage that, although Birobidzhan has changed since 1929, he has not returned to witness the changes firsthand. The summary of advancements in electrification, production output, and transportation improvements replicates official statements on Birobidzhan and closely follows James Brown's much earlier vision of what Birobidzhan would become. The only sentence in the novel that claims to describe Birobidzhan in the present ends with an ellipsis before moving on to summarizing the fate of the novel's main protagonist.

Gordon himself, the narrator heard, had become a set designer for Birobidzhan's Yiddish theater. An unsuccessful artist in Palestine, he now becomes a purveyor of Socialist Realist art for the Soviet state. In this role, Gordon could conceivably create stage sets that depicted a Birobidzhan that existed nowhere in reality. These stage sets—painted schools, factories, apiaries, and rice fields—could all be seen as evidence of, to borrow the famous dictum about Socialist Realism attributed to Maxim Gorky, "reality in its revolutionary development," as manifestations of an aesthetic product that was meant not to represent any kind of reality but rather to create it. As a creative artist, Gordon, too, might have made use of substitution in the way Gekht did: before coming to Birobidzhan, Gordon wandered around the hills and valleys of Palestine with his easel and paints. In promising the reader a sequel, Gekht appears to suggest that the protagonist of his novel might have continued to replace the details of the new Soviet Jewish homeland with ones drawn from the scenery associated with the Middle East, just as the author had.

Both Viktor Fink and Semyon Gekht traced their narrative routes through the ideologically constructed regimes of state-imposed resettlement, and both relied on idiosyncratic repertoires of mobility. They also substituted other people and places for the people and places they ostensibly described. The two writers' game of substitution was, on the surface, a way to cast the project of the Jewish homeland in the USSR in a positive light. When read closely, however, their texts reveal that the Soviet Jew—the ostensibly chief protagonist of the Birobidzhan narrative—was a figure that never tangibly arrived there.

* * *

In 1930, a year after he visited Birobidzhan and six years before he released his novel about Alexander Gordon's wanderings, Semyon Gekht wrote *The Budler Family's Resettlement* (*Pereselenie semeistva Budlerov*), a children's book. Children comprised an important audience for literature about the government's migration regime associated with the Far Eastern region; Gekht's was just one of several children's books about Birobidzhan. The Society for the Settlement of Toiling Jews on the Land (OZET), among its many activities, approached Soviet children as both targets and disseminators of propaganda. All Soviet children, Jewish and not—and especially young members of the Pioneer organization—were invited to read OZET's promotional materials, discuss the question of Jewish agricultural settlement with their parents, and convince their parents to subscribe to OZET's periodical, *Tribuna*. These activities were aimed at drawing wider public support for Jewish resettlement in Birobidzhan.

The dust jacket of *Misha from a Jewish Settlement* (*Misha iz evreiskogo posëlka*)—another children's book about Jewish agricultural activity—indicated that OZET had established a special children's division, Friends of OZET. This network of clubs, one of many networks at the time that deployed this kind of organizational infrastructure and agitational work, was tasked with "explaining to children the issue of Jewish agricultural settlement."[105] The writer Alexander Solzhenitsyn recalled soliciting financial contributions for Birobidzhan after OZET representatives touted it in his school in 1927–1928.[106]

Gekht's *The Budler Family's Resettlement* was published at a transitional moment in the evolution of Soviet children's literature, between the campaign against the fairy tale within the educational establishment in the 1920s and the fairy tale's return as a permitted and encouraged genre in the early 1930s. At first glance, the book echoes OZET's didactic and doctrinaire child-centered activities and educational curriculum. But it also contains a twist. Though ostensibly about the Jewish migration to Birobidzhan, the story dwells on the traumatic expulsion of Jews from their customary places of residence in the former Pale of Settlement, the uncertainty of their destination, and the indeterminate nature of their uprootedness. It marks Birobidzhan not as the permanent home for Jews in the USSR but as a place where the Soviet Jew failed to arrive.

A 1930 pamphlet, *OZET's Work among Children,* outlined a set of approaches for integrating children into its project of "organizing and sending migrants and arousing interest [. . .] among workers of all nationalities."[107] Citing OZET's work among Jewish and non-Jewish audiences alike, its authors emphasized that Jewish agricultural resettlement was a "powerful weapon" against antisemitism in Soviet society.[108] Children's literature had a role to play in this fight.

Indeed, children's literature has customarily been seen as a conduit for the transmission of societal norms and values to the younger generation. "Proletarian tales," which were created by socialist writers in Weimar Germany, provide a useful comparison with the Birobidzhan stories created in the USSR at the same time. Socialist children's literature in Germany after the First World War aimed "to instill a sense of hope that a new egalitarian society could be realized if people correctly identified the supposed true enemy— namely, capitalism in various disguised forms—and learned together to defeat that enemy."[109] In the Soviet Union, the transformation of Jews was seen as one of several tasks in the battle against capitalism after the Bolshevik Revolution: as economic middlemen in the Pale of Settlement, Jews had been iconic figures of imperial-era capitalism. Children were an important target audience for stories about Birobidzhan—a place where Jews in the USSR could move so as to be transformed.

Evolving views about the place of family in society and the meaning of childhood more generally shaped the role assigned to children's literature in the USSR. The orphan or the child who ran away from home was, in many ways, an ideal candidate for being reforged as a Soviet citizen; such children became key protagonists in children's and young adult literature and cinema—most famously in the 1931 film *A Ticket to Life* (*Putëvka v zhizn'*).[110] Hostility to the family as a bourgeois institution, dominant in the years immediately after the revolution, began to wane in the 1930s when the Bolsheviks realized that they needed to rely on families for raising children. But if the family were to be relied on in caring for the young, it had to be remade: children needed to be reached through reeducation efforts so that entire families could follow suit.[111]

Throughout the 1920s, the USSR's education professionals, aided by other high-ranking officials, fought a number of battles against the traditional folk tale, because folktales and fairy tales, in their opinion, did not possess sufficiently "class-oriented content."[112] This view of fairy tales dovetailed with the general perception that folklore reflected the bourgeois ideology that had only recently been displaced. One of the institutions dedicated to shaping new children's literature "sought to eradicate folktales on the basis that they glorified tsars and tsareviches [princes], corrupted children and instigated sickly fantasies in them, developed the kulak attitude, and strengthened bourgeois ideals."[113] Lenin's widow Nadezhda Krupskaia, who was instrumental in shaping the USSR's education policies, stated that children's literature was "one of the mightiest weapons in the socialist education of the new generation."[114] After its initial rejection, however, the fairy tale was "rehabilitated" at the First All-Union Congress of Soviet Writers in 1934, where Maxim Gorky praised "both folklore and the folktale for their lack of pessimism and their participation in the struggle for 'the renovation of life.'"[115] The literary establishment understood that realist stories for children may have failed to transmit the ideological message of the state; by contrast, the fairy tale could deliver.

Gekht's children's story about the relocation of a Jewish family to Birobidzhan was published in 1930, when the "realist" approach to children's stories was still dominant. Nonetheless, when compared with S. Epshtein's *Misha from a Jewish Settlement,* which was written in the realist genre, Gekht's strategic use of folktale and magic becomes clear. But Gekht doesn't use these genres in the way that Gorky intended; instead, he deploys them to sketch out the contours of the Soviet Jew marked by this figure's non-arrival in Birobidzhan.

In *Morphology of the Folktale,* published in the USSR two years before Gekht's story about the Budlers, Vladimir Propp famously identified thirty-one functions of the folktale. The beginning of *The Budler Family's Resettlement* fulfills three of these functions. The first function is absentation (*otluchka*), the disappearance or death of a family member, usually an adult; the second is interdiction (*zapret*), in which the hero is warned against taking a particular step or action; and the third is the violation (*narushenie*) of the interdiction, which sets the story's chain of events in motion.[116] When mapped over Propp's functions, the folkloric subtext of Gekht's story challenges the regime of Jewish migration to Birobidzhan. It implies that the family's travel to Birobidzhan is not a willful, ideologically motivated act but rather one prompted by a random and tragic confluence of events.

The story opens as the ten-year-old Munya Budler says, "I would really like to run into a White Army soldier out in the street."[117] Munia's father reacts with fear: "father Budler looked at [Munya's] mother with fright and got up."[118] At this point, the family appears to include father, mother, and son; the Proppian function of the absentation of a family member seems not to apply. Toward the end of this short chapter, however, the mother mentioned in the story's opening is no longer there. The chapter concludes with the premonition: "Neither the tanner Budler from [the shtetl] Logoisk, nor his ten-year old son knew that three months hence they would encounter the Whites closer than they had ever encountered them in their lives."[119] Only the elder Budler and his son are mentioned; throughout the rest of the story, only the two of them remain (figure 3.2).

What happened to Munya's mother? Gekht's narrative situates Munia's birth in the year 1919, the worst period of anti-Jewish violence during the Russian civil war. Raised with the memory of that era's pogroms still raw, Munya would have internalized the danger of genocidal violence that prevailed around the time of his birth. Cathy Caruth has written that a traumatic event can remain outside the boundaries of narration, that it can be inaccessible to narrative because of its unspeakable nature.[120] The mention of the boy's mother, the hint at the year 1919, and its associations in Jewish cultural memory with the worst wave of pogroms suggest that the unsayable event in Gekht's story is the mother's death in a pogrom, likely just a short while after she gave birth to Munya. Earlier, when Munya's father is said to

Figure 3.2. Cover of Semyon Gekht's *The Budler Family's Resettlement* (Moscow, 1930); illustration by P. Staronosov. Courtesy of the National Library of Russia.

have looked at both his son and his wife in fright upon Munya's mentioning of a White Army soldier, it is likely just the memory of the by-then deceased mother—or, perhaps, her photographic portrait hung within the father's view—that the narrator evokes. The mother's disappearance from the text and the implication that she may have died in a pogrom establish a frightening subtext that gives the story—which is ostensibly a realistic text about one family's resettlement—a narrative structure that resembles a fairy tale.

Munya's mother is mentioned at the beginning of the story just before the introduction of the second Proppian function: the interdiction. In response to Munya's stated wish to meet a White soldier, the boy's father admonishes him for even expressing such a thought. He does so by first asking his son how old he is (Munya replies that he is ten); second, he asks him to name the current year (the son answers that the year is 1929). Finally, the father asks Munya what a White soldier would want to do to him were he to run into one. Munya answers, "He would want . . . to make a corpse out of me."[121] We don't know why Munya desires to run into such a villainous figure, but he appears to be fully aware of the threat.

Any representative of the Whites, which were among the forces that opposed the Bolsheviks during the Russian civil war, would have appeared as a folkloric villain in the consciousness of children at the time. Grotesque and monstrous White protagonists had, by then, shown up in some of the most famous texts for children. In one iconic children's story—Arkady Gaidar's 1933 "A Tale about a Military Secret" (Skazka o voennoi taine)—a young boy is pitted against a band of evil Whites and their bourgeois accomplices. In Gekht's story, the father's warning to his son against conjuring up any encounter with the Whites is effectively Propp's second folkloric function, the interdiction. The exchange between Munya and his father places the danger posed by the Whites at the center of the story: the ending of the first chapter, instead of hinting at the father's and son's happy relocation to Birobidzhan, suggests that a subsequent encounter with the Whites would define the narrative and that the family's resettlement to the Far East wouldn't go smoothly.

Following established ideological tropes about the relocation of Jews from the former Pale of Settlement to the Far East, Gekht's story sets up Birobidzhan as the antithesis of the shtetl in decline. The shtetl briefly turns up in a background scene early on in the book: referring to Munya Gekht writes, "He ran out to the wet streets of Logoisk and headed down, past the black and collapsing houses where, having sorrowfully folded their arms, the unemployed residents of Logoisk were sitting on their porches with nothing to occupy them."[122] Epshtein's *Misha From a Jewish Settlement* paints a similar shtetl backdrop as the origin point of the Birobidzhan-bound migrants. Misha visits a group of young Pioneers elsewhere in the Soviet Union to tell them about Birobidzhan, where he now lives. When asked about his family's background, he answers, "'Those of us who live there [in Birobidzhan] are all Jews. Before that, we lived in the Podolia region [of Ukraine], in the shtetl Lipki. Our parents used to be different kinds of artisans and merchants there. Our life was bad. Oh, how bad!' And the boy took a deep sigh, as if sensing the whole burden of the life of Jews in the shtetls before their resettlement."[123] Misha's answer to the other schoolchildren has a much weaker narrative justification than the background shtetl scene in Gekht's book. The inclusion of shtetl scenes in both books reveals the rough stitching that links Birobidzhan to the shtetl in the ideological discourse of leaving the former to resettle in the latter. However, Gekht's Munya is not as happy in his new home as is Epshtein's Misha.

The second chapter of Gekht's story finds the Budlers—father and son—aboard a train. The story surveys the geography of the USSR as the train speeds toward Birobidzhan. A flashback offers the backstory of how the Budlers ended up on that train. Back in their native shtetl, the father—a tanner by profession—had sent his son to inquire about the price of animal hides. Encountering two queues of people in the town square, Munya joins the longer one—a classic folkloric motif of the split in the road that forces the hero to choose one of two or more available paths. Munya has joined the wrong queue, which turns out to be a group of people waiting to meet an OZET representative. Instead of finding out the price of hides as his father had asked, Munya signs the family up for relocation to Birobidzhan. Munya's unwitting choice has the effect of enacting the state's ideology: the main economic argument for the resettlement of Jews had to do with changing their occupations from middlemen, independent artisans, and tradesmen to tillers of the soil and factory workers.

Once the Budlers arrive in Birobidzhan, another Proppian folktale element determines the development of the plot: the acquisition of a magical agent that is meant to help the tale's hero overcome the difficulties he faces. The excavator serves as such a magical agent. It is described in a way that calls attention to the fairy-tale motifs implicit in Gekht's narrative: "Then an excavator appeared in the taiga. It left such a wide and deep mark in the ground that even those boys who did not believe in fairytales [*dazhe ne veriashchie skazkam mal'chiki*] thought that a heretofore unheard of giant was walking through here in iron-clad boots."[124] On the one hand, the comparison of the excavator with a giant seems perfectly fitting for a story written during the First Five-Year Plan.[125] On the other hand, the mentioning of fairy tales brings into focus the apparent absence of the fairy-tale genre from Soviet children's literature of the time. Gekht focuses not only on the excavator that comes to the help of Birobidzhan's settlers; he also emphasizes the imagination of children who, though they are said not to believe in fairytales, wonder how the machine's track marks in the soil measure against the footprints of a mythic giant.

Given the sustained campaign against the fairy tale in the 1920s, the children Gekht mentions in his story would have been raised to question the magic plots of fairy tales. But there is something in the children's encounter with the excavator that makes them unable to reconcile the giant they see with the objective reality that they had been taught to recognize. The children react to the excavator similarly to the way the elderly Cossacks respond to the new machinery introduced by Jewish settlers in Fink's *Jews in the Taiga*. The encounter with a piece of heavy machinery, a commonplace in the literature of the initial Five-Year Plans, here calls attention to the presence of fairy tale motifs in a narrative about the resettlement of Jews in the Far East.

Once the Budlers arrive in Birobidzhan, heavy rains cause disastrous flooding. When the father and son venture out to locate some of their collective farm's lost cattle, they are captured by enemy soldiers lurking near the border with Manchuria. These soldiers are working with White army divisions in exile in China to plan their incursion into the USSR. Just before the Budlers are taken captive and brought to Manchuria, they recall Logoisk, their native shtetl. Given the text's "repressed" narrative about pogrom violence, this flashback suggests a frightful comparison between Birobidzhan and Logoisk. Although it is depicted in propagandistic terms as the opposite of the shtetl, Birobidzhan takes on the appearance of a dangerous place because the Whites, who are long gone from Logoisk, are still a threat in the place that had been touted as the Jewish homeland.[126]

When the attackers take the Budlers deeper into Manchuria, they lead the family through an unnamed town full of storefronts with awnings lettered in prerevolutionary Russian orthography: a sign of the local presence of White immigrants from Bolshevik Russia.[127] The Budlers are thrown in a jail cell along with forty-eight Russian prisoners who have been captured on their way from Sakhalin Island to the city of Harbin in northeast China. Eventually, Munya faces interrogation by a man described as "a real White soldier [*nastoiashchii belogvardeets*]."[128] Munya's wish has come true: he has, in the end, met a White soldier. His father's interdiction has been violated. The run-in with the Whites replicates and builds on the fears associated with the Budlers' old domicile in the former Pale, even though Birobidzhan was touted as the opposite of the backward—and dangerous—shtetl.

Munya's interrogation, begun by the White officer, continues with a different official: an older Jewish man with the last name Bukhshtab. Bukhshtab, whose name means "letter of the alphabet," interrogates Munya in Yiddish rather than Russian, expecting that the boy would more readily disclose the desired information in his mother tongue. The Whites in the story seek intelligence about the appearance and design of Soviet trains, the number of settlers in Birobidzhan, and the weapons at their disposal. Gekht hints that, regardless of the rhetoric of Birobidzhan as a homeland for Jews, the region's military value to the USSR was an important motivation for the settlement scheme.[129]

Instead of presenting Birobidzhan as a haven for Jews from the former Pale, Gekht implicitly suggests that the region poses dangers for Jewish residents who are defenseless against the counterrevolutionary forces plotting to invade the USSR. Munya's questioning is a case in point: the Whites threaten to kill Munya's dad if the boy refuses to answer his interrogators. Bukhshtab tells Munya, "Oh, we know how to hold a grudge! For example, take a boy who lives minding his own business, it just goes on like that for a long time. He lives like this for ten years and then one fine day he suddenly becomes an orphan."[130] Bukhshtab's threat here is essentially to kill Munya's father, and it taps into a traumatic and unarticulated memory of violence that Munya experienced when he presumably lost his mother in a pogrom in the Pale of Settlement. Munya's native shtetl and Birobidzhan are linked in a way that contradicts the rhetoric about the resettlement of Jews.

Gekht's story for children ends abruptly, its sudden conclusion anticipating the similarly hasty ending of *A Ship Sails to Jaffa and Back,* which Gekht would write six years later. It takes just eight lines to describe the captives' sudden liberation by the Red Army. Immediately before the captives find out that the Reds have taken the prison, they comprehend the disappearance of the Whites as a clue that they would be sent on to Harbin, which was their original destination before their imprisonment by the Whites: "Someone's coming for us. We'll be sent on to Harbin."[131] The next line of the narrator's comment, "They were mistaken," is followed by the concluding lines of the story, which state that the Red troops entered the fortress on October 12, 1929—a date that falls during the IKOR expedition when Gekht was touring the region himself.[132] The reader never finds out what happens to the forty-eight prisoners.

Munya's observation about the prisoners arrested on their way to Harbin highlights one of the text's important details: most of the prisoners were fleeing the Soviet Union when they were taken captive. Harbin, established as a stop on the Chinese Eastern Railway, was at the time a major center of Russian immigration.[133] These forty-eight prisoners would indeed have hoped to continue their journey to Harbin, which at the time had a sizable community of Russian-Jewish expats with their own synagogues, Jewish-run businesses, and communal organizations. At this point in the story, it is already known that the season's crops in Birobidzhan had failed because of the heavy flooding: the Budlers would have had nothing to return to. They could easily have joined the group of liberated prisoners and gone to Harbin, leaving Birobidzhan behind.

The ending of the story is inconclusive: did the prisoners, including the Budlers, return to the Soviet Union or not? Such inconclusiveness leaves open the possibility that none of the prisoners went back to the USSR. Given the sheer number of Harbin-bound migrants who had joined the two people from Birobidzhan in Gekht's story, it is plausible that the Budlers themselves would not have returned. The Budlers were accidental rather than ideological migrants to Birobidzhan to begin with—and so Munya and his father would have been likely to follow those they met in captivity. The date that Gekht gives at the end of *The Budler Family's Resettlement* is the autumn of 1929, when floods had decimated much of the early settlement in Birobidzhan, including its harvest. A significant number of new arrivals did, in fact, leave that year: some went on to Khabarovsk, outside the territory designated for Jewish settlement but still in the Soviet Union's Far East, whereas others returned to their homes elsewhere in the Soviet Union.[134] The inconclusive ending of the book makes it likely that Gekht's is a children's story about a vanishing act, a tale of the migrants' disappearance from Birobidzhan rather than their arrival there.

The Budlers' vanishing act was not unusual in the literature of Jewish non-arrival in Birobidzhan. Working within the context of children's literature about the region, Gekht creates Jewish protagonists who never arrived in what had been trumpeted as their new homeland. Disappearances and substitutions are a regular feature of children's literature. In the way it deploys such possibilities of the plot, *The Budler Family's Resettlement* brings the larger issue explored in this chapter into sharper relief: when it came to Birobidzhan, the Soviet Jew was not a figure who successfully settled in a place that the USSR designated as his home, but one who never arrived.

* * *

In August 1931, Warsaw's mass-circulation Yiddish-language daily *Haynt* ran a translated five-part series of excerpts from Victor Fink's Birobidzhan reportage. The series appeared under the headline "What Does Jewish Life Look like in Biro-Bidzhan?" The editor's introduction noted that *Haynt*'s series was a Yiddish translation of an English translation of Fink's original Russian-language travel essay. The English version, in Leon Dennen's translation, had appeared in an American Jewish periodical, *The Menorah Journal,* earlier that summer.[135] Titled "The Colonies on the Taiga Steppes," the piece was one installment in the journal's regular series called "Letters from Abroad," which had previously printed dispatches on Jewish life in Rio de Janeiro, Tel Aviv, Warsaw, Vienna, and Shiraz.[136] To the journal's American Jewish readership, which *Haynt* referred to as its intellectual elite (*amerikanishe yidishe inteligents*), Birobidzhan was one exotic site among other places as far from New York as Brazil and Persia. Fink's article did not offer a charitable look at the USSR's Jewish region. The translated excerpts came from the first edition of *Jews in the Taiga,* in which Fink describes Birobidzhan's inhospitable climate and the mistakes of local leadership. *The Menorah Journal* did not editorialize on the subject, but for the Yiddish readers in *Haynt,* Fink's report was framed explicitly as a critical exposé. The subtitle appended to the series reads, "A Soviet Writer Reveals the Bluff [*blof*] of the 'Jewish State' in Soviet Russia."

Birobidzhan, located at the edge of the world—in a godforsaken *ek velt,* as a Yiddish idiom would have it—was very much on the global map of the Jewish experience by the 1930s. It was not at all certain, however, whether the place made sense to readers as a plausible homeland for Jews. Writings by Viktor Fink and his colleague Semyon Gekht left equally unclear whether the ostensible subject matter of their work—Jews in the territory designated as a Jewish home—could be adequately described and assessed, or even found in sufficient numbers to warrant a convincing description. The opposite, in fact, appeared to be the case: contrary to propagandistic pronouncements about the Jews' settlement in their new place of refuge in the USSR, the Soviet Jew was a figure who disappeared from the place officially designated as his home. As Birobidzhan drew international attention, the figure of the Soviet Jew became defined by his non-arrival and continued wanderings, across the USSR and around the world.

4

Back in the USSR

The Wandering Jew on the Soviet Screen

In Ilya Il'f and Evgeny Petrov's 1931 novel *The Little Golden Calf* (*Zolotoi telënok*), the itinerant protagonist Ostap Bender, Soviet literature's most famous trickster, joins workers headed to one of the First Five-Year Plan's massive construction sites. Aboard the train, Bender meets Hiram Burman, an American Jew and likely an earlier émigré from the Pale of Settlement, who speaks a "decently clear and correct Russian." Burman came to the USSR because of his interest in reporting on "the Jewish question." Soviet journalists on the train, assigned to report on the progress of the construction of the Turkestan-Siberia railway (Turksib), assure Burman that the Bolshevik Revolution has settled this age-old issue: there are Jews in the USSR, they tell him, but "the Jewish question" no longer exists and many ethnic groups build socialism together as one family of nations.[1]

The "Jewish question" refers to a debate, beginning in the late eighteenth century, about the place of Jews as would-be citizens of European polities. But the USSR has rendered it irrelevant, the journalists assure Burman: the Bolshevik state granted Jews citizenship and welcomed them without any concerns about their ethnic origins. *The Little Golden Calf* highlights the uneasy relationship between the supposedly decisive end of the unsettled and unassimilable figure of the prerevolutionary Jew, the subject of "the Jewish question," and the rumors about this figure's persistence after the revolution. The topic of Jews like Burman visiting the Soviet Union from abroad offered a fruitful space for Il'f and Petrov, as well as other writers and filmmakers, to explore the USSR's inclusive rhetoric toward Jews. These works traced a process by which the figure of the Jew—often presented as a Jewish émigré from the Russian Empire now returning "home"—had the potential to become the New Soviet Man, but who instead became the Soviet Jew, a figure never fully freed from "the Jewish question" of old and still marked both by his origins in the shtetl and his subsequent travel in foreign lands.

On the train, when Burman steps away for a moment, Ostap Bender tells the journalists a parable about the Wandering Jew, one in which this eternal, undying figure finally dies. The legend of the Wandering Jew, which dates to the early modern period in Europe, is about a Jerusalem cobbler condemned to interminable peregrinations for failing to allow Christ to rest at his doorstep on his way to Golgotha.[2] The figure of the Wandering Jew persisted in the Russophone sphere under the moniker *vechnyi zhid,* which translates as "the eternal Jew." In Bender's unusual take on this old legend, the Wandering Jew dies at the hands of Ukrainian nationalists during the Russian civil war, when violence against Jews was rampant.[3]

Bender's version of the legend imagines the revolution as the end of history: it carries with it both the promise of the messianic end-times and the fulfillment of the conviction, articulated by the socialist thinker Karl Kautsky, that the Wandering Jew "will at last have found a haven of rest."[4] Bender relays the story in response to a fellow traveler, an Austrian journalist, who suggests that, on the contrary, the Wandering Jew will continue wandering and history will keep repeating itself. Bender responds to this assertion by exclaiming that "the Eternal Jew will never wander again!"[5] When Burman returns to his seat, the Austrian journalist, knowing of Burman's interest in "the Jewish question," conveys Bender's story to him. Burman, in turn, sends the story—with its twist on the classic Wandering Jew legend—to his newspaper in America. The novel's reader is asked to imagine that Bender's story about the end of millennia-old Jewish wanderings, under Burman's byline, continues to circulate in the periodical press in the United States and on the global stage.

The Soviet Union encouraged American visitors to tour Soviet construction sites during the era of industrialization under Stalin and touted its achievements to global audiences through English-language publications like *USSR in Construction.* American Jewish visitors, especially those who had left Russia a generation earlier, offered a particular opportunity for writers to reflect both on Jewish migration (literal wandering) and the symbolic discourse about the "end" of Jewish wandering thanks to the revolution. The fictional Hiram Burman is a case in point.

One of Petrov's subsequent essays, written after Il'f's death in 1937, uses another encounter with an American Jew as a prompt to discuss "the Jewish question." In this travel sketch about the Jewish Autonomous Region in the Soviet Far East, published in the mass-circulation weekly *Ogonëk,* Petrov recalls an encounter with a Jewish barbershop owner that was said to have taken place during Petrov's and Il'f's trip to the United States three years earlier:

> Once an American Jew asked me:
> "Tell me, what is the state of the Jewish question in your country?"
> I answered that in our country the Jewish question does not exist.[6]

The writer claims to have been reminded of this earlier conversation as his train was pulling into Birobidzhan in 1938—at a time when the Jewish Autonomous Region was central to the claim that the Soviet state had successfully resolved "the Jewish question" by designating the area for Jewish settlement.

The similarity between the American Jewish barber and Hiram Burman, the American Jewish journalist who speaks good Russian, suggests a composite figure: the Jew who had emigrated from the Russian Empire long before the Bolshevik Revolution. In *The Little Golden Calf,* Burman is a literal itinerant who has come to visit his rediscovered homeland, which is now known as the Soviet Union and is presumed to be the last stop on his—like that of the mythical Wandering Jew's—journey. Bender, too, is an itinerant and a vagrant shapeshifter: at the end of the novel, he attempts to slip out of the USSR across the same border where the Wandering Jew in his story was killed.[7] The escape fails when border guards rob Bender and send him back, but Bender survives and is released, presumably to wander the land of the Soviets forever. Bender and Burman are the two instantiations of the same phenomenon: the Wandering Jew who appears to have found the promise of a permanent home in the USSR but who nonetheless continues to be propelled on his eternal journey. Pronounced dead but still very much alive, the Wandering Jew informs the emergence of the Soviet Jew in the space between the telos of ideologically constructed heroism and the early Soviet realities of indeterminacy, migration, and incomplete transformation. The Soviet Jew is not simply the Wandering Jew in a new form, however. Rather, this figure symbolizes the indeterminacy of the early Soviet period for historically sus-pect ethnic minorities who found themselves included in a newly proclaimed brotherhood of peoples.

The story of the fictional Hiram Burman, his trip to the USSR, and his pre-sumed English-language publication of Bender's unusual story about the Wandering Jew unfolded against the background of foreign travelers visiting the Soviet Union in the 1920s and 1930s. Although some were inspired simply by increased access to middle-class leisure travel, Jewish travelers often had deeper motivations. Having lived in the United States, Palestine, or Western Europe for several years or even decades after leaving the Pale of Settlement, some were nostalgic for their former homes, remaining family, and friends.[8] Others were involved in interest groups that sent representatives to report on conditions in the USSR and assess projects of Jewish agricultural coloniza-tion, first in Crimea and then in the Far East.[9] Soviet officials and culture makers readily picked up on this trend and sought to encourage travel, offering visitors ideologically motivated commentary about the places they visited. Some visitors longed to see their nostalgically beloved homeland transformed by the revolution and were more than willing to be convinced.[10]

* * *

The increased availability of travel to the USSR, both by foreigners and re-turnees, coincided with the growth of the Soviet film industry and the in-ternational distribution of Soviet motion pictures.[11] At the same time, Holly-wood films were available and popular in the USSR, exerting their influence on Soviet audiences' tastes and on Soviet directors' craft. Starting in the 1920s and throughout the 1930s, Soviet films incorporated plotlines about Western travel to the Soviet Union. *The Extraordinary Adventures of Mr. West in the Land of the Bolsheviks* (1924)—Lev Kuleshov's foundational film in this genre—hilariously imagines a naïve, satirically named American who arrive in a country he had known only from anti-Bolshevik articles in the U.S. press. Mr. West resembles Woodrow Wilson, the U.S. president who had declined to extend diplomatic recognition to the Bolshevik regime after the revolu-tion. As a cinematic protagonist, Mr. West offered Kuleshov the opportunity to use cut-on-action editing, which he felt the incipient Soviet film industry could learn from Hollywood, and to satirize Western attitudes toward the

USSR by stereotyping the figure of the American visitor in light of the Bolsheviks' own propaganda.[12]

Soviet cinema was gaining an international reputation with the help of works by directors like Kuleshov, Sergei Eisenstein, and Dziga Vertov, who made immeasurable contributions to the development of film as an emergent art form. In this context, films about Westerners imagining the USSR from far away and traveling there to see it with their own eyes could both attract receptive audiences abroad and show domestic viewers their own country reflected through the global imagination. As Stalin solidified control of the government and inaugurated an era of rapid industrial development with the First Five-Year Plan (1928–1932), visiting foreigners—increasingly typecast as industrial saboteurs—proliferated on the Soviet screen.[13] Some were engineers and other specialists lending their expertise to the country's industrial production efforts. Others were travelers who had left Russia when it was a society dominated by peasants and were now returning to witness the USSR's widely touted strides toward collectivized agriculture. Dispatched to the West through film distribution networks, these images were, in turn, projected to the foreign viewer. They also suggested free movement between the USSR and other countries—all at a time when the Soviet state's growing security apparatus was beginning to tether foreignness to criminality.[14] As they encountered stories of real Jews from abroad, Soviet filmmakers deployed similar fictional protagonists, creating a subgenre of films about visiting foreigners that centered specifically on Jews. Such figures reflected the real phenomenon of Jewish mobility in the interwar period, including the resettlement of some in the USSR. Such characters' existence highlighted deeper anxieties about the limits of Jewish transformation and the literal and figurative multidirectionality of Jewish journeys toward but also away from dominant ideological currents.

This chapter foregrounds one such film, *The Return of Neitan Bekker*, released in 1932 in both Russian (*Vozvrashchenie Neitana Bekkera*) and Yiddish (*Nosn Beker fort aheym*), which centers on a story of repatriation to the Soviet Union and was distributed on both sides of the Atlantic. I examine this film in relation to several other contemporary Soviet films that outline the contours of the Soviet Jew as an ambivalent figure, even despite its apparent transformation. I further focus on cinematic techniques used during the era of transition from silent to sound film in the USSR within the context of

Stalin-era cultural politics and explore the making of the figure of the Soviet Jew, which emerged within and represented a transition between eras.

The screenplay for *The Return of Neitan Bekker* was cowritten by the avant-garde Yiddish poet Peretz Markish and the screenwriter and director Rashel' Mil'man; Mil'man later codirected the film with Boris Shpis. Both Mil'man and Shpis were students of avant-garde filmmakers of the preceding generation, and they carried bits of what they had learned just after the revolution into the film they made at the dawn of Socialist Realism. In 1934, two years after the release of the film, Markish adapted the Russian-language screenplay into a Yiddish-language novel, which was also published in Russian translation that same year.[15] *The Return of Neitan Bekker,* which establishes the Soviet Jew as a figure who returns to the USSR from the West, is significant in several ways: as an early Socialist Realist film made by one-time exponents of both the Russian and Yiddish avant-garde; as a cultural text that existed both on the silver screen and the printed page; and as one of the first Soviet sound films, made during a period when sound technology in cinema was being commandeered into the service of ideology.[16]

At the beginning of the film, Neitan Bekker, played by the actor David Gutman, returns from New York to his native shtetl in the former Pale; the shtetl had become part of the Soviet Union after Bekker's departure prior to the revolution. Bekker, a bricklayer by trade who had worked on numerous construction sites in New York City, had journeyed home with a Black man named Jim, played by the Senegalese actor Kador Ben-Salim, who garnered an extensive resume of roles in Soviet cinema.[17] In the film, Jim stands in for the many Black Americans drawn to the Soviet Union at the height of the Jim Crow era, including the high-profile writers and cultural figures Claude McKay and Langston Hughes (figure 4.1). As a member of the working class and of a persecuted American racial minority, Jim illustrates the global appeal of the Bolsheviks' commitment to internationalism and racial equality.[18] Bekker's wife Meika is played by Yelena Kashnitskaya as a stereotypically matronly Jewish woman, whose episodic and comical appearances highlight the fact that the figure of the Soviet Jew evolving in this film—as in other texts of the time—is coded as male.

Back in his native shtetl, Bekker falls under the influence of his father Tsale, who has become an enthusiastic supporter of the Soviet state. Tsale, a figure with a comic demeanor and gestures, is played by the famous Yiddish actor

Figure 4.1. Tsale Bekker (played by Solomon Mikhoels) is questioned about Jim (played by Kador Ben-Salim) by an unidentified townsman (*The Return of Neitan Bekker,* 1932). Courtesy of the National Center for Jewish Film.

Solomon Mikhoels. Tsale is particularly fond of the state's industrialization efforts. He appreciates the sound of the word "Magnitogorsk" and invokes it as a general byword for Soviet construction sites, though, when pressed, doesn't know exactly what the name refers to.[19] Also a bricklayer, Tsale encourages his son (whom he calls by the Yiddish version of his name, Nosn), to help build the Soviet motherland. Both father and son participate in the construction of a factory somewhere within a short truck ride of their native shtetl. In some of the American Jewish travelers' accounts of this time, as in Soviet ethnography, the shtetl became the locus for a negative analysis of the old world, a remnant of a bygone society.[20] Moving a part of the film's action to a construction site was consistent with the implicit ideology of return narratives: the anticipated death of the shtetl and its replacement by different ways of organizing society as exemplified by iconic Soviet construction projects.

Yet Tsale finds it hard to convince Neitan of the superiority of Soviet labor practices. The prodigal son does not easily obey either his father or the state his father has come to represent in his own idiosyncratic way. Instead, despite the ongoing Great Depression that likely cast him out of his adopted home, Neitan adamantly defends American worker training methods, which he got to know on New York's construction sites, against Soviet practices. In particular, he disagrees with a Soviet approach championed by the Central Institute of Labor (known by its Russian acronym as TsIT, which stands for Tsentral'nyi institut truda)—an organization founded in Moscow in 1920 for the study of labor and labor practices. He believes that his approach to bricklaying—physically exerting the body to the point of exhaustion and collapse, which serves as evidence of hard work for his capitalist bosses—was superior to the TsIT method, which saw the worker's body as a machine that needed to be carefully calibrated to be consistently efficient. And so he challenges the Soviet system to a competition.[21]

During the competition, Bekker faces off against a construction worker trained according to Soviet methods, some of which were inspired, ironically, by the assembly line model that Henry Ford perfected in his Michigan car factories. Curiously, in the film—unlike in the screenplay—the competition is set in a circus arena. Bekker loses this competition and, preparing to be fired, begins packing for his seemingly unavoidable return to the United States. But the Central Institute of Labor has a different idea. There is plenty that the Soviet side can learn from Bekker's American technique, they tell him, suggesting that it could help increase the pace of the country's industrialization if combined with Soviet methods. Humbled by his loss and impressed by the TsIT's pragmatism, Bekker confesses to Meika that he has changed his beliefs and implores her to unpack their bags. Bekker stays in the USSR as an instructor at the Central Institute of Labor. The last sequence of the film, to which I'll return later in this chapter, shows him in the company of his father and Jim at the construction site. Tsale is teaching Jim how to hum a *niggun,* a traditional wordless Hasidic melody; Bekker picks up the tune in the film's concluding shot.

Several other contemporary films offer seemingly straightforward narratives about Jews from outside the USSR undergoing similar ideological transformations. The first of these, Kuleshov's 1932 film *Gorizont,* is about an eponymous protagonist disaffected by the United States and drawn to the promise of the Soviet Union. One of the famed director's least-studied films, dismissed by contemporary critics as sloppily made and overly episodic,[22] the film shows Lyova Gorizont (whose last name means "horizon") fleeing to America from the Pale of Settlement, having become upset with the way rising antisemitism has undermined his dignity as a man and a Jew. In the United States, however, he discovers that he is subjugated in a different way: as a member of the working class who is just as denigrated as a Jew in the Pale. Gorizont returns to Russia with the U.S. Army, which has come to support counterrevolutionary forces during the Russian civil war, but he soon defects to the Bolshevik side, acting on the promise of becoming a free man as both a Jew and a worker. The film concludes with a flash-forward to Gorizont's transformation into a cheerful Soviet train engineer.

The second film, Mikhail Dubson's 1935 film *Border* (*Granitsa*), seems to provide a clear propagandistic portrait of the Soviet Union's superiority as well. Also known by the title *Old Dudino* (*Staroe Dudino*), the film depicts life in a fictional shtetl located in a part of the former Pale of Settlement that became part of Poland after 1918. While the modernizing Soviet Union is forging ahead, life in Old Dudino has continued unchanged more than a decade after the revolution. Capitalist ways still rule, and the local Jewish bourgeoisie manipulates the Jews' belief in the power of ritual to drive away the "plague" of communism. Jewish and non-Jewish workers in Old Dudino, however, begin to identify as members of the working class exploited by the bourgeoisie in general and by one local Jewish factory owner in particular; they start to covet the life their brethren are said to be enjoying on a collective farm just a few miles away on the Soviet side of the border.

Finally, Vladimir Korsh-Sablin's 1936 film *Seekers of Happiness* (*Iskateli schast'ia*) introduces a Jewish family who, years after moving from the Pale of Settlement to Palestine, resettles in Birobidzhan. Working through the cultural stereotype of the unproductive Jew, the film offers a memorable portrait of Pinya Kopman, an old-world shtetl dweller that after spending several years abroad, fails to become a productive member of Soviet society following his return. Pinya is drawn against ideological portrayals of characters who embody positive features associated with the New Soviet Man. One of them—the collective farm chairman Natan—is the exemplary Soviet citizen who displaces Pinya from his own family.

When read against the ideological grain, however, these films show how the Soviet Jew is made through references to Jewish figures whose "Sovietness" is in doubt. As they entered the developing system of global film circulation, these motion pictures also made their appearance outside the USSR, bringing the figure of the Soviet Jew abroad with them. Reviewing *The Return of Neitan Bekker* after its New York premiere in April 1933, the Communist Yiddish daily *Morgn frayhayt* commended the film for showing "how the Soviet state straightens the back of the Jewish masses and makes yesterday's *luftmentshn* [literally, "men of air," people who contribute nothing to society] into [b]uilders of [s]ocialism."[23] At the same time, the *New York Herald Tribune* criticized *Gorizont* for its "rambling and rather pointless scenario," making for "neither good propaganda nor good cinema."[24]

Films about returning Jews made during Stalin's industrialization campaign centered on building and production: Neitan Bekker competed to build the tallest brick wall; Pinya Kopman failed—while the rest of his family thrived—at socialist construction; the shtetl Jews of Old Dudino dreamt of joining their brethren on a Soviet collective farm; and Lyova Gorizont gleefully drove a train—an essential if clichéd symbol of industrial progress—around the time of the First Five-Year Plan. Quipping that the cultural output of "the epoch of great construction sites was mostly about great construction sites," Yuri Slezkine has noted that not much actually got built in Stalin-era cultural texts about construction. Instead, these cultural artifacts were "construction stories—or, since human souls are also under construction—construction-cum-conversion stories." Stories of physical construction doubled as stories about the development of their key character, the New Soviet Man. What mattered most in these narratives, Slezkine argues, was "the act of building" as such.[25] In turn, films about the repatriation of Jews to the USSR traced the making of a kind of Jewish variant of the New Soviet Man at or near Stalin-era construction sites and collective farms; in these charged ideological settings, "conversion" to Soviet ideology was an essential part of the plot.

Released between the early and mid-1930s, films about Jewish return to the USSR circulated globally and were screened before domestic and foreign audiences. As a cultural phenomenon of the Stalin era, they imagined the emergent figure of the Soviet Jew as a variation not only on the figure of the New

Soviet Man but also on the age-old figure of the Wandering Jew. On the one hand, the returning Jew projected on the silver screen in the USSR and abroad attested to the gravitational pull of the Soviet Union during the country's rapid industrialization and collectivization. On the other hand, because any return to the Soviet Union required protagonists to confront and reevaluate the prerevolutionary Jewish past, the shtetl continued to weigh the Soviet Jew down and prevent him from becoming the New Soviet Man that Soviet cinema ostensibly propagated. The issue was made more acute because the Jew's peregrinations in capitalist countries after his departure from the shtetl, but before his return to the USSR, added yet more potentially inassimilable foreignness to his already retrograde profile. The Soviet Union might have officially resolved the "Jewish question" but so long as Jews, including visiting or repatriating Jews, bore traces of the "old country" and the detritus of their travels in foreign capitalist lands, the figure of the Soviet Jew retained tinges of the Wandering Jew whose eternal peregrinations could never be over.

∗ ∗ ∗

In 1932, when the Yiddish writer Peretz Markish and Rashel' Mil'man wrote their Russian-language screenplay, *The Adventures of Neitan Bekker,* the USSR's first Five-Year Plan was promising to eliminate the sociocultural ills that stemmed from the Russian Empire's economic backwardness. As the new state built a new society and left this past behind, it aimed to create the "New Soviet Man"—a healthy, muscular type who was to become the new society's chief builder. The New Soviet Man, imagined as the representative of all newly minted Soviets regardless of ethnic or cultural background, was explicitly a man. "The image of the revolutionary proletarian had strongly marked male characteristics in Bolshevik mythology," Sheila Fitzpatrick has written, as did the Bolshevik revolutionary project writ large.[26]

Set directions for one scene in the resulting film, *The Return of Neitan Bekker,* offer an optimistic assessment of this transformation. "There is no fortress that the Bolsheviks couldn't conquer," the screenplay reads. "There are no socially crippled freaks [*sotsial'no iskalechennykh urodov*] whom the Bolsheviks can't reforge into useful and necessary people who are in demand under the conditions of new socialist society's construction."[27] The language of construction at the core of this sentence was quickly becoming commonplace in Soviet culture, literature, and cinema. However, although this optimistic idiom outwardly emphasized the state's ability to cure social ills, the set directions could not have been vaguer: how exactly was one to translate the locution "socially crippled freak" from the pages of the screenplay to the silver screen—and how did this disability fit with the Stalin-era masculine ideal?

This note in the screenplay set the scene for one of the film's ideological storylines: how to take a man whose body had been trained in a bourgeois system designed to exploit an individual's labor for profit and incorporate him into the socialist collective. The "socially crippled" body slated for such a revival was the body of a Jewish man who had left the Russian Empire before the revolution and later returned to his native shtetl at the start of the Stalin-era industrialization, carrying within himself traces of both his shtetl childhood and his wanderings in the capitalist world. This narrative about return presents as a story about a socially unfit body, the collective that seeks to reform it, and the traces of the Pale that differentiate the emerging Soviet Jew from the New Soviet man. The locution "socially crippled freak"—a peculiar turn of phrase—emphasizes the body as the site of social fitness or unfitness and thus the locus of a process of physical reforging.

The word "freak" from the screenplay for *The Return of Neitan Bekker*, suggests that the body is "perpetually significant" in the web of discourses into which it is inscribed. Extraordinary bodies, argues Rosemary Garland Thomson in her work about bodies deemed culturally atypical, bear the cultural resonances of the specific historical contexts in which they have emerged.[28] Moreover, Thomson notes, "singular bodies become politicized when culture maps its concerns upon them as meditations on individual as well as national values, identity, and direction."[29] Neitan Bekker's "socially crippled" body is the result of two layered sets of experiences: that of a Jew from the Pale of Settlement and that of an American construction worker trained in the capitalist system. Bekker is "crippled" in the context of the industrialization-era values associated with masculinity and productive labor that become superimposed with the language of physical disability. The question of how to integrate this doubly compromised body into the Soviet collective is at the core of the conflict in the film—and at the core of the larger discussion in early Soviet culture about whether Jews could become exponents of the figure of the New Soviet Man.

The Return of Neitan Bekker thus existed in the broader context of Stalin-era representations of male workers' bodies. The film scholar Lilya Kaganovsky has observed that the heroes of novels and films at the time were often "[b]lind or paralyzed, limping, one-legged, or wearing prostheses" and that the cultural milieu was "filled with damaged male bodies." Kaganovsky notes that such characters often became disabled in the process of serving the larger Soviet good and were, as a result, elevated to the status of heroes, "yet their extreme forms of physical disability reveal what might be called an ideological and cultural fantasy of Stalinism: the radical dismemberment of its male subjects."[30] She contrasts the presence of these mutilated bodies in Stalinist discourse with a simultaneous cult of the ideal, healthy, strong male bodies of the aviator, border guard, explorer, and worker.

Bodies "crippled" in different ways are at the core of Neitan Bekker's adventures—and Bekker's adventures sit at the core of the larger depiction in early Soviet culture of shtetl-born Jews returning to the USSR after years-long sojourns abroad. The screenplay describes a scene in which Bekker, aboard the ship sailing away from America, remembers his native shtetl and his grandfather, who, like Neitan and his father, was a bricklayer: "His grandfather had six fingers on his left hand and one of his legs was missing. In the olden days he worked on the construction of the Treasury building and fell from the scaffolding during work." The screenplay continues: "Then the old man started taking him, Neitan, when Neitan was still a little boy, along to work. The old man would lie on the ground and using his crutch he would gesture to Neitan for his shovel or hammer."[31] The screenplay posits a family legacy of bricklaying as part of Bekker's identity and even a kind of genetic inheritance. Nature and nurture, a kind of heredity and socially acquired disability combine here: Bekker's grandfather is a "freak" of nature in the sense that he has a sixth finger on one of his hands, yet he is also disabled as the result of a workplace accident; Neitan is a "freak" of a different sort but a "freak" nonetheless.

Suggesting that Stalin embodied the ideal of centralized power that was projected onto the idealized male body, Kaganovsky contends that the emerging Soviet subject was "almost like but never the same as" Stalin. The focus of Stalinist culture, then, "is on the production of a circumscribed masculinity that openly acknowledges and privileges its own undoing, that insists on weakness, on blindness, on distance from power."[32] In this context, the physical disabilities of male heroes mark their distance from power. Bekker's grandfather's physical disability, his phantom limb, is a Gothic remnant from the family's history. This phantom still haunts Bekker when he returns to the shtetl where his disabled grandfather once lived—even though the shtetl is now under the forward-oriented control of the Soviet state.

Peretz Markish's subsequent novel, in contrast to the screenplay and film, includes a description of a funeral procession to bury the severed leg of Neitan's grandfather after his workplace accident, years before the man himself died. The burial of the amputated limb is said to have been carried out in accordance with Judaism's prescription that all parts of the body need to be interred together to ensure bodily integrity in the messianic end-times.[33] His grandfather's disfigurement and the religious ceremony undertaken thereafter emphasize for Bekker his own social "disability." Though he is presumed to be "crippled" by his origins in the shtetl and his work in capitalist America, the ethnographic Jewish components of Bekker's family history establish his own body, even before these injuries, as a cultural site resistant to integration into the Soviet collective. The film thus locates the body of the Soviet Jew, as this figure was emerging in the years after the revolution, in a richly woven web of cultural significance.

* * *

The film *The Return of Neitan Bekker,* unlike both the 1932 screenplay for its production and the 1934 novel published two years after its release, stages the protagonist's integration into the Soviet collective as a competition in a circus arena. The circus is itself a cultural site where different types of "freakishness" have historically been put on display, including in freak sideshows where differently abled bodies acquired performative dimensions.[34] The selection of the circus as the improbable setting for a showdown over socialist labor practices, during which the contours of the figure of the Soviet Jew become visible, is significant to the analysis of *Neitan Bekker* for two reasons. First, the circus is associated with avant-garde and silent film practices that persisted, often in traces, into the period of sound cinema, which coincided with the beginnings of Socialist Realism. Therefore, it is a fitting site for exploring a figure defined by persistent traces of the past. Second, the circus is a site employed in depictions of Stalinist show trials and so lends itself to a discussion of the discourses of reformability and irreformability in Soviet culture in the first two decades after the revolution.

To explore how discourses about aesthetic and technical innovations in filmmaking evoke Soviet discourses about human, and specifically Jewish, transformation, let's turn first to the intellectual biographies of the film's directors. Boris Shpis and Rashel' Mil'man were veterans of the Factory of the Eccentric Actor, an avant-garde collective founded in 1921 by Leonid Kozintsev and Grigorii Trauberg and commonly known by its Russian acronym, FEKS; the group dissolved in 1926. Artists and filmmakers affiliated with FEKS rejected the traditional emphasis on the psychological underpinnings of art and performance, instead arguing for the primacy of the body. In their 1921 manifesto, the group identified the circus as a model for a new approach to acting that focused on gestures. The first tenet read: "1. to the actor: [move] from emotions to the machine, from straining to tricks. The technique: Circus. Psychology: [throw it] upside down."[35] The conceptualization of the body as a machine, coupled with the negation of the psychological motivations behind characters' actions, circulated widely across Russian avant-garde movements.[36]

FEKS proclaimed that popular American genres of entertainment such as boxing, the circus, and the music hall could serve a liberating function in Russia's postrevolutionary culture and make art accessible to the masses. Their aesthetic program relied on the use of eccentric gestures that would evoke clear associations for viewers without the need for much verbal explanation. As Oksana Bulgakova has noted, FEKS was oriented to a kind of "genetic memory, the memory of genre and stereotype that could provoke an instant reaction" because the gesture would be immediately familiar from popular entertainment.[37] By insisting on democratizing art by deploying "low genres" and exaggerated gestures that edged out verbal and psychologically motivated content, Kozintsev, Trauberg, and their colleagues shifted attention from word to gesture in Russia's famously logocentric high culture. In the group's staging, in 1922, of Nikolai Gogol's play *The Wedding* (*Zhenit'ba*), they reimagined the text as a circus show, and the movement of shadows drove an alternate plot of its own in their first film, *The Overcoat* (*Shinel'*, 1926), based on a different famous text by Gogol. The eccentric gesture, they believed, had the capacity to decenter verbally based plots.[38]

Although *The Return of Neitan Bekker* came out a decade after the heyday of FEKS, the film directors' experiences with the group earlier in their careers had been profound and influential. Boris Shpis had served as Kozintsev and Trauberg's assistant on all the FEKS workshop's films. When Kozintsev and Trauberg wanted to abandon their work on *Someone Else's Coat* (*Chuzhoi pidzhak*) in 1927, Shpis, together with Mil'man, convinced Kozintsev and Trauberg to allow the artistic pair to continue the work independently; this became the only FEKS film that Kozintsev and Trauberg did not direct themselves. The film was the first collaboration by Shpis and Mil'man, who later moved to the Belorussian Film Studio, where *The Return of Neitan Bekker* would be made in 1932. *Neitan Bekker,* a film that at first glance appears to be motivated by the increasingly dominant Socialist Realist aesthetic, which relied on the new technology of film sound, also contains within it the remnants of avant-garde eccentricity. These vestiges of the artistic avant-garde and silent film, preserved as spectral remains within the centralized ideological project of Socialist Realism, dovetail with the portrayal of the Soviet Jew on the screen. The Soviet Jew was learning to speak the language of the state—and, given the rise of film sound, not just metaphorically so—while continuing to rely on vestigial gestures from the bygone era of the shtetl and the retrograde capitalist West.

Bulgakova has noted that the American elements in the FEKS aesthetics were not "real items"—that is, not actual genre-specific set pieces borrowed from American culture—but rather "signs [symbols] of America."[39] If *The Return of Neitan Bekker* were to be viewed as an extension of the FEKS aesthetics into the 1930s, a symbolic conflict between two different Americas becomes visible: the America of the Soviet popular imagination in the early 1930s and the America captured in the aesthetics of the FEKS collective a decade earlier. The image of America in the early 1930s was shaped by the Great Depression and the Great Migration. *Neitan Bekker* highlights the two entwined stories of a Jewish worker "socially crippled" by the capitalist system and its collapse and of a Black man fleeing America's racial inequality. The Soviet image of America from the 1920s, in contrast, had been typified in avant-garde circles by the circus, a symbolic space that could shake loose the established genres of high art. In this fashion, a film that is outwardly a creation well on its way to Socialist Realism mixes the rapidly solidifying symbols of socialist production with identifiable remnants of the avant-garde. Along with the residues of a different aesthetic epoch, some remnants and traces of the Pale of Settlement, channeled through the shtetl Jew's adventures in the capitalist West, get mixed in as well.

Yuri Tsivian and Yuri Lotman have noted that FEKS broke through patterns of representational history by using aestheticized signs and symbolic attributes pried loose from their respective contexts. The "symbols" that FEKS deployed as markers of "American" culture worked to detach aspects of Russian culture from their established representational milieus and shift them in new, unexpected directions. For example, FEKS would depict a Russian tavern as an American saloon and model an aristocrat's behavior on that of a heroine in an American Western.[40] This kind of shift was also evident in *The Return of Neitan Bekker:* whereas the construction site figures in both the screenplay and in Markish's subsequent novel, this space is shifted in the film to a circus arena. When the construction site, the epitome of a productive "socialist" space in the era of the First Five-Year Plan, is restaged in the film as a circus act in an inherently performative space previously considered "American" and "eccentric," the film destabilizes the meaning of the construction site as an emergent Soviet space.

Along with displacing and substituting the site of construction, the film also shifts the meaning of its associated figures and acts. The "socially crippled freak," who contributes labor to the construction of a factory in both the screenplay and the novel, now becomes more akin to a clown. The labor expended during the competition in the circus, unlike in the construction of a factory, is unproductive: the wall of bricks laid inside a circus arena is not the wall of an actual factory, so its building is of little value to Soviet industry. As such, it stands apart from the industrialization-era's discourse on maximizing productivity.[41] But the "work" completed during the competition is unproductive only if assessed in terms of the physical edifice that it creates. As a confrontation that pits the "American" system against the ideologically preferable Soviet one, the staged competition is immensely productive insofar as it shows Soviet approaches to physical labor in an advantageous light. Measured in this fashion, productivity refers not only to the height of a finished wall or the number of bricks laid but also to the show of Soviet ideological and labor superiority. The circus arena is a fitting space for staging a spectacle of this kind of discursive "productivity," even if this context works to the detriment of productivity, strictly speaking (figures 4.2 and 4.3).

The labor competition operates according to the rules and conventions of a circus performance. The screenplay notes that Neitan Bekker and the representative from the Central Institute of Labor compete in an event known

Figure 4.2. Neitan Bekker (played by David Gutman) with Jim in the circus arena at the start of the construction competition. *The Return of Neitan Bekker,* Belgoskino, 1932.

at the time as a "storm night" (*shturmovaia noch'*). Generally, a storm night was a short period of accelerated construction when teams of workers competed to reach a production target in record time. In the film, by contrast, the competition takes place before a passive audience of construction workers, for whom the event is entertainment. Actually, most members of the audience are Jews who had just moved to the construction site from the shtetl. They are witnessing not the construction of a new Soviet factory but the performative emergence of the figure of the Soviet Jew—guided by the semiotic rules of the circus.

Bekker, who initiated the competition, is a short, heavyset figure. His body moves in intense and overdetermined ways, particularly when he is shown laying bricks. His opponent, the worker from TsIT, is, by contrast, tall and lean and his movements appear natural rather than forced; to emphasize the

Figure 4.3. Neitan at the end of the construction competition. *The Return of Neitan Bekker*, Belgoskino, 1932.

contrast, the mise-en-scène includes a large banner depicting an idealized Soviet male worker. The film uses the physical appearance of each figure and their respective heights to showcase Bekker's ideological opposition to the training regimen devised by TsIT for Soviet workers, and particularly to its emphasis on upper body workouts. Under its regimen, bodies would have been positioned alongside pulleys that elevated bricks to the level of the workers' torsos so that workers could remain upright instead of having to bend down. Bekker, however, insists that a true bricklayer needs to constantly bend down to reach for his bricks. The film portrays Bekker's bent-over figure as a product of years of exploitation and neglect by the capitalist system, which has so indoctrinated him that he cannot see the advantages of Soviet worker-centered approaches to labor. The film's competition scene makes this difference in method plainly visible: because Bekker's opposition to the TsIT system forces him to bend down each time he needs to pick up bricks, his body is constantly lower than his opponent's. Because the competition's winner will be the participant who builds the taller wall in a set span of time, the downward pull of Bekker's body, compared to the relative height of his opponent's, predetermines the eventual outcome even before the time is up.

Set amidst the symbols and characters of a circus arena, Bekker resembles a clown while his opponent evokes a trapeze artist or tightrope walker. The simultaneous presence of the clown and the aerial performer, a staple of circus routines, bring to mind one scene in Charlie Chaplin's *Circus* (1927), a film that was known and screened in the Soviet Union. In Chaplin's film, the tramp tries to win over a woman who is in love with a handsome aerial performer by attempting to walk the tightrope in the performer's absence. In contrast to the graceful performance of the tall, lean, tightrope walker, Chaplin's tramp—with his comic weighted-down walk—turns the performance into a mockery.[42] Grigorii Alexandrov's *Circus* (*Tsirk*) made four years after *Neitan Bekker* and hailed as an exemplary Socialist Realist film, pays homage to Chaplin's tramp, whose lookalike appears as a sidekick in the aerial performance act at the center of the film.

The acrobat and the clown appear as opposite, contrasting types. The acrobat's act is dependent on an "utterly self-reliant" body, "preserved by skill and strength, never by faith, fate or magic," and admired "precisely for its independence, resourcefulness and self-reliance: its ability to survive and to reach new heights of ascendancy over nature."[43] Such physical feats possess ideological symbolism as well. The acrobatic performance of Bekker's opponent dovetails with industrialization-era aspirations to overcome the body's natural limitations, exceed production quotas, and complete construction goals in record time. In extending his body upward in his attempt to build his structure during the labor competition, Bekker's opponent aims to use the TsIT's training regimen to override nature and to achieve new ideological and industrial goals.

Whereas the acrobat evokes the conquest of nature, the clown exemplifies human folly and frailty: "at one end the gravity-defying grace and strength of aerialists and high-wire acts and, at the other, the clumsy, pie-flinging, barbarous clowns."[44] The simultaneous presence of these opposite personages in both the circus arena and in the same frames of the film resembles mockery: the clown, by way of his exaggerated movements, mocks the aerialist in an attempt to attract the audience's attention and become the centerpiece of the show. In the context of the competition that is unfolding in *Neitan Bekker*, the aerialist is the New Soviet Man. The clown mocking the aerialist is the shtetl Jew who, by way of his adventures in the capitalist West, is on his way to becoming the Soviet Jew.

Mockery is a crucial part of the competition sequence in *The Return of Neitan Bekker*. By the end of the faceoff—in its eighth hour according to a clock whose ticking hands are prominent throughout—Bekker is visibly exhausted. For a moment, as his opponent continues to work, Bekker ducks out of the arena for a drink of water. Thirsty, his face perspiring, he looks as though he is melting. Bekker's "melting" in this sequence serves as a visual representation of the ideological reforging (*perekovka*) or recasting (*pereplavka*) associated with the policies of industrialization during the First Five-Year Plan: both words analogize human beings to metal that can be melted down and subsequently recast.[45] When Bekker returns to the set and realizes that he is about to lose the competition, he expresses this awareness through physical mockery, which, in the absence of any voice-over narration, adds to the visual language associated with the concept of "reforging." For Bekker to be proven wrong, he must first be reminded of that which he had opposed, and he is reminded of it by mocking it.

Bekker directs his mockery at the methods championed by the Central Institute of Labor. As Bekker returns to the arena, he experiences a flashback to an earlier sequence depicting a gymnastics class at TsIT where muscular workers are training their upper bodies using arm and hand exercises to help them increase their efficiency on the construction site. In that earlier sequence, Bekker had considered this exercise mere "theater" and called the technique useless, insisting that a worker should strain to his limit instead. This flashback is crucial to Bekker's realization that he had been wrong, although unable to openly admit it. Then, the camera cuts from the flashback of workers exercising their upper bodies to a shot of Bekker in the circus arena moving his arms in a way that mocks those movements. These exaggerated, eccentric gestures also mock the arm movements of Bekker's opponent, who had himself been trained in the TsIT system. The competition scene is built on such an opposition: on one side of the arena, a worker represents the normative culture of Soviet construction; on the other side, a clown mocks it.

Placing Bekker's mocking gesture in the middle of the frame calls attention to his body, while his failure in the construction competition appears to be the direct result of his inadequate training. Ultimately, Bekker is forced to realize that the Soviet system of training workers' bodies is superior to what he had come to know in America, where workers are exploited to maximize profits. With the audience gathered around him, the capitalist system is itself on trial as the film focuses on the body of a worker whom that system still holds in its clutches.

Bekker's realization of his failure, expressed first through the deployment of mockery, is confirmed at the end of the circus scene through another shot built from starkly opposite details. The sequence contrasts shots of Bekker's hands mocking the hands of Soviet workers with shots of Soviet workers doing their exercises. The final shot of the circus sequence shows Bekker's exhausted body leaning back and sliding down against the wall that he built. Bekker then looks across the circus arena at the wall that was built by his opponent. The two structures are placed in the shot opposite one another. The opposition between the performance of normative culture and a clown's mockery of it is a staple of a circus performance.[46] In *The Return of Neitan Bekker,* the normative, represented by the taller and efficiently built wall, is associated with the New Soviet Man, and the mockery of the norm with the emergent figure of the Soviet Jew.

* * *

The Return of Neitan Bekker is thought to be the first Soviet sound film in Yiddish. No full Yiddish print of the film appears to have survived, though roughly fifteen minutes from the first reel, originally dubbed in Yiddish, are available.[47] *Neitan Bekker* is also one of the first sound films produced in the USSR in any language during the Soviet film industry's transition from the silent era, which firmly defined the beginning of Soviet cinema.[48] In a sense, the Factory of the Eccentric Actor had previously introduced a seemingly inverse shift—deemphasizing the verbal in favor of the visual—when the collective first premiered its work on stage and screen in the 1920s. By the early 1930s, the exaggerated gestures associated with FEKS—and more broadly with silent cinema, because silent films needed to convey emotions without the use of sound—appeared as a site of resistance to the introduction of sound in cinema. Sound, unlike eccentric grimaces and gestures, was supposed to aid cinema in its transition to an aesthetic medium better suited for a crisper, clearer, and less ambiguous articulation of ideology. The "eccentric" preference for the gesture, however, was preserved within sound films via remnants of techniques that had developed in silent cinema. In *The Return of Neitan Bekker*—a film made at a moment of shifting aesthetic and ideological priorities—the emergent figure of the Soviet Jew, caught between eras, dovetailed with the cultural politics and anxieties of the time.

Like eccentric gestures, montage also represented an earlier aesthetic practice in Soviet silent films that were made during the first decade after the revolution; when it appeared in films in the 1930s, it, too, encoded anxieties about the persistence of the past into a new political era under Stalin. During the 1920s, Soviet cinema had been dominated by theoreticians and practitioners of montage, including Sergei Eisenstein, Dziga Vertov, and Vsevolod Pudovkin. In juxtaposing shots varying in visual intensity, as in Sergei Eisenstein's "montage of attractions," Soviet directors expected viewers to use their own comprehension to compile disjointed images into a narrative.[49] Sequences would often be shown so quickly that they appeared to violate the natural space-time continuum and form a new kind of cinematic one.[50]

Early cinema fixed the attention of the viewer on the moving image: the Lumière brothers' *The Arrival of the Train*—the world's first moving picture screened to a sizable audience—demonstrated cinema's ability to depict movement as such.[51] In contrast, audio technologies at the dawn of the sound era directed cinemagoers to notice sound by placing it at the center of many film plots. Unsurprisingly, as the film scholar Evgeny Margolit has written, early sound films fixated on the sound produced by objects, and not on their size or shape, to show off the cutting-edge technology.[52] "In early Soviet sound film," Lilya Kaganovsky has noted, "there is a preponderance of loudspeakers, radios, and other devices for reproducing sound that underscore sound cinema's ability to directly address the viewer."[53] Paying attention to how human characters produced sound was equally in vogue: in *The Jazz Singer* (1927), considered the first Hollywood film that made use of synchronized sound, the plot revolves around a protagonist who makes a living as a singer. The vocal apparatus itself offers a kind of meta-commentary on the way sound films are made: "Recalling the predilection of silent pictures for visual images—objects, lines, contours—it is no wonder that singers, musicians, and other 'sources of sound' became heroes of the first talking film."[54] One of the first Soviet sound films, Kozintsev and Trauberg's *Alone* (*Odna*), opens with a close-up of a ringing alarm clock that pierces the audience's expectation of silent cinema with its loud mechanical trill; writing about the film, the scholar Neya Zorkaya recalled her parents' astonished reactions to the film when they returned home after seeing it upon its release in 1931.[55]

In 1928, at the dawn of the sound era, leading Soviet directors, including Eisenstein and Pudovkin, issued a statement on the challenges that film sound posed to their experiments in montage, which they regarded as the foundational building block of Soviet cinema. Fearing that synchronized sound would disrupt the "innocence and purity of the initial concept of cinema's new textural possibilities," they instead suggested integrating it through the "contrapuntal use of sound vis-à-vis the visual fragment of montage" instead of more straightforwardly matching sound to a film's visual cues.[56] By then, Eisenstein had already been attacked by critics for his 1927 film *October* and its supposed elitism and formalism: his use of "intellectual montage," the critics thought, left too much to the viewer's imagination. In the context of the ideological shift to the codified practices of Socialist Realism, Soviet critics increasingly felt that cinema could and should be used to convey clearer political messages. At the same time, they sensed that Soviet audiences, which included many uneducated viewers, found films like Eisenstein's unengaging because these films lacked easily graspable narratives. Despite the success of Eisenstein's films abroad, they could not compete in the USSR against the widely popular movies imported from Hollywood.[57] The desire of Eisenstein and his colleagues to add sound as another layer of intellectual montage ran counter to the proposals to use such technology for more straightforward, accessible, and comprehensible messaging—including to deliver state ideology.

Between ideological pressures for clearer narratives, on the one hand, and the viewing public's preference for American-style editing on the other, the introduction of sound came to be viewed as an opportunity to merge new technology with new ideological objectives. Denise Youngblood, a historian of Soviet film, has written that montage, which served as the "hallmark of the great silent cinema, produced a cutting style that was often rapid and unrealistic"—and which was impossible in sound film "[b]ecause the ear understands more slowly than the eye sees." A trend toward realism accompanied sound cinema everywhere in the world but had "a special significance in the Soviet case, where realism in the arts was already becoming aesthetic dogma for political reasons."[58] Another scholar of Soviet film has remarked that in sound cinema, "the aesthetics of the fragment [associated with montage] is replaced by a reorientation onto a human figure": continuity editing, which came to replace Soviet montage practices, facilitated narrative cohesion and coherence in its preference for character-based plots over disjointed, discontinuous shots.[59] This transition altered the role of the audience, too: the viewer was no longer "joining different fragments together" to produce meaning but, instead, transforming from "an active participant in the process of deciphering meaning into a listener of an apostrophe addressed to them."[60] The introduction of sound technology in cinema—and its ability to deliver explicit verbal messages—overlapped in the USSR with a move toward greater accessibility of ideological messaging across the arts.

The transition from silent to sound film and from discontinuous montage to sound-assisted continuity editing did not occur all at once. Few movie theaters in the USSR had the equipment necessary to screen sound films; this fact limited not only the quantity of sound films that could be imported but also the number of films produced domestically.[61] During the drawn-out process of technological transition, different approaches to film coexisted uneasily. Just as the emphasis that FEKS had placed on gesture over voice in the 1920s survived into the 1930s, the 1920s practices of silent cinema persisted into the 1930s as audio technology gained ground but had not yet fully taken over. *Neitan Bekker* was made during this transitional moment in the history of Soviet cinema, placing at its center the figure of the Soviet Jew as a cultural artifact that reflected anxieties about transition to Soviet industrial modernity and contained in it the residues of layered Jewish pasts.

The juxtaposition of sound and montage in *The Return of Neitan Bekker* sharpens the central issue of the film: the attempted reintegration of Bekker's body, crippled by both the old world of the shtetl and American capitalism, into the Soviet body politic. At the beginning of the film, in what remains of its first Yiddish-language reel, Neitan and his entourage—his wife Meika and his Black friend Jim—are aboard the ship sailing from America to the Soviet Union. Neitan removes a stack of papers from his suitcase and declares, "Let's see the visas to our new land." The use of sound is theatrical, and the phrase fulfills only the referential function of language: the sound accomplishes what a close-up of Bekker's visas alone could have achieved but does not harness its own potential to convey a clear message about those visas' meaning in Bekker's life. One critic noted this problem when the film came out: "The sound is not used consistently well," the reviewer for *Kino* wrote in November 1932, "the dialogues and monologues [of the actors] don't always contribute to the development of the cinematic potential at the director's disposal but stay as remnants of theater in cinema."[62] The use of sound in this sequence fails, in the critic's view, because the directors use sound merely to replicate the worn-out approaches from cinema's silent era. After displaying his Soviet visa and announcing its existence, Bekker discusses another document, his "Party membership card." Bekker is not, in fact, a member of the Communist Party, but in the subsequent shot he demonstratively looks at his hands and exclaims that both his and Jim's hands had become their "Party membership cards [*partbiletn*]" over "twenty-eight years of forced labor [*akht un tsvantsik yor katorge*]" while "working for Rockefeller." Bekker claims symbolic membership in the Party by virtue of his membership in the working class; in so doing, he effectively attempts to justify his long absence from the old country during the revolution. We weren't there during the revolution, he implies to Jim, but our callused hands are our true Party cards.[63]

Another sequence, which occurs midway through the film and is also focused on hands, reflects the uneasy overlap of silent and sound film norms and the indeterminacy of Bekker's attempted transformation into a Soviet person. A hand holds a list containing more than fifty names in Yiddish, with signatures next to them. The subsequent shot reveals that the hand is that of the Soviet factory director, while the voiceover makes clear that the list contains names of workers from the shtetl whom one of the factory's representatives had brought to the construction site. Referring to the list, construction site managers discuss the fact that the factory now has a sufficient workforce thanks to this influx of Jewish workers. This sequence consists of two shots, the first of which is constructed without sound while the second uses sound to explain the meaning of the preceding shot. Yiddish and Russian are stitched together as well: the silent shot displays Yiddish text, whereas the subsequent shot has Russian voiceover. Moyshe Olgin, reviewing the film upon its New York premiere in 1933, noted that one audience member he encountered was astonished by the sight of the hand-held Yiddish document in this sequence, taking this very fact as evidence of amazing prospects for Jews in the USSR: "they write in Yiddish, they organize in Yiddish . . . [This is] the road to Communism."[64] *The Return of Neitan Bekker* could appear to Jewish audiences in the Unites States as a propaganda film that successfully advertised optimistic possibilities for Jews in the land of the Soviets.

There is, however, a discrepancy suggested by the two sequences: Bekker's name is likely on the Yiddish-language list of workers from the shtetl who have been brought to the construction site, yet his claims to being a member of the Soviet collective is informed by his work experience in the United States. Unlike other Jewish workers in the film, Bekker's arrival at the site of socialist construction is circuitous and comes by way of working for the Rockefellers in America, rather than directly from the shtetl. His subsequent loss in the competition to a worker presented as the New Soviet Man requires not merely an acknowledgment of his failure, not merely a renunciation of the shtetl, but a more pronounced ideological confession about his understanding of the superiority of Soviet construction practices to the ones he learned in the capitalist world.

This confession takes the form of a speech Bekker delivers the morning after his failed performance, following a long night when he is beset by nightmares of being fired from his job and being expelled from the USSR. First, Bekker tells his wife to pack their bags and prepare for the couple's return to the United States; he then sets out for the TsIT offices to request his severance pay. Much to his astonishment, however, he discovers that TsIT will both keep him on as an instructor and will also endeavor to learn from his bricklaying techniques so long as Bekker proves willing to learn the TsIT method in turn. Bekker then returns home and excitedly informs his wife that they are not going back to America after all. Meika is perplexed and comically displays her fatigue at the demands to pack and unpack their belongings but realizes that the need to unpack means that the couple's homecoming is now complete. This is the context in which Bekker must explain to his wife both what happened and how he was converted to the methods of socialist construction.

As Bekker prepares to verbally acknowledge his Soviet "conversion," however, he finds himself suddenly at a loss for words. Bekker's father Tsale had consistently urged his son to accept the rules of his newly rediscovered homeland and to drop his earlier protestations. Now, as Neitan tries but fails to express his newly realized commitments, Tsale literally puts the words in his son's mouth. In this sequence, Tsale initiates a string of words and short phrases and Bekker repeats them:

Tsale: "We are here [*My zdes'*]."   *Neitan:* "Yes, here [*Da, zdes'*]."
Tsale: "We build [*My stroim*]."   *Neitan:* "[We] build [*Stroim*]."
Tsale: "We work [*My rabotaem*]."   *Neitan:* "[We] work." [*Rabotaem*]."
Tsale: "Socialism [*Sotsializm*]."   *Neitan:* "Socialism."
Tsale: "We lay bricks [*My kladem   *Neitan:* "Four thousand per day."
         kirpich'*]."   [*Chetyre tysiachi v den'*]."

This conversation between father and son then dissolves into a comedy consisting solely of gestures. Having professed his belief in the Soviet system in this parroted fashion, Bekker moves to the back of the room, and he and his father continue to gesticulate. Occasionally, their gestures are interspersed by three monosyllabic words: "yes [*da*]," "but [*no*]," and the Slavic-origin Yiddish particle *nu,* which means something akin to "so."

The arc of Bekker's development becomes clear as the movie nears its end. At the start, Bekker is fully conversant; he speaks words captured through sound technology. He expresses his opposition to the Soviet system and his support of the American system of labor. He then tries to present the marks of exploitive labor imprinted on his body from his time in America as his form of identification, as though he had earned his membership in the Soviet collective. Then, a silent sequence about the competition in the circus arena shows Bekker experiencing, in his own failing body, the superiority of the Soviet system. Finally, Bekker's voice returns: he states his belief in the superiority of the Soviet system but only by parroting his father's words. In repeating Tsale's statements, moreover, Neitan appears to be driving his total output of words closer to zero: he reduces by half the number of words his father said in two of the sentences, implying the first-person plural pronoun Tsale had spoken but no longer enunciating it. Having stated his belief, Bekker again loses his speech and, except for occasional grunts, communicates only in eccentric gestures. While narrating the story of Bekker's development from an American returnee to a good Soviet citizen who believes in the ideology and methods of socialist construction, the film also seems to be telling a narrative about Bekker's progressive loss of voice. One of the first Soviet sound films, *The Return of Neitan Bekker* calls attention to voice itself and to the limitations of ideological refashioning. In returning to the USSR, the Soviet Jew loses his ability to speak.

* * *

In the scene of his "conversion," Bekker doesn't merely repeat his father's words; rather, he appropriates them and uses them as the building blocks of a statement of belief in the Soviet system. In so doing, he answers the call of the state insofar as Tsale's statements give voice to the reigning ideological line on socialist construction. The call of the state is connected to Tsale's words in another way as well: earlier in the film, while chastising his son for not playing by the state's rules, Tsale spoke to Neitan on behalf of the collective: "You are quarrelling with us, Neitan! [*Ty sporish' s nami, Nosn!*]" Tsale's "us" refers to his new understanding of himself as part of the collective of Soviet workers and the Soviet people, in stark opposition to Bekker's individualist approach to labor. Despite his exaggerated comic features, emphasized in Mikhoels's performance, Tsale plays the role of an ideological mentor, a commonplace figure in Socialist Realism who guides a mentee in ideological matters. As Tsale ventriloquizes the state's ideology, Bekker accepts and repeats it.

Lilya Kaganovsky has written about the call of the state in Soviet cinema during its transition from silent to sound. She focuses on the protagonist of Kozintsev and Trauberg's 1931 film *Alone,* who answers the call of the state when she is sent from Leningrad to teach in Russia's faraway Altai region in southern Siberia. Noting that *Alone,* the first Soviet sound film, had brought attention to sound as such, Kaganovsky notes that "the film relies on the new technology of sound to deliver its ideological message."[65] Beginning with its opening shot of an alarm clock that suddenly breaks into sound, the film continuously operates through the "baring of the cinematic device itself." Writes Kaganovsky, "Like the heroine, we, the audience, are addressed by the new technology and learn to accept our new position as 'auditors' as well as viewers."[66] The film's foregrounding of mechanized noises, including typewriters, alarm clocks, and loudspeakers, motivates her analysis of "the ideological impact of transition, the ways in which the introduction of synchronized sound coincided and, in some ways, made possible the shift in

Soviet film-making away from avant-garde cinema of the 1920s, to Socialist Realist cinema of the 1930s and beyond."[67] *Alone* is the first film in which the "voice of power" could be heard directly from the screen as it was quite literally part of the film's diegetic soundtrack.

Kaganovsky concentrates on the loudspeakers that deliver the central message of *Alone:* the call to bring education to faraway regions, which the film's protagonist hears and obeys. The sound emanating from loudspeakers in the middle of an empty square spreads the message of the state. "Whether or not there is anyone there to listen," writes Kaganovsky, "this call neither demands nor forces anyone to respond, 'to take call,' or to answer its appeal. Yet once answered [. . .] the call becomes a duty."[68] Those who do answer the call "find themselves forever in debt, always paying for the charges."[69] By answering the call of the state, notes Kaganovsky, the film's heroine is constituted as a Soviet subject who realizes her duty to others and fulfills it by sacrificing her preferred urban lifestyle and becoming an educator in an underserved region. The call of the state is portrayed in the film as a literal appeal that conveys the ideological agenda of the state operating off-screen.

Though there are no loudspeakers in *The Return of Neitan Bekker,* the screenplay for the film does describe a planned scene that involves them; a version of this scene is also present in Markish's novel two years later. It takes place in a public square near the construction site, where loudspeakers project a radio broadcast of the "national" melodies of different ethnic groups in the USSR.[70] According to the screenplay, the sound attracts the attention of Bekker and his wife as they pass by, causing Bekker, who had experienced antisemitism in the Pale of Settlement before the revolution, to marvel at a Jewish melody playing in the middle of a city square. The sound here is taken as evidence that the Soviet state to which Bekker has returned is committed to the project of a new Jewish culture and identity: "Rather than tying Jews to their traditional Jewish past," Harriet Murav has written about this scene, "the use of Yiddish in the new media shows that the state is creating a new kind of Jewish identity with Yiddish as the primary marker of Jewish difference."[71] As drafted in the screenplay, the scene ends comically: a dog comes up to Meika as she stands listening to the music and urinates on her leg.[72] She has failed to see the dog approach because her eyes had been directed upward, toward the loudspeaker and the sound issuing from it. Meika doesn't notice the dog because she's looking at the source of sound the way the viewer of an early sound film would look in astonishment at the sound emanating from moving images on the screen.

In the screenplay for *Neitan Bekker,* the ideological message of ethnic diversity is encoded in a Jewish melody played from a loudspeaker in the middle of a Soviet public square. In the film that resulted from the screenplay, this message is still transmitted through sound, but the loudspeaker is no longer the device tasked with its delivery. Instead, Bekker's father Tsale hums a Jewish melody known as a *niggun*—a wordless Hasidic tune. Tsale's humming makes up a significant portion of the film's diegetic sound. Like the insistent call of the state through loudspeakers in *Alone,* the oft-repeated melody of the *niggun* becomes an insistent appeal in its own right. Both the loudspeaker and Tsale's voice herald the message that the USSR is a welcoming multiethnic entity.

Because the film played abroad, it was meant to appeal to foreign viewers who, like the fictional Neitan Bekker, might have considered returning to their one-time homeland now claiming to be a haven for ethnic minorities in general and for Jews in particular. This claim would have been especially poignant for New York audiences because, as the film historian J. Hoberman has noted, the film opened within weeks of the Nazi Party's victory in Germany's March 5, 1933, parliamentary elections and the promulgation of the first discriminatory laws banning Jews from the civil service and legal professions.[73] Earlier in the film, when Tsale chastises Bekker for not being part of the workers' collective, his humming of the *niggun* adds an ethnically specific element to the earlier "call of the state" that he is trying to channel for his wayward son's benefit. In the ways he uses his voice, Tsale becomes not only a model worker but also a model Jewish worker. Tsale is a shtetl Jew from the former Pale of Settlement who is successfully reforged as a kind of diminutive Jewish version of the New Soviet Man, opening up the possibility that his son—who has now returned to his birthplace from both capitalist America and the shtetl of long ago—could become a New Soviet Man himself.

In an article published in *Kino* after *Neitan Bekker* was released in 1932, the composer of the film's score, E. Brusilovskii, foregrounded the issue of Jewish music in the film. Composing music for a sound film dealing with a Jewish subject matter was going to be a difficult task, he feared: "Unfortunately, Jewish music tends to be thought of as something grotesque, as a joke, as music that does not have any deep or serious meaning." "Considering such attitudes," the critic continued, "[. . .] I set myself the goal of supplying music that would reveal the considerable underlying content [*znachitel'noe soderzhanie*] of both the entire film and its most significant moments."[74] The composer's statement exemplifies the critical and self-conscious attention to sound in the film industry during this transitional period at the conclusion of the silent era. Tsale's *niggun* is part of the film's deliberately created musical score and, according to the score's composer, one of the major ways by which the film transmits its primary storyline.

Tsale is a stutterer, and his near-constant humming of the *niggun* is inextricably connected to his speech impediment. Marc Shell has pointed out that, "if a stutterer must talk, he or she might fluently sing the words as song—or smoothly recite them as poetry" and that, furthermore, "most stutterers cease to stutter when they singsong."[75] The singsong as a technique to break through stuttering evokes Shpis and Mil'man's reflections on their use of sound in *The Return of Neitan Bekker*: "We were forced [*prinuzhdeny*] to emphasize the strict reality of sounds in the film. [We] completely refused to use music as background for dialogue and in a similar way tied every instance of speech precisely and everywhere to the speaking character."[76] In claiming that there is no background music in the film, the codirectors suggest that Tsale's humming resembles speech that contributes to dialogue and that his *niggun* should be viewed as advancing the film's narrative arc.

Following Neitan Bekker's affirmation of his new convictions, which he makes by parroting his father's stuttering speech, he, Tsale, and Jim meet while on a work break at the construction site. All three are seated high up on the scaffolding. A closeup focuses on Tsale and Jim as Tsale teaches Jim how to hum the wordless *niggun* (figure 4.4), Jim repeats the tune, makes a mistake, and Tsale repeats it again. An old shtetl Jew newly remade by the Soviet society is teaching a traditional Jewish melody to a Black refugee from the United States during the Jim Crow era—significantly, on a Soviet construction site. Through this sequence of shots, the film seeks to portray the USSR as a multiethnic haven both for those within the country who had faced discrimination before 1917 and for the oppressed from anywhere in the world.

Interrupting Jim's singing lesson for a moment, the newly reforged Neitan Bekker makes another pronouncement that results from a kind of epiphany about Soviet workers. Staring dreamily into the distance when he turns to

Figure 4.4. Tsale teaching Jim and Neitan the melody of the wordless *niggun* in the concluding shot of the film. *The Return of Neitan Bekker,* Belgoskino, 1932.

his father, he says, "Here they work not only with this"—Bekker points to his head—"but also with this," as Bekker points to his heart. The statement seems on the surface to confirm that the Soviet Union inspires its workers both intellectually and emotionally. But Bekker never articulates the two most important words: "head / mind" and "heart." Likewise, while making his earlier ideological statement by repeating after his father, he omitted crucial words needed to make those pronouncements sound like grammatically coherent sentences. On the one hand, Bekker's use of gestures in the middle of a spoken sentence is consistent with the film's larger indecisiveness around the use of sound. The exaggerated emphasis on gestures also might be another throwback to the eccentricity associated with the avant-garde. At the same time, Bekker's gesturing at parts of his body while speaking a sentence that is short on words might suggest that his physical reforging has come at the expense of fluent speech.

As a bricklayer trained in the capitalist system, Bekker had been primarily directed by a misguided cerebral understanding of labor efficiency.

The process of becoming reforged as a Soviet worker taught him that correct training needed to be combined with a kind of "spiritual" belief that lay beyond his intellectual faculties. The Soviet worker—not unlike a devout Christian—needed to be guided by his heart to function efficiently as a member of the spiritual and ideological collective. Neitan Bekker, pointing at his heart, anoints himself a New Soviet Man who arrives at this status through a kind of conversion. However, by pointing at his heart instead of saying that his heart is now changed, Bekker suggests that his conversion marked not only the acquisition of a new faith but also a loss of familiar speech.

The Return of Neitan Bekker was one of many Stalin-era cultural artifacts that focused on protagonists who converted to Soviet ideology but lost the ability to speak when time came for them to describe their transformation. As I discussed in Chapter 1, the writer David Bergelson populated his novel *Judgment* with characters unable to convincingly voice their "conversion" to Bolshevism either because they weren't articulate speakers or because, at the critical moments when their speeches were most needed to move the ideological plot along, their voices couldn't reach others. Mikhail Dubson's *The Border*, a 1934 film centered on characters who wish to cross into the USSR, relies on the use of sound to convey, paradoxically, the loss of voice at the moment of conversion and offers a helpful set of details for better understanding the ending of *Neitan Bekker*.

As mentioned, *The Border* is set in Old Dudino, a shtetl a few miles from the Soviet border, in Poland. At the beginning of the film, Arye, the accountant to Novik, the wealthiest Jewish man in town, is shown counting his boss's money and writing down his calculations in a ledger. As he carries out his duties, Arye hums a wordless Hasidic *niggun* and then begins singing out the numbers he is counting to the melody's tune (figure 4.5). The numbers are the rich man's profits, earned from running a factory where he refuses to employ any of Old Dudino's Jews out of fear that Jewish workers would try to organize the non-Jews he employs and "infect" them with socialism. As one of the reviewers at the time noted, Arye's subdued humming of the *niggun* adds to the sense of the shtetl as a backward place impoverished by oppressive capitalist practices.[77] The sequence firmly tethers the capitalist foundations of the shtetl's economy to a melody associated with Jewish piety: Dubson builds on one of the tenets of Soviet antireligious propaganda, which

Figure 4.5. Arye (played by Veniamin Zuskin) at his desk, humming a wordless *niggun*. *The Border,* Lenfilm, 1935.

habitually framed religious devotion as a tool manipulated by the moneyed classes to exploit workers and peasants.[78]

In the concluding shots of the film, Arye—who had by then journeyed across the Soviet border and back to his shtetl in Poland—reports on the happy and productive life he had observed on a Jewish collective farm a few miles away. He is particularly impressed by a Jewish song that he heard on the Soviet side, "a song in minor key but with its meaning in major key [*minornaia pesnia s mazhornym soderzhaniem*]." He then launches into a platitudes-filled speech about how good a life Jews lead on the collective farm, subsequently stating that "if [he] only knew how [*esli by ia umel*]," he would have sung the happy song of the Jews from the Soviet side of the border. However, Arye doesn't know the words and so, in the film's final moments, he breaks into a wordless Hasidic *niggun,* to the tune of which the Jewish collective farmers' song was likely set and which a non-Jewish man standing near Arye picks up on his accordion.

Similarly, at the end of *The Return of Neitan Bekker*, the wordless *niggun* replaces the articulation of a newly acquired ideological outlook. In the concluding shot of the film, as Tsale teaches Jim how to sing the wordless *niggun*, Bekker picks up the tune for the first time himself. Earlier I suggested that the *niggun* that Tsale hums throughout the film also projected the image of the Soviet Union as a multiethnic state and facilitated the flow of Tsale's stuttering speech. The two functions of the melody are united in the film's concluding sequence. Neitan Bekker's body is in focus as it produces the *niggun* that both identifies him as a Jew and marks him as a stutterer. In the process of answering the "call of the state" and reforging his body, damaged by capitalism, into the body of a Soviet worker, Bekker loses the fluidity of his speech. Though he is apparently transformed in body and spirit, he lacks speech to articulate his understanding of the demands of the Soviet state where he has been repatriated. Neitan Bekker completes his transformation into the figure of the Soviet Jew—a figure who has been "converted" and changed but who can never be fully made over and, as such, is one whose existence calls into questions the transformative power of the Soviet project.

* * *

Neitan, his wife Meika, and Jim, the screenplay notes in its opening lines, set sail to the Soviet Union "during the twelfth year of the revolution [*na 12yi god revoliuitsii*]."[79] "The twelfth year of the revolution" means that the action is set between November 1928 (the eleventh anniversary of the Bolshevik Revolution) and November 1929, one year later. This period precedes the 1932 screenplay and film by three years and corresponds both to Stalin's consolidation of power and the onset of the Great Depression, which would have contributed to Bekker's readiness to leave the United States and return to the USSR.[80] The film's central scene, the competition in the circus, where the figure of the Soviet Jew is defined is staged as a variant on the era's other dominant form of performance, the show trial.

The circus arena was not only a source of "eccentric gestures" stemming from the history of the avant-garde; it was also a space that became associated with the political show trials of the Stalin era. *Circus*, released four years after *The Return of Neitan Bekker* and, like *Neitan Bekker*, centered on an ideological conflict between the USSR and the West, stages a more meta-phorical version of such a trial in a circus arena. Anna Wexler Katsnelson has suggested that *Circus* "treats the elements of the courtroom symbolically, referencing reality, not reproducing it."[81] In the climactic scene of *Circus*, the film's villain—a figure who conflates the racial ideologies of Nazism and Jim Crow America—is exposed as a racist and his views are proclaimed unacceptable in the USSR. The villain is then chased away by the public from the middle of the circus arena. Commenting on this scene, Katsnelson compares the film's "unmasking of the enemy" with the Stalinist show trial. By the 1930s, show trials had come to dominate Soviet political narratives, and references to them would have been apparent to audiences.

The Return of Neitan Bekker was filmed shortly after the much-publicized 1930 show trial of the so-called Industrial Party, in which several scientists and economists were falsely accused of planning a coup against the Soviet government.[82] The circus scene in *Neitan Bekker* treats the elements of the courtroom symbolically in a way that alludes both to the earlier performative tradition of "agitation trials" in the 1920s—scripted and staged performances that aimed to educate the public about the importance of new Soviet norms—and to the emerging reality of the show trials in the 1930s.[83] Julie Cassiday has argued that the melodramatic plots of the agitation trials of the 1920s were beginning to lose their propagandistic value by the 1930s: they had become diffused among a number of other genres.[84] *Neitan Bekker* participates in shaping the visual idiom of the show trial by substituting an actual trial—a trial of a foreign worker who has erred on the job—with a circus performance.

The 1928 Shakhty trial, in particular, shaped the language and the aesthetics of subsequent show trials, including the traces of them that made their way into *The Return of Neitan Bekker*. That trial followed the arrest of a group of engineers—three of them German nationals—in the coal mining town of Shakhty in the North Caucuses on charges of "sabotage" and "wrecking" (*vreditel'stvo*). Coal production had declined in the early years of the Bolshevik regime and outdated prerevolutionary equipment couldn't be harnessed to meet increased output quotas. Charging the arrestees with sabotage was meant to concretely assign blame to individuals for the production slump: in this fashion, the government could clear itself of any wrongdoing on the eve of the major industrialization effort at the beginning of the

First Five-Year Plan. The foreign origin of some of the defendants was among the central features of the Shakhty Affair. During the trial, the three German engineers who were among the accused started to be referred to as "foreign specialists" purposefully sabotaging the Soviet Union's efforts to industrialize. They, along with home-grown "specialists," were accused of conspiring with the former "bourgeois" owners of the Shakhty coal mines—all of them living abroad as émigrés at the time of the trial—with the intent to derail the growing Soviet economy.[85] The Shakhty Affair, and the attention it brought to foreigners in the USSR, would have been impossible to ignore a few short months before the fictional Neitan Bekker returned from bourgeois America to the USSR and vocally disagreed with the latter's methods of socialist construction.

Bekker works at the Soviet construction site under a foreman named Hans who is clearly himself a "foreign specialist" from Germany. When Bekker initially refuses to accept the methods of socialist construction, he resembles one of the "saboteurs" accused at the Shakhty trial. At the time, any resistance to new mechanized modes of work came to be seen as a form of industrial sabotage.[86] Given the rhetoric of the Central Institute of Labor, according to which the worker's body was to be calibrated like a well-functioning machine, Bekker's refusal to reshape his body and to educate workers' bodies in this fashion would have fallen dangerously within the parameters of "wrecking." By the early 1930s, reintegration into the Soviet collective became impossible for those accused of industrial sabotage: although Bekker's story appears to end well, the Jewish returnee's story might not be one with a happy ending.

The agitation trials (the singular, in Russian, is *agitsud*) of the 1920s were staged performances based on fictional scripts, which were intended to educate the mostly illiterate public about the important social issues of the day. Focusing on a given defendant's "almost religious conversion to the new way of life," they relied on a tripartite, almost "religious" formula of confession, repentance, and reintegration to demonstrate the unappealing nature of old ways that were to be rooted out by the revolution.[87] Such performative conversions would have been familiar to the public because the audience at an agitation trial would have been invited to participate in determining the defendant's verdict. The trial's dramatic structure guided the public toward allowing the defendant to reintegrate into society.

In the 1930s, by contrast, the dramatic origins of agitation trials became obscured. The show trials that emerged in their stead no longer relied on lay audiences to issue judgment: the focus of show trials shifted from the audiences and their role in the spectacle to the defendants themselves, who were placed under increased scrutiny. Even though the defendant at a show trial was still expected to repeat the formula associated with the agitation trials, his or her reintegration into society was no longer possible, nor was it expected.[88] Indirectly, this shift resembled—and coincided with—the shift from silent films to sound cinema. Silent films relied on audiences to make connections between juxtaposed shots in a montage; similarly, agitation trials relied on members of the audience to piece together information about the case to offer a verdict. In contrast, Soviet cinema in the sound era was explicitly tasked with controlling and guiding the audience's comprehension of a given film's unambiguous ideological messages.

In these changed circumstances, the defendant's repentance was no longer seen as trustworthy. The accused "saboteurs" who were the show trial's protagonists came to be seen as conspirators against the state, while their acts to undermine the state's industrialization efforts were now widely understood to be premeditated. Because the state's underlying goal in all of this was to conceal the lack of progress in restructuring entire sectors of Soviet economy, the search for "saboteurs" was effectively a way of identifying scapegoats. Unlike the subjects of agitation trials soon after the revolution—the erring citizens of the 1920s who were not yet familiar with the new ways of life and work—the scapegoats of the 1930s could not be reintegrated; they could only be removed. Moreover, in the model that was invented for the Shakhty trial and subsequently perfected during the purges, the enemy was perceived as invisible, dangerous, and ubiquitous.[89]

The outlines of the show trials that the 1928 Shakhty affair introduced into Soviet culture contradict the apparent narrative of *The Return of Neitan Bekker*. The 1932 film, about events set in 1928 or 1929, appears to be about the successful reforging of a one-time Jewish refugee from the Pale of Settlement, who subsequently became an American worker, into a Soviet citizen on his return to his homeland. However, given the historical context and the resemblance of the circus arena to a symbolic courtroom, it is almost impossible not to see the film as also telling the story of a "foreign specialist" and "saboteur" who has not, in fact, been reintegrated and whose body remains too "socially crippled" for the Soviet collective to absorb. Stuttering, which begins to be noticeable gradually as Bekker attempts to admit the apparently misguided nature of his past beliefs, hints at this foreign specialist's forced loss of his voice. Bekker begins to lose the fluency of speech and hum a wordless *niggun* in what can be seen as a kind of symbolic manifestation of the inherited cultural traits that mark Bekker not only as a "wrecker" from a foreign land but also as an unreformed shtetl Jew.

Bekker was not the only Jewish protagonist on the Soviet screen to suffer such a fate. Pinya Kopman in *Seekers of Happiness,* released four years later in 1936, is a further evolution of this type of protagonist during the Stalin era. His story helps us better understand Bekker's. Pinya was born in the Pale of Settlement; his shtetl origins turned him into an aspiring capitalist in a foreign land, where he spent a period of time after leaving the Russian Empire and before resettling in the Soviet Union. Pinya dreams of owning a small clothing factory and being known as "Pinya Kopman, the King of Suspenders [*Pinya Kopman, korol' podtiazhek*]." Pinya has relocated to the USSR "from far away [*izdaleka*]," as he puts it. Though this location is never explicitly named, Pinya's residence prior to his return was likely in Palestine, then under British rule. Pinya says that he moved from a sunny place where he could pray to his heart's content; one contemporary review of the film noted that members of Pinya's family had "fle[d] from joblessness in 'the Promised Land' [*iz 'zemli obetovannoi'*] to the Soviet Union."[90] If Bekker's work on America's construction sites briefly turned the exploited laborer into an industrial "wrecker" and an advocate of worker exploitation, the patriarchal traditionalism from Pinya's shtetl days amplified his qualities as a *luftmentsh*—Yiddish for "man of air," someone who produces nothing of value for society. The figure of the *luftmentsh*, a "shtetl fabulist [*mestechkovyi fantazër*] and 'a man of air,' had been carefully developed in Yiddish literature," wrote one reviewer when the film premiered. He proceeded to commend the filmmakers and screenwriters involved in the making of *Seekers of Happiness* for having successfully "expressed this type through cinematic means."[91]

The one-time shtetl *luftmentsh* in *Seekers of Happiness* is even more avaricious than the typical "man of air" of Yiddish literature because of his foreign travels—or perhaps this trait is more noticeable against the backdrop of the supposed workers' paradise where he now finds himself. Pinya's story unfolds in Birobidzhan, designated as a territory for Jewish settlement on the model of other ethnonational territories in the USSR. Once there, Pinya finds himself at odds with both the members of his multigenerational family and other Jewish colonists. Every member of the Red Field (in Yiddish, *royter feld*) collective farm, where Pinya settles and which is led by a chairman known by his first name, Natan, is excited to get to work building the new socialist homeland for the Jewish people. However, Pinya has trouble believing that the people giddily felling trees and blasting rock to build roads are actually Jews. Jews, to Pinya, are people like him who aspire to make money rather than work in agriculture or construction for the sake of a nebulous collective good.

While in transit to Birobidzhan, Pinya had initially resisted joining his family in settling on the collective farm, but he relented after reading in the newspaper that another Jewish migrant, Katz, had found gold there. Katz had turned the gold over to the state, but Pinya does not intend to do any such thing. After arriving at the collective farm, he refuses to join others in their communal labor and strikes out on his own to look for treasure. He is so unconcerned about the collective's undertaking that he abandons his assigned watchman's post—this after declining more strenuous tasks—and thereby allows a herd of pigs unfettered access to the farm's vegetable patch.[92] As he occupies himself with panning for gold in a stream, Pinya hums a wordless Hasidic *niggun:* here, the film combines its focus on Pinya's personal greed with a soundtrack featuring a traditional Jewish melody. This combination of antisemitic tropes about Jewish avarice and religious traditionalism undergirds *Seekers of Happiness.*

In one key sequence in *Seekers of Happiness,* the film juxtaposes the images on the screen with a contrapuntal soundtrack, creating a contrast between what we see on screen and the sound we hear. A large group of collective farm members sing joyfully in unison as they work in the field. Their tune is interspersed with shots of Pinya, off searching for gold alone and far from others. Commenting on the camera's oscillating focus between Pinya panning for gold and his brother-in-law Lyova and sister-in-law Rosa working in the fields, one reviewer at the time noted that this sequence depicted "two philosophies of life, two systems of social relations, which collided in this film about struggle and contradictions."[93] The contrast between Pinya's greedy obsession with personal gain and the collective's priorities, expressed in their joyful singing about labor, becomes all the more apparent as Pinya, thinking he has discovered gold, resumes humming the *niggun*. Pinya is both an unreformed shtetl Jew and someone corrupted by fantasies of personal wealth acquired during his years of wandering after leaving the Pale but before resettling in the USSR. He is too far gone to be changed by the collectivist values his family members have joyously accepted.

Seekers of Happiness coarsely contrasts the corrupted and unchangeable Pinya with Natan, who is presented as an idealized version of what a Jew in the Soviet Union was supposed to become. As one reviewer noted at the time, Natan comes across as static and didactic, "merely a pale shadow" of a realistic collective farm chairman, but this accomplishes the trick of showing him as a regnant cultural type of the era.[94] Pinya, played by the actor Veniamin Zuskin, wears dark, baggy clothing and is filmed in hunched-over poses. He is weighed down and pulled toward the ground, as though toward the gold he is hoping to find. Natan, in contrast, tends to wear white and walks with his back straight. Pinya wears a cap on his head; at one point he uses it to gather soil he falsely thinks contains gold shavings (figure 4.6). This cap makes Pinya resemble the elderly man whose photograph hangs on the wall of the family's hut—presumably, Pinya's deceased father-in-law, Avrom-Ber. Avrom-Ber had died either before his family left the shtetl for Palestine or in Palestine before his family resettled in the USSR: his framed portrait shows a shtetl Jew wearing a traditional man's head covering.

Pinya's resemblance to Avrom-Ber, coupled with his thirst for gold, makes Pinya an example of something known in the Soviet parlance of the day as a "vestige of the past" (*perezhitok proshlogo*), a specter of the bygone prerevolutionary times haunting the new Soviet life. One reviewer, writing in the same issue of *Evening Moscow* that advertised the opening of Alexandrov's *Circus,* praised Zuskin's portrayal of Pinya and emphasized how well the actor captured the protagonist's "capitalist [*sobstvennicheskuiu*] psychology." Nonetheless, he criticized the actor for his "excessive emphasis [*izlishnii nazhim*] on the specificity of [Pinya's] gestures and speech intonations."[95] Pinya's depiction as a folkloric old-world Jew, however, is what leads him to reject the opportunity to become the Jewish exponent of the New Soviet Man that Natan, the chairman of the collective farm, has become.

In 1932, *The Return of Neitan Bekker* apparently offered the Jewish returnee a symbolic rehabilitation, even if coupled with symbolic punishment—Neitan

Figure 4.6. Pinya Kopman (played by Veniamin Zuskin) with a bottle of what he believes to be gold shavings (*Seekers of Happiness*, 1936). Courtesy of the National Center for Jewish Film.

Bekker, after all, may have lost his ability to speak but he still enjoyed his freedom. Four years later in 1936, however, *Seekers of Happiness* treats Pinya as a vestige of the shtetl and a foreign element subject to removal from the body politic. Having nearly murdered his brother-in-law Lyova after Lyova stumbles on him prospecting for gold, Pinya attempts to escape across the Amur River to Manchuria. Another man had already been arrested as a suspect in the near-fatal beating of Lëva, but the collective farm chairman Natan says that he saw footprints left by "boots with foreign tread patterns [*botinki s zagranichnymi shipami*]" near the scene of the crime. Natan immediately suspects Pinya and sets out in pursuit of him. A portrait of Stalin hangs in Natan's office, so the viewer comes to associate Natan's authority with the central power of the state embodied in its iconic leader. Pinya's arrest by uniformed agents of the state leads to a ritualized expulsion of the inassimilable foreigner, as the official rhetoric of the day demanded.

In more recent Jewish cultural memory of the Soviet era, *Seekers of Happiness* has come to represent the opposite of what the film intended to depict. In the decade after the USSR's dissolution, the oral historian Anna Shternshis conducted interviews with elderly Jews who grew up and came of age in the Soviet 1930s. Shternshis noted that her respondents remembered *Seekers of Happiness* being popular with Jewish audiences simply because "it was [a film] about Jews and Jewish life in the Soviet Union."[96] Pinya's old-world mannerisms evoked for Jewish viewers in the USSR a pleasant nostalgia for a culturally rich lost world. The film critic J. Hoberman has noted that the film "was occasionally revived in 1960s Moscow, appreciated as a rare example of 'Jewish humor.'" This was likely the period to which Shternshis's respondents traced their own memories.[97] The propagandistic intent of the film when it was made was to paint Pinya with a negative brush, the antithesis of both Natan and the film's other "positive" characters, Shternshis has noted. But she concludes that "in preferring Pinya's 'negative' character [. . .] the Jewish viewers were expressing their silent protest against Soviet rhetoric and ideology."[98] Miron Chernenko has made a similar point, writing that Zuskin's performance as Pinya shifted the popular memory about the film into the realm of comedy—comedy not based on humor intended to provoke disdain for the unproductive and unassimilable Jew but, instead, comedy that provokes nostalgia for the old world that Pinya was taken to represent.[99]

But even if some Jews from the former USSR fondly remembered their reactions to *Seekers of Happiness* decades after they first saw it, Pinya's arrest by the authorities, in a film released on the eve of Stalin's Great Terror, is hardly a comic matter. His arrest signals his removal not merely as a foreign body shaped outside the new state but also as an anachronistic vestige shaped in the shtetl prior to the new state's coming into existence. Pinya, if allowed to remain, would have prevented his family members, who were otherwise on their way toward becoming Jewish versions of the New Soviet Man, from thriving in the land they have returned to. "Go away, you stranger [*chuzhoi chelovek*]," says Dvoira, Pinya's elderly mother-in-law, as Pinya is arrested. There is no place for Pinya even among his kin.

At the conclusion of the film, Rosa, one of Dvoira's daughters and Pinya's sister-in-law, marries a non-Jewish man. Uncertain about the intermarriage at first, Dvoira turns to Natan for advice, just as she says she would have turned to a rabbi back in the shtetl. He approves of the union. His appearance and authority already identified with Stalin's, Natan enters Dvoira's family as a local incarnation of the leader referred to in Soviet culture as "Father of Peoples" (*otets narodov*).[100] At the wedding, Natan invites another of Dvoira's daughters, Pinya's wife Basya, for a dance. Though still married, she is newly available as a romantic prospect now that Pinya has been locked up. Pinya, symbolically identified with Dvoira's deceased husband and cast out as a vestige of the old world, is replaced by a man identified with Stalin. As Dvoira recalls the hardships and material deprivations of the shtetl, she offers a toast to "our new, wonderful life [*za nashu novuiu, zamechatel'nuiu zhizn'*]." The idealized Jewish version of the New Soviet Man has come into existence by literally displacing the Jew from the Pale of Settlement, who has proven to be too corrupted by his shtetl past and travels in foreign lands to join productive Soviet life.

Yet, decades later, it was the *luftmentsh* Pinya, not the collective farm chairman Natan, who evoked warm recollections among Jews in the Soviet Union. Natan, in contrast, was nearly erased from the popular imagination. The seemingly rigid reification of the two opposite Jewish types in *Seekers of Happiness*—the unreformed and the fully reformed—obscures the evolution of a far more ambiguous figure, the Soviet Jew. Commenting on the ending of *The Return of Neitan Bekker,* in which Tsale, the elderly shtetl Jew, teaches Jim, a Black American, how to sing a traditional Jewish tune, Harriet Murav has noted that the pair is "sitting on top of the vast scaffolding of a [Soviet] construction site." Emphasizing that the "wordless melody is a form of traditional prayer in the Hasidic community," Murav suggests that "[t]he vertical axis of the last shot, showing Mikhoels [who plays Tsale] perched at the very tip of the scaffolding, visually underscores the role of the Jew as *luftmensch*, 'a person of air,' and further suggests the link between the *luftmensch* and the divine."[101] Murav's framing of Tsale in *Neitan Bekker* echoes Shternshis's observations in centering Pinya within the collective cultural memory about *Seekers of Happiness*. But Murav leaves the film's central protagonist, Neitan Bekker, out of the picture.

In fact, the shot Murav describes is not the last shot of the film. In the shot that follows it, we see Neitan Bekker again, picking up his father's *niggun*. The *niggun* offers Bekker a way to disguise his newly emergent stutter, a marker of the body that can never be fully assimilated into the Soviet collective. The low angle of the camera in the film's final sequence is a cinematic trick that underscores the importance of a protagonist by showing him from below. The central figure here is not Tsale or Jim; it is, instead, Neitan Bekker.

Bekker is the Soviet Jew, a figure that is neither the unreformed shtetl *luft-mentsh* made all the more ungrounded by his foreign travels nor the Jew who might have hoped to become the New Soviet Man of propagandistic clichés. The figure of the Soviet Jew—in this case, a man from the shtetl who has taken a long detour through capitalist foreign lands—might have been made a member of the Soviet collective but he still carries remnants of the shtetl inside him. These vestigial aspects thwart this figure's full assimilation into the Soviet collective.

* * *

The establishing shot of *Seekers of Happiness* focuses on a ship adrift at sea, ferrying Dvoira and her family to the Soviet Union. The sequence that follows carries an extra-diegetic soundtrack—a song in Yiddish about the interminable nature of Jewish wanderings around the world: "*di velt iz groys . . .*" the song goes, "the world is big." The camera then focuses on Pinya, who hums and mumbles in Russian to a tune of his own: "We're traveling, traveling, and keep not arriving." The film that opens on endless water concludes on terra firma with the wedding of Pinya's sister-in-law to a non-Jewish man. In the final sequence of the film, representatives of multiple Soviet peoples dance to the merry musical score composed for the film by Isaak Dunaevsky.[102] As the music plays, Dvoira toasts her new homeland. "Pour some wine," she pronounces, the camera framing her in a low-angle shot signaling the importance of the message she is delivering, "and we'll drink to our motherland and to those who gave us such a good life!" Dvoira's toast presents the Soviet Union as a kind of "promised land" where Jews— long a wandering people and still a wandering folk at the beginning of the film—can settle and live in harmony as part of a happy extended family of nations.

Of all the endings in the films discussed in this chapter, Dvoira's toast is the most articulate. It both conveys the prevailing ideological message of the day and concludes a narrative arc that has, over the course of the film, primed the viewer to clearly hear and receive Dvoira's words. Other films about returning Jews lack such coherent endings. Lev Kuleshov's *Gorizont,* which depicts a protagonist's flight from Tsarist Russia to America and his subsequent return to Bolshevik Russia around 1918, ends with his defection from the U.S. Army's counterrevolutionary forces to the Red Army's side. In the film's concluding moments, the narrative jumps forward a decade and a half to the era of the First Five-Year Plan; its sudden final sequence shows Gorizont as a train engineer. As a reviewer for the *New York Herald Tribune* wrote on the film's U.S. release in 1933, the scene of Gorizont "finally driving a locomotive in present-day Russia is curiously unrelated to the earlier episodes," which set up no smooth ideological transition to such an abrupt ending.[103] Dubson's *The Border* and Shpis and Mil'man's *The Return of Neitan Bekker* also end on more ambiguous notes of ideological uplift: the protagonists of each film make ideological declarations about the happy return of Jews to the Soviet Union but become inarticulate while doing so. In both films, the protagonists' words dissolve into wordless melodies.

But even with Dvoira's toast to the happy life of Jews and their supposedly permanent settlement in the Soviet Union, *Seekers of Happiness* also contains traces of the peripatetic, in-between figure of the Soviet Jew. These traces can be found in the details provided about Dvoira's family's journey from Palestine to Birobidzhan—the journey that seemingly represented the transition from interminable Jewish wanderings to rootedness in the USSR. To get to Birobidzhan from Palestine, the family must have disembarked at a port of arrival, likely Odessa, where they boarded a train that, via Kiev and Moscow, eventually took them to the Far East. The railroad sequence in the film opens inside the train car, with a left-to-right tracking shot of the passengers moving against the right-to-left direction of the train's motion as detected from the landscape seen through the train car's windows. The progression of the film's narrative sets the passengers' displacement against the direction marked by the forward-moving train. Although the Jewish returnees to the Soviet Union appear to be traveling in the only conceivable ideological direction—forward, toward the proverbial bright future—they are being moved as though in the opposite direction. The scene on the train, a typical if overused symbol of forward progress, also suggests a countercurrent of a history whose outcome is far from clear.

Well into its journey across the Soviet interior, and amidst the train passengers' nervous discussions of what life would be like in the new place, a peculiar figure appears: a man playing a mournful tune on his clarinet (figure 4.7). He identifies the tune as "Israel's Lament on the Banks of the Amur" (Plach' Izrailia na beregakh Amura). The title of the tune calls to mind the lines of Psalm 137 concerning the exile of the people of Israel to ancient

Figure 4.7. The unnamed clarinetist playing a melody he calls "Israel's Lament on the Banks of the Amur." *Seekers of Happiness,* Belgoskino, 1936.

Babylon in the sixth century BCE: "By the rivers of Babylon, there we sat down and wept, when we remembered Zion." By transposing the toponym of "the rivers of Babylon" onto the "banks of the Amur," the river that forms the border between Manchuria and the Jewish Autonomous Region where the passengers on the train are headed, the song turns Birobidzhan not into a Soviet Zion, as it was commonly depicted in official rhetoric, but into yet another version of Babylon, one more stage in a long Jewish history of dispersal and wandering. The destination inside the USSR, touted as the Jewish promised land, becomes a site of Jewish exile.

The man playing the clarinet, apparently speaking to his own experience in the Far East, advises the migrants that it will be hard in Birobidzhan. Pinya takes a keen interest in the clarinetist's words: "Quite the motherland you've got there! [*Nu vot vam i rodina!*]," he comments, sensing in the clarinetist's story and tune a critique of the state's propaganda about Birobidzhan. Natan, in contrast, responds by inviting Pinya's family to join the collective farm he chairs when they arrive at their destination. The visual details of the sequence suggest that the man with the clarinet is, counterintuitively, returning from Birobidzhan even though he—like Dvoira's family—is aboard the train headed to the region. At the end of the sequence, the man puts on his hat and parts with Dvoira's family, bidding them farewell and asking them to write him a letter if they find their new life satisfactory. The strange man with the clarinet appears to take his leave, even though it would be impossible to step off a moving train. The unidirectional narrative of *Seekers of Happiness* appears to be somehow reversed as the film depicts the crucial part of the family's journey to their Soviet destination. Just as Pinya and his family arrive, there are Jews—some with experience abroad—who are departing or attempting to depart from there. This story of the Jewish return to the Soviet Union coexists with a narrative that implies a different kind of Jewish mobility: one that questions Jewish return to and resettlement in the USSR.

The man with the clarinet resembles the mythic figure of the Wandering Jew. He speaks of his experience in Birobidzhan using language that draws on the storied Jewish exile. Some of this language is articulated through music that connects the history of Jewish displacement from the Land of Israel to the Jews' ongoing relocation to the supposed "promised land" in the Soviet Far East. The clarinetist speaks as someone who has been wandering for a long time. His reverse movement relative to the onward direction of the train creates a figure moving against the onward push of Soviet modernity. The figure of the Wandering Jew moves circuitously, over the many centuries and geographies of the myth's transmission and against the linear march of modern time. *Seekers of Happiness* contains traces of a counternarrative about the failure of return to the USSR within its larger, more apparent narrative of such a return taking place. As I noted at the beginning of this chapter, Ostap Bender of Il'f and Petrov's *The Little Golden Calf* claimed that the "Jewish question" had been resolved through the fact of the Soviet Union's very existence. In the counternarrative, visible in the contours of the train sequence in *Seekers of Happiness,* the Wandering Jew appears to have escaped the territory designated as his final home.

The Wandering Jew, as Karen Grumberg has noted, is a Gothic figure associated with the endless nature of Jewish displacement. He reflects the instability inherent in modernity and has provided a screen onto which Europeans have projected anxieties about these transformations since the early modern period.¹⁰⁴ "It is [. . .] the very instability embodied in the figure of the Wandering Jew, and in the Jews in general," writes Galit Hasan-Rokem, "which has served as one of the factors by which European consciousness has interpreted itself as rooted in stability and locality."¹⁰⁵ In *Seekers of Happiness,* the Wandering Jew is the remnant of the past that serves as an unwelcome reminder of the unsettledness inherent in all modernization projects, including the Soviet one. In contributing its traces, it muddles the film's seemingly Manichean view of the anachronistic globe-trotting shtetl Jew, represented by Pinya, as set against the Jew as a New Soviet Man, represented by Natan. The emergent Soviet Jew, a partially transformed figure that contains the unsettled traces of the Wandering Jew, is somewhere in between these polarities, and it haunts the Soviet project with its continued presence.

The Return of Neitan Bekker—the central cultural text of the 1930s about the return of Jews to the USSR—contains traces of this haunting presence. Writing about sound in Stalin-era cinema, Lilya Kaganovsky has noted that Shpis and Mil'man's work was one of a number of early Soviet sound films that emphasized "non-Russian speech as incoherent or incomprehensible (song, delirium, wordless melody) and, more importantly, as 'traditional' and premodern."¹⁰⁶ The wordless *niggun,* which the Jewish returnee to the USSR abruptly picks up in the concluding shot of the film, suspends the possibility that the Soviet Jew and the New Soviet Man could ever be one and the same. On a circuitous journey from the prerevolutionary shtetl, via foreign lands, and back to the USSR, the figure of the Soviet Jew can never fully separate from the Wandering Jew's ceaseless travels or ever learn to speak in ways that don't contain lingering traces of its inassimilable past.

5

The Soviet Jew as a Trickster

Isaac Babel and Hershele Ostropoler

On March 16, 1918, five months after the Bolshevik Revolution, Isaac Babel's short story "Shabos-nakhamu" was published in Petrograd's daily, *The Evening Star (Vecherniaia zvezda).*[1] The work was an adaptation of a tale about Hershele Ostropoler, a trickster from Yiddish folklore. Its subtitle, "From the *Hershele* Cycle," presented the story as an installment in a series. In the years since its publication, critics have viewed "Shabos-nakhamu" not as part of an explicit cycle like Babel's well-known *Odessa Tales* and *Red Cavalry* but, rather, as simply a young writer's one-time attempt to adapt a character from Jewish folklore.[2] Some have taken this story, alongside a few others, as proof that Babel was definitively a "Jewish writer"; that is, an author conversant with Jewish literary, folkloric, and traditional sources and uniquely suited to subtly communicate distinctly Jewish cultural content to savvy readers.[3]

I argue in this chapter, however, that the Hershele cycle that Babel signaled in "Shabos-nakhamu" did in fact materialize—but not in the way his more discrete cycles of short stories did. Instead, Hershele functions as a thematic link, a critical accretion of motifs and associations across Babel's oeuvre. Babel transposes the figure of Hershele from the domain of Yiddish folklore, nurtured in the former Pale of Settlement, into the realm of Russian literature as a model for the figure of the Soviet Jew. In the guise of Babel's Hershele, the Soviet Jew reaches beyond specifically Jewish concerns and becomes, through his Soviet-era engagement with Jewish cultural intertexts, a trickster learning to navigate the Soviet project writ large.

In "Shabos-nakhamu," Hershele sets out to earn money after his wife berates him for failing to provide for their family. He embarks on a sixty-mile journey south from Ostropol, the Ukrainian shtetl where he lives, to Medzhibozh.

A peculiar opportunity awaits him there: he will become a jester to Borukhl, the depressive leader of the most powerful dynasty within Hasidism, the new spiritual movement sweeping across East European Jewish communities at the time. The story unfolds on the road as Hershele undergoes a transformation of his identity. This transformation, in turn, provides Babel with a model both for constantly reinventing himself as an author and for mapping out the figure of the Soviet Jew.

Hungry and freezing in the middle of his journey, Hershele stumbles on a tavern, where he meets Zelda, the tavern keeper's pregnant wife. Home alone, she asks whether Hershele knows when Shabos-nakhamu is expected to arrive. Zelda shares with Hershele that her husband was waiting for that time to purchase a new wig for her and to take a trip out of town to seek a blessing from his rebbe that the child she is carrying be a boy. She is upset about these delays and speculates about Shabos-nakhamu: "I think that this is someone from the world to come, right?"[4] As far as she knows, the long-awaited Shabos-nakhamu is a guest set to appear at her doorstep. Seizing the opportunity created by her question, Hershele responds that *he* is Shabos-nakhamu and that he has, as Zelda suspected, arrived from the world to come. He tells Zelda that he is famished because food is scarce in the world beyond the grave and that the woman's relatives already there are cold and in need of warm clothes. Zelda finds comfort in Hershele's assurance that she could help ease her relatives' situation in the afterlife by treating him as a courier between the living and the dead. The tavern keeper's wife feeds Hershele a generous meal and gives him clothes intended for her deceased relatives. Hershele, fed and supplied with warm garments, walks off with his loot.

The tavern keeper eventually catches up with the thief in the forest. Having anticipated this eventuality, Hershele had stripped naked and hidden his things. When the tavern keeper encounters Hershele, he sees a naked man standing by a tree. Hershele tells him that he had fallen victim to the same impostor who had robbed Zelda. Hershele convinces the tavern keeper to "lend" him his clothes and his horse so that he can find the criminal. He leaves the man standing naked by the tree, picks up the things he had hidden at the edge of the forest, and resumes his journey to Medzhibozh.[5]

Hershele uses linguistic tricks, a staple of folkloric trickster tales, at each step of his story.[6] Because Zelda lacks the systematic religious education that has traditionally been available only to men, she appears to be unaware that

"Shabos-nakhamu" is not a person at all but rather a date on the Jewish calendar. The name, meaning "the Sabbath of Comforting," comes from the section of the Book of Isaiah read in synagogues on one particular Saturday each year: "be comforted, be comforted, my people" (*nakhamu, nakhamu, 'ami*). The day is the restorative Sabbath (in Yiddish, *Shabos* or *Shabes*) immediately following the summertime fast of Tisha B'Av, which commemorates the destructions of both the First and Second Temples in Jerusalem and concludes a three-week period of ritual mourning. Tisha B'Av and the ceremonial cycle around it, including the Sabbath of Comforting, demarcate foundational aspects of Jewish cultural memory: the loss of sovereignty and of a ritual center in ancient Jerusalem and the beginning of centuries of exile and diaspora.

In accordance with tradition, some activities must be delayed until the end of this three-week ritual cycle: buying new clothes, preparing festive foods, and sexual intercourse are prohibited during the mourning period and especially in its final nine days. At the time of Hershele's arrival, Tisha B'Av had just passed and, following the fast, the tavern keeper had resumed his work schedule and rode off to take care of some pressing financial matters. Zelda, obligated to stay at home to cook for the festive Sabbath ahead, had been promised that she could take up her delayed business only after Shabos-nakhamu had come and gone. Sidelined, she has reasons to be upset.

Hershele arrives at the tavern to find Zelda unhappy with both her husband and the terms of the pious lifestyle that he controls. "I didn't study [Jewish texts] with anyone [*Ia ni u kogo ne uchilas'*]," she tells him. The prescriptive nature of Jewish practice is as alien to her as the ritualized comforting, which in any case doesn't address her desire to feel at ease.[7] For Zelda, the "Shabos-nakhamu" she was told to expect could just as well have been the man now identifying himself as a guest from the other world. The comfort he offers is more tangible than anything regimented that Jewish ritual could provide. Hershele exploits the opportunity that Zelda has given him because of her lack of systematic knowledge of Judaism.

When he appropriates the temporal concept of Shabos-nakhamu as his name, Hershele reimagines a set of traditional customs. Meanwhile, he gives the appearance of comforting Zelda without explicitly dismantling the calendar of Jewish observance: now that Tisha B'Av is over, he is not violating Jewish law by acquiring new clothes and feasting on celebratory foods. With or without Hershele's mischief, the actual Shabos-nakhamu is still going to arrive exactly when it's supposed to, but there is room for the trickster to strike in the short window of time before it does.

As a date on the Jewish calendar, Shabos-nakhamu remains part of what James C. Scott has called the "public transcript"—a culture's official record that wields prescriptive power over the members of the community defined by its tenets.[8] In Judaism's public transcript, Tisha B'Av and the Sabbath of Comforting are dates that establish the centrality of the Temple and of the memory of its existence long ago to the legal, religious, and communal system developed after ancient Jerusalem's demise. In contrast, when Zelda takes Shabos-nakhamu to be a person, she contributes to a "hidden transcript," one that exists in parallel to normative religion, offers the underprivileged a space for airing grievances, and lets elites respond to those grievances without meaningfully ceding any of their power.[9] Zelda's contribution to the hidden transcript—a subversive communication by a woman, a member of one of Judaism's underprivileged groups—challenges the tenets of a culture arbitrated by men. Zelda's intervention may well have been an uninformed act. At the same time, she might have feigned ignorance so as to take symbolic revenge on her husband and the patriarchal system. Perhaps, perfectly aware of what Shabos-nakhamu was, Zelda acted as though she were uninformed, knowing that her ignorance would have been believable—for the purpose of getting back at her husband, jolting him out of complacency, and alerting him to her needs. Zelda may have played by the rules of the hidden transcript, deploying her subject position as a woman to reveal the patriarchal structure of the system in which she lived.

Hershele, meanwhile, enacts a multivalent performance in his encounter with Zelda. The trickster seizes on the alternative meaning of Shabos-nakhamu that Zelda suggested and participates in promulgating the hidden transcript in his own struggle against the well-to-do Jews, waged not on gender but on class grounds. Unlike Zelda, however, Hershele has access to the community of learned men and displays no interest in dismantling the male-centered culture of Judaism as such. Hershele's livelihood as a jester to powerful men presupposes the unequal gender roles built into traditional East European Jewish culture. An intermediary between the oppressed and the powerful, who feels affinity to both groups, Hershele puts on a kind of double mask. The trickster exploits cracks in the larger ideological system to destabilize the culture's coherence through a bit of mischief. At the same time, with Zelda's prodding, he opts for "active manipulation of rituals of subordination to turn them to good personal advantage" and uses an ideological pretense of resistance to Judaism's prescriptive practices to camouflage his own interest in material survival.[10]

Hershele acquires food and clothing while preserving the religious and social system in which Zelda lives. Within the boundaries of what's permitted by Jewish custom, Hershele cuts an iconoclastic figure while keeping those traditional boundaries intact. His tall tales about Zelda's relatives in the world to come prove comforting to the despondent woman: in effect, the trickster's stories console Zelda better than traditional customs. When he obtains food and clothing for his own survival, Hershele associates himself with the promise of comfort and merriment offered by the commemoration of an historical tragedy. His wit pokes holes in the fabric of lives centered on piety and ritual observance without ripping that fabric apart. Isaac Babel, publishing "Shabos-nakhamu" at the start of his career, effectively set up Hershele Ostropoler, the Jewish trickster, as a model for his authorial persona. The figure of the Soviet Jew that I observe across texts and over the course of Babel's entire career would follow a similar trajectory.

* * *

Hershele Ostropoler, whose career as a trickster gave rise to numerous prerevolutionary Yiddish folktales, was, in fact, an historical figure. He is said to have once been a butcher in the town of Ostropol in the late eighteenth century. Either because he didn't earn enough in that line of work or because he made too many enemies in town with his jokes, he found himself wandering around Ukraine earning money by his wit alone.[11] Hershele's wittiness was linked to the pietistic movement of Hasidism, a joyful and populist Jewish movement that painted the Rabbinic Judaism of the time as overly cerebral and legalistic. Hasidism brought much-needed rejoicing to Jewish communities in Ukraine and Poland several decades after the Cossack uprising of 1648, which killed tens of thousands of Jews.[12] Like the mass movements led by messianic pretenders Shabtai Tzvi and Joseph Frank, also following the 1648 massacres, Hasidism tapped into an overflowing well of messianic expectations instigated by the communal tragedy. Hershele was rumored to have had a familial connection to at least one victim of the 1648 violence: Shimshen, the rabbi of Ostropol, who sacrificed himself to spare his community.[13]

The historical Hershele's career as a wandering entertainer brought him to Rebbe Borukhl's court in Medzhibozh. The figure of the rebbe—an affectionate form of "rabbi"—is central to Hasidism. Each of the movement's many sects coalesced around one rebbe, a righteous communal leader and authority figure who instructed his followers through parables and songs. This group of followers was collectively referred to as the rebbe's *hoyf*—his court.[14] The Hasidic movement itself had been founded by Borukhl's grandfather, Rabbi Israel Ben Eliezer, more commonly known as the Baal Shem Tov (which translates from Hebrew as "Master of the Good Name")—or, as the Besht, the acronym of that name. Medzhibozh, where the Besht first established Hasidism, became the most prominent dynastic seat of Hasidic power. By employing Hershele as his court jester, Borukhl placed Heshele near the physical and symbolic center of the Hasidic movement and its claims to authority.

Although integral to Hasidism's emphasis on responding to despair with joy, Hershele's humor also offered a comic salve for lingering disappointment with the movement itself. Like all messianic movements, the redemptive expectations attached to Hasidim were inevitably inflated and unrealized. The ensuing disappointment and thwarted hopes mirrored those associated with other early modern messianic movements.[15] Some accounts locate the origin of Borukhl's melancholia in his inability to hasten the Messiah's arrival.[16] Borukhl's followers, struggling to live with a depressive leader in a community ostensibly dedicated to joy, invited Hershele to entertain their rebbe.

Though jesters were not uncommon in the larger Hasidic courts of Ukraine, Hershele became by far the most prominent jester in Yiddish lore.[17] He appears in folk narratives where Hasidism fails in practice to offer a joyful corrective to Judaism's elite scholarly tradition. Charismatic leaders, the object of so much admiration and expectation, were bound to be accused of human failures and fakery because of the inevitable discrepancies between their mythologized personalities and reality. Hershele is, in Ruth R. Wisse's formulation, a "comic corrective to the corrective, a countervoice within the revolutionary religious movement, the irrepressible and joyous skeptic who cannot be inhibited from telling the truth."[18] But Hershele does not neatly resemble this romanticized portrait of a subversive dissident. He disguises his words as humor because he is inhibited from telling the truth openly. The "truth" in Hershele's jokes, moreover, relies on his preserving, rather than overturning, the status quo: without a larger system in need of them, Hershele's jokes would lack a context in which to circulate. His jokes could deflate the authority of the rebbe just enough to expose his human foibles to his followers but not too much so as not to topple the entire system. Hershele was complicit in maintaining rather than dismantling the authority of Hasidism over people's lives, even as he cut it down to size and used humor to make it more comprehensible to the movement's followers. On the one hand, Hershele's trickery did reveal some cracks within the boundaries of the existing Hasidic power structure. On the other hand, cutting more vigorously or destructively through Hasidism's authority would have endangered both the Hasidic movement and Hershele's own livelihood and source of creativity.

When, in Babel's story, Hershele offers Zelda the consolation she seeks, he subverts the parameters created by the very religious tradition that has conditioned Zelda to see him as a concrete agent who could alleviate her grief. Hershele does not question the premise of the custom. Rather, he sheds a tiny bit of light onto the workings of the belief system, but the system itself remains intact: though a subversive figure, Hershele is not an advocate for dismantling authority.

In "Shabos-nakhamu," Babel transplants Hershele from the Hasidic milieu into the context of Bolshevik Russia. This Hershele offers a corrective voice to a new cultural system that, like Hasidism, failed to supply its followers with the relief it had promised them but, at the same time, he helps maintain the system itself. Babel's protagonist does this not only in the context of Hasidism, the ostensible subject of the story, but also within the emerging political and cultural system in which this story appears. Both allegorically and by analogy, Babel's Hershele, given this figure's appearance in 1918, challenges not just Hasidism but also the messianic ideology embodied in the new Bolshevik state; he anticipates its failure to deliver on its utopian promises while keeping its emerging structure intact.

When Babel's story about Hershele came out in March 1918 in Petrograd, the city was devastated, and the country was in the first months of a brutal civil war. Babel re-deployed Hershele during the Bolsheviks' war against Poland in 1920, which brought the writer into close contact with Hasidic Jews in the former Pale of Settlement. Babel gestured in Hershele's direction against the backdrop of the Stalin-era's universalizing discourse about the "brotherhood of the peoples," which sought to erase deep-seated ethnic and religious markers while highlighting some of the differences within the USSR's diverse population as a way of appealing to all Soviet peoples, whatever their backgrounds. During a time charged both with ideological promise and large-scale devastation, Babel's Hershele had a role to play that resembled the one played by the historical Hershele in the context of Hasidism. As a figure of merriment and relief, he could poke holes in the system without destroying it as such.

In "Shabos-nakhamu," Babel's Hershele prefigures the development of a rich tradition of tricksters, swindlers, and conmen in Soviet culture, particularly during the early Soviet period. Analyzing Ostap Bender, the protagonist of popular novels by Ilya Il'f and Evgeny Petrov, Sheila Fitzpatrick has noted that the trickster's success was predicated on mastering the new Bolshevik idiom while its rules were still fluid and not clear to all Soviet citizens.[19] Such fictional protagonists were based on real contemporary individuals who knew how to manipulate the evolving language of Soviet officialdom.[20] Their swindles involved playing in the interstices of what their victims understood—and did not yet understand—about the rules of the new state power and rhetorically adapting the state's rules without subjecting them to scrutiny. Tricksters, both in real life and in early Soviet cultural production, evolved in tandem with the New Soviet Man. In a polity full of pre-Soviet people trying to "reforge" themselves, no one could remain what he or she had been: everyone had to become an impostor. If Soviet culture depended on the construction of a new person in a new society, "impersonation, the trickster's specialty" could be an integral part of the game.[21] Within the repertoire of folkloric tricksters, the act of becoming someone else was nothing new, but when Babel drew on the Hershele narrative shortly after the revolution, he underscored its unique utility in the early days of the Bolshevik state.

Trickster figures permeated Soviet culture and mediated between the symbolic production of Soviet ideology and the real-life experiences of Soviet citizens. Mark Lipovetsky has argued that the closed reality of Soviet society in practice existed alongside a parallel symbolic reality that was enabled by its constantly shifting goals and unclear expectations. Historical and fictional actors operated in two "parallel realities," symbolic and practical, and existed alongside "each other and constantly collide[d] with one another in the space of subjectivity but lack[ed] any systematic mechanisms for social communication with each other."[22] The trickster emerges from the mostly closed Soviet society and, through his use of symbols, creates interstitial zones of openness within it. In Babel's work, Hershele relies on a compensatory mechanism that converts cynicism into a form of merriment; this process yields ways of negotiating the horror, violence, and ideological coercion of the early Soviet years.

At the roadside tavern in "Shabos-nakhamu," Hershele takes on the "identity" of the Sabbath of Comforting during the transitional period between a mournful day of fasting and the day of consolation that follows soon after. The anthropologist Victor Turner has famously noted that "liminal entities are neither here nor there; they are betwixt and between the positions assigned and arrayed by law, custom [and] convention."[23] Building on Turner's connecting liminality with rituals that upend the existing social order but are nonetheless balanced by the existence of that order, Lipovetsky has suggested that the Soviet trickster "implants anti-structural elements into the social and cultural order, uncovering and at times creating liminal zones *inside* hierarchies and stratifications."[24] The Soviet trickster, like his Hasidic relation, is not an antinomian creature: he does not destroy existing structures but rather plays within them and, in the process, manipulates and expands their meaning. Babel's Hershele becomes one of the prototypes of the figure of the Soviet Jew as a trickster who enters and disorders ideologically charged spaces while safeguarding them at the same time. Ever the peripatetic creature, he does so with the help of the cultural baggage of Jewish allusions that he brings with him.

Language is the trickster's primary tool for creating alternative meanings and playing on ambivalences, oppositions, and discrepancies in the larger cultural and linguistic sphere in which he operates. Writing about the Signifying Monkey, a figure from Black American folklore, Henry Louis Gates Jr., has suggested that the structure of the trickster's language sits at the intersection of "signification"—the literal meaning of a linguistic sign—and "Signification" (capital S), the use of rhetorical games and vernacular or nonstandard English. Gates maps these two processes onto Ferdinand de Saussure's semiotic model of the two relational axes of language along which sentences are formed. Whereas signification occurs on the syntagmatic axis, which specifies the rules by which words can be configured into sentences, the more unpredictable and playful process of Signification occurs on the paradigmatic axis, which allows for the substitution of the sentence's different elements. The trickster is the master of both Signification and the paradigmatic axis: he deftly substitutes alternative words and meanings and takes on the injustices of the surrounding reality with the help of clever disguises. "Whereas signification depends for order and coherence on the exclusion of unconscious associations which any given word yields at any given time," notes Gates, "Signification luxuriates in the inclusion of the free play of these associative rhetorical and semantic relations."[25] Gates's trickster "luxuriates" in his clever quips: the aesthetic nature of trickery is something meant to be enjoyed.

However, a successful trick's enjoyment has a somber underside: it disrupts but does not abolish the power of those who are the butt of the joke. Puns and punch lines get chosen from the paradigmatic axis but are fit into the expectations of existing syntagmatic structures because the undisguised meaning can never be stated directly: the linguistic trickery "allow[s] us to bring the repressed meanings of a word, the meanings that lie in wait on the paradigmatic axis of discourse, to bear upon the syntagmatic axis."[26] Sigmund Freud's theory of humor rests on a similar premise: that which brings merriment is inextricably tied to that which is repressed, unarticulated, and cannot be looked at directly. The Signifying Monkey eviscerates the powerful in America's slave-owning society before an audience of the weak who find relief in his verbal tricks. The oppressive institution of slavery remains intact, however, and the pain it inflicts cannot be avoided. Babel's Hershele also resorts to tricks to avoid looking directly at difficult issues: his trickery allows him both to subvert the complicated reality around him and preserve the world order that is coming into being.

Hershele is a remnant of Yiddish folklore from the Pale of Settlement that seeped into Babel's work during the early Bolshevik years. Once a part of the Hasidic cultural world, Hershele became dislodged from that context. Likewise, the Signifying Monkey—originally a sidekick of Esu-Elegbara, a trickster in several African cultures—became a standalone figure in Black folklore in America.[27] Esu-Elegbara, an independent character in folk narratives on the African continent, did not survive the passage on slave ships across the Atlantic. The Signifying Monkey, dislodged and diffused on his own, took on the features of an archaic—but no longer directly accessible—cultural tradition after a major historical upheaval displaced entire communities to new locations and new cultural and political contexts.[28] Following S. An-sky's expeditions to collect and, in effect, salvage Jewish folklore in parts of the Pale of Settlement on the eve of the First World War and coinciding with the larger flowering of neoprimitivism in Russian modernism, Hershele's debut in Isaac Babel's "Shabos-nakhamu" in 1918 can be seen in the context of a larger concern with the recovery of preindustrial cultural artifacts amidst rapid modernization and industrialization.[29] Babel's Hershele, it bears emphasizing, is not synonymous with the Hershele of Jewish folklore and is not a nostalgic figure through which Babel seeks to re-create the old world. Hershele's peripatetic existence and reliance on linguistic substitution, trickery, and playing on more than a single side at once allow Babel to adopt the trickster's playfulness as a model of authorship. This strategy enables him to become a skilled literary interpreter of the Soviet experience and a chronicler of the emergence of the Soviet Jew.

* * *

All sightings of Hershele in Isaac Babel's work are connected to walking; these many acts of walking, in turn, enable the subversion of linguistic and ideological itineraries. In "Shabos-nakhamu," Babel links Hershele's linguistic tricks to walking on foot, and Hershele's peregrinations in this story model his wanderings through the writer's work. Hershele's walks—starting with "Shabos-nakhamu" and continuing into later stories where the Hershele motif is traceable—include detours that create alternative routes through space, time, and language as he navigates the terrain of the immediate postrevolutionary years and well into the Soviet experience. Through Hershele, Babel locates the figure of the Soviet Jew as a trickster who, by linking speech and walking, illuminates gaps between the language and practices associated with state ideology (figure 5.1).

Babel's Russian-language story about Hershele, which transposes the scattered culture of the Pale into another language, differs considerably from its likely Yiddish original. Hershele stories were part of the prolific folkloric corpus that circulated as part of oral culture, so Babel would not have needed to rely on a printed source. However, at least one version of the Yiddish

Figure 5.1. Isaac Babel in 1915. Courtesy of the Odessa Literary Museum.

original of "Shabos-nakhamu," one-fifth the length of Babel's subsequent re-make, was published in 1890 and again in 1895, around the time of Babel's birth. The story, bearing the same title as Babel's own, appeared in a chapbook of Hershele stories published by the Bletnitsky brothers' publishing house, based in Babel's native Odessa (figure 5.2).[30] In addition to the publishing house, the Bletnitsky brothers also ran a bookstore in Odessa where these chapbooks would have been available; given their frequent republication, they would have easily circulated among Babel's relatives and other people in the city who would have likely told him the story when he was a child.

In contrast to the Yiddish folktale as it was published in the 1890s, Babel's 1918 text is an inventive rewriting of the narrative. Babel displays a commanding grasp of the Russian language's linguistic possibilities, effectively turning the Yiddish folktale into a story of authorial self-invention in the mold of his other meta-literary texts like "My First Fee."[31] By maximizing the specific expressive capacity of Russian and adopting the folkloric

Figure 5.2. Title page of *The Joyous Hershele Ostropoler* (*Dos freylikhe Hershele Ostropolier*), published by Odessa's Bletnitsky brothers and printed in Warsaw (1895). The imprint of the Bletnitsky brothers, with reference to their location in Odessa, in Russian, Hebrew, and German is on the page facing the title page.

trickster's methods as his own, Babel invents a kind of literary Russian suitable both for his creative intervention and as a tool in the creative arsenal of the Soviet Jew.

Let's compare those differences between the Yiddish folktale about Shabos-nakhamu and Babel's version of this story that pertain to acts of walking. The Yiddish story opens:

> The tavern keeper's wife heard from her husband that it was soon going to be [*az es darf bald zayn*] Shabos-nakhamu. She was certain that Shabos-nakhamu was a man from the other world. It just so happened that the tavern keeper was away from home precisely when the destitute Hershele Ostropoler arrived [*iz . . . ongekumen*] at the tavern. The

tavern keeper's wife thought that this was a poor man going around begging. She gave him charity and asked him: "They say that Shabos-nakhamu is coming soon [*me'zogt az Shabos-nakhamu darf bald onkumen*]. Has he already been at your house? [*bay aykh iz er shoyn geven?*]" Hershele, having heard what the woman said, had already figured out that she wasn't particularly bright, and answered her promptly: "What kind of a question is that? I am Shabos-nakhamu!"[32]

In this Yiddish passage, the verbs that allude to the proximate arrival of the mysterious Shabos-nakhamu switch between the future-oriented "coming soon" and the past tense "arrived" (*darf bald onkumen* and *ongekumen*), and also between "was soon going to be" and "has already been" (*darf bald zayn* and *shoyn geven*). The woman, left nameless in this version, immediately signals to Hershele that she expects Shabos-nakhamu to be a man. The verbs used in the story accentuate the woman's apparent stupidity: what she hears from her husband literally means, "It will soon be" Shabos-nakhamu—a locution that clearly alludes to an event or period of time, rather than to a person. However, when she asks Hershele about the proximate arrival of Shabos-nakhamu she talks about "him [*er*]" as "coming soon." The very premise of her question anthropomorphizes Shabos-nakhamu as a man, even though the language her husband used earlier in the story did not suggest this possibility. In this Yiddish version, Hershele's ruse is wholly enabled by the woman's stupidity; she, in turn, is simply a dupe.

Babel's story in Russian, however, pursues linguistic details absent in the Yiddish text and, in so doing, recasts the folkloric material into a new idiom. Now, the tavern keeper's wife becomes a cocreator of Hershele's trickery through turns of phrase available in Russian, even though the text makes clear its conceit that the language of exchange in the story could only have been Yiddish—Zelda and Hershele would not have spoken Russian to each other. Babel produces a kind of "translated" Russian version of an implied Yiddish original, in which he explores possibilities available only in Russian, the target language of such a "translation."

The linguistic subtlety Babel exploits is the Russian language's complex and precise distinctions around verbs of motion. Specifically, Russian grammar distinguishes between verbs for motion that occurs with an aid of a horse or vehicle and verbs indicating movement by foot. Hershele first intends to ride ("*poedem,*" literally, "we shall ride") straight to Rebbe Borukhl's court; the verb refers to riding inside a wagon or astride a horse. But Hershele's vehicle—a hungry horse—is uncooperative, so the trickster decides to walk: "*poidu peshkom*"—literally, "I shall walk on foot."[33]

The precision of the verbs of motion in Russian helps explain why Babel's Zelda is not surprised by Hershele's claims to be Shabos-nakhamu. She asks Hershele, "*Skoro li pridët k nam Shabos-nakhamu*"—idiomatically, "How long before Shabos-nakhamu arrives?" but literally, "When will Shabos-nakhamu walk into our place?"[34] Reimagined by Babel in Russian, the woman uses a verb that demonstrates to Hershele that she has conjured up a visitor who would arrive (*pridët*) on foot. Linguistic distinctions around grammatical gender are also crucial here: "Shabos-nakhamu" is a feminine noun in Yiddish but a masculine one in Russian, so Babel's Zelda is primed to expect a male-identified visitor. Arriving at the tavern on foot, Hershele ignites Zelda's linguistic imagination in a way possible in Russian but not in Yiddish. Babel's Zelda is not the stupid woman of the Yiddish story who doesn't realize that Shabos-nakhamu is not a person: instead, she expects Shabos-nakhamu's arrival on foot and his gender to be male, because such are the grammatical presuppositions of the Russian text. Walking into Zelda's tavern, Babel has Hershele act out the nuances of the Russian language and literally step into the linguistic opportunity offered him by the tavern keeper's wife.

The difference between the endings of the two stories also hinges on Babel's use of verbs of motion. When the tavern keeper catches up with Hershele in the forest, the trickster convinces the man to "lend" him clothes so he can "search" for the "real" thief. In Yiddish, it reads, "Hershele dressed in the tavern keeper's clothes and took off in the man's horse-drawn cart for the other side of the forest, where he hid his things. There, he loaded the sack with his things onto the cart and rode off on his way [*un iz zikh avek geforn zayn veg*]."[35] Babel's Hershele, we recall, wished to travel on horseback from the start, just as the Hershele of the Yiddish original had. But when he has the opportunity to do so by getting his hands on the tavern keeper's horse, the trickster in Babel's Russian story makes a choice that seemingly contradicts his initial intentions: "Hershele got in the [tavern keeper's horse-drawn] cart and rode off. He dug up his things, loaded them on the wagon, and rode to the edge of the forest. There, Hershele slung the bundle over his back again, let the horse go, and started walking along the road [*zashagal po doroge*] that led to the house of the holy Rebbe Borukhl."[36] Hershele did not simply dismount and begin to walk, but if we interpret the Russian literally, he "started taking steps with his feet" in the direction of Borukhl's court. This odd and impractical choice of how to move, given that he had a horse and wagon at his disposal, is consistent with the language of walking that had facilitated Hershele's trick in the first place. To suddenly switch the mode of travel would have lessened Hershele's power as a trickster who could appropriate a calendrical observance as his identity. En route to Rebbe Borukhl's court, Hershele becomes a trickster through the act of walking on foot.

"Shabos-nakhamu" is set in the Ukrainian countryside, but the audience for this text included urban dwellers: the story appeared in Petrograd in March 1918 when Babel resided there. In transplanting the figure of Hershele from Yiddish folklore into the sphere of Bolshevik-era literary culture, Babel sought to translate Hershele's experience on the rural road to Medzhibozh into a template that could inform the urban experience after the revolution.

Writing about spatial practices associated with cities, Michel de Certeau has emphasized the distinction between "place," which exists as a product of top-down urban planning, and "space," which individuals can "practice" by walking through existing places on their own terms. Maps prescribe routes that link one place to another and suggest an outline for walkers' itineraries. However, walkers themselves are free to devise their own routes through existing places. Drawing on J. L. Austen's notion of the speech act—an utterance that serves as a unit of communication—de Certeau uses the term "pedestrian speech act" for each idiosyncratic instance of "practicing" space. "The act of walking," writes de Certeau, "is to the urban system what the speech act is to language or to the statements uttered."[37] Overriding the "places" demarcated by the map, walkers realize their own routes and "spaces" by "speaking" with the movements of their bodies. In comparing walking to speech, de Certeau has challenged Michel Foucault's concept of totalitarian space exemplified by the Panopticon—a structure that allows those in power an unobstructed view of everyone under their surveillance. Whereas, for Foucault, citizens of modern societies are always under the watchful eye of the state, de Certeau's walkers rely on "pedestrian speech acts" to free themselves to "practice" space according to their own itineraries, improvising within the confines of the map.

A pedestrian speech act links walking to speech. Though the map prescribes a set of choices, alternative possibilities arise in both language and place through substitution. Like speakers who improvise on the conventions of language within the existing structures of speech, pedestrians substitute their own itineraries for those printed on the map, even as they are limited by physical and geographic constraints. Spatial practices "secretly structure the determining conditions of social life," and much like James C. Scott's "hidden transcript," these "multiform, resistant, tricky and stubborn procedures" of appropriating the map "elude discipline without being outside the field in which it is exercised."[38] Practitioners of space substitute idiosyncratic spatial practices for prescribed itineraries. Babel draws on the symbolic resonances of Hershele's meandering route and the trickster's false identity to provide comfort to city dwellers in wartime Petrograd. Publishing "Shabos-nakhamu" in the winter of 1918, Babel offered Jewish cultural frameworks for dealing with destruction, such as the ritual paradigm of "Shabos-nakhamu," to urban dwellers after the revolution.

* * *

A story about Hershele's adventures on the roads of rural Ukraine, "Shabos-nakhamu" came out as Babel was launching his career in Petrograd amidst urban unrest and upheaval. It appeared in the pages of Petrograd's daily press in 1918, alongside the writer's journalistic work in and around the city. In the latter, Babel reveals the chasm between the imagined and the built environment and, implicitly, between the glorious revolutionary Bolshevik rhetoric and the urban dwellers' visceral experiences of destruction. As an urban reporter and exemplar of de Certeau's practitioner of space, Babel wanders the streets on a self-directed tour of morgues, hospitals, and slaughterhouses. As he surveys the devastation around him in Petrograd, he reflects on it through a series of allusions to Hershele and to historical Jewish displacement. In particular, Babel appropriates references to the Babylonian exile of 587 BCE, the *locus classicus* of Jewish destruction, as a roundabout way of discussing the Russian capital's desolation after the revolution. A vestige of folkloric culture from the former Pale of Settlement, Babel's Hershele brings with him a set of Jewish references that help the writer make sense of the new reality and begin to shape the figure of the Soviet Jew after the revolution.

On March 21, 1918, five days after "Shabos-nakhamu" came out in *The Evening Star,* Babel published the second and last installment in his short series of literary sketches about Odessa on the pages of the same paper.[39] This was not the first time that Babel wrote about his native city for the Petrograd press. Two years earlier, in "Odessa," Babel had identified the sunny seaside city as the place from which the literary "messiah" would come and revitalize the dreary literary tradition of Petersburg with his freer, merrier touch.[40] This literary messiah unapologetically resembled the young writer himself; however, his promised arrival was delayed by war and revolution. A city flooded with First World War refugees, the Odessa that Babel described in *The Evening Star* two years later differed markedly from the city of his 1916 manifesto. In his 1918 dispatch, Babel yearns for the speedy revival of the city's port—identified in the 1916 article as the source of Odessa's uniquely free-wheeling spirit—and wishes to see its cafés filled with music again. "Soon," writes Babel about the impending departure of Russian troops from the city at the war's end, "the time will come when officers, who had gotten used to Petrograd and to their tiny garrisons of Medzhibozh [*k svoim malen'kim polkovym medzhibozham*], will take their leave of us."[41]

Babel's reference to Medzhibozh in his 1918 sketch about Odessa is notable because of the town's connection to Hershele. Medzhibozh was, as Babel notes, the place where a Russian military garrison had been stationed in an old castle since the middle of the nineteenth century. Its barracks were located next to Rebbe Borukhl's court, and some of the stories of Hershele's adventures took place near or inside the garrison.[42] The Medzhibozh of Babel's Odessa sketch, published five days after the Russian story of Hershele's adventures on his way to Medzhibozh, indexes Medzhibozh as both a military outpost and the seat of the powerful Hasidic dynasty where the jester Hershele entertained the depressive Rebbe Borukhl. Two years after presenting himself as a joyful, redemptive messianic figure, Babel confronts the Bolshevik regime's own very different messianic claims and destructive realities and begins to identify with a figure who could offer consolation instead of merriment: Hershele, the jester of Medzhibozh, ready to make sense of thwarted messianic expectations in a landscape marked by destruction.

Hershele's adventures in "Shabos-nakhamu" offered a model of consolation at a time when the Bolshevik regime's practical inability to fulfill the messianic promise of the revolution was beginning to lead to disappointment and devastation. Babel wrote his sketches as an urban reporter for *The New Life* (*Novaia zhizn'*), a short-lived Social Democratic periodical edited by Maxim Gorky, whom Babel had met a year and a half earlier and whom he considered a mentor.[43] *The New Life* opposed the Bolshevik takeover and the suppression of political freedoms that followed.[44] Babel wrote regularly about the city's gruesome sites and events throughout the spring and summer of 1918; his articles joined the better-known Petrograd observations by Viktor Shklovsky, Zinaida Gippius, Evgeny Zamyatin, and other writers at the time.[45] Records of wandering, Babel's essays raised awareness about aspects of present-day issues that were obscured by Bolshevism's messianic ideology and suggested to urban denizens a response to despair that could be adapted from Jewish cultural sources.

In "First Aid," published in *The New Life* on March 9, 1918, a week before "Shabos-nakhamu" came out in *The Evening Star,* Babel notes that unlike first-aid stations in other European cities, those in Petrograd did not preserve any material evidence for archives or public exhibits. In the face of this lack of historical awareness, Babel saw his articles for *The New Life* as "a living and mournful chronicle [*letopis'*] of urban life" and a warning against the ideologically expedient staging of the city as a fulfillment of revolutionary messianism.[46] His self-proclaimed literary messiah waylaid, Babel switched his cultural role to one of an observer documenting the city's deprivations. The destruction of the Temple in ancient Jerusalem became Babel's historical parallel when he documented the demise of Petrograd. This was the same parallel suggested by the day on Judaism's liturgical calendar that forms the crux of the fictional story "Shabos-nakhamu," published the same year.

As Petrograd audiences read Babel's journalistic accounts about 1918, the Bolsheviks' messianic promises were facing the headwinds of internecine conflict, and Babel found his initial messianic project, bringing the spirit of Odessa into the Russian literary tradition, cast into turmoil. In 1932, fourteen years after the end of Babel's urban beat for *The New Life,* his story "The Road" (Doroga) revisited the cold winter following the Bolshevik Revolution. The narrator, having left the collapsing First World War front in November 1917, sets out on a seemingly straightforward train journey to Petrograd. It does not proceed smoothly. A soldier in the Red Army, whose official policy was to defend Jews against antisemitic attacks but which, at the same time, had antisemitic recruits in its ranks, identifies the traveler as a Jew by feeling inside his pants for his circumcision. The soldier spares the narrator's life when he discovers money sewn into his underwear. "Get lost, Chaim [*ankloyf, khayim*]," the non-Jewish soldier tells the narrator, using a stereotypical Jewish name and a bit of Yiddish he might have picked up from his other Jewish victims in the bloody civil war that was then starting.[47] The narrator is thrown off the train and, like Hershele in "Shabos-nakhamu," proceeds to his destination on foot.

"My destination was Petersburg," says the narrator at the beginning of "The Road," before his journey gets literally derailed. Finally, his feet frostbitten, the narrator approaches the city at the end of a long journey. The iconic Nevsky Avenue, described by Pushkin, Gogol, and Dostoevsky among other canonic Russian writers, stretches before him. The youthful narrator of "Odessa" had envisioned himself redeeming the dreariness of literary Petersburg with an infusion of merriment from his sunny hometown. The first-person narrator of "The Road," finally poised to enter the Petersburg of his dreams after a long journey, is a version of that self-anointed messiah. But instead of seeing the city shaped in his imagination by Russia's literary tradition, the narrator sees a cityscape that is "marked off by the carcasses of horses as by so many milestones." The sight of devastation makes the narrator despair: "'Thus does the need to conquer Petersburg pass,' I thought, trying to remember the name of the man who was trampled to death by the hooves of Arab chargers at the very end of his journey. It was Yehuda Halevi."[48] Here, Babel marks Petersburg as an imagined, unreachable destination through a reference to Jerusalem that transposes a key element of the rich Jewish cultural vocabulary onto the postrevolutionary context.

Yehuda Halevi was a twelfth-century Hebrew poet from Andalusia who undertook a lengthy journey to Jerusalem and, according to legend, was killed at the gates of the city he so wanted to reach. He had expressed this longing in the oft-cited lines, "My heart is in the East— / And I am at the edge of the West," which mark Jerusalem as the *axis mundi* of the Jewish experience.[49] Commenting on the relationship of Halevi's poetry to the legend of his death, the literary scholar Sidra Ezrahi asks, "When Yehuda Halevi sets out for the Holy Land, does not the image that pointed to that place 'beyond,' now about to be fully realized *as itself*, render the 'beyond' palpable and concrete, entailing a shift in poetic sensibility as the symbolic connection is materialized—and thus effectively annihilated?"[50] Were Halevi to have entered the city of Jerusalem, he would have seen that the Jerusalem of his poetry and of his longing was effectively destroyed. When Babel's narrator in "The Road" reaches the devastated Petrograd, the city of his imagination is shattered as well.

After Jerusalem's second destruction, by the Romans in 70 CE, a notion took root in Jewish tradition that there were two Jerusalems. One is the heavenly or celestial Jerusalem (*Yerushalayim shel ma'alah*), the embodiment of collective longing in exile; the other is the earthly Jerusalem (*Yerushalayim shel matah*)—the physical city destroyed first by the Babylonians and then by the Romans and still in a state of waste. The eventual restoration of the earthly city to its heavenly status has been imagined as a hallmark of the messianic age. This dualist view of the city was expressed in *midrash* (exegetical texts) and commentary, which posited that the heavenly Jerusalem was created concurrently with the earthly one and that the two would eventually be reunited, but only when the physical city was rebuilt.[51] Were he to enter the earthly Jerusalem—an imperial backwater then controlled by the Crusaders—at the end of his journey in 1141, Halevi would have realized that it did not correspond to the heavenly Jerusalem that he had longed for in verse. Halevi's death, according to the legend, was the price paid to allow the imagined Jerusalem of his poetry to endure.

Babel's narrator in "The Road" had been traveling to a kind of heavenly Petersburg, which the self-proclaimed literary messiah of "Odessa" had associated with Russia's high culture. But when he arrives, he realizes that he has come to an earthly city that is frozen and starving. Tellingly, he continuously refers to his destination as "Petersburg"—he does not call it "Petrograd," as the city had been renamed four years earlier, at the start of the First World War, to make it sound less German. Babel's contemporaries also referred to the city as Petersburg, both out of habit and to emphasize the semantic and emotional meaning of Petersburg as "primarily a literary city, a city-text."[52] The journey of Babel's protagonist is a literary one, a budding writer's quest to "conquer" the Petersburg of Russian literature. Yet at the city gates, Petersburg manifests itself as the devastated Petrograd. Babel's self-proclaimed literary messiah has little to offer: looking at the evidence of destruction, he realizes that the promise of the revolution appears not to have panned out. Instead, the narrator is now faced with the inevitability of redefining his purpose.

Babel also evoked traditional Jewish tropes of destruction with the *nom de plume* under which he published "Odessa": Bab-El. The two syllables, a broken-up version of Babel's name, form the Aramaic word for Babylonia, the place to which Jews were exiled after Jerusalem's destruction in 587 BCE. Babylonia is vividly described in the Book of Lamentations as a site of extreme suffering. By the time Babel became "Bab-El," as the author of "Odessa," the First World War had already severely disrupted the food supply in Petrograd, forcing the city's denizens to endure long bread lines in the bitter cold. "Shabos-nakhamu" implicitly refers to Babylonia, as a story about an impostor who takes on the identity of a day connected to the collective Jewish memory of the Babylonian exile. In "Odessa," his manifesto about his messianic role as a writer, Babel assumes the identity of Bab-El. He evokes it again in "The Road" by associating the gap between the literary Petersburg and the destroyed Petrograd with the gap between the celestial Jerusalem of Jewish collective imagination and the destroyed, earthly Jerusalem. The trickster Hershele as Shabos-nakhamu provides a model for the writer Babel as literary messiah Bab-El.

Babel was not the only writer at the time to reference the Babylonian exile and destroyed Jerusalem in relation to Petrograd. In his reminiscences about the city after the revolution, Viktor Shklovsky drew on biblical literature for imagery of destruction: "I write about a terrible year and about a city under siege. Ezekiel and Jeremiah fried bread in manure in order to show Jerusalem what awaits it under siege [by the Babylonians]. During weekdays bread would be fried in human excrement, on holidays, in horse excrement."[53] Babel went even further: wandering the streets of Petrograd in 1918, he did not simply observe the biblical proportions of urban devastation but styled himself after the Jewish prophets whose words testified to Jerusalem's demise. A walker amidst the ruins, Babel was, in effect, creating a protagonist who served as the fallen city's scribe. The figure that Babel began to create during and about the cold winter of 1918 was the Jew in the new Bolshevik state beginning to make sense of the revolution with the help of Jewish literature of destruction, from biblical prophets to the folkloric corpus of stories about Hershele Ostropoler. With time, this figure would become in Babel's Russian-language oeuvre the writer's version of the Soviet Jew.

*　*　*

The references to Hershele throughout Babel's oeuvre operate through a method similar to what linguists call recursion. Like clauses, which can be added in infinite number to a sentence, plot elements, allusions, and aspects of meaning repeat and become nested within each other in an evolving chain of associations. Hershele's recurrent appearances across a growing number of contexts bring out interrelated allusions to destruction. These sightings, in turn, evoke the very aspects of Jewish collective memory that motivate Hershele's recurring appearances in the first place.

"The Road," published in 1932, participates in this process of recursion by revisiting Babel's journalistic treatment of events immediately following the revolution and resituating this material in the context of the new ideological realities of the early 1930s. Babel's 1918 work on Petrograd ran in *The New Life,* which the Bolsheviks promptly shut down for calling attention to early failures of the new state. Its editor Maxim Gorky would eventually embrace the new regime and become its central cultural figure by the time Babel published "The Road." Babel, like other "fellow travelers," would reluctantly come around to accepting the new regime as well.

"The Road" can be read as Babel's attempt to resituate his initial observations about the revolution in a new political climate, to retrofit his earlier, more ambivalent narrative about his journey to Petrograd in 1918 into a plausible autobiography that would be more ideologically suitable for the Stalin era. Indeed, the story ends by suggesting that its narrator, who resembles the author, was embraced by the Bolsheviks right after the revolution—a proposition for which Babel's 1918 dispatches provide no evidence. "The Road" thus recursively inserts new details into Babel's narrative of his involvement in the revolution that seek to change the way the narrative could be read in retrospect.

Though, as noted, the story was published in 1932, it is dated "1920–1930." These dates, which Babel included right underneath the concluding paragraph of the story, imply that the writer took a full decade to write these ten pages, but they can also be read as part of the story's fictional universe. The "1920–1930" range reflects a journey that unfolded within a time frame that differs from the story's narrative present in 1918. The tale told by this alternative time frame is less about the narrator's trip to Petrograd in 1918 than about the development of his views about the revolution into the early 1930s. Babel had practice making temporal substitutions of this sort: in presenting himself as "Shabos-nakhamu," the writer's version of Hershele seizes on his interlocutor's inability to distinguish between the chronological, linear time associated with the narrative present and the cyclical time of the Jewish calendar. "The Road," likewise, manipulates time with a touch of Hershele-like trickery.

At the end of "The Road," Babel's narrator takes a job as a translator with the Bolshevik secret police, the Cheka. The story's final line then retrospectively assesses the narrator's life since the events of 1918: "Thus, thirteen years ago, did my wonderful life begin, a life full of thought and merriment."[54] This sentence, seemingly an aside, suggests that the first-person narrator has embraced the regime and that his allegiance to it has been long-standing. A connection between the narrator of the story and its author is strongly implied in the dating of the events of 1917–1918 to "thirteen years ago." This temporal marker situates the year 1930—the end date of the story's composition according to Babel the author—thirteen years after the events described by Babel the journalist and narrated in "The Road."

The concluding sentence of "The Road" reads like a tacked-on ending, and its sudden appearance is jarring. The meaning of the word "merriment" (*vesel'e*) is particularly elusive given its dissonance relative to the horrors that the story recounts. On the one hand, "merriment" originates in the narrator's acquisition of "clothes, food, work and comrades faithful in friendship and death" through his new association with the Cheka.[55] On the other hand, the word implies a macabre rejoicing amidst the rampant destruction, violence, and fear that the newly arrived narrator found in the war-torn city. This second, more ambivalent (and even grotesque) type of "merriment" contains a further reference to Hershele and, through him, to the Jewish collective memory of destruction. During the period between publishing "Shabos-nakhamu" and "The Road"—the decade of the 1920s alluded to in the dating of "The Road"—Babel published his masterpiece, *Red Cavalry*. In this cycle of stories, set in 1920, the writer's thinking about the project of the revolution circles yet again to Hershele and the question of Jewish destruction associated with him.

During the Bolsheviks' war with Poland in 1920, Babel joined Semyon Budyonny's First Cavalry Army; his duties included writing for the army's propaganda newspaper, *The Red Cavalryman* (*Krasnyi kavalerist*). The military rank and file were Cossacks who were considered ideologically unreliable and whose support of the Bolsheviks could not be taken for granted; *The Red Cavalryman*'s mission was to educate them about the political goals of their army service.[56] Babel wrote five articles for *The Red Cavalryman*, all published in August and September 1920 under the pseudonym Kirill Lyutov. Babel went on to give the same name to the narrator of *Red Cavalry*. Stories from this cycle—many of them fictionalized retellings of the writer's wartime experiences—appeared in periodicals between 1923 and 1926 and, in 1926, as the book that catapulted Babel to national and international fame.

With a surname originating in the Russian root for "fierce" (*liutyi*), Lyutov was an ill-fitting *nom de guerre* both for the short, bespectacled Babel and for the similarly built protagonist of *Red Cavalry*. The pen name Lyutov concealed Babel's Jewishness from the Cossacks while he worked as an army propagandist during the 1920 war; the fictionalized propagandist of *Red Cavalry* disguised himself in much the same fashion. Lyutov became a literary mask for Babel, a new iteration of the earlier figure of the self-proclaimed literary messiah, Bab-El.

In 1916, Bab-El warned the denizens of Petrograd that the fate of their city resembled that of the destroyed Jerusalem. In 1918, Hershele's transformation into "Shabos-nakhamu" modeled Babel's subsequent authorial reinvention as a consoler during a time of destruction. Then, while traveling with the troops in 1920 in the former Pale of Settlement, Babel rediscovered Hershele and relied on him as his and Lyutov's guide to wartime violence. The propagandist Lyutov—the disguise of both Babel and his literary alter ego—was officially tasked with explaining the need to deploy violence in achieving the revolution's ideological objectives. But Lyutov was not his only disguise: the propagandist who hid behind a mask also took on the persona of the peripatetic folkloric trickster.

A state in the midst of chaotic transition, the literary scholar Michael Gorham has written, "depends heavily on public discourse for the dissemination of its ideas"; consequently, Russian writers after the revolution, "given their primary focus on verbal and symbolic representation, play[ed] a formidable role in generating and legitimating the central value system of that state."[57] The Bolsheviks saw language as a tool for establishing the legitimacy of their nascent government; Babel, as a wartime propagandist for the new regime, was expected to be on the frontlines of its official discourse.[58] Unlike his contemporary Dmitry Furmanov in his civil war novel *Chapaev* (1923), Babel did not directly channel the language of the state in *Red Cavalry*. But the writer did produce propaganda in his articles for *The Red Cavalryman*. Likewise, Lyutov, the Babel-like protagonist of *Red Cavalry,* alludes to his method of writing articles and promulgating state ideology. These two types of texts—journalistic and fictional—are interrelated. Babel was involved in the double-edged project of producing the language of the state through his propaganda work while questioning it in his fiction. This dual function would recur several times in Babel's work.

Through a series of cryptic references to Hershele's made-up stories, which substituted cultural concepts, subverted expectations, and tricked people, Babel's literary texts about the 1920 Bolshevik-Polish War question the very propaganda that he himself produced. Enlisted in the military campaign to expand the Bolsheviks' sphere of influence, the narrator of *Red Cavalry* stumbles on Hasidic Jews in war-torn areas of the former Pale. These encounters divert Lyutov both from his duties as a propagandist and, more literally, from his prescribed itinerary. As he veers off the route that the regime intended for him, he takes detours—on foot—through Jewish spaces.

Babel's references to Hershele in *Red Cavalry* recast the task of a wartime propagandist as a trickster's game amidst devastation. This macabre game resembles the "merriment" at the end of "The Road." In each text, the narrator evokes "merriment" while playing the role of mediator between the state and those newly under its jurisdiction: in "The Road," an interpreter for the secret police is tasked with translating "statements that had been made by diplomats, *agents provocateurs* and spies,"[59] whereas in *Red Cavalry,* the term arises in the context of Lyutov's making the new ideology accessible to the troops. The "merriment" in *Red Cavalry* thus references Babel's earlier work on Hershele as commentary on the making of propaganda itself.

"Merriment" pops up in a cluster of *Red Cavalry* stories set on a Friday evening in the summer of 1920. In "Gedali," Lyutov's army train has made a stop in Zhitomir, and he decides to take a walk through the town. A visit to the deserted marketplace and a subsequent encounter with the elderly shop-keeper Gedali vividly remind Lyutov of his Jewish grandparents and his childhood in Odessa. In "Rebbe," set later that evening, Lyutov joins the town's Hasidic Jews for their Sabbath celebration at their rebbe's court. Lyutov and the rebbe, who sits with his eyes closed, converse:

> "From where has the Jew come?" he asked, raising his eyelids.
> "Odessa," I replied.
> "A pious city," the rebbe said suddenly, with extraordinary vigor. "The star of our banishment, the involuntary well of our tribulations! . . . What does the Jew do?"
> "I am putting into verse the adventures of Hershele Ostropoler [*Ia pere-kladyvaiu v stikhi pokhozhdeniia Gersha iz Ostropolia*]."
> "A great labor," the rebbe whispered, closing his eyelids again. "The jackal moans when it is hungry, every fool is foolish enough to be un-happy, and only the wise man rends the veil of existence with laughter. . . . What has the Jew studied?"
> "The Bible."
> "What does the Jew seek? [*Chego ishchet evrei?*]"
> "Merriment [*vesel'ia*]."[60]

Babel's first-person narrator in "The Road" claims to have found "merri-ment" in his work as a translator for the Cheka; Lyutov in *Red Cavalry*, a propagandist for the state, appears to be seeking it still. His answer to the rebbe's question about his occupation situates his search for "merriment" alongside his claim that he is "putting into verse" the adventures of Hershele. The enigmatic overlap between "merriment" and "verse"—and the connec-tion of these two concepts to Hershele—recalls Babel's own earlier work about the Yiddish trickster. In "Shabos-nakhamu," upset with his failure to pro-vide for the family, Hershele's wife "hurled reproaches. Each one of those reproaches was as heavy as a cobblestone. Hershele would reply in verse [*Gershele otvechal stikhami*]."[61] "Merriment," read intertextually between "The Road" and "Rebbe," has to do with finding relief in grave situations. But "verse," read in a similarly comparative fashion between "Rebbe" and "Shabos-nakhamu," hints at deceitful storytelling and the promulgation of lies.

"Verse" here has nothing to do with Hershele's—or, later, Lyutov's—poetic inclinations. In "Shabos-nakhamu," Hershele's "reply[ing] in verse" alludes to distracting his wife with verbal antics so as to stave off her anger about his failure to make a living. In "Rebbe," Lyutov's claim of "putting" Hershele's adventures "into verse" is a way to lie about himself at the rebbe's court because he knows that he could never gain the Hasidic Jews' trust as a Bolshevik. In stating his occupation the way he does—in a roundabout, recursive way that resembles his circuitous detour in Zhitomir—Lyutov lets the Hasidic Jews gathered at their rebbe's know that his task, like Hershele's, is to deal in mischief.

The "verses" Lyutov euphemistically evokes in his answer to the rebbe are the verbal concoctions of Bolshevik propaganda he cooks up for the illiterate Cossacks. The Jews of Zhitomir distrust Lyutov because, as an army propagandist, he represents the revolution, which has so far manifested as ceaseless violence whose goals have left them confused. Lyutov's allusion to Hershele's trickery is a roundabout way of describing his own occupation. It allows the propagandist to style himself after the folkloric trickster who becomes Borukhl's jester, stories about whom would have been familiar to Lyutov's interlocutors at the rebbe's court. Amidst the devastation of war, Lyutov becomes a kind of Hershele who tells stories to Zhitomir Jews not only to lighten their mood but also, through his craftiness, antics, and jokes, to reassure them about his own work as an army propagandist.

The stories "Gedali" and "Rebbe" recount events from this single evening in Zhitomir. As the Sabbath begins at the end of "Gedali," Lyutov follows the eponymous shopkeeper to the rebbe's court, where the two arrive and stay for a Sabbath meal, described in the story "Rebbe." These two stories were presented in a curious way in *Red Cavalry:* despite being the first and second parts of one narrative, they were not printed one after the other. Rather, a seemingly unrelated story, "My First Goose," is placed between them.[62] I see this disruption as a suggestion that Lyutov told a tale to those gathered at the court of Zhitomir's rebbe, and this tale might very well have been a story not unlike "My First Goose," a trickster tale in which Lyutov styles himself after Hershele.

"My First Goose" is an initiation story in which Lyutov seeks the acceptance of the Cossacks in his billet. At its start, the soldiers are rude to the bespectacled interloper whose eyeglasses, both here and elsewhere in *Red Cavalry,* mark him as a member of the educated elite and a sickly Jew: "you get cut to pieces for glasses around here," Lyutov is warned after being called "one of those pansies" and "a little louse."[63] Lyutov emphasizes his puny stature when he relates his admiration for the division commander's muscular body. An intellectual carrying a typewriter and manuscripts, he is nonetheless on a mission to make it among the brutes. A sympathetic quartermaster tells Lyutov that there is only one way for him to earn the respect of his fellow soldiers: he must "mess up a lady [*a isport' vy damu*]," Lyutov is told, "and a good lady at that [*samuiu chisten'kuiu damu*]."[64] Lyutov has been instructed to rape a woman to prove his manliness. Instead, he opts for a different violent act: he kills a goose and intimidates his landlady into cooking it for him. The killing of the bird, described in detail with graphic attention paid to its bloodied virginal-white feathers, does the trick of symbolically substituting for rape: the Cossacks accept Lyutov.

Similar substitutions of less transgressive acts for truly violent ones appear in other Hershele stories in the Yiddish folkloric corpus. In one tale, the proprietress of a tavern, after learning that Hershele has no means of settling his bill, tells him that she has run out of food. Hershele retorts, "In that case, I'm afraid I'll have to do what my father did." The woman requests a clarification. "Never mind," Hershele says, "my father did what he did!" Frightened, she serves Hershele a full meal and later asks about Hershele's father. "Oh, my father?" Hershele responds. "Whenever my father didn't have any supper, he went to bed without it."[65] Hershele intended no physical harm in the first place: the threat of violence exists only as a locution that allows him to get what he seeks.

Focusing on playfulness in culture, Johann Huizinga has examined the alternative, unexpected answers that can suddenly turn up even when a question appears to have only one response: "Should it prove that a second answer is possible, in accord with the rules but not suspected by the questioner, then it will go badly with him: he is caught in his own trap."[66] Such ludic alternatives prove essential in Hershele folktales. The tavern's proprietress expects violence—a fear likely informed by her previous lodgers' outbursts—but Hershele's oblique locution lets him get what he wants without intending physical harm. Lyutov in "My First Goose" resembles the folkloric Hershele in the tavern: the less brutal act he commits is violent enough for those he needs to impress. Both, moreover, are rewarded for their craft with food: the tavern keeper feeds Hershele, and the Cossacks invite Lyutov to join them at mealtime.

With a ludic survival strategy at its center, "My First Goose" serves a double narrative purpose in *Red Cavalry*. Most evidently, it appears between two other stories that together recount Lyutov's experience among Zhitomir's pious Jews and the nostalgia for his childhood that this experience evokes for him: "On Sabbath eves, I am tormented by the rich sorrow of memories."[67] At the same time, the story about Lyutov tricking his way into acceptance by the Cossacks, because of its placement in the story cycle, turns into a tale that Lyutov would tell to Zhitomir's Jews, who he also hopes will accept him despite the fact that they suspect and fear the Bolsheviks.

In this set of stories, Lyutov plays on two teams at once. First, he tricks the Cossacks by substituting a less violent act of killing a goose for rape; in doing so, he earns the trust that allows him to exert political influence on the soldiers. Second, he uses the story of tricking the Cossacks to trick the Jews of Zhitomir into accepting the Bolshevik ideology, which they, like the Cossacks of the First Cavalry Army, have been subjected to. Between the story related in "My First Goose" and the implied telling of this story to Zhitomir's Jews in "Rebbe," Lyutov emerges cloaked in the circuitous logic and devious disguise of a trickster whose behavior resembles Hershele's.

In placing Lyutov in this context, Babel ponders the evolution of the figure that would become the Soviet Jew. This figure is not at home in traditional Jewish culture, but neither has he become nostalgic for it after being alienated by the emerging Bolshevik society. Instead, this is a figure whose very existence, like Hershele's, is defined by alienation from both societies and cultures, combined with the ability to be engaged in both. Styling himself after Hershele, Lyutov can navigate two distinct cultural systems and play them off one another.

After gaining the Cossack's trust and sharing a meal with them, Lyutov reads the Cossacks the ideological text du jour: Lenin's July 1920 speech at the Second Congress of the Communist International that made the case for the global proletarian revolution: "And loudly, like a deaf man triumphant [*kak torzhestvuiushchii glukhoi*], I read Lenin's speech to the Cossacks."[68]

A "deaf man triumphant" is Lyutov's revealing assessment of his role as the Bolsheviks' representative. His engagement with the Cossacks is a unidirectional affair: Lyutov celebrates his success in reaching out to them but remains "deaf" to the crowd of unresponsive listeners. "The public transcript is, to put it crudely, the self-portrait of dominant elites as they would have themselves seen," James C. Scott has written, in what can serve as an appraisal of Lyutov when he presents himself to the soldiers as a conduit of the state ideology they must violently impose on others. "Given the usual power of dominant elites to compel performances from others, the discourse of the public transcript is a decidedly lopsided discussion," Scott continues, emphasizing that subordinate classes comprehend the public transcript very differently than elites intend them to.[69] This assessment captures the Cossacks' reaction to Lyutov's performance of Lenin's speech: "'Truth tickles every nostril,' [one soldier] said when I'd finished. 'Question is, how do you pull it out of the pile? But Lenin hits it straight away, like a hen pecking at a grain.'"[70] The Cossack affirms that Lyutov has indeed transmitted state ideology but, at the same time, also communicates that he hasn't understood the complex logic of Lenin's address. Instead, Lenin's words, whatever their intricate meaning might be, could simply be invoked further down the line—like Lenin's words would be by a different soldier in another *Red Cavalry* story as his rationalization for murdering his prerevolutionary master—as a justification for violence.

Lyutov experiences the same text very differently: "I read and rejoiced, and caught, rejoicing, the mysterious curve of Lenin's straight line [*tainstvennuiu priamuiu leninskoi krivoi*]."[71] Lyutov's rejoicing displays the delight of the Party insider who has gained access to the hidden transcript of power. It also reflects the trickster's "luxuriating" in his own cleverness, to borrow the word Henry Louis Gates uses to describe how the Signifying Monkey delights in his linguistic mischief. Lyutov knows that the Cossacks whom he convinced to accept him see only the "straight line" of Lenin's speech: they take what they hear at face value, as a motivation to follow the command to keep on fighting. Lyutov, acting as a representative of the revolutionary elite, understands how Lenin's words could defy the seeming straightness of their own logic. The curving of a straight line recalls the unexpectedly curving paths of "The Road" and "Shabos-nakhamu," in which protagonists "practicing" seemingly clear-cut spaces find that their journeys unspool into wanderings and lateral moves. Cognizant of the "curviness" of Lenin's speech even as he reads it aloud to Cossacks who can only see its straightness, Lyutov peddles "verse": in his role as a propagandist, he tricks them into complicity, into following orders they might not fully understand— just as he tricks Zhitomir's pious Jews in "Rebbe" to accept him as someone who could pass as one of their own. In telling a story to the Hasidim about how he had lied to the Cossacks, Lyutov also makes clear that the same story contains the mechanism of its own subversion.

These interrelated, deception-filled stories strategically use trickery to avoid looking directly at the horrors of war. Babel made these horrors clear in a diary entry written during the 1920 war that records an exchange he had with a rebbe in Zhitomir, the likely prototype of the exchange in *Red Cavalry:*

"Where are you from, young man?"

"From Odessa."

"How do people live there?"

"People are alive there [*Tam liudi zhivy*]."

"And here it's horror [*A zdes' uzhas*]."[72]

Let's compare this exchange with the fictional one we noted earlier between Lyutov and the rebbe in the story "Rebbe" in *Red Cavalry:*

"What does the Jew seek?"

"Merriment."[73]

Horror (*uzhas*) from the diary turns into merriment (*vesel'e*) as Babel reworks his personal observations into a literary exchange. This substitution underscores the uncanny proximity of merriment and horror in the rapid, confused barrage of nightmarish wartime experiences. It also recalls the Freudian notion of dream work, a mental process by which people avoid mimetic representations of troubling latent experiences by replacing them with manifest content that may appear in an altered form. Babel, in his diary, had already tried to process his nightmarish experience of the 1920 war by instantaneously linking "horror" (*uzhas*) and "alive" (*zhivy*) through the repetition of the *zh* sound in both Russian words. As Babel modified this exchange for the short story, he found it too burdensome to acknowledge the "horror" he had observed as a diarist. In the dialogue in "Rebbe," "merriment" replaces "horror"; "merriment," in turn, is mentioned right after Lyutov describes his occupation as "putting into verse the adventures of Hershele Ostropoler." Horror, merriment, and Hershele's adventures are all linked in Babel's diary and his fictional prose about the war: like the relief Hershele provides to Rebbe Borukhl, Lyutov, whose allegiances are split between the Cossacks and the Jews, uses trickery to underscore the presence of the problem it aims to alleviate. Hershele's tricks would not have been needed had it not been for Borukhl's melancholia, which threatened the future of Hasidism. Lyutov's trickery, likewise, highlights the horrors that war inflicted on Jews in the former Pale.

Lyutov encounters Zhitomir's Jews while the cultural and material environment of Hasidism is under assault. As Gedali, the old man guiding Lyutov at the rebbe's court, leads the Red Army propagandist into a room "empty and of stone, like a morgue," he notes that "the windows and doors of the passionate edifice of Hasidism have been knocked out."[74] When he referred to Hasidic Jews in his 1918 sketch about Odessa, Babel mentioned that this community, many of them refugees in the city, was pious in ways utterly foreign to the freewheeling Odessan spirit. It seems surprising, then, that the rebbe in *Red Cavalry* would offer Lyutov a positive assessment of Odessa when Lyutov tells him—just as Babel himself did in the exchange with the rebbe he described in his wartime diary in 1920—that this is where he comes from: "A pious city . . . The star of our banishment, the involuntary well of our tribulations!"[75] This locution is both tongue-in-cheek and desperate. Surrounded by the horrors and devastation of Jewish life in Zhitomir, Odessa offers a glimmer of hope even for the Hasidic Jews, who had generally objected to the secular and hedonistic culture that the city famously represented.[76]

In 1920, in turn, Babel has Lyutov observe the destruction of the Hasidic environment—and tries to comprehend it himself. Both the diarist and his fictional alter ego in *Red Cavalry* appeal to Hershele for help as they do so. In a diary entry on July 23, Babel discusses a damaged synagogue in Dubno as an example of the broader destruction of Jewish life in the former Pale. A month after his visit to Zhitomir, Babel stands among "stunted little figures" and "emaciated faces" during a religious service. Babel notes, in what could be literally translated into English as, "I pray, rather I almost pray, and think about Hershele, how would I describe [*Ia molius', vernee pochti molius' i dumaiu o Gershele, vot kak by opisat'*]." Babel's language in the diary is schematic; some sentences are mere sketches of thoughts rather than complete statements. The clause after Hershele's name signals not an assertive full stop but an implied question mark. What Babel means here can be more idiomatically rendered as, "I pray, rather I almost pray, and think about Hershele; how could I ever describe what I see?"[77] Babel thinks about Hershele as he ponders the difficulty of describing the destruction that he sees around him in Dubno.

Babel penned this diary entry two days before Tisha b'Av—or, the 9th of Av—in 1920. The resonance of this timing did not elude Babel when, a day later, he noted that he remained silent and hid his familiarity with Jewish custom when his army companion forced a group of local Jews to cook: "Main cause of discord—today is the Sabbath. Prischepa tries to make them fry potatoes but tomorrow is a fast day, the 9th of Av, and I keep quiet, because I'm a Russian."[78] In an entry made on the day of the fast itself, Babel referred to the "torturous two hours" when some Jewish women in Demidovka were awakened before dawn and forced to boil meat—"and this on the 9th of Av."[79] Babel's diary references the commemoration of the fall of Jerusalem on Tisha b'Av in the context of 1920. Two years earlier, "Shabos-nakhamu" likewise referred to this annual date on the Jewish calendar to allude to the wartime destruction of Petersburg. Given Babel's work on Hershele in "Shabos-nakhamu," it is not surprising that Babel would have recalled the trickster from Yiddish folklore in 1920 as he witnessed the destruction of Jewish life in the former Pale.

The end of "Rebbe" emphasizes that Lyutov's encounter with Zhitomir's Jews, which had begun in "Gedali," took place because Lyutov took a detour and wandered into the town when his army train stopped for the night. As he leaves the rebbe's court in Zhitomir and returns to the train that had brought him there, Lyutov reminds the reader of the unfinished assignment waiting for him in the editorial offices of the army newspaper. "There, at the station, on the propaganda train of the First Cavalry," Lyutov concludes the story, "I was greeted by the sparkle of hundreds of lights, the enchanted glitter of the radio transmitter, the stubborn rolling of the printing presses, and my unfinished article for *The Red Cavalryman*."[80] The contrast between the brightly lit train and the moribund court of Zhitomir's rebbe is striking, as is the apparent dichotomy between the positively charged "Soviet" train and the negatively depicted "Jewish" town.

Yet, Lyutov's walk through Zhitomir while his train is parked at the station, maps the contours of a "practiced space" resistant to a binary reading. The "unfinished article" that Lyutov left on the train is a *nedopisannaia stat'ia*: the literal translation of this phrase is "an article whose writing has commenced but has not yet been finished." The locution emphasizes not only the unfinished propaganda essay itself but also Lyutov's interrupted process of writing it. The narrative explored in "Gedali" and "Rebbe" involves a propagandist whose writing had to be temporarily put on hold when his train came to a halt. Pausing his work in service of a regime whose revolutionary progress was frequently analogized to the forward motion of a speeding train, Lyutov switches to both a different kind of mobility and a different temporality.

While Lyutov's propaganda article remains unfinished and the train sits motionless, the narrator takes a detour on foot. This detour thrusts him back into a space and time associated with the prerevolutionary Jewish experience and, in the process, offers a meditation on Bolshevik propaganda. He is not so much distracted from his main textual project as he is creatively substituting another text in its place. The propagandist who steps off the train in Zhitomir turns into a trickster when he walks into town. Searching for the words to finish an article intended to motivate Red Army soldiers, Lyutov engages in a linguistic game with the Jews whom he encounters.

During his circuitous detour on foot, Lyutov tells the Hasidim in Zhitomir a tale about how he had tricked the group of Red Army soldiers into accepting him. Like Hershele who peddles "verse" to escape his wife's anger, and like Lyutov who peddles "verse" to both the Jews of Zhitomir and the Cossacks of the Red Army, the Soviet Jew Babel invents here is a trickster. This trickster uses techniques of substitution to "practice" a space seemingly predetermined by the route of the propaganda train. Instead of offering (only) propaganda, the trickster turns to the euphemistically labeled task of "putting into verse the adventures of Hershele"; that is, engaging in linguistic trickery that calls the revolution into question. Hershele's play unfolds within the colliding worlds of folkloric Jewish storytelling, the brutish culture of newly recruited Cossack soldiers, and Bolshevik propaganda harnessed for the revolutionary education of both Jews and Cossacks. The capacity for this kind of play becomes the defining trait of the Soviet Jew that Babel invents in these narratives.

* * *

Babel puts his final touches on the figure of the Soviet Jew, via tales of Hershele-inspired trickery, in the story "Karl-Yankel." "Karl-Yankel" was published in the journal *The Star* (*Zvezda*) in 1931 at the time of antireligious campaigns that aimed to eradicate parochial or traditional lifestyles and practices among the numerous ethnocultural groups of the USSR.[81] Achieving "the brotherhood of the peoples," later rendered as "the friendship of the peoples" in Stalin's 1936 constitution, required transforming the country's ethnically distinct groups into Soviet citizens.[82] But the Soviet Union did not wish to eliminate ethnic difference itself; rather, its project depended on marking ethnic difference so as to increase the appeal and unifying potential of Soviet ideology. The combination of cultural diversity and ideological compliance helped solidify the state's claim of uniting all people in class struggle regardless of ethnic origin. At the same time, the state took interest in stripping away specific ethnocultural markers that threatened its rhetoric about workers and peasants of all ethnicities equally striving toward a shared state. "Karl-Yankel" sketches the figure of the Soviet Jew as a trickster who picks apart some of these aspirations and illuminates their broader inconsistency.

"Karl-Yankel" playfully engages with the tension between these two desiderata—ethnic marking and the erasure of ethnic difference—by presenting the body of a Jewish male as a cipher for lingering cultural difference. The Bolsheviks saw circumcision, the traditional marking of the Jewish male body, as anachronistic; they feared that this practice could prove to be a site of resistance to the project of creating ideological uniformity across ethnic populations.[83] However, unlike clothing, facial features of those who didn't look stereotypically "Jewish," or other external markers, circumcision is not a publicly visible site of ethnic difference. If it is not discovered, it can coexist with full participation in Soviet public life. In "Karl-Yankel," the male Jew is specifically marked and made different in this way so as to enable him to conceal his identity and participate in Soviet public life. The story, focused on the Jewish body of a Soviet boy, suggests an alternative paradigm for "the brotherhood of the people" that is defined neither by visible, essentialized difference nor by the removal of difference but rather by a particularity that can be concealed. The Soviet Jew emerges here as a universal figure that is marked by hidden difference; as such, it is also a paradigm for other ethnocultural minorities that may in various ways resist becoming part of the Soviet people.

In "Karl-Yankel," a Jewish resident of Odessa, Ovsey Belotserkovsky, finds his upward mobility jeopardized after the birth of his son. A candidate for

Communist Party membership, he does not want his child circumcised, but the boy's grandmother, intent on preserving traditional customs, wants to make sure the ritual is observed. Such generational tension would have resonated with Babel's readers: narratives proliferated at the time about circumcision and other unwelcome "holdovers from the past"—*perezhitki proshlogo* in Soviet parlance—which also included Christian rituals like baptism.[84] While Belotserkovsky is away, his boy's grandmother obtains the services of the *mohel* Naftula, a colorful character with a long career circumcising boys in Odessa. The newborn, his flesh now marked, acquires a double name: Karl-Yankel. Karl (after Marx) is the name by which the Party aspirant Belotserkovsky calls his son; Yankel, a Jewish name (a diminutive of Jacob), is given to the boy during the circumcision ceremony, which, in the Jewish tradition, also includes the naming ritual.

Karl-Yankel's grandmother and others involved in the affair are put on trial in Odessa; the story's first-person narrator attends it while visiting his hometown.[85] Staged in the assembly hall of a factory, the trial attracts a large audience of locals and visitors from across the USSR and abroad, including a group of Hasidic Jews from Poland. Although the legal proceedings are the core of the story, the narrator takes a break from the state-sponsored spectacle to embark on a detour. Outside the courtroom, he comes upon a wet nurse breastfeeding Karl-Yankel; she is said to have the appearance of an ethnic Kyrgyz. The Central Asian wet nurse and a Russian woman, who is also present at the scene, start discussing the perfect Soviet future in store for the boy: one thinks he will grow up to become a military man; the other, a pilot. The scene is an apparent homage to the pervasive contemporary rhetoric of "the brotherhood of peoples" in the USSR and a celebration of the boy's potential to become a full-fledged Soviet citizen despite his Jewish difference.[86]

Babel's story might suggest, at first glance, that Karl-Yankel is a kind of deracinated Soviet everyman, stripped of his past and full of potential. However, Karl-Yankel is also a prototype for the figure of the Soviet Jew, who is located at the complex intersection of cultural systems. At one point the narrator remarks on the grandmother's religiosity: she "was devout, with a fanatical devotion." He continues,

In Volhynia, her native land, in the shtetl of Medzhibozh, the doctrine of Hasidism was born. The old woman went to the synagogue twice a week—on Friday evening and Saturday morning; the synagogue was a Hasidic one, and there at Passover people would dance themselves into a frenzy, like dervishes. [She] paid tribute to the emissaries whom the Galician *tsadiks* [rebbes] sent into the southern provinces. [Her husband] did not interfere in his wife's relations with God.[87]

Medzhibozh, the birthplace of Hasidism, played a significant role in the cultural geography of Babel's oeuvre. It was a garrison town whose troops were stationed in Odessa during the First World War and was mentioned in Babel's 1918 sketch about the coastal city. That article about Odessa, in turn, was published the same week as "Shabos-nakhamu," a story in which Medzhibozh—the dynastic seat of Borukhl's court and the place of Hershele's employment as the powerful rebbe's jester—figured as the destination of Hershele's meandering journey by foot.

The reference to Medzhibozh as the grandmother's birthplace in "Karl-Yankel" hints at Babel's idiosyncratic sense of geography. The town's persistence as a signpost in Babel's fiction helps explain the writer's mistaken placement of it in the wrong part of Ukraine: in Volhynia, instead of the neighboring region of Podolia. This error appeared in the first edition of the story in 1931; it was corrected in most subsequent editions. But "an error has an aura," as the literary scholar Svetlana Boym has quipped in her writing about the ludic, and so it warrants a further discussion.[88]

Medzhibozh's misplacement suggests that the toponym's meaning for Babel evolved over time. Lyutov's—and Babel's—wanderings in *Red Cavalry* took place in Volhynia, where the writer was attuned to the destruction of the region's Jewish communities. The first page of *Red Cavalry* captures Babel's awareness of its geography: "The quiet Volhynia bends. Volhynia recedes from us into the mist of birch groves and creeps into the flowery hills."[89] Babel's liberties with geography in "Karl-Yankel" follow his larger interest in "practiced space"—often at the expense of fidelity to the location of real places on a map.[90] Moving Medzhibozh from Podolia to Volhynia suggests that, like the other shtetls Babel visited during the 1920 war, Medzhibozh became somehow abstract for the writer as a physical place but accessible as an imagined space. "Karl-Yankel" considers how a universalizing Soviet discourse threatens to destroy and displace specific cultural sites, but at the same time, alternative cultural meanings linger and infuse these sites with unexpected interpretations.

Medzhibozh in the story effectively becomes a cultural remnant that points the narrative back to the trickster Hershele and his persistent presence in Babel's creative world.

The first published version of "Karl-Yankel," in which Babel erroneously placed Medzhibozh in Volhynia instead of Podolia, became the source for the Yiddish translation of the story published in the antireligious periodical *The Apostate (Der apikoyres)*. Printed alongside propaganda, the story in Yiddish appeared less like a work of fiction than like a narrative about the state's war on religion. The sentence that incorrectly locates Medzhibozh in Volhynia instead of Podolia contains another error: it refers to the grandmother's birthplace as "*voliner shtetl medzhibozh.*" In other words, the Yiddish transliterates the place name as "Medzhibozh," from the Russian, instead of using the accepted Yiddish spelling "Mezhbizh," which follows the spelling of the shtetl's name in Ukrainian.[91] Babel's spelling of the shtetl's name emphasizes the Yiddish translation's fidelity to the source text in Russian and calls attention to the text as one mediated through literal translation.

Babel's playful geographic dislocations and interlinguistic miscommunication manifest in Lyutov's discussion about Hershele with the Hasidic Jews in Zhitomir. Although "Rebbe" is written in Russian, its characters could not have interacted in any language other than Yiddish on a Sabbath eve in a Volhynian town heavily populated by Jews. Let's return to the phrase that precedes Lyutov's response about Hershele, "*Otkuda priekhal evrei?*" This is a direct Russian calque of the Yiddish phrase "*Fun vanen kumt a yid?*" (Where has the Jew come from?) At first glance, the wording of the rebbe's question seems no more than a direct rendering of the implied Yiddish original. However, the Yiddish *a yid* is idiomatic and does not actually mean *evrei* (Jew) in translation. Because Yiddish assumes its speakers to be Jews, *a yid* in this and other similar locutions means "a person" or, simply, "you." An idiomatic translation of the implied Yiddish phrase would be, simply, "Where are you from?"

The difference between the idiomatic and the calqued text is significant for three reasons. First, the rebbe's question is the only instance in *Red Cavalry* where Lyutov is openly—rather than implicitly, as has happened on other occasions—called a Jew. Second, this is the only time in *Red Cavalry* when Lyutov unambiguously self-identifies as a Jew by accepting the premise of the rebbe's question and engaging with it in his reply. This self-identification is aimed not at the rebbe in Zhitomir, who already understands that his Yiddish-speaking interlocutor is Jewish, but at the Russian-language reader of *Red Cavalry*. This reader is likely not aware that the dialogue between Lyutov and the rebbe should not have contained the word "Jew" to begin with—to this reader, the word simply identifies Lyutov as Jewish. By comparison, Lyutov does not directly confirm his Jewishness to First Cavalry Army personnel in other stories. Third, the calqued idiom in "Rebbe" sacrifices idiomatic language for a non-idiomatic and overly literal translated phrase in Russian. Through it, the text of the story indicates the existence of an implied Yiddish text beneath its surface, calling attention to Babel's Russian text itself as a translation—paradoxically, because there is actually no Yiddish original of "Rebbe."

Immediately after answering the question about his origins, Lyutov responds to the question about his occupation: "I am putting into verse [*perekladyvaiu v stikhi*] the adventures of Hershele Ostropoler." This Russian verb's morphological structure also calques an implied Yiddish original: the Russian prefix *pere-* is close in meaning to the Yiddish prefix *iber-,* whereas the Russian root *klast'* calques the Yiddish root *zetsen*. Given the numerous Russian calques in "Rebbe," the Russian for "I'm putting into [verse]"—*perekladyvaiu*—could be "translated" back into the implied Yiddish original as *ikh zets iber*—the first-person conjugation of the Yiddish verb *iber-zetsen:* "I'm translating" or "I translate."

Babel's use of *perekladyvaiu,* like other bits of literally translated Yiddish in *Red Cavalry,* is what Lawrence Venuti has called a "foreignizing" translation: in its lack of fluidity and awkward structure, the Russian text calls attention to its having been first imagined in another language.[92] That the phrase indicating this foreign context could be read as "I translate" reinforces the presence of an implied translation in the text. Likewise, "Karl-Yankel" associatively engages with the topic of translation in its focus on circumcision.

Circumcision and translation share a critical vocabulary that dates to early Christian polemics against Judaism. Practitioners of "word-for-word" translation, which privileges the source text over fluidity in the target language, have long been pitted against advocates of "sense-for-sense" translation, which prioritizes the target audience's reading experience over fidelity to the original. Circumcision became a proxy for this debate among early Christians who compared Judaism's emphasis on ritual observance to the pedantic "word-for-word" sort of translation. Early Christians sought converts to their redefined form of Judaism and saw the practice of male circumcision as an impediment to the spread of the new faith. At the same time, reinterpreting the Hebrew Bible as a universal text and translating it into non-Jewish languages, they wanted to promote the "spirit" of the new faith rather than obedience to the letter of the obsolete law. Paul famously expressed this dichotomy between spirit and law when he drew a distinction between the "circumcision of the heart"—a phrase initially found in Deuteronomy—and the circumcision of the flesh, the Jewish practice now deemed obsolete: "No, a person is a Jew who is one inwardly; and circumcision is circumcision of the heart, by the Spirit, not by the written code" (Romans 2:29). In the second century, the Greek translator Aquila of Sinope, a convert to Judaism who underwent circumcision as an adult, resisted early Christianity's imperative to make the biblical text universally appealing through sense-for-sense translation. Instead, he offered a literal and doggedly pedantic translation of the Hebrew Bible into Greek. In Aquila's translation, the scholar Naomi Seidman has noted, "Hebrew is inscribed into the Greek, we might almost say circumcised on it, as a mark that signals both Jewish affiliation and divine mimesis."[93] The circumcision of Aquila's flesh seemed to be reflected in his pedantic translation, which undermined the new faith's efforts to disseminate the Hebrew Bible as a universally accessible prequel to the emergent New Testament.

In "Karl-Yankel," the universalizing discourse of the nascent Soviet ideology is analogous to that of early Christianity. Communism's universality, centered on its appeal to all peoples regardless of ethnic, cultural, and religious differences, conflicted with the particularity of the circumcision ritual. The Soviet Jewish child's body in the story is marked as a culturally specific and pedantic text whose distinct physical features threaten to detract from the universal spirit of the new ideology. Babel offers a comparison between Karl-Yankel's circumcised body and a printed text through the words of the mohel Naftula. In Odessa people tell stories about how Naftula used to shout at women during circumcision ceremonies: "Fat mamas [. . .] print boys [*pechataite mal'chikov*] for Naftula [. . .] Print boys, fat mamas . . ."[94] Referring to the biblical commandment to reproduce, the mohel equates the birthing of male children with the production of texts.

Venuti has argued that the translator can become visible in the text through a "foreignizing" rendering that calls attention to itself as a translation—as opposed to a universalizing "sense-for-sense" translation that leads to "the translator's invisibility."[95] The narrator in Babel's story is akin to the translator: he perceptively observes established Jewish cultural codes and emerging Soviet cultural codes and makes himself visible by playing skillfully in their interstices. In "Karl-Yankel," circumcision is not merely a religious practice that threatens the aspirations of the boy's Party-bound father; it might also prevent the newborn from becoming a Soviet man. Circumcision marks the male Jew as a potentially destabilizing figure: although he may have the outward appearance of a Soviet person in terms of his clothing and in that not all Jews look phenotypically "Jewish," a look inside his pants—as in "The Road"—complicates matters. The Jewish body in Babel's story is a cultural text that resists a universalizing idiom, which, in turn, conceals the process of translation: Karl-Yankel cannot be seamlessly brought into a Sovietness that depends on the appeal of the new ideology across ethnocultural boundaries.

Although "Karl-Yankel" presumes the gradual disappearance of difference and shows all ethnic groups as equally committed to the Bolshevik cause, its emphasis on circumcision destabilizes the universalizing discourse about the "brotherhood of the peoples." With the trial still in progress, the narrator sees the child outside the courtroom in the factory's "red corner," in the arms of a wet nurse described as having the appearance of a Kyrgyz woman.[96] The Soviet red corner, a ubiquitous cultural appropriation of the Russian Orthodox space for hanging holy icons, was used to present the secular communist "covenant of the spirit" through displays of posters, slogans, and images. This is where Babel locates the baby Karl-Yankel, whose Jewish covenant is inscribed in his flesh, and his wet nurse, who imagines the boy's bright Soviet future while breastfeeding him. This Soviet Madonna with child serves as Babel's depiction of multiethnic unity: individuals will continue to be visibly identified as members of different groups only insofar as that difference proves the new ideology's universal appeal across lines of difference.

Scholars have scoffed at the breastfeeding scene, calling it Babel's forced, compromising nod to the Soviet regime and "a sugary vignette illustrative of the indestructible friendship of the peoples of the USSR."[97] However, Babel's noticeably awkward language makes the scene more complex.

The woman who nurses Karl-Yankel is not a "Kyrgyz worker," as numerous translations into English have put it, but rather "*rabotnitsa s litsom kirgizki*"; literally, "a worker with the face of a Kyrgyz woman."[98] This character is not, in other words, necessarily an ethnic Kyrgyz. The "face of a Kyrgyz woman" is more akin to an ethnic mask that matches the narrator's stereotype of a Central Asian person. The narrator might have absorbed this stereotype as a child in prerevolutionary Odessa, the port through which many devout Muslims from the Russian Empire's Central Asian colonies, as well as from China, India, and Persia, passed during the Hajj, the annual pilgrimage to Mecca.[99] The character with "the face of a Kyrgyz woman," if we are to understand her as symbolic of Central Asia more generally, invites the reader to consider the contemporary plight of several ethnic groups in that region of the USSR. During the Stalin-era industrialization and collectivization, local inhabitants there were forced to work on massive water engineering projects that diverted rivers for the irrigation of cotton fields; they were also herded onto collective farms on which this water-guzzling monoculture crop was cultivated. The resulting displacement, starvation, and spread of diseases like typhus and malaria affected whole population groups, disrupting their local agriculture and traditional ways of life.[100] Babel's story, then, doesn't so much depict the "brotherhood of the peoples" as grotesquely stages a performance of it that hints at the economic extraction and coerced transformation that continually underlay it.

In staging an aspect of Soviet ideology in a scene that contains elements of its own undoing, "Karl-Yankel" posits the circumcised body as both a stereotypical Jewish "mask" and a rich cultural text. But the motivation Babel provides for the circumcision suggests that the ritual's meaning goes beyond the physical appearance of the body. The newborn's grandmother wanted the boy circumcised not because she simply wished to maintain the Jewish custom but because, as the story puts it, she "needed a grandson to whom she could tell stories about the Baal Shem Tov."[101] On trial for enabling a Jewish lifecycle ritual, the grandmother in fact represents a less visible threat: Karl-Yankel's body has the potential to destabilize the state's ideological program not only because circumcision is perceived as a retrograde religious rite but also because the boy's grandmother believes that being ushered into Judaism's traditional covenant will make her grandson receptive to Jewish storytelling. The pedantic, subversive, "circumcised" text of a Jewish story might pose a far more serious challenge to state ideology than a physical mark identifying the boy as a Jew.

In "Shabos-nakhamu," Hershele steps into the role—or, rather, the cultural site—of the Sabbath of Comforting, thanks to the tavern keeper's wife's misunderstanding of Jewish custom. Karl-Yankel, circumcised at the request of a grandmother who cares less about the rite than about the continuity of Jewish storytelling, becomes a similar kind of cultural site open to idiosyncratic misreading and reinterpretation. The stories that the grandmother has in mind for Karl-Yankel feature her own hometown of Medzhibozh, which she shares with the founder of Hasidism, the Baal Shem Tov. As jester to Borukhl, the Baal Shem Tov's grandson, the trickster Hershele is associated with Medzhibozh as well.

Babel has repeatedly identified Hershele's hometown of Medzhibozh with a precarious nexus of creativity, subversion, and destruction. In his imaginative geography, Babel displaced Medzhibozh from Podolia, where Hasidism began as a joyous movement among Jewish communities facing despair, to Volhynia, where Babel had witnessed the Jewish community's destruction during the 1920 war between Poland and Bolshevik Russia. This substitution is a trickster's mischief: the toponym remains the same, but it moves into a symbolic position different from the one defined by the map. The new imaginative location of Medzhibozh belongs not in the world of actual geography but in the imaginative landscape marked by Babel's—and his trickster-narrators'—previous adventures.

Babel's textual trick in "Karl-Yankel" is more consequential than it first appears. It becomes visible only when viewed in connection with his earlier texts and the linkage they made between destruction and Hershele's trickery. Both the worker "with the face of a Kyrgyz woman" and Karl-Yankel contribute to the propagandistic iconography of the "brotherhood of peoples." Her flat ethnic mask, however, is out of balance with the Jewish boy's intertextually defined cultural mark. Her appearance positions her as a stereotype of a Central Asian woman, whereas the baby's circumcision codes him as part of a much more nuanced intergenerational tradition of Jewish storytelling. In setting up a structurally mismatched pair to represent the "brotherhood of the peoples," Babel suggests the existence of a hidden story beneath the surface of the text—a story about Hershele and, as such, a story about destruction. That missing narrative pertains to another ethnic group in the seemingly happy family of Soviet peoples that is threatened with destruction: Ukrainian peasants during the era of collectivization.

Ovsey Belotserkovsky was not home when his son was born. His absence from Odessa is what allows Karl-Yankel's grandmother to have the boy circumcised despite Belotserkovsky's objections. At the subsequent trial, Belotserkovsky testifies to that fact as his alibi. He further specifies that he was on a Party assignment far away from the city during the state's push to collectivize agriculture. By obliquely referring to Belotserkovsky's activities in the countryside, Babel smuggles into "Karl-Yankel" the story of the destruction that collectivization has wrought on Ukrainian peasantry.

During his court testimony, Belotserkovsky hints at his whereabouts during his absence:

> According to Ovsey [Belotserkovsky], the Tiraspol and Balta district Party committees had cooperated fully in the procuring of oilcake [*po zagotovke zhmykhov*]. When the work was in full swing he had received a telegram with the news of the birth of the son. After having a word with the organization manager of the Balta district committee, he decided not to interrupt the procurement and to confine himself to the dispatch of a congratulatory telegram . . . He himself returned only two weeks later. In all, sixty-four thousand poods [approximately 2.3 million pounds] of oilcake had been collected. No one was home, except for the witness Kharchenko—a neighbor and laundress by profession—and his infant son. His wife was away at the hospital, and the witness Kharchenko was rocking the cradle and was engaged in the now-obsolete practice of singing a lullaby. Knowing the witness to be an alcoholic, he did not find it necessary to try making out the words of this song, but he was taken aback to hear her call the boy Yasha [a diminutive of the Russian version of Yankel], when he had expressly given instructions that his son be named Karl, in honor of our esteemed teacher Karl Marx. Unwrapping the child's swaddling clothes, he came face-to-face with his misfortune.[102]

On assignment facilitating the procurement of oilcake (*zhmykh*), used as livestock feed, Belotserkovsky doesn't leave work and return home when his son is born. The job demands his undivided attention and he is eager to prove himself to his superiors. His testimony is full of upbeat reports

about his activities in the countryside but ends with his seeing his son's circumcised penis.

Belotserkovsky's testimony outlines the nature of his duties and the results
of his work during his expedition to the countryside. But there is a fissure in
Belotserkovsky's testimony: he notes but does not account for the gap of two
weeks separating the birth of his son from his return to Odessa. The ellipsis
between Belotserkovsky's description of his trip to Balta and the narrative of
his return to Odessa—printed in the first publication of the story in the
journal *Zvezda* in 1931 but removed from subsequent editions of this story—
suggests a pause in his court statement. Both the time gap in the account and
the pause in Belotserkovsky's testimony demarcate a boundary between what
had occurred in the vicinity of Balta and what happened later, in Odessa.
Tasked with producing an account of his activities for the public, Belotserkovsky lets it slip at the trial that there exists also a hidden narrative,
which the public never hears. As a candidate for Party membership, he can't
divulge this untold story—about the horrors of collectivization in Ukraine—
and so the task of making the hidden visible falls to the author, who resorts
to tricks from Hershele's repertoire. Babel had witnessed these horrors but
could not describe them directly, yet he could imply them through the testimony of a fictional character.

In 1930, Babel traveled to the Ukrainian countryside to observe the process of collectivization. His work for *The New Life* in 1918 had brought him
to some of the more macabre places in Petrograd just after the revolution.
His assignment with *The Red Cavalryman* during the 1920 war made him a
witness to violence experienced by Jews in Eastern Poland and Western
Ukraine. Babel's trip to Ukraine in 1930, meanwhile, exposed him to terror
that, according to one of the letters he wrote to his mother and sister, left "one
of the sharpest impressions in [his] life [*odno iz samykh rezkikh vospominanii
v moei zhizni*]."[103] These horrors, including the intentional starving of Ukrainians that would come to be known as the Holodomor, were a taboo subject
at the time of Babel's trip, when collectivization was trumpeted as a mile-
stone in the USSR's economic restructuring.

In 1918 and 1920, Babel produced both journalistic accounts and literary
fiction about Petrograd and the Bolsheviks' war with Poland, but he did not
manage to produce any nonfictional texts about what he had seen in Ukraine
in 1930. Nonetheless, "Karl-Yankel," published one year after Babel's trip,

includes in the protagonist's court testimony the sort of precise statistics that Babel would have included in a journalistic report had he written one. Belotserkovsky's testimony—with an absent account of terror hiding in its gaps—is an act of narrative trickery modeled on Hershele's mischief. Hershele's strategy of intimidation by omission is on display in the folktale about his empty threat to show a tavern keeper "what [his] father did" in response to not being given food. In Belotserkovsky's testimony, this strategy of omission takes the form of an elision. Like Lyutov's substitutions of "merriment" for "horror," it masks the horror that actually occurred and, in so doing, makes the narrative of that horror all the more apparent for the reader.

Karl-Yankel's father likely participated in requisitioning crops from Ukrainian peasants during collectivization. He would have considered this work important enough to keep him from traveling home soon after the birth of his son. The Yiddish translation of "Karl-Yankel" in *Der apikoyres* was laid out next to a report on the collectivization of recently established Jewish agricultural settlements in Crimea: the subtext of collectivization in "Karl-Yankel" would have been easily apparent to those who read both stories in the same issue of the journal. Belotserkovsky's testimony mentions one activity in particular—*zagotovka zhmykhov,* the preparation of oilcake. *Zhmykh* is made from the sunflower seeds discarded after extracting oil from sunflowers. A common livestock feed, *zhmykh* was used in place of flour during collectivization when wheat and other grains were routinely expropriated from peasants.

As a byproduct of the sunflower plant, oilcake also points to the sunflower itself. Sunflowers feature in "Gapa Guzhva," one of only two short stories Babel wrote about collectivization in Ukraine. Gapa, known for her sexual promiscuity, visits a Party representative who had been sent to oversee the requisitioning of crops.[104] His predecessor had been inefficient and was replaced; the new Party representative ruthlessly strives to exceed the state's quotas, driving local peasants to suicide. The village appears doomed. Visiting his office, "Gapa took a bag of sunflower seeds from under her skirt."[105] In Russian, the phrase—"*Gapa vyvernula iz-pod iubki koshel' s podsolnukhami*"—names the direct object "a pouch of sunflowers" rather than "a bag of sunflower seeds": Babel refers to the seeds as a synechdoche for the entire plant, symbolically preserving the whole sunflower plant in the text.[106]

"Gapa Guzhva," with its mention of sunflowers, appeared in October 1931, three months after "Karl-Yankel" and its mention of oilcake—the squeezed remnant of the same plant. Babel would have been aware of the symbolic connection between sunflowers and Ukraine, especially from late 1929 through the early 1930s when it was undergoing collectivization. The Ukrainian film director Oleksandr Dovzhenko made the image of the sunflower central to *Earth*, released in the fall of 1929 and publicly denounced by the spring of 1930. The film's most iconic shot juxtaposes a sunflower plant with the face of a young woman: a montage of organic images of fertility, femininity, and youthfulness representative of Ukraine itself.[107]

"Karl-Yankel" ends as the narrator looks out of a factory window onto the streets of Odessa, with the trial still in progress inside the building. Lyutov, the narrator of *Red Cavalry* who told the group of Hasidic Jews in Zhitomir that he, like Hershele, peddles "verse" and deals in trickery, also looks out of the window of their rebbe's court as his Sabbath meal there draws to a close: "The wilderness of war gaped outside the window."[108] Images of destruction, attached to the wandering figure of Hershele, are woven through Babel's oeuvre via interlinked allusions to the trickster. They also appear at the end of "Gapa Guzhva," a story about collectivization linked implicitly to "Karl-Yankel": "The piercing, frenzied night hurled itself down on her with thickets of low-hanging clouds—twisted ice floes lit up by black sparks. Silence spread over [the village], over the flat, sepulchral, frozen desert of the village night."[109] Babel's interest in Hershele contains dark undertones. It turns the trickster into an embodiment and literary marker of instability, indirectness, and manipulation. Babel's Hershele, a cipher for the early Bolshevik years, marks this period of revolutionary promise as unstable and tragic.

In creating an idiosyncratic version of Hershele at the intersection of Jewish storytelling and Soviet ideology, Babel molds a new cultural type, the Soviet Jew. Karl-Yankel, whose body is marked through an ethnoculturally specific rite, is a prototype of the Soviet Jew deployed to create new and unexpected meanings within the confines of state ideology. Babel reinterprets circumcision as more than merely a vestige of a Jew's former rootedness in a cohesive traditional community of the former Pale of Settlement: in "Karl-Yankel" circumcision becomes a proxy for the cultural specificity of narrative, an indication of the possibility of creating new narratives suitable to emerging historical realities with the help of techniques from Jewish storytelling. The figure of the Soviet Jew that emerges in "Karl-Yankel," moreover, is capable of narrating not only the experience of Jews in the USSR but also the submerged experiences of other groups in "the brotherhood of the peoples."

* * *

"From the window flew the straight streets that I had walked all over in my childhood and youth," the narrator of "Karl-Yankel" observes. "Pushkin Street stretched toward the station, and Malo-Arnautskaya Street extended into the park beside the sea."[110] The literary scholar Efraim Sicher offers a straightforward interpretation of these place names: "Pushkin Street clearly speaks for the Russian literary tradition and the cultural memory of [the Russian poet Alexander] Pushkin's exile in Odessa in 1823–1824 [. . .] but [Malo-Arnautskaya] is where [the Hebrew poet Chaim Nachman] Bialik lived until 1921, as every Odessa Jew knew."[111] Sicher sees these two streets as representing a rigid dichotomy between fixed Russian and Jewish cultural markers: Pushkin Street is "clearly" the domain of "Russian" culture, whereas Malo-Arnautskaya, "as every Odessa Jew knew," is "Jewish." For Sicher, the "Jewish" meaning of the toponym makes "Karl-Yankel" a reliably "Jewish" story and displays the writer's ethnocultural allegiances within the text. The plot about a challenge to a religious rite, Sicher suggests, is to be read as an assault on Judaism in the USSR.

However, there is a different way to walk Odessa's streets: not as straight, unidirectional vectors but instead as loci fit for a more idiosyncratic "practice of space." The Soviet Jew whom Babel sketches in his work is a pedestrian capable of navigating this map. He is a figure whose Jewishness manifests not in the stable cultural markers that Sicher envisions but, instead, remaps cultural elements that became dislodged from their traditional contexts in the former Pale of Settlement and became diffused within the evolving Soviet culture.

The trial in "Karl-Yankel" takes place inside the Petrovsky tobacco factory located, as the text notes, at the corner of Pushkin and Malo-Arnautskaya Streets.[112] This intersection was a geographic reality before it became symbolic evidence for what Sicher takes to be the clash of Russian and Jewish cultures. Although Sicher assigns a fixed symbolic significance to these streets, the text of the story points to a more malleable, open-ended set of meanings, rooted in the cultural landscape of the narrator's native Odessa.

Assessing the view from the factory window, the narrator comments on what he sees in the narrative present while superimposing his childhood memories on the landscape in front of him: "From the window flew [*iz okna leteli*] the straight [*priamye*] streets that I had walked all over in my childhood and youth [*iskhozhennye detstvom moim i iunostiu*] [. . .] I had grown up in these streets, and now it was Karl-Yankel's turn [. . .]"[113] The narrator's vision is shaped both by the point of view of an observer looking from an elevated distance and by the perspective of someone who had once been a pedestrian familiar with navigating the city at the street level. A view at once from both above and below, the narrator's idiosyncratic assessment of the scene captures both the prescriptive sense of geographic place and the idiosyncratic practice of space.

There are at least two ways for understanding the narrator's vision in "Karl-Yankel" as aligned with the state's institutions and symbols of authority. First, he looks out at the street from the window of the factory's "red corner," which houses Lenin's portraits, the factory's production statistics, and ideological slogans—all markers of state power. Second, other parts of the story—including the transcript of the speech by Karl-Yankel's father and the prosecutor's questioning of the boy's mother and the mohel Naftula—point to the possibility that the narrator attended the trial as a journalist reporting on antireligious campaigns. In this sense, the story's narrator resembles Babel, who reported on Petrograd in 1918 and who participated in the 1920 Polish campaign as a member of the propagandistic press. The Yiddish translation of "Karl-Yankel" came out in an antireligious periodical and contained narrative threads that could have belonged in a reported news story rather than in a piece of fiction.

At the same time, the narrator of "Karl-Yankel" supplants his perspective as an observer proximate to state power with the alternative perspective of an urban pedestrian who covertly resists such a top-down gaze. He had "practiced" this space when he was a child, and his experience allowed him to challenge the apparent "straightness" of the streets he now observes from above. Like *Red Cavalry*'s Lyutov, who participates both in the creation and subversion of state rhetoric, and like Hershele in "Shabos-nakhamu" who helps uphold Hasidic power while circuitously questioning it from within, the narrator of "Karl-Yankel" plays two sides at once.

When he was a child, the narrator made his own way through Odessa's streets. He knows that the streets he now depicts as "straight" could be experienced, instead, as labyrinthine. When the narrator comments that "Karl-Yankel's turn" has come, he suggests that he wants Karl-Yankel to someday master these implicitly twisting paths, not the straight roads visible from the factory window. The straightness of Pushkin Street that the narrator now sees is akin to the straightness of Lenin's speech as it appears to the Cossacks when Lyutov reads them the army newspaper in "My First Goose." Lyutov can both perform this supposedly straightforward text for others and appreciate its "curved" and indirect nature; Babel's autobiographical narrator in "Karl-Yankel" can similarly see both the directness and the twisted nature of such trajectories at one and the same time.

From the factory window, the narrator of "Karl-Yankel" sees Pushkin Street oriented not toward the center of Odessa but toward the train station on the opposite side of the city: "Pushkin Street stretched toward the station," he notes. This detail marks Pushkin Street less as a fixed topos of things indisputably "Russian" but more as a route that situates Odessa's train station, at the end of Pushkin Street, as a point of departure—literally and figuratively. The narrator's nostalgic tone about the Odessa of his childhood suggests that he may have returned to the city after leaving it some years earlier for a place more central to Soviet culture, in which he has become a participant. Given Babel's messianic dreams, stated in his 1916 manifesto "Odessa," of bringing the fun-loving and sunny spirit of his native city to the literary tradition based in gray and dreary Petersburg, and the desires of the first-person narrator of "The Road" to conquer Russia's literary capital, "Karl-Yankel" might also be read as a story of authorial self-invention. The street named after Russia's national poet leads to the train station and out of Odessa—the path that the autobiographic narrator of "The Road" took when he set out, via Kiev, toward the city he imagined as the Petersburg of Russian literature.

When Sicher draws a straight line from the toponym of Malo-Arnautskaya Street to the Hebrew poet Bialik, he suggests that the intersecting streets refer to a "Jewish cultural context [that] unlock[s] the subtext of a 'double book-keeping.'" He argues that "Karl-Yankel" contains a "Jewish" meaning hidden from all but those who know how to look for it.[114] By this logic, Pushkin Street is the Russian half of the elusive Russian-Jewish identity, for which Babel has been made a kind of standard-bearer. But the narrator has reminded us that long before he saw these streets as "straight" from a factory window, he used to walk them as a child at his own pace—as a one-time "practitioner of space." Malo-Arnautskaya Street does not have to be associated solely with Bialik as a stand-in for "Jewish culture," and Pushkin Street, too, may have associations other than the obvious connection to its namesake.

Near the opposite end of Odessa's Pushkin Street, farthest away from the train station, stands a statue of the preeminent Russian poet after whom the street is named. Yuri Slezkine cites a scene from Babel's story "Di Grasso" that is set in front of this statue to illustrate his thesis about the affinity for Russian high culture among Jewish writers of Babel's generation. These writers, Slezkine argues, had to "convert" to the "Pushkin faith," mastering the Russian language and high culture.[115] Like Sicher, who considers Pushkin Street in Babel's topography as symbolic of Russian (as opposed to Jewish) culture, Slezkine sees a fixed opposition between that which is "Russian" and represented by the figure of Pushkin and that which is "Jewish." Slezkine concludes, "If the Russian world stood for speech, knowledge, freedom, and light, then the Jewish world represented silence, ignorance, bondage, and darkness."[116] For Sicher, the "Jewishly" coded part of Odessa's topography possesses a kind of hidden but positively marked meaning, whereas for Slezkine the same part of the equation represents a place from which Babel and his Jewish contemporaries needed to escape. The opposite assessments of the two scholars are two sides of the same coin: both presume a conflict and a rigid separation between that which is "Russian" and that which is "Jewish." However, this understanding is misleading.

In "Di Grasso," which Slezkine uses as a prooftext for his argument about Jewish writers' attraction to the "Pushkin faith," Babel deploys the protagonist's first-person perspective to recall his childhood in Odessa: "I stood there alone, clutching my watch, and suddenly, with a clarity such as I had never experienced before, I saw the soaring columns of the Duma, the illuminated foliage on the boulevard, and Pushkin's bronze head touched by a dim reflection of the moon. For the first time in my life, I saw the world around me the way it really was: serene and beautiful."[117] Presenting Babel as the paradigmatic practitioner of the "Pushkin faith," Slezkine sees Pushkin's statue in Odessa as a clear symbol of Russian literary culture—much like Sicher sees Malo-Arnautskaya Street as an unambiguous reference to Jewish culture produced for a knowing Jewish reader. However, Slezkine overlooks the historical context. Like the young walker in the streets whom the older narrator remembers from his elevated perch in "Karl-Yankel," Babel's narrator in "Di Grasso" is a pedestrian. He stands near the beginning of Pushkin Street, in front of the statue erected by the citizens of Odessa to commemorate the poet's yearlong stay in the city in the 1820s. Babel's narrator would not only have seen Pushkin from that spot but he would also have seen the City Duma right behind the statue. An urban legend has it that the Pushkin statue faces away from the Duma in defiance of the city government that had refused to contribute funds for its construction.

One of the last stories published in Babel's lifetime, "Di Grasso" came out in *Ogonëk* in 1937 and appeared alongside extensive coverage of two events celebrated during the height of Stalin's purges: the revolution's twentieth anniversary and the centennial of Pushkin's death. The elevation of Pushkin to the status of "the great poet [*velikii poet*]" in public discourse in 1937 placed him on a pedestal next to another outsized personality of the time—Stalin.[118] In 1937, the building of the Odessa Duma, before which the Pushkin statue stands, housed Odessa's regional committee of the Communist Party. In the context in which "Di Grasso" was first published, the poet's statue is not just a symbol of Russian high culture; it is also closely associated with the cultural symbolism of High Stalinism. By 1937, the Pushkin statue's position in front of the Party headquarters made it a complex cultural site. When the narrator "Di Grasso" experiences an epiphany in front of Pushkin's statue in Odessa, Babel describes not the process of a Jew escaping Jewishness into Russianness but the evolution of a new figure, the Soviet Jew, who dwelt in the extensive complexities of culture after the revolution.

* * *

When Babel published "Shabos-nakhamu" in 1918, the young writer from Odessa offered his Russian readers a story about Hershele Ostropoler as a paradigm, informed by Jewish storytelling, for dealing with destruction and despair. Through the story's subtitle, which appeared to identify it as an installment "from the *Hershele* cycle," Babel seemed to promise that "Shabos-nakhamu" would be one in a series of stories about the folkloric Yiddish trickster. This cycle never materialized as a clearly delineated collection of short stories.

However, Babel's apparent promise contained a couple of linguistic tricks: the phrase "*Iz tsikla 'Gershele'*" in the subtitle of "Shabos-nakhamu" does not mean only, literally, "from the cycle [entitled] 'Hershele'"—or, rather, "from the *Hershele* cycle" as the subtitle has been translated into English. In the Russian original, the word "Hershele" is in quotation marks, suggesting the title of an unrealized cycle of short stories. But the conventions of Russian grammar also allow for these quotation marks to be read as ironic scare quotes. In this reading, someone purporting to be Hershele—or, rather, *like* Hershele—is the apparent author (rather than only the subject) of "Shabos-nakhamu." In such a reading, both the words "cycle" and "Hershele" would be in the Russian genitive case and the phrase could be read as "from the cycle of 'Hershele.'" "Shabos-nakhamu," then, can be read as a tale from a cycle of stories by someone pretending to be—or humorously but knowingly comparing himself to—the famous Yiddish trickster. When all the direct and implicit references to Hershele Ostopoler are assembled from across Isaac Babel's oeuvre, Babel emerges as a writer who, posing as a trickster not unlike Hershele, generated a repertoire of stories that illustrate how narrative playfulness worked in a range of complicated historical contexts during the first two decades after the Bolshevik Revolution.

Hershele, whose shenanigans Babel instrumentalized to create a model of authorship for himself, at times appeared interchangeable with Babel the author. The Soviet Jew that the writer created over the course of his literary career, tragically cut short by Babel's arrest in 1939 and execution in 1940, was a trickster, too. Babel's implicit thematic cycle of work about Hershele, a figure associated with prerevolutionary Jewish culture, is a sequence of scattered moments in which Babel—along with his protagonists—negotiates major features of the early Soviet experience: the messianic import of the revolution, its accompanying destruction, the creation of state propaganda, and the repercussions of Soviet universalism. When, in doing so, he adopts terms from the layers of Jewish culture, he intends neither to highlight exclusively Jewish concerns nor to escape Jewishness and convert to "the Pushkin faith." As a journalist, propagandist, and nonfiction writer—and as a writer of literary fiction—Babel was deeply engaged with the issues of his day. Filled with linguistic trickery and symbolic substitution drawn from the Hershele Ostropoler of Yiddish folklore, the apparent cycle of Hershele stories that Babel began to present to his readers in 1918 became, as it were, Hershele's cycle: a cycle of texts *by* someone like Hershele rather than only *about* Hershele. Over the course of two decades, Hershele—like Babel—cycles through an idiosyncratically "practiced" space, negotiates some of the most pressing challenges of the early Soviet years, and repeatedly calls its culture's utopian promises into question. In Isaac Babel's work, Hershele's cycle became a cultural site where the figure of the Soviet Jew is playfully woven together from the seemingly disjointed bits of multiple cultural systems during the first twenty years of the Soviet experiment.

Epilogue

Returns to the Shtetl

Isaac Babel was not the only writer to turn to Hershele Ostropoler—part of the now-scattered cultural ecosystem of the former Pale of Settlement—for inspiration in telling stories of the Soviet experience, nor were the two decades after the Bolshevik Revolution the only time when the Yiddish folkloric trickster influenced Soviet culture. In the late 1970s, Hirsh (Grigorii) Polyanker (1911–1998) wrote a novel called *The Teacher from Medzhibozh*. This text transplanted Hershele into a narrative of the Second World War, which continued to loom large over Soviet history more than three decades after Nazi Germany's defeat in 1945.

The novel's protagonist, Ilya Frenkis, was born in Medzhibozh not long after the revolution and became known as a jokester and prankster as a child. In a town associated with the historical figure who became a folkloric jester, Ilya's tricks quickly earned him a reputation as "Hershele Ostropoler's descendant or grandson."[1] Ilya acquired German-Russian interpretation skills as part of his army training, which would have taken place during the two-year period of cooperation between Nazi Germany and the USSR. The short-lived alliance ended when Germany broke the August 1939 nonaggression pact and invaded the Soviet Union in June 1941. Within months, Jews residing in the territory of the former Pale of Settlement fell victim to the genocidal violence of the Holocaust.[2] The fictional Ilya, intended to represent the half-million Jews in the USSR who served in the Red Army, headed to the front while his family and townsmen who hadn't managed to evacuate into the Soviet interior faced destruction at mass execution sites in or near their home shtetls and cities.

At the front, Ilya's fellow soldiers appreciate his sense of humor, and he tells them that he learned how to jest from listening to the tales about Hershele that had been popular with his townsfolk. When he is wounded and taken captive by the Nazis in a Ukrainian town, the quick-witted Ilya burns his papers to thwart being identified as a Jew, renames himself Ernst, and claims to have come from a town that had been populated by the so-called Volga Germans (or Russian Germans) since the eighteenth century.[3] The Wehrmacht officer to whom he surrenders accepts Ilya's cover story and appoints Ilya/Ernst as his translator. Ilya uses his skills and position as an interpreter to share classified military information with Soviet citizens living under German occupation. Ilya compares his life-saving identity stunt to a trick deftly executed by Hershele, and the novel presents Hershele as the inspiration for his acts of deliberate mistranslation. As the Nazis attempt to suppress information to spin their own wartime propaganda more effectively, Ilya's acts of mistranslation give his fellow Soviets a clearer sense of the course of the war.

In its Russian translation, printed in an impressive run of 65,000 copies, *The Teacher from Medzhibozh* appeared in a style accessible to school-age readers as one of numerous hagiographic texts about real and fictionalized wartime heroes. Though Polyanker's Hershele, like Babel's, emerged from Yiddish folklore, he could also reach far beyond Jewish audiences. Ukrainian peasants, like Hasidic Jews, had their traumatic stories refracted in Babel's Hershele. Likewise, Polyanker's incarnation of the trickster helped save the lives of non-Jewish Soviet citizens after their Jewish neighbors who hadn't managed to evacuate had already been murdered.

Like Hershele, the shtetl itself persisted after the Pale's dissolution. Despite being imagined "as a foil, or simply a wellspring from which Jewish modernity has emerged," as the historian Jeffrey Veidlinger has written, the shtetl continued to exist long into the Soviet period. On the basis of oral histories conducted in the 2000s with elderly Jews in the Podolia region of Ukraine, where Hershele's Medzhibozh is located, Veidlinger describes Jews who continued to live in their small towns in the former Pale between the revolution and the Second World War. After surviving the war at the front, in hiding, or in evacuation, some of Veidlinger's informants returned to their native towns and continued living there—albeit in vastly diminished numbers—through the remainder of the Soviet era and beyond.[4] As the shtetl persisted in situ in a significantly reduced form, its culture disseminated far more widely via storytelling. The figure of the Soviet Jew, formed out of the displaced cultural elements of the Pale, was propelled into the vortex of Bolshevik modernity and would journey through the Soviet century and beyond while carrying baggage still stamped with its place of origin.

The original Hershele, like most Jews living in the Pale before the revolution, spoke Yiddish. In the two decades after the revolution, this Yiddish became inflected with a "Sovietizing" Russian vocabulary and syntax. As they learned Russian, the Jews' speech and writing in that state language retained elements of the worldview and folkways expressed in Yiddish. The Soviet Jew was a survivor of pogroms in the years after the revolution. This experience of trauma was obliquely narrated as this figure's defining feature in a language influenced by the then-new Bolshevik-speak. The Soviet Jew was also a collector of ethnographic and linguistic tidbits from a familial, Yiddish-speaking space that was being submerged into larger Soviet cities. Such cultural fragments could appear to some as items of salvage destined for the proverbial dustbin of history but be deemed by others as worthy of preservation and ongoing interpretation. The government considered the Jew capable of becoming, like a representative of any other "national" group, an ethnic variant of the New Soviet Man. In official rhetoric, this transformation would occur both through being resettled in faraway Birobidzhan, designated as a Jewish "national" territory with Yiddish as its official language, and by repatriating to the USSR from abroad and experiencing a process of ideological conversion. But the resettled or repatriated Jew ultimately became a figure of non-arrival. The Soviet Jew retained bits and pieces of Yiddish language and folkways within coded patterns of speech, wordless melodies, and narrative associations that resisted the official linguistic and political push to resettle, whether physically or ideologically. And then there was, of course, Isaac Babel's Hershele—an especially persistent example of a figure from Yiddish folklore who became a kind of cipher for the Soviet Jew.

Yiddish did not disappear in the first two decades after the revolution, nor did it vanish later; literature in Yiddish continues to be written and Yiddish literature written in the Soviet Union continues to be translated.[5] Nonetheless, with the passage of time, its cohort of speakers aged as younger generations abandoned the Jewish vernacular due to the linguistic pressure exerted by Russian. The vast majority of Yiddish speakers were killed in the Holocaust. Before the Holocaust, Yiddish shaped Russian as a language of the Soviet Jewish experience in a way that resembled its effect on the English of Ashkenazi Jews in the United States in the same period. As in the United States at the time, many Jews in the Soviet Union before the Second World War would have grown up in Yiddish-speaking homes, only to move more firmly into their country's dominant language by the century's middle. But dialectical variants of Russian shaped by Yiddish speech patterns continued to resonate in literary work. American readers are familiar with the Yiddish-inflected English in *Portnoy's Complaint,* published in 1969 by the American writer Philip Roth. Likewise, the Russian writer Fridrikh Gorenshtein, who was Roth's contemporary, participated in what literary scholar Adrien Smith has termed "a broader trend in which major-language writers have suggested that the dialects of their country's margins are, at times, better equipped to expand the literary tradition than the standard, publicly available language."[6]

Gorenshtein's play *Berdichev*—written, set, and published (at first, abroad) in the mid-1970s but staged for the first time only in the twenty-first century—kept the Yiddish-influenced language of the USSR's margins within the orbit of Russian culture. "Yiddish inhabits Russian, ignoring its rules and usages completely," Harriet Murav has written of the play's characteristic style.[7] Similarly, the well-known satirist and stand-up performer Mikhail Zhvanetsky (1934–2020) studded his work with Odessa's Jewish dialect of Russian, which remained at the center of Soviet and post-Soviet public cultures well into the twenty-first century. The margins from which this defamiliarizing language came, in this case, were heavily Jewish shtetls and bigger cities in what had been the Pale of Settlement, including Gorenshtein's Berdichev and Zhvanetsky's Odessa. Though these spaces were irrevocably changed by decades of violent turbulence, they retained attributes of Jewishness that became uniquely identified with the figure of the Soviet Jew. These attributes, in turn, continued to circulate in Russia's cultural centers.

In important ways, as literary scholar Evgeny Dobrenko has observed, the USSR's 1941–1945 war against Nazi Germany—known to this day in Russia and across most of the former Soviet Union as the Great Patriotic War—created a rupture in the Soviet historical narrative so significant that it effectively replaced the Bolshevik Revolution of 1917 as the foundational event of the Soviet experience. The regime associated with the industrialization era and the purges of the late 1930s—which swept up Moyshe Kulbak (executed in 1937) and Isaac Babel (executed in 1940), along with many others—reflected Stalin's attempts to appropriate a revolution that he did not personally helm. Late Stalinism—the period between the war's end and Stalin's death in 1953— was an entirely different phenomenon. Convincingly presenting himself as an undisputed leader in the Third Reich's ultimate defeat, Stalin no longer struggled for dominance under the long shadow of Lenin's revolution.[8]

This shift in domestic politics brought about the foreign policy reorientation that became known as the Cold War. Both altered the dimensions of the Soviet Jewish experience. Before the Second World War, the Soviet Jew came into being within an idiosyncratic and culturally rich response to the Soviet state's attempts to reform Jews, like other non-Russian ethnic groups, into model Soviet citizens. After the war, in contrast, Jews started to be seen as a fifth column undermining the state from within. The high-profile, state-sanctioned Jewish Antifascist Committee (1941–1948) that raised foreign funds for the Soviet war effort became, in the late 1940s, the exemplary target of this growing suspicion. Solomon Mikhoels, who, among numerous other theatrical and cinematic roles, played Tsale in *The Return of Neitan Bekker,* was murdered in 1948 as a public antisemitic campaign against a euphemistically identified "cosmopolitanism" engulfed the Soviet Union. David Bergelson—like Mikhoels, a member of the Jewish Antifascist Committee—was arrested in 1949 and executed in 1952, as were Peretz Markish and other notable Soviet Yiddish literary figures who served, along with several Jewish functionaries with no connection to the arts, as committee members. Semyon Gekht was arrested earlier, in 1944, on made-up charges of anti-Soviet propaganda; in some ways, he was "lucky" to have spent these turbulent years far away from the changing political winds. By the time of Stalin's violent final years, the author of the novel about Birobidzhan was already in the Gulag, from which he was released in 1952. Gekht went on to live another decade, during which, in the war's aftermath, he wrote about its legacy.[9]

In many ways, the tragic fate of these notable Jewish cultural figures at the end of Stalin's reign came to be associated with the Soviet Jewish experience writ large. "Tragic history is a narrative strategy whose crafters select particular historical moments for the telling; it puts the end of the story before the story itself, and in its most extreme case, puts death before life," wrote the historian David Shneer, who meditated on the way later associations cast their shadow backward onto earlier periods.[10] The historical trauma of the Holocaust and of the immediate postwar years did, indeed, loom so large over lived experience and cultural imagination that it colored all that came before it—and much that came after it—in singularly tragic tones. This has, on occasion, resulted in scholars overlooking important literary texts written long before the devastations of the mid-century because they found it hard to see them as anything more than a prelude to this overdetermined history. Yet, one cannot ignore the tragic fact that so many of the individuals who created the cultural texts discussed in this book did not survive Stalin's regime. Perhaps, then, it is important to recognize that the Soviet Jew developed in response to one historical rupture and on the eve of another, which would reshape it yet further. Before the Soviet Jew came to be seen, especially among Jews in North America, in entirely tragic tones as a victim of cruel historical forces, this figure evolved in far more polyvalent circumstances. This book has been an attempt less to outline a prehistory of the Soviet Jew who was emblazoned on Cold War–era posters, banners, and pins as a figure in need of being "saved" by the West, than an effort to explore the Soviet Jew as a phenomenon all its own.

* * *

In the short story "The End of the Almshouse," with which I began this book, Isaac Babel describes a band of elderly Jews as a "heap of rags" stranded in the middle of the road. This image gives way, nearly eight decades after it was penned, to the group of protagonists introduced by the writer Margarita Khemlin (1960–2015) in her tellingly named 2008 short story collection *A Living Queue (Zhivaia ochered')*. Babel's old Jews were already nearing the end of their lives just after the revolution when they were expelled from an old-age home near the cemetery. That moment was when most of Khemlin's protagonists were just beginning to be born into the turbulent Soviet century; their stories narrate the ebbs and flows of the Jewish experience in the Soviet Union from the Bolshevik Revolution until after the USSR's demise. The "heap of rags"—symbolic of the scattered cultural attributes of the former Pale of Settlement—becomes "a living queue" of Soviet Jewish voices that resonate through the decades. An especially striking story in *A Living Queue*, "About Zhenya" (Pro Zheniu), centers the difficulty of retrospectively narrating a Soviet Jewish experience in which the past continues to haunt the present.

Solomon—whose grandson's wife is the title character and narrator of "About Zhenya"—was a wealthy merchant in Chernobyl who made his fortune shipping timber down the Dnieper River before 1917. When the revolution takes place, Solomon gathers the local Jews in the synagogue and encourages them to close shop, sell their houses, pack up the synagogue's sacred books and ritual objects, and flee to Palestine. Local Jews protest—Chernobyl had been the seat of an important Hasidic dynasty and they don't want the shtetl to empty out—but Solomon insists, "Let it stand empty. Our holy men [*tsadiki,* from Hebrew] lie in the ground here—it will never be empty."[11] Nonetheless, two of Solomon's three sons refuse to accompany him and their mother and instead run off to join the Red Army as the civil war engulfs the region. Solomon's departure is delayed when marauders begin to plunder the area, making their flight impossible. Solomon, his wife, and their then-youngest son Aronchik—who, when he grows up, begets Zhenya's future husband—find their way to Ostyor, a shtetl a hundred kilometers away on the eastern bank of the Dnieper.

Ostyor is not far from the city of Chernigov, where Margarita Khemlin grew up in the 1960s; the shtetl also appears as a kind of gravitational pole of the Soviet Jewish story in several of Khemlin's other works.[12] Once there, Solomon is installed as a rabbi to replace the community head, who had been murdered along with all of Solomon's relatives in the shtetl. He continues serving a community of older Jews who had survived the antisemitic violence of the civil war until, in 1925, the Soviets are finally firmly established and local authorities decide to close the synagogue. The Bolshevik official charged with the task of shutting down the synagogue is Isaac, Zhenya's own grandfather. Solomon resists the eviction order with all his might, giving rise to a rumor that "scratches left by Solomon's fingernails remained on the stone floor when he was being dragged over the threshold."[13] Like Broydin, the official in charge of expelling the elderly Jews in Babel's "The End of the Almshouse" from their abode near the cemetery, Isaac is also Jewish: the commonplace story of communities and families riven by divergent political affiliations repeats here in the retelling by Khemlin's narrator.

This rift between two families in one shtetl in the early years after the revolution, and the circumstances that led to it in the first place, simmers for decades and spills over into multiple other tragedies that continue to haunt the family for decades. In his role as a Bolshevik official whose accomplishments included evicting local Jews from the synagogue, Isaac is given a sheepskin coat (*kozhukh*). Several sizes too big, the garment passes on to his elder son who, because he was wearing it when taken captive by the Germans during the Second World War, is incorrectly identified as a Soviet official and hung. Solomon's daughter—his and his wife's last child—is shot during the German occupation by a Ukrainian neighbor. Solomon, the once-wealthy timber merchant, was rumored to have buried his gold in his wife's grave in Ostyor before heading back to Chernobyl within a few months of his expulsion from the synagogue. When the Germans arrive in Ostyor and line up the Jews to be shot, one man, in a last-ditch effort to save his life, volunteers to lead the soldiers to the presumed site of the hidden treasure. When the grave is opened, however, the Germans learn that what Solomon had buried was not gold at all but the synagogue's Torah scrolls and prayer books. These are set on fire by the Nazis, along with the Jewish man who had them unearthed. Rumors about defiled Jewish graves continue to haunt the region. Khemlin's narrator accepts the commonplace belief that the 1986 nuclear accident in Chernobyl, which leaves Zhenya's husband with radiation poisoning and eventually leads to his early death, occurred because a grave from the town's Hasidic past had been disturbed. "They said," Zhenya relates, "that the tragedy took place because they had dug up the grave of a Jewish holy man, and a famous one, too [*evreiskogo sviatogo, znamenitogo*]."[14] On top of everything, Zhenya's in-laws nurse a lifelong grudge against her for her grandfather's role in displacing their kin, which continues to manifest as resentment in everyday matters through the Soviet period and beyond.

The past and the present, both marked by historical tragedies and intergenerational traumas, merge in Zhenya's first-person account at the center of Khemlin's story. As though to confirm that she is of sound mind, Zhenya identifies her age (she's seventy-two years old) and the year in which she is telling her story (2007). As the story comes to an end, Zhenya clarifies another detail as well: her daughter Lyuba, who had emigrated to Israel and then to America, has asked her to compose a will bequeathing her both Zhenya's apartment in Chernigov and Zhenya's father-in-law's former home in Ostyor. The chilling revelation in the final paragraph of "About Zhenya" is that the meandering first-person narrative, which switches between the faraway past and the present, *is* this last will and testament. What it bequeaths, however, is not property but trauma.

Zhenya conveys her first-person narrative as the last surviving member of a Soviet Jewish family still living in the former Soviet Union at the beginning of the twenty-first century. Written from the perspective of a woman, it leaves the reader with the question of how the figure of the Soviet Jew might have appeared differently had female protagonists like Khemlin's been present alongside the voices of men who made the figure of the Soviet Jew so markedly male in the first two decades after the revolution. The Soviet Jew is coded as male both because the figure of the Jew in religious, cultural, and political texts—both Jewish and not—had always been gendered male and because the New Soviet Man, in whose shadow the Soviet Jew was made, was also seen as ipso facto male. The women who turn up in the male-authored texts hold secondary, if significant, roles throughout. The literature of pogroms is conscious of the gendered nature of antisemitic violence. The doctrinaire protagonist espousing Bolshevik clichés in Kulbak's *The Zelmenyaners* is a woman. The disappearance of a mother figure, likely murdered, prompts at least one relocation in the literature on Birobidzhan. Neitan Bekker's wife Meika repatriates to the USSR along with her husband. Nonetheless, only he can be the expert bricklayer needed for socialist constriction and for the film's and the Stalin-era's main plot. Meanwhile, Dvoira, the family's matriarch in *Seekers of Happiness,* delivers the curse that blends the old shtetl together with the new Soviet ethos, onto the *luftmentsh*—a Yiddish word for a good-for-nothing that literally translates as "a *man* made of air"—who is her son-in-law. The tavern keeper's wife Zelda invites the trickery of Babel's Hershele Ostropoler that launches this folkloric figure into the postrevolutionary era, and in another story by Babel, "Karl-Yankel," a grandmother has her grandson circumcised because she wants to keep telling him other Yiddish stories. Women are present throughout the story of the Soviet Jew, and they are central to the cultural construction of this figure—but they do not get to tell their own stories.

In "About Zhenya," Khemlin's female first-person narrator, situated in what had been the Pale of Settlement, tells a story that returns us to the time when the Soviet Jew was being made after the revolution. Through her narrative, she links several instantiations of the Soviet Jew across generational divides. In the final sentence, just after we discern that the family's bequest is narrative, not property, Khemlin has Zhenya make another unexpected move with enormous repercussions for how and even whether this story might continue to be told. Zhenya has picked up and related family stories from her grandmother, her mother, her in-laws, and even a town fool who turned himself into a custodian of the shtetl's cemetery—but she makes clear that the transmission of the narrative ends with her. She might tell her estranged daughter these tales, Zhenya muses, before concluding, in the story's final line: "But even better—I won't tell."[15] A survivor of the Soviet century, a granddaughter of the era when the Soviet Jew was first made, she knows that that particular story has come to an end and finds a measure of freedom in not passing it on to her descendants, who would be protagonists in a different, post-Soviet set of evolving narratives. Instead, Khemlin makes us, her readers, through the lenses of our own dislocations and incomplete transformations, the true inheritors of Soviet Jewish stories.

Notes

Introduction

1. On the Jewish communal poorhouse (*hekdesh*), see Natan M. Meir, *Stepchildren of the Shtetl: The Destitute, Disabled, and Mad of Jewish Eastern Europe, 1800–1939* (Stanford: Stanford University Press, 2020), 63–88.

2. Isaac Babel, *Collected Stories,* ed. Efraim Sicher, trans. David McDuff (New York: Penguin, 1994), 299.

3. On the 1812 plague epidemic in Odessa, see Andrew Robarts, *Migration and Disease in the Black Sea Region: Ottoman-Russian Relations in the Late Eighteenth and Early Nineteenth Centuries* (London: Bloomsbury, 2017), 147–148.

4. Isaak Babel', *Sobranie sochinenii,* vol. 1 (Moscow: Vremia, 2006), 140. The title of the story in Russian is "Konets bogadel'ni."

5. On Soviet policies on nationalities, see Terry Martin, *The Affirmative Action Empire: Nations and Nationalism in the Soviet Union, 1923–1939* (Ithaca, NY: Cornell University Press, 2001); Ronald Grigor Suny and Terry Martin, eds., *A State of Nations: Empire and Nation-Making in the Age of Lenin and Stalin* (Oxford: Oxford University Press, 2001).

6. On the USSR's non-Ashkenazi Jews—including Georgian Jews, Jews from Central Asia, and Mountain Jews—see Zvi Y. Gitelman, *A Century of Ambivalence: The Jews of Russia and the Soviet Union, 1881 to the Present* (Bloomington: Indiana University Press, 2001), 196–211. From among an emerging body of scholarly literature on Jewish languages of non-Ashkenazi Jews in the USSR, see, for example, Vitaly Shalem, "Judeo-Tat in the Eastern Caucasus," in *Languages in Jewish Communities, Past and Present,* edited by Benjamin Hary and Sarah Bunin Benor (Berlin: De Gruyter Mouton, 2018), 313–356.

7. ChaeRan Y. Freeze and Jay M. Harris, eds., *Everyday Jewish Life in Imperial Russia: Select Documents, 1772–1914* (Waltham, MA: Brandeis University Press, 2013), 5.

8. Benjamin Nathans, *Beyond the Pale: The Jewish Encounter with Late Imperial Russia* (Berkeley: University of California Press, 2002).

9. Eugene M. Avrutin, *Jews and the Imperial State: Identification Politics in Tsarist Russia* (Ithaca, NY: Cornell University Press, 2010), 116–146.

10. Rebecca Kobrin, *Jewish Bialystok and Its Diaspora* (Bloomington: Indiana University Press, 2010), 1–18. On Jewish journeys inside and outside the Pale of Settlement in modern Yiddish literature, see Leah V. Garrett, *Journeys beyond the Pale: Yiddish Travel Writing in the Modern World* (Madison: University of Wisconsin Press, 2003).

11. Elissa Bemporad, *Becoming Soviet Jews: The Bolshevik Experiment in Minsk* (Bloomington: Indiana University Press, 2012), 4.

12. Yuri Slezkine, *The Jewish Century* (Princeton, NJ: Princeton University Press, 2004), 217. For demographic data on Jews in the USSR in the interwar period, see Mordechai Altshuler, *Soviet Jewry on the Eve of the Holocaust: A Social and Demographic Profile* (Jerusalem: Yad Vashem, 1998).

13. Jeffrey Veidlinger, *In the Midst of Civilized Europe: The Pogroms of 1918–1921 and the Onset of the Holocaust* (New York: Metropolitan Books, 2021), 7–9.

14. David L. Hoffman, *Peasant Metropolis: Social Identities in Moscow, 1929–1941* (Ithaca, NY: Cornell University Press, 1994).

15. Lewis H. Siegelbaum and Leslie Page Moch, *Broad Is My Native Land: Repertoires and Regimes of Migration in Russia's Twentieth Century* (Ithaca, NY: Cornell University Press, 2014).

16. Slezkine, *The Jewish Century*, 206.

17. Elissa Bemporad, *Legacy of Blood: Jews, Pogroms, and Ritual Murder in the Lands of the Soviets* (Oxford: Oxford University Press, 2019), 32.

18. Jeffrey Shandler, *Shtetl: A Vernacular Intellectual History* (New Brunswick, NJ: Rutgers University Press, 2014). On the shtetl's representation in Yiddish literature, see Dan Miron, *The Image of the Shtetl and Other Studies of Modern Jewish Literary Imagination* (Syracuse, NY: Syracuse University Press, 2000), 1–48.

19. Jonathan L. Dekel-Chen, *Farming the Red Land: Jewish Agricultural Colonization and Local Soviet Power, 1924–1941* (New Haven: Yale University Press, 2005).

20. Laura Engelstein, *Russia in Flames: War, Revolution, Civil War, 1914–1921* (Oxford: Oxford University Press, 2017).

21. Timothy Snyder, *Bloodlands: Europe between Hitler and Stalin* (New York: Basic Books, 2010).

22. Gal Beckerman, *When They Come for Us, We'll Be Gone: The Epic Struggle to Save Soviet Jewry* (Boston: Houghton Mifflin Harcourt, 2010).

23. Shaul Kelner, "Ritualized Protest and Redemptive Politics: Cultural Consequences of the American Mobilization to Free Soviet Jewry," *Jewish Social Studies* 14, no. 3 (2008): 1–37; Shaul Kelner, "The Bureaucratization of Ritual Innovation:

The Festive Cycle of the American Soviet Jewry Movement," in *Revisioning Ritual: Jewish Traditions in Transition,* ed. Simon J. Bronner, 2011, 360–391.

24. Zvi Y. Gitelman, *Jewish Identities in Postcommunist Russia and Ukraine: An Uncertain Ethnicity* (Cambridge: Cambridge University Press, 2012), 22–23.

25. Sasha Senderovich, "Scenes of Encounter: The 'Soviet Jew' in Fiction by Russian Jewish Writers in America," *Prooftexts* 35, no. 1 (2015): 98–132.

26. Shaye J. D. Cohen, *Why Aren't Jewish Women Circumcised? Gender and Covenant in Judaism* (Berkeley: University of California Press, 2005).

27. Galit Hasan-Rokem and Alan Dundes, *The Wandering Jew: Essays in the Interpretation of a Christian Legend* (Bloomington: Indiana University Press, 1986).

28. Daniel Boyarin, *Unheroic Conduct: The Rise of Heterosexuality and the Invention of the Jewish Man* (Berkeley: University of California Press, 1997).

29. Sander L. Gilman, *The Jew's Body* (New York: Routledge, 1991); George L. Mosse, "Max Nordau, Liberalism and the New Jew," *Journal of Contemporary History* 27, no. 4 (October 1992): 565–581; Todd Samuel Presner, *Muscular Judaism: The Jewish Body and the Politics of Regeneration* (New York: Routledge, 2007).

30. Todd Samuel Presner, "'Clear Heads, Solid Stomachs, and Hard Muscles': Max Nordau and the Aesthetics of Jewish Regeneration," *Modernism/Modernity* 10, no. 2 (April 2003): 269–296.

31. Eliot Borenstein, *Men without Women: Masculinity and Revolution in Russian Fiction, 1917–1929* (Durham: Duke University Press, 2000); John Haynes, *New Soviet Man: Gender and Masculinity in Stalinist Soviet Cinema* (Manchester: Manchester University Press, 2003).

32. Victoria Smolkin, *A Sacred Space Is Never Empty: A History of Soviet Atheism* (Princeton: Princeton University Press, 2018), 21–56.

33. Gregory Freidin, "Introduction," in *Isaac Babel's Selected Writings,* ed. Gregory Freidin, trans. Peter Constantine (New York: W.W. Norton, 2010), x–xi.

34. Known for its freethinking ways, Odessa was seen as a godless place by more traditional Jews elsewhere in the Pale: "seven miles around Odessa burn the fires of hell" is a famous Yiddish expression about the city. Steven J. Zipperstein, *The Jews of Odessa: A Cultural History, 1794–1881* (Stanford: Stanford University Press, 1985), 1.

35. Isaac Babel, *The Essential Fictions,* trans. Val Vinokur (Evanston, IL: Northwestern University Press, 2018), 147.

36. Babel, *Collected Stories,* 294.

37. Elena M. Katz, *Neither with Them, nor without Them: The Russian Writer and the Jew in the Age of Realism* (Syracuse, NY: Syracuse University Press, 2008); Leonid Livak, *The Jewish Persona in the European Imagination: A Case of Russian Literature* (Stanford: Stanford University Press, 2010); Gabriella Safran, *Rewriting the Jew: Assimilation Narratives in the Russian Empire* (Stanford: Stanford University Press, 2000).

38. On the Bolshevik hero, see Rufus W. Mathewson, *The Positive Hero in Russian Literature* (Stanford: Stanford University Press, 1975), 179–210. For the discussion of the Bolshevik hero as a Jew, see Alice Stone Nakhimovsky, *Russian-Jewish Literature and Identity: Jabotinsky, Babel, Grossman, Galich, Roziner, Markish* (Baltimore: Johns Hopkins University Press, 1992), 20–24. See also Maxim Shrayer, *Russian Poet / Soviet Jew: The Legacy of Eduard Bagritskii* (Lanham, MD: Rowman & Littlefield, 2000).

39. Scholarship on the New Soviet Man investigates the roots of this figure in Russian modernism and in notions of masculinity and gender politics in the Stalin era. See, for example: Haynes, *New Soviet Man;* Lilya Kaganovsky, *How the Soviet Man Was Unmade: Cultural Fantasy and Male Subjectivity under Stalin* (Pittsburgh: University of Pittsburgh Press, 2008). Margulies of Valentin Kataev's 1932 novel *Time, Forward!* is a famous Jewish protagonist in a novel exploring the New Soviet Man phenomenon.

40. Paul Hanebrink, *A Specter Haunting Europe: The Myth of Judeo-Bolshevism* (Cambridge, MA: Harvard University Press, 2018).

41. Brendan McGeever, *The Bolshevik Response to Antisemitism in the Russian Revolution* (Cambridge: Cambridge University Press, 2019).

42. Slezkine, *The Jewish Century.* Jewish backgrounds of a range of highly placed Soviet officials and other members of the Soviet elite in Stalin's USSR are also discussed intermittently in Yuri Slezkine, *The House of Government: A Saga of the Russian Revolution* (Princeton, NJ: Princeton University Press, 2017).

43. Nakhimovsky, *Russian-Jewish Literature and Identity,* x.

44. Zsuzsa Hetényi, *In a Maelstrom: The History of Russian-Jewish Prose (1860–1940)* (Budapest: Central European University Press, 2008); Nakhimovsky, *Russian-Jewish Literature and Identity;* Maxim D. Shrayer, ed., *An Anthology of Jewish-Russian Literature: Two Centuries of Dual Identity in Prose and Poetry,* 2 vols., (Armonk, NY: M. E. Sharpe, 2007); Efraim Sicher, *Jews in Russian Literature after the October Revolution: Writers and Artists between Hope and Apostasy* (Cambridge: Cambridge University Press, 1995).

45. Osip Mandelshtam, *The Noise of Time: Selected Prose,* trans. Clarence Brown (Evanston, IL: Northwestern University Press, 2002), 78.

46. Outside the focus of the current book on the 1920s and the 1930s, David Shneer, Marat Grinberg, and Maya Balakirsky Katz, among others, have approached the question of Jewish identities of Soviet culture makers with an eye toward identifying the imprint of these identities in creative works. See David Shneer, *Through Soviet Jewish Eyes: Photography, War, and the Holocaust* (New Brunswick, NJ: Rutgers University Press, 2011); Marat Grinberg, *"I Am to Be Read Not from Left to Right, but in Jewish: From Right to Left": The Poetics of Boris Slutsky* (Brighton, MA: Academic Studies Press, 2011); Maya Balakirsky Katz, *Drawing the Iron Curtain: Jews and the Golden Age of Soviet Animation* (New Brunswick, NJ: Rutgers University Press, 2016). Klavdia Smola, in contrast, attempts to sidestep the category

of identity as a defining feature of Russian-language literature written by Jews in the late Soviet period. Relying on approaches developed in the 1980s and the 1990s by scholars like David G. Roskies, who worked with Yiddish-language literature and was conversant with traditional Jewish sources, Smola claims to find a kind of traditionally informed Jewish textuality that seemingly exists irrespective of languages. Klavdia Smola, *Izobretaia traditsiiu: Sovremennaia russko-evreiskaia literatura* (Moscow: Novoe literaturnoe obozrenie, 2021).

47. Nakhimovsky, *Russian-Jewish Literature and Identity*, xii.

48. Shrayer, *An Anthology of Jewish-Russian Literature*, 1: xxiv–xxv.

49. Harriet Murav, *Music from a Speeding Train: Soviet Yiddish and Russian-Jewish Literature of the Twentieth Century* (Stanford: Stanford University Press, 2011), 9–11.

50. Amelia M. Glaser, *Songs in Dark Times: Yiddish Poetry of Struggle from Scottsboro to Palestine* (Cambridge, MA: Harvard University Press, 2020), 10. Similarly, their own experience of marginality turned some Jewish writers in Ukraine toward a cultural and political identification with Ukraine's anti-imperial struggles in the Russian Empire and during the Soviet period: Yohanan Petrovsky-Shtern, *The Anti-Imperial Choice: The Making of the Ukrainian Jew* (New Haven: Yale University Press, 2009).

51. Anna Shternshis cites the proportion of native Yiddish speakers in Russia in 1917 at 90 percent. Anna Shternshis, *Soviet and Kosher: Jewish Popular Culture in the Soviet Union, 1923–1939* (Bloomington: Indiana University Press, 2006), xv.

52. Ken Frieden, *Classic Yiddish Fiction: Abramovitsh, Sholem Aleichem, and Peretz* (Albany: State University of New York Press, 1995).

53. Gennady Estraikh, *Soviet Yiddish: Language Planning and Linguistic Development* (New York: Oxford University Press, 1999); Gennady Estraikh, *In Harness: Yiddish Writers' Romance with Communism* (Syracuse, NY: Syracuse University Press, 2005); David Shneer, *Yiddish and the Creation of Soviet Jewish Culture, 1918–1930* (Cambridge: Cambridge University Press, 2004); Shternshis, *Soviet and Kosher*.

54. Kenneth B. Moss, *Jewish Renaissance in the Russian Revolution* (Cambridge, MA: Harvard University Press, 2009), 225–227.

55. Ruth R. Wisse, *The Modern Jewish Canon: A Journey through Language and Culture* (Chicago: University of Chicago Press, 2000), 119–120.

56. Mikhail Krutikov, *From Kabbalah to Class Struggle: Expressionism, Marxism, and Yiddish Literature in the Life and Work of Meir Wiener* (Stanford: Stanford University Press, 2010); Mikhail Krutikov, *Der Nister's Soviet Years: Yiddish Writer as Witness to the People* (Bloomington: Indiana University Press, 2019); Moss, *Jewish Renaissance in the Russian Revolution;* Murav, *Music from a Speeding Train;* Harriet Murav, *David Bergelson's Strange New World: Untimeliness and Futurity* (Bloomington: Indiana University Press, 2019); Jeffrey Veidlinger, *The Moscow State Yiddish Theater: Jewish Culture on the Soviet Stage* (Bloomington: Indiana

University Press, 2000); Joseph Sherman and Gennady Estraikh, eds., *David Bergelson: From Modernism to Socialist Realism* (London: Legenda, 2007); Joseph Sherman, *A Captive of the Dawn: The Life and Work of Peretz Markish (1895–1952)* (Leeds: Legenda, 2011).

57. Murav, *Music from a Speeding Train*, 2.

58. Todd Samuel Presner, *Mobile Modernity: Germans, Jews, Trains* (New York: Columbia University Press, 2007), 7.

59. Nakhimovsky, *Russian-Jewish Literature and Identity*, xii.

60. Sicher, *Jews in Russian Literature after the October Revolution*, 14.

61. Shrayer, *An Anthology of Jewish-Russian Literature*, 1:xlvii.

62. See, for example, Elaine Pomper Snyderman and Margaret Thomas Witkovsky, eds., *Line Five, the Internal Passport: Jewish Family Odysseys from the USSR to the USA* (Chicago: Review Press, 1992).

63. Francine Hirsch, *Empire of Nations: Ethnographic Knowledge and the Making of the Soviet Union* (Ithaca, NY: Cornell University Press, 2005).

64. Avrutin, *Jews and the Imperial State*, 127–135.

65. Marc Garcelon, "Colonizing the Subject: The Genealogy and Legacy of the Soviet Internal Passport," in *Documenting Individual Identity: The Development of State Practices in the Modern World*, ed. Jane Caplan and John Torpey (Princeton, NJ: Princeton University Press, 2001), 83–100.

66. Hirsch, *Empire of Nations*, 293–307.

1. Haunted by Pogroms

1. For a detailed account of the numerous political and military forces involved in contesting Ukraine, see Jeffrey Veidlinger, *In the Midst of Civilized Europe: The Pogroms of 1918–1921 and the Onset of the Holocaust* (New York: Metropolitan Books, 2021).

2. John J. Dziak, *Chekisty: A History of the KGB* (Lexington, MA: Lexington Books, 1988), 1–38.

3. The exact date is not mentioned in the novel. However, the reference to one protagonist, Dr. Babitsky, notes that he had taught his illegitimate son the word "revolution" "just three years earlier" than the novel's narrative present, "in the first, festive weeks of the revolution." The weeks just after the February Revolution in 1917, then, preceded the novel's narrative present—ipso facto, in 1920—by three years. David Bergelson, *Judgment: A Novel*, trans. Harriet Murav and Sasha Senderovich (Evanston, IL: Northwestern University Press, 2017), 22.

4. Scott B. Smith, *Captives of Revolution: The Socialist Revolutionaries and the Bolshevik Dictatorship, 1918–1923* (Pittsburgh: University of Pittsburgh Press, 2011).

5. On the ethnographer and writer S. An-sky's involvement with the SRs, see Gabriella Safran, *Wandering Soul: The Dybbuk's Creator, S. An-Sky* (Cambridge, MA: Harvard University Press, 2011), 95–148.

6. Bergelson, *Judgment*, 154.

7. Elissa Bemporad, *Legacy of Blood: Jews, Pogroms, and Ritual Murder in the Lands of the Soviets* (Oxford: Oxford University Press, 2019), 14–34.

8. Amelia M. Glaser, ed., *Stories of Khmelnytsky: Competing Literary Legacies of the 1648 Ukrainian Cossack Uprising* (Stanford: Stanford University Press, 2015), 4, 12.

9. Bergelson, *Judgment*, 158.

10. Bergelson, 154.

11. Bergelson, 154.

12. A. A. Shlyakher, "Ekonomicheskaia kontrabanda i bor'ba s nei v SSSR, 1917–1941 gg.," in *Istoricheskie chteniia na Lubianke* (Moscow: Kuchkovo pole, 2008), 71.

13. Bemporad, *Legacy of Blood*, 21.

14. Oleg Budnitskii, *Russian Jews between the Reds and the Whites, 1917–1920*, trans. Timothy J. Portice (Philadelphia: University of Pennsylvania Press, 2012), 90.

15. James E. Young, *Writing and Rewriting the Holocaust: Narrative and the Consequences of Interpretation* (Bloomington: Indiana University Press, 1988), 85–89.

16. Laura Engelstein, *Russia in Flames: War, Revolution, Civil War, 1914–1921* (Oxford: Oxford University Press, 2017), 588–605.

17. Marquis de Sade, *The Crimes of Love: Heroic and Tragic Tales, Preceded by an Essay on Novels,* trans. David Coward (Oxford: Oxford University Press, 2008), 13.

18. Dale Peterson, "Russian Gothic: The Deathless Paradoxes of Bunin's Dry Valley," *Slavic and East European Journal* 31, no. 1 (1987): 37.

19. Eric Naiman, *Sex in Public: The Incarnation of Early Soviet Ideology* (Princeton, NJ: Princeton University Press, 1997), 148–180.

20. Bergelson, *Judgment,* 157; Dovid Bergelson, *Mides-hadin*, Geklibene verk, vol. 7 (Vilna: B. Kletskin, 1929), 200.

21. Peterson, "Russian Gothic," 37.

22. Valeria Sobol, "'Tis Eighty Years Since: Panteleimon Kulish's Gothic Ukraine," *Slavic Review* 78, no. 2 (2019): 393.

23. M. M. Bakhtin, *The Dialogic Imagination: Four Essays,* ed. Michael Holquist, trans. Caryl Emerson and Michael Holquist (Austin: University of Texas Press, 1981), 245.

24. Bakhtin, 246.

25. Valeria Sobol, *Haunted Empire: Gothic and the Russian Imperial Uncanny* (Ithaca, NY: Cornell University Press, 2020), 5.

26. William Hughes, David Punter, and Andrew Smith, eds., *The Encyclopedia of the Gothic* (Chichester: Wiley Blackwell, 2016), 270–273.

27. Bergelson, *Judgment*, 63.

28. Bergelson, 53–54; Maya Barzilai, *Golem: Modern Wars and Their Monsters* (New York: New York University Press, 2016), 27–68.

29. Bergelson, *Judgment,* 46–47.

30. Bergelson, 161.

31. Kenneth B. Moss, *Jewish Renaissance in the Russian Revolution* (Cambridge, MA: Harvard University Press, 2009), 37–38, 91.

32. For Bergelson's detailed biography, see Joseph Sherman and Gennady Estraikh, eds., *David Bergelson: From Modernism to Socialist Realism* (London: Legenda, 2007), 7–78.

33. I. M. Cherikover, *Antisemitizm i pogromy na Ukraine 1917–1918 gg.: K istorii ukrainsko-evreiskikh otnoshenii* (Berlin: Ostjüdisches Historisches Archiv, 1923); I. M. Cherikover, *Antisemitizm un pogromen in Ukraine, 1917–1918: tsu der geshikhte fun Ukrainish-Yidishe batsiyungen (mit a hakdome fun S. Dubnov)* (Berlin: Mizreh-Yidishn historishn arkhiv, 1923).

34. On Bergelson's Berlin stories, see Marc Caplan, *Yiddish Writers in Weimar Berlin: A Fugitive Modernism* (Bloomington: Indiana University Press, 2021), 91–133; Harriet Murav, *David Bergelson's Strange New World: Untimeliness and Futurity* (Bloomington: Indiana University Press, 2019), 179–204; Allison Schachter, *Diasporic Modernisms: Hebrew and Yiddish Literature in the Twentieth Century* (Oxford: Oxford University Press, 2011), 84–91; Sasha Senderovich, "In Search of Readership: Bergelson among the Refugees," in *David Bergelson: From Modernism to Socialist Realism,* ed. Joseph Sherman and Gennady Estraikh (London: Legenda, 2007), 150–166.

35. S. Gekht, *Syn sapozhnika* (Moscow: Molodaia gvardiia, 1931), 30.

36. Bemporad, *Legacy of Blood,* 17.

37. S. Gekht, *Chelovek, kotoryi zabyl svoiu zhizn'* (Kharkov: Proletarii, 1927), 124–125; R. Edelmann, "Ahasuerus, the Wandering Jew: Origin and Background," in *The Wandering Jew: Essays in the Interpretation of a Christian Legend,* ed. Galit Hasan-Rokem and Alan Dundes (Bloomington: Indiana University Press, 1986), 16–18.

38. George K. Anderson, *The Legend of the Wandering Jew* (Providence, RI: Brown University Press, 1965).

39. Karen Grumberg, *Hebrew Gothic: History and the Poetics of Persecution* (Bloomington: Indiana University Press, 2019), 16–17.

40. Gekht, *Chelovek, kotoryi zabyl svoiu zhizn',* 19.

41. Irina Astashkevich, *Gendered Violence: Jewish Women in the Pogroms of 1917 to 1921* (Boston: Academic Studies Press, 2018), 128.

42. Grumberg, *Hebrew Gothic,* 40.

43. Amelia Glaser, *Jews and Ukrainians in Russia's Literary Borderlands: From the Shtetl Fair to the Petersburg Bookshop* (Evanston, IL: Northwestern University Press, 2012), 132.

44. As translated in Seth L. Wolitz, *Yiddish Modernism: Studies in Twentieth-Century Eastern European Jewish Culture* (Bloomington: Slavica Publishers, 2014), 280.

45. Glaser, *Jews and Ukrainians in Russia's Literary Borderlands*, 135.

46. Harriet Murav, *Music from a Speeding Train: Soviet Yiddish and Russian-Jewish Literature of the Twentieth Century* (Stanford: Stanford University Press, 2011), 35.

47. A. Tarasov-Rodionov, *Shokolad* (Kharkov: Proletarii, 1927), 89.

48. Tarasov-Rodionov, *Shokolad*, 64–65.

49. A. Lunacharskii, "Iosif Utkin: 'Povest' o ryzhem Motele, gospodine inspektore, ravvine Isaiie i komissare Blokh,' Biblioteka 'Prozhektor,'" *Pravda*, June 6, 1926, 7.

50. Iosif Utkin, *Stikhotvoreniia i poemy* (Moscow: Sovetskii pisatel', 1966), 267, 287.

51. Steven J. Zipperstein, *Pogrom: Kishinev and the Tilt of History* (New York: Liveright Publishing, 2018), xiii.

52. Utkin, *Stikhotvoreniia i poemy*, 270.

53. Brendan McGeever, *The Bolshevik Response to Antisemitism in the Russian Revolution* (Cambridge: Cambridge University Press, 2019), 53–87.

54. Bergelson, *Judgment*, 62.

55. Harriet Murav, "Archive of Violence: Neighbors, Strangers, and Creatures in Itsik Kipnis's 'Months and Days,'" *Quest: Issues in Contemporary Jewish History*, no. 15 (August 2019): 53.

56. Leib Kvitko, *1919* (Berlin: Yidisher literarisher farlag, 1923).

57. I. Erenburg, *Staryi skorniak i drugie proizvedeniia*, ed. M. Vainshtein, vol. 1 (Jerusalem: n.p., 1983), 35.

58. Erenburg, *Staryi skorniak i drugie proizvedeniia* 1:36.

59. Astashkevich, *Gendered Violence*, 54–55.

60. Erenburg, *Staryi skorniak i drugie proizvedeniia*, 1:37.

61. Erenburg, 1:52.

62. Erenburg, 1:49.

63. On the Jewish sections (*evsektsii*), see Zvi Y. Gitelman, *Jewish Nationality and Soviet Politics: The Jewish Sections of the CPSU, 1917–1930* (Princeton, NJ: Princeton University Press, 1972).

64. Paul Hanebrink, *A Specter Haunting Europe: The Myth of Judeo-Bolshevism* (Cambridge, MA: Harvard University Press, 2018), 42–43. Brendan McGeever, writing about Trotsky's two rejections, in 1917 and 1922, of Lenin's offers to take up senior positions in the government, noted that "despite his assimilatory internationalism, Trotsky could not [including by his own later admission] fail to be cognizant of the force of the antisemitic projection: acutely aware that he was its object, he refused senior roles in the government to avoid confirming those projections." McGeever, *The Bolshevik Response to Antisemitism in the Russian Revolution*, 209–210.

65. Robert Weinberg, "Demonizing Judaism in the Soviet Union during the 1920s," *Slavic Review* 67, no. 1 (Spring 2008): 120–153.

66. Isaac Babel, *1920 Diary,* ed. Carol Avins, trans. H. T Willetts (New Haven: Yale University Press, 1995), 4.

67. Hanebrink, *A Specter Haunting Europe,* 48.

68. Modified translation from Vasily Grossman, *The Road: Stories, Journalism, and Essays,* ed. Robert Chandler (New York: NYRB Classics, 2010), 29; Vasilii Grossman, *Chetyre dnia: rasskazy* (Moscow: Khudozhestvennaia literatura, 1936), 263.

69. Erenburg, *Staryi skorniak i drugie proizvedeniia,* 1:49.

70. Veidlinger, *In the Midst of Civilized Europe,* 270–286.

71. Bergelson, *Judgment,* 30.

72. Mikhail Krutikov, "Rediscovering the Shtetl as a New Reality: David Bergelson and Itsik Kipnis," in *The Shtetl: New Evaluations,* ed. Steven T. Katz (New York: New York University Press, 2007), 227.

73. David Bergelson, "At the Depot," in *A Shtetl and Other Yiddish Novellas,* trans. Ruth R. Wisse (Detroit: Wayne State University Press, 1986), 84–139; David Bergelson, *The End of Everything,* trans. Joseph Sherman (New Haven: Yale University Press, 2009); David Bergelson, *Descent,* trans. Joseph Sherman (New York: Modern Language Association of America, 1999).

74. Murav, *David Bergelson's Strange New World,* 212, 223–224. For influences of Soviet montage across the visual and literary arts, see Il'ia Kukulin, *Mashiny zashumevshego vremeni: Kak sovetskii montazh stal metodom neofitsial'noi kul'tury* (Moscow: Novoe literaturnoe obozrenie, 2015).

75. Bergelson, *Judgment,* 42.

76. Bergelson, 61.

77. Muireann Maguire, *Stalin's Ghosts: Gothic Themes in Early Soviet Literature* (Oxford: Peter Lang, 2012), 47.

78. Bergelson, *Judgment,* 61–62.

79. David Punter, *The Literature of Terror: A History of Gothic Fictions from 1765 to the Present Day* (London: Longman, 1996), 5.

80. Bergelson, *Judgment,* 5; Bergelson, *Mides-hadin,* 8.

81. Bergelson, *Judgment,* 8.

82. Bergelson, 5.

83. Naiman, *Sex in Public,* 148–180.

84. Anne Applebaum, *Gulag: A History* (New York: Doubleday, 2003), 3–17.

85. Bergelson, *Judgment,* 17.

86. Bergelson, 50.

87. Robert Gerwarth, *The Vanquished: Why the First World War Failed to End, 1917–1923* (London: Allen Lane, 2016).

88. Bergelson, *Judgment,* 128.

89. Bergelson, 49.

90. Bergelson, 52.

91. Bergelson, 17.

92. Daniela Montovan, "Language and Style in *Nokh alemen* (1913): Bergelson's Debt to Flaubert," in *David Bergelson: From Modernism to Socialist Realism,* ed. Joseph Sherman and Gennady Estraikh (London: Legenda, 2007), 89–112.

93. Bergelson, *Judgment,* 20.

94. Bergelson, 27.

95. Bergelson, 22.

96. Bergelson, 34.

97. Iu. Libedinskii, *Izbrannye proizvedeniia,* vol. 1 (Moscow: Gosudarstvennoe izdatel'stvo khudozhestvennoi literatury, 1958), 10–11.

98. Il'ia Erenburg, *Zhizn' i gibel' Nikolaia Kurbova* (Berlin: Gelikon, 1923).

99. Bergelson, *Judgment,* 5.

100. T. M. Smirnova, *"Byvshie liudi" Sovetskoi Rossii: strategii vyzhivaniia i puti integratsii, 1917–1936 gody* (Moscow: Mir istorii, 2003), 24.

101. Bergelson, *Judgment,* 5; Bergelson, *Mides-hadin,* 8.

102. Bergelson, *Judgment,* 4; Bergelson, *Mides-hadin,* 7.

103. Bergelson, *Judgment,* 53.

104. Bergelson, 54–55.

105. Bergelson, 23.

106. Bergelson, 16.

107. Bergelson, 57.

108. For a detailed study of the mutilated bodies of Stalin-era literary and cinematic heroes, see Lilya Kaganovsky, *How the Soviet Man Was Unmade: Cultural Fantasy and Male Subjectivity under Stalin* (Pittsburgh: University of Pittsburgh Press, 2008).

109. Tarasov-Rodionov, *Shokolad,* 213–214.

110. Vladimir Zazubrin, "Shchepka," in *Obshchezhitie* (Novosibirsk: Novosibirskoe knizhnoe isdatel'stvo, 1990), 90. "Schepka" was written in 1922–1923 but not published until six and a half decades later.

111. Libedinskii, *Izbrannye proizvedeniia,* 1:9.

112. Bergelson, *Judgment,* 160.

113. Bergelson, 197.

114. Bergelson, 197.

115. Bergelson, 59.

116. Bergelson, 196.

117. Murav, *David Bergelson's Strange New World,* 205–206.

118. Dovid Bergelson, "Dray tsentren," *In shpan,* no. 1 (1926): 84–96; David Bergelson, "Three Centers (Characteristics)," in *David Bergelson: From Modernism to Socialist Realism,* 347–354.

119. Gennady Estraikh, "Bergelson in and out of America," in *David Bergelson: From Modernism to Socialist Realism,* 210–212.

120. Sherman and Estraikh, *David Bergelson,* 51.

121. Shifres, "Vegn D. Bergelsons 'Mides hadin,'" *Shtern,* no. 5–6 (1929): 75–81.

122. In the 1930s, Bronshteyn headed the literary division of the Institute for Proletarian Jewish Culture at the Belorussian Academy of Sciences; see Elissa Bemporad, *Becoming Soviet Jews: The Bolshevik Experiment in Minsk* (Bloomington: Indiana University Press, 2012), 103. He was also secretary of the Belorussian Writers' Union between 1932 and 1937; see Gennady Estraikh, *In Harness: Yiddish Writers' Romance with Communism* (Syracuse, NY: Syracuse University Press, 2005), 138.

123. A. Mapovets [Yasha Bronshteyn], "Unter dem last fun yerushe," *Prolit,* no. 6 (June 1929): 71.

124. A. Mapovets [Yasha Bronshteyn], 70.

125. Susan Ann Slotnick, "The Novel Form in the Works of David Bergelson" (PhD diss., Columbia University, 1978), 233.

126. Mikhail Krutikov, "Narrating the Revolution: From 'Tsugvintn' (1922) to 'Mides-Hadin' (1929)," in *David Bergelson: From Modernism to Socialist Realism,* ed. Joseph Sherman and Gennady Estraikh (London: Legenda, 2007), 175.

127. Caplan, *Yiddish Writers in Weimar Berlin,* 47.

128. Sasha Senderovich and Harriet Murav, "David Bergelson's *Judgment:* A Critical Introduction," in *Judgment: A Novel,* by David Bergelson, trans. Harriet Murav and Sasha Senderovich (Evanston, IL: Northwestern University Press, 2017), xviii–xxiv.

129. Rokhl Korn, "Dovid Bergelson: fun mides-harakhamim biz mides-hadin," *Di goldene keyt,* no. 43 (1962): 20. On the Jewish Anti-Fascist Committee, see Joshua Rubenstein and V. P. Naumov, eds., *Stalin's Secret Pogrom: The Postwar Inquisition of the Jewish Anti-Fascist Committee* (New Haven: Yale University Press, 2001), 1–64.

130. Irving Howe and Eliezer Greenberg, eds., *Ashes out of Hope: Fiction by Soviet-Yiddish Writers* (New York: Schocken Books, 1977), 25.

131. David Bergelson, *When All Is Said and Done,* trans. Bernard Martin (Athens: Ohio University Press, 1977), xx.

132. Krutikov, "Narrating the Revolution," 175.

133. Senderovich and Murav, "David Bergelson's *Judgment,*" xxi.

134. Sherman and Estraikh, *David Bergelson,* 40.

135. Krutikov, "Narrating the Revolution," 175.

136. Bergelson, *Judgment,* 209.

137. Bergelson, 211.

138. Bergelson, 211.

139. Isaac Babel, *The Essential Fictions,* trans. Val Vinokur (Evanston, IL: Northwestern University Press, 2018), 250.

140. Bergelson, *Judgment,* 209.

141. Isaak Babel', *Sobranie sochinenii,* vol. 2 (Moscow: Vremia, 2006), 215.

142. A. Erlikh, "U pogranichnogo stolba," *30 dnei,* no. 8 (1925): 51, 53.

143. Andrey Shlyakhter, "Smuggler States: Poland, Latvia, Estonia, and Contraband Trade across the Soviet Frontier, 1919–1924" (PhD diss., University of Chicago, 2020), 371–405.

144. Bergelson, *Judgment*, 13.

145. Erlikh, "U pogranichnogo stolba," 52.

146. Bergelson, *Judgment*, 52.

147. O. Varshavskii, *Spekulianty*, ed. Andrei Sobol', trans. Ia. Slonim, 2nd ed. (Moscow and Leningrad: Gosudarstvennoe izdatel'stvo, 1927). In a December 1927 article about Ilya Ehrenburg's visit to Warsaw, the writer is quoted as saying, in reference specifically to the Russian translation of Varshavsky's novel, "In regard to Yiddish [*evreiskoi*] literature, I know very little of it. Of the young Jewish writers [*pisatelei-evreev*] who write about Jews, I would like to single out the mighty talent of Varshavsky"; see Viacheslav Popov and B. Frezinskii, *Il'ia Erenburg: khronika zhizni i tvorchestva v dokumentakh, pis'makh, vyskazyvaniiakh i soobshcheniiakh pressy, svidetel'stvakh sovremennikov*, vol. 2 (Saint Petersburg: Lina, 1993), 232. In some ways, Erenburg's own picaresque novel *The Stormy Life of Lazik Roytshvants* (*Burnaia zhizn' Lazika Roitshvantsa*), published in Russian in Berlin in 1928—in which there are scattered references to pogroms—could be seen as influenced by Varshavsky's work; see Miriam Udel, *Never Better: The Modern Jewish Picaresque* (Ann Arbor: University of Michigan Press, 2016), 145–146.

148. Andrew Sloin, *The Jewish Revolution in Belorussia: Economy, Race, and Bolshevik Power* (Bloomington: Indiana University Press, 2017), 82.

149. McGeever, *The Bolshevik Response to Antisemitism in the Russian Revolution*, 205.

150. Bergelson, *Judgment*, 53.

151. Bergelson, 52.

152. Bergelson, 54.

153. Bergelson, 54.

154. Bergelson, 54.

155. Bergelson, 54; Bergelson, *Mides-hadin*, 69.

156. Murav, *David Bergelson's Strange New World*, 213–214.

157. Bergelson, *Judgment*, 56; Bergelson, *Mides-hadin*, 71.

158. A. Mapovets [Yasha Bronshteyn], "Unter dem last fun yerushe," 69–70.

159. Bergelson, *Judgment*, 55; Bergelson, *Mides-hadin*, 70.

160. Jay Geller, *The Other Jewish Question: Identifying the Jew and Making Sense of Modernity* (New York: Fordham University Press, 2011), 222–223.

161. Grumberg, *Hebrew Gothic*, 15.

162. Bergelson, *Judgment*, 88; Bergelson, *Mides-hadin*, 113.

163. Sloin, *The Jewish Revolution in Belorussia*, 59–73.

164. Bergelson, *Judgment*, 88.

165. Isaac Babel, *The Complete Works of Isaac Babel,* ed. Nathalie Babel, trans. Peter Constantine (New York: Norton, 2002), 332.

166. Bergelson, *Judgment,* 97.

167. Bergelson, 99.

168. A. Mapovets [Yasha Bronshteyn], "Unter dem last fun yerushe," 72.

169. Bergelson, *Judgment,* 97.

170. Bergelson, 4.

171. Bergelson, 4.

172. Hughes, Punter, and Smith, *The Encyclopedia of the Gothic,* 639.

173. Bergelson, *Judgment,* 4.

174. Bergelson, 109.

175. H. Kazakevitch, "D. Bergelson. 'Midas hadin,'" *Prolit,* no. 6 (1929): 199.

176. Julia Kristeva, *Black Sun: Depression and Melancholia* (New York: Columbia University Press, 1989), 113.

177. Boris Dralyuk, ed., *1917: Stories and Poems from the Russian Revolution* (London: Pushkin Press, 2016), 63. On the figure of Christ in Yiddish modernism, see Matthew Hoffman, *From Rebel to Rabbi: Reclaiming Jesus and the Making of Modern Jewish Culture* (Stanford: Stanford University Press, 2007), 117–169.

178. Hughes, Punter, and Smith, *The Encyclopedia of the Gothic,* 344–345.

179. Bergelson, *Judgment,* 117.

180. Bergelson, 118; Bergelson, *Mides-hadin,* 154.

181. Bergelson, 119.

182. Bergelson, 200.

183. Bergelson, 201.

184. Bergelson, 204.

185. Bergelson, 206.

186. Bergelson, 199.

187. Bergelson, 170.

188. Bergelson, 170–171; Bergelson, *Mides-hadin,* 215.

189. Peterson, "Russian Gothic," 38.

190. Joseph Sherman, ed., *From Revolution to Repression: Soviet Yiddish Writing 1917–1952* (Nottingham: Five Leaves, 2012), 61; Dovid Bergelson, "Onheyb kislev tar'at," *Milgroym,* no. 1 (1922): 25.

191. Sherman, *From Revolution to Repression,* 63.

192. Murav, *David Bergelson's Strange New World,* 190.

2. Salvaged Fragments

1. Modified translation from Moyshe Kulbak, *The Zelmenyaners: A Family Saga,* trans. Hillel Halkin and with introduction and notes by Sasha Senderovich (New Haven: Yale University Press, 2013), 3. For the Yiddish original, see Moyshe Kulbak, *Zelmenyaner: ershter bukh* (Minsk: Tsentraler felker farlag fun F.S.S.R,

1931), 5. On the cultural history of the courtyard in Russian and Soviet Jewish cultures, see my introduction in Kulbak, *The Zelmenyaners*, viii–x.

2. Kulbak, *The Zelmenyaners*, 4.

3. Kulbak, 4; Kulbak, *Zelmenyaner: ershter bukh*, 6.

4. Elissa Bemporad, *Becoming Soviet Jews: The Bolshevik Experiment in Minsk* (Bloomington: Indiana University Press, 2012), 74. Bemporad points to the discussion, in 1926, nearly a decade after the legal dissolution of the Pale, involving a possible relocation of the editorial offices of the Moscow-based Yiddish newspaper *Der Emes* to "the 'Pale of Settlement,' namely, to Minsk or Kharkov" (75).

5. Deborah Yalen, "On the Social-Economic Front: The Polemics of Shtetl Research during the Stalin Revolution," *Science in Context* 20, no. 2 (2007): 239–301.

6. On Jews as paradigmatic Soviets, see the fourth chapter of Yuri Slezkine, *The Jewish Century* (Princeton, NJ: Princeton University Press, 2004).

7. On Kulbak's Berlin period, see Marc Caplan, "Belarus in Berlin, Berlin in Belarus: Moyshe Kulbak's 'Raysn' and 'Meshiekh Ben-Efrayim' between Nostalgia and Apocalypse," in *Yiddish in Weimar Berlin: At the Crossroads of Diaspora Politics and Culture,* ed. Gennady Estraikh and Mikhail Krutikov (London: Modern Humanities Research Association, 2010), 89–104; Rachel Seelig, "A Yiddish Bard in Berlin: Moyshe Kulbak and the Flourishing of Yiddish Poetry in Exile," *Jewish Quarterly Review* 102, no. 1 (2012): 19–49. Kulbak is the likely prototype of the destitute Yiddish poet Max Wentzl in "One Night Less," one of the stories that David Bergelson wrote about Berlin: David Bergelson, *The Shadows of Berlin: The Berlin Stories of Dovid Bergelson,* trans. Joachim Neugroschel (San Francisco: City Lights Books, 2005), 103–115.

8. Il'ia Kukulin, *Mashiny zashumevshego vremeni: Kak sovetskii montazh stal metodom neofitsial'noi kul'tury* (Moscow: Novoe literaturnoe obozrenie, 2015), 14.

9. Robert Adler Peckerar and Aaron Rubinstein, "Moyshe Kulbak," in *Dictionary of Literary Biography,* ed. Joseph Sherman, vol. 333: Writers in Yiddish (Detroit: Thomson Gale, 2007), 121–129; Avraham Novershtern, "Kulbak, Moyshe," *YIVO Encyclopedia of Jews in Eastern Europe,* accessed November 17, 2021, http://www .yivoencyclopedia.org/article.aspx/Kulbak_Moyshe.

10. M. M. Bakhtin, *The Dialogic Imagination: Four Essays,* ed. Michael Holquist, trans. Caryl Emerson and Michael Holquist (Austin: University of Texas Press, 1981), 284.

11. A. Damesek, "Der realizm fun Kulbaks 'Zelmenyaner,'" *Shtern* no. 7 (1936): 83.

12. *Rabochii* (Minsk), October 15, 1929, 5.

13. "Tak svershilos' prishestviie tramvaia," *Rabochii,* October 15, 1929, 7.

14. I. Stalin, "God velikogo pereloma," *Rabochii,* November 6, 1929, 7.

15. Modified translation from Kulbak, *The Zelmenyaners*, 105; Kulbak, *Zelmenyaner: ershter bukh*, 134–135.

16. Sasha Senderovich and David Coons, "A Clan on the Move: A Zelmenyaner Family Tree," *In Geveb,* October 2015, http://ingeveb.org/blog/a-clan-on-the-move -a-zelmenyaner-family-tree.

17. Chapters that would constitute part one were serialized between December 1929 and November 1930; chapters that later became part two, between March 1933 and June 1935.

18. Bemporad, *Becoming Soviet Jews,* 87; Gennady Estraikh, *In Harness: Yiddish Writers' Romance with Communism* (Syracuse, NY: Syracuse University Press, 2005), 102.

19. Kulbak, *The Zelmenyaners,* 65.

20. Kulbak, 42; Kulbak, *Zelmenyaner: ershter bukh,* 55.

21. Speaking during the Russian civil war, in 1920, Lenin drew a distinction between the older and the younger generations and their role in the building of the new society. He suggested that "[t]he generation of people who are now at the age of fifty cannot expect to see a communist society. This generation will be gone before then. But the generation of those who are now fifteen will see a communist society, and will itself build this society." Quoted in Rex A. Wade, "Generations in Russian and Soviet History," *Soviet and Post-Soviet Review* 32, no. 2–3 (2005): 130.

22. Kulbak, *Zelmenyaner: ershter bukh,* 31–32. Modified translation from Irving Howe and Eliezer Greenberg, eds., *Ashes out of Hope: Fiction by Soviet-Yiddish Writers* (New York: Schocken Books, 1977), 143.

23. Kulbak, *The Zelmenyaners,* 38.

24. Kulbak, 124.

25. Julia Bekman Chadaga, *Optical Play: Glass, Vision, and Spectacle in Russian Culture* (Evanston, IL: Northwestern University Press, 2014), 174–184.

26. Modified translation from Kulbak, *The Zelmenyaners,* 37; Kulbak, *Zelmenyaner: ershter bukh,* 48.

27. Kulbak, *The Zelmenyaners,* 44.

28. Modified translation from Kulbak, 33.

29. Kulbak, 12.

30. Kulbak, 44–45.

31. Kulbak, 46.

32. Reviewers also focused on how *The Zelmenyaners* fit into the larger corpus of work by Moyshe Kulbak, who by the time of the novel's publication had mainly been known as a poet. Writing for *The Red World* (*Royte velt*) based in Kharkov, USSR, one critic in 1931 saw the completed first part of the novel as Kulbak's failed project to cast away the prior "bourgeois" aestheticism of his earlier poetry and prose; such casting away appeared, according to the critic, to have been the novel's intention that didn't pan out: A. H. Tsveyg [Ayzik Rozentsvayg], "Afn breytn shlyakh fun der Sovetisher literatur (vegn Kulbaks 'Zelmenyaner')," *Royte velt,* no. 7 (1931): 101–116.

33. Anonym., "Zelmenyaner," *Der moment*, July 4, 1930, 7.

34. Kh[aim] Sh[lomo] Kazdan, "Der 'Zelmenyanisher poet' un 'di Zelmenyaner,'" *Vokhnshrtift far literatur* 80, no. 30 (July 22, 1932): 2, 8.

35. Kulbak, *The Zelmenyaners*, 15.

36. Kulbak, 38.

37. Kulbak, 78; Kulbak, *Zelmenyaner: ershter bukh*, 108.

38. Rokhl Tsukerman and M. Litvak, "Elektrifikatsie un radiofikatsie fun Reb-zehoyf," *Der khaver* no. 6 (56) (1935): 167–171; Rokhl Tsukerman and M. Litvak, "Elektrifikatsie un radiofikatsie fun Rebzehoyf," *Der khaver*, no. 7 (57) (1935): 197–201. A revue show in Warsaw in 1933, which included scenes based on Kulbak's novel, received a positive review: N. M. [Nakhmen Mayzel], "'Nisht geshtoygn—nisht gefloygn' in 'Novoshtshi'-teater," *Literarishe bleter*, no. 45 (November 10, 1933): 720.

39. Quoted in Katerina Clark, "Little Heroes and Big Deeds: Literature Re-sponds to the First Five-Year Plan," in *Cultural Revolution in Russia, 1928–1931*, ed. Sheila Fitzpatrick (Bloomington: Indiana University Press, 1978), 191.

40. Clark, 202.

41. Nakhmen Mayzel, "Moyshe Kulbaks nay verk 'Zelmenyaner,'" *Haynt*, no. 31 (February 5, 1937): 7. Mayzel published a similar review in another journal at the time as well: Nakhmen Mayzel, "Moyshe Kulbaks 'Zelmenyaner,'" *Literarishe bleter*, no. 11 (670) (March 12, 1937): 174.

42. Nakhmen Mayzel, "Dos bukh vos ikh hob akorsht ibergeleyent: Moyshe Kulbaks 'Zelmenyaner,'" *Literarishe bleter*, no. 14 (413) (April 1, 1932): 224–225.

43. Y. Bronshteyn, "Kegn biologizm un folkizm (vegn Moyshe Kulbaks literarish veg fun 'Shtot' biz 'Zelmenyaner,'" in *Farfestike pozitsies* (Moscow: Emes, 1934), 159.

44. Katerina Clark, *The Soviet Novel: History as Ritual* (Chicago: University of Chicago Press, 1981), 15.

45. Clark, 16.

46. Bronshteyn, "Kegn biologizm un folkizm," 174.

47. Bronshteyn, 176.

48. The publication data on the final page of Bronshteyn's book *Farfestike pozitsies*, in which the article on Kulbak was printed, indicate that it went to press on February 2, 1934: Bronshteyn, 292.

49. William M. Todd III, "Anna on the Installment Plan: Teaching Anna Kare-nina through the History of Its Serial Publication," in *Approaches to Teaching Tolstoy's Anna Karenina*, ed. Liza Knapp and Amy Mandelker (New York: Modern Language Association of America, 2003), 53–59.

50. National Archive of the Republic of Belarus [NARB] f. 238, op. 8, d. 27, l. 55.

51. NARB f. 238, op. 8, d. 27, l. 60.

52. On the impact of purges on Minsk's Jewish culture scene, see Bemporad, *Becoming Soviet Jews*, 193–201.

53. The Yiddish phrase on the title page was the calque of *literaturnaia ob-rabotka* from the Russian.

54. Nikolai Ostrovskii, *Vi shtol hot zikh farkhatevet: roman in tsvey teyln,* ed. M. Kulbak (Minsk: Melukhe farlag, 1937).

55. Nikolai Vasilievich Gogol, *Revizor,* trans. Moyshe Kulbak (Minsk: Melukhe-farlag, 1937).

56. M. Kul'bak, "Vyiti na shirokuiu chitatel'skuiu arenu," *Rabochii,* September 18, 1934, 3.

57. M. Kulbak, "Der veg fun a folks-dikhter," *Shtern,* no. 10 (n.d.): 71–72.

58. A. Damesek, "Farakhte soynim unter a literarishe maske," *Shtern,* no. 10 (1936): 67–70.

59. Clark, *The Soviet Novel,* 103. On the prominence of civil war heroes among the protagonists of emerging Soviet literature, see also Rufus W. Mathewson, *The Positive Hero in Russian Literature* (Stanford: Stanford University Press, 1975), 180–210.

60. Kulbak, *The Zelmenyaners,* 11.

61. Bronshteyn, "Kegn biologizm un folkizm," 175–176.

62. Kulbak, *The Zelmenyaners,* 11.

63. M. Kulbak, "Bere (kapitlen funem tsveytn bukh Zelmenyaner): a prolog vegn a lefl," *Shtern,* no. 3 (1933): 9–15.

64. M. Kulbak, "Oysgeveyntlikhe pasirungen mit Beren untervegns," *Shtern,* no. 1 (1935): 6–14.

65. Such autobiographies were "less a record of what had actually happened to the applicant than an account of how he had ascribed meanings to what he had experienced." Igal Halfin, *Red Autobiographies: Initiating the Bolshevik Self* (Seattle: University of Washington Press, 2011), 10.

66. Kulbak, *The Zelmenyaners,* 143–144.

67. Sh. Y. Abramovitsh, *Tales of Mendele the Book Peddler: Fishke the Lame and Benjamin the Third,* ed. Ken Frieden, trans. Hillel Halkin (New York: Schocken Books, 1996), 307.

68. Modified translation from Kulbak, *The Zelmenyaners,* 134.

69. M. Kulbak, "Bere un feter Folye shlogn zikh far dem nayem mentshn," *Shtern,* no. 8–9 (1934): 34–39.

70. Kulbak, *The Zelmenyaners,* 235.

71. Modified translation from Kulbak, 238; Moyshe Kulbak, *Zelmenyaner: tsveyter bukh* (Minsk: Melukhe-farlag fun Vaysrusland, 1935), 181.

72. Kulbak, *The Zelmenyaners,* 239.

73. Kulbak, 241.

74. Kulbak, 254.

75. Kulbak, 255.

76. Kulbak, 261.

77. Kulbak, 45. The Yiddish original uses the ideologically charged Russian term *vreditel'*: Kulbak, *Zelmenyaner: ershter bukh*, 59.

78. Kulbak, *The Zelmenyaners*, 258.

79. Kulbak, 262.

80. Kulbak, 260.

81. Modified translation from Kulbak, 260.

82. Modified quotation from Kulbak, 260–261.

83. A. Kardushin, "Rabochie okrainy priblizilis' k tsentru," *Rabochii*, October 14, 1929, 7.

84. Modified translation from Kulbak, *The Zelmenyaners*, 89.

85. Demi, "Nanuk," *Rabochii*, October 17, 1929, 5.

86. Jay Ruby, *Picturing Culture: Explorations of Film and Anthropology* (Chicago: University of Chicago Press, 2000), 76.

87. Fatimah Tobing Rony, *The Third Eye: Race, Cinema, and Ethnographic Spectacle* (Durham, NC: Duke University Press, 1996), 101.

88. Kulbak, *Zelmenyaner: tsveyter bukh*, 97. Modified translation from Kulbak, *The Zelmenyaners*, 186.

89. The confirmation of Kulbak's employment as the Academy of Sciences' research associate was issued posthumously on May 22, 1957, at the request of Zelda Kulbak who was seeking a pension on behalf of her late husband per the 1956 rehabilitation laws (The Central Archive of the National Academy of Sciences of the Republic of Belarus f. 2, d. 3682, l. 6). A separate reconstruction of the notes of the meeting of the presidium of the Academy on November 29, 1930, confirms Kulbak's appointment as a stylistic editor of Yiddish publications beginning December 1, 1930 (The Central Archive of the National Academy of Sciences of the Republic of Belarus f. 2, d. 3682. l. 5).

90. Alfred Abraham Greenbaum, *Jewish Scholarship and Scholarly Institutions in Soviet Russia, 1918–1953* (Jerusalem: Centre for Research and Documentation of East European Jewry at the Hebrew University, 1978), 30. Also, David Shneer, "A Study in Red: Jewish Scholarship in the 1920s Soviet Union," *Science in Context*, 20, no. 2 (2007): 206–207. See also Cecile Esther Kuznitz, *YIVO and the Making of Modern Jewish Culture: Scholarship for the Yiddish Nation* (Cambridge: Cambridge University Press, 2014), 106.

91. Greenbaum, *Jewish Scholarship and Scholarly Institutions in Soviet Russia*, 31.

92. Greenbaum, 32–33.

93. Kulbak, *The Zelmenyaners*, 23; Kulbak, *Zelmenyaner: ershter bukh*, 30–31.

94. I thank Raya Kulbak for making her mother's unpublished notebooks available to me during my research.

95. Two approaches to local ethnography are of note here. One is the Jewish Society for Landkentenish / Krajoznawstvo, which was founded in Warsaw in 1926. The aim of the society was "to foster *doikayt* (hereness), a deep sense of root-

edness to the Polish lands where Jews had lived for hundreds of years." Samuel Kassow, "Travel and Local History as a National Mission: Polish Jews and the Landkentenish Movement in the 1920s and 1930s," in *Jewish Topographies: Visions of Space, Traditions of Place,* ed. Julia Brauch, Anna Lipphardt, and Alexandra Nocke (Hampshire: Ashgate, 2008), 243. The second overlapping phenomenon is Russian local ethnography, known as *kraevedenie*; see Emily D. Johnson, *How St. Petersburg Learned to Study Itself: The Russian Idea of Kraevedenie* (University Park: Pennsylvania State University Press, 2006). On the local approach to the study of Belorussian Jewish culture, see Bemporad, *Becoming Soviet Jews,* 104–109.

96. Iurii Tyn'ianov, "Dostoevskii i Gogol': k teorii parodii," in *Poetika: Istoriia literatury. Kino* (Moscow: Nauka, 1977), 226.

97. Kulbak, *The Zelmenyaners,* 186. Kulbak, *Zelmenyaner: tsveyter bukh,* 97.

98. Modified translation from Kulbak, *The Zelmenyaners,* 186–192. Kulbak, *Zelmenyaner: tsveyter bukh,* 97–108.

99. Deborah Yalen, "Red Kasrilevke: Ethnographies of Economic Transformation in the Soviet Shtetl 1917–1939" (PhD diss., University of California Berkeley, 2007), 4.

100. Yuri Slezkine, *Arctic Mirrors: Russia and the Small Peoples of the North* (Ithaca, NY: Cornell University Press, 1994), 219–263.

101. Francine Hirsch, *Empire of Nations: Ethnographic Knowledge and the Making of the Soviet Union* (Ithaca, NY: Cornell University Press, 2005), 8–9.

102. Yalen, "Red Kasrilevke," 2.

103. H. Aleksandrov, *Forsht ayer shtetl!* (Minsk: Institut far Vaysruslandisher kultur—Yidisher sektor, 1928), 10–16.

104. Bemporad, *Becoming Soviet Jews,* 107–108.

105. Damesek, "Der realizm fun Kulbaks 'Zelmenyaner,'" 80.

106. Charles Moser, *Esthetics as Nightmare: Russian Literary Theory, 1855–1870* (Princeton: Princeton University Press, 1989), 27.

107. Damesek, "Der realizm fun Kulbaks 'Zelmenyaner,'" 80.

108. Damesek, 80.

109. Damesek, 81.

110. Maxim Mikulak, "Darwinism, Soviet Genetics, and Marxism-Leninism," *Journal of the History of Ideas* 31, no. 3 (1970): 369–370.

111. Damesek, "Der realizm fun Kulbaks 'Zelmenyaner,'" 92.

112. Damesek, 92.

113. Terry Martin, *The Affirmative Action Empire: Nations and Nationalism in the Soviet Union, 1923–1939* (Ithaca, NY: Cornell University Press, 2001), 182.

114. Shmuel Niger, reviewing the first part of *The Zelmenyaners* in 1931, pointed out the dissatisfaction of Soviet critics with Kulbak's novel: "They [the proletarian critics] want revolutionary pathos, and Kulbak came along with a smile on his lips . . . Their weapon is satire, while he provides humor." Sh[muel] Niger, "Di Zelmenyaner,"

in *Yidishe shrayber in Sovet-Rusland* (New York: Sh. Niger bukh-komitet baym alveltlekhn Yidishn kultur-kongres, 1958), 115.

115. Modified translation from Kulbak, *The Zelmenyaners*, 260–261.

116. Kenneth Martin Pinnow, *Lost to the Collective: Suicide and the Promise of Soviet Socialism, 1921–1929* (Ithaca, NY: Cornell University Press, 2010), 247.

117. Pinnow, 248. Nikolai Erdman's satirical play *The Suicide* (*Samoubiitsa*) was written in 1928; in the play, members of different aggrieved constituencies try to convince a would-be suicide to leave a note, in which he would present himself as a martyr for one of their causes.

118. Kulbak, *The Zelmenyaners*, 58; Kulbak, *Zelmenyaner: ershter bukh*, 77.

119. Kulbak, *The Zelmenyaners*, 52; Kulbak, *Zelmenyaner: ershter bukh*, 69.

120. Kulbak, *The Zelmenyaners*, 52.

121. Kulbak, 52–53; Kulbak, *Zelmenyaner: ershter bukh*, 70.

122. Kulbak, *The Zelmenyaners*, 54.

123. Kulbak, *Zelmenyaner: ershter bukh*, 72.

124. Ruth R. Wisse, *The Modern Jewish Canon: A Journey through Language and Culture* (Chicago: University of Chicago Press, 2000), 123.

125. Bronshteyn, "Kegn biologizm un folkizm," 162.

126. Kulbak, *The Zelmenyaners*, 54.

127. Kulbak, 7.

128. Kulbak, *Zelmenyaner: ershter bukh*, 32.

129. Kulbak, 54.

130. Kulbak, *The Zelmenyaners*, 40–41; Kulbak, *Zelmenyaner: ershter bukh*, 53–54.

131. Galit Hasan-Rokem, "Material Mobility versus Concentric Cosmology in the Sukkah: The House of the Wandering Jew or a Ubiquitous Temple?" in *Things: Religion and the Question of Materiality*, ed. Dick Houtman and Brigit Meyer (New York: Fordham University Press, 2012), 153–179.

132. Kulbak, *The Zelmenyaners*, 266; Kulbak, *Zelmenyaner: tsveyter bukh*, 225.

133. Kulbak, *The Zelmenyaners*, 3; Kulbak, *Zelmenyaner: ershter bukh*, 5.

134. Kulbak, *The Zelmenyaners*, 189.

135. Kulbak, 5.

136. Kulbak, 144.

137. Kulbak, 145.

138. Kulbak, *Zelmenyaner: ershter bukh*, 53–54.

139. Kulbak, 26.

140. Modified translation from Kulbak, *The Zelmenyaners*, 20; Kulbak, *Zelmenyaner: ershter bukh*, 26.

141. Kulbak, *The Zelmenyaners*, 253.

142. Moyshe Kulbak, "From *Byelorussia*," trans. by Leonard Wolf, in Irving Howe, Ruth R. Wisse, and Khone Shmeruk, eds., *The Penguin Book of Modern Yiddish Verse* (New York: Viking, 1987), 388.

143. Shlomo Beylis, "Gezangen tsum erdishn (notitsn vegn Moyshe Kulbak)," *Di goldene keyt*, no. 105 (1981): 96–107. On the poetics of "hereness" in Moyshe Kulbak's novel, see Madeline Atkins Cohen, "Here and Now: The Modernist Poetics of Do'ikayt" (PhD diss., Berkeley, University of California, 2016), 75–121.

144. Moyshe Kulbak, *Naye lider* (Warsaw: Kultur-lige, 1922), 27.

145. Kulbak, 28–29.

3. The Edge of the World

1. Viktor Fink, *Evrei v taige* (Moscow: Federatsiia, 1930), 107. The title page of this—first—edition of the book noted on the title page that this was "Book Two" of *Jews on the Land* (*Evrei na zemle*)—positioning *Jews in the Taiga* as a continuation of Fink's earlier book, published in 1929, about Jewish agricultural settlements in Crimea. The second edition of *Jews in the Taiga* in 1932 made no such allusion to the Crimean experiment.

2. Masha Gessen, *Where the Jews Aren't: The Sad and Absurd Story of Birobidzhan, Russia's Jewish Autonomous Region* (New York: Schocken, 2016), 51.

3. Henry Srebrnik, "Territorialism and the ICOR 'American Commission of Scientists and Experts' to the Soviet Far East," in *1929: Mapping the Jewish World*, ed. Hasia Diner and Gennady Estraikh (New York: New York University Press, 2013), 109.

4. On the history of Jewish colonization before Birobidzhan, see Jonathan Dekel-Chen, *Farming the Red Land: Jewish Agricultural Colonization and Local Soviet Power, 1924–1941* (New Haven: Yale University Press, 2005).

5. See, for example, Zvi Y. Gitelman's introduction in Robert Weinberg, *Stalin's Forgotten Zion: Birobidzhan and the Making of a Soviet Jewish Homeland: An Illustrated History, 1928–1996* (Berkeley: University of California Press, 1998), 5.

6. The notion of how Soviet peoples were constituted of different ethnic (or, in Soviet parlance, "national") groups varied in the early years of Soviet power; these categories were not constant. See Francine Hirsch, *Empire of Nations: Ethnographic Knowledge and the Making of the Soviet Union* (Ithaca, NY: Cornell University Press, 2005).

7. Henry Srebrnik, "Diaspora, Ethnicity and Dreams of Nationhood: American Jewish Communists and the Birobidzhan Project," in *Yiddish and the Left*, ed. Gennady Estraikh and Mikhail Krutikov (London: Legenda, 2001), 80–108.

8. *Otchët ekspertov: doklad amerikanskoi komissii "Ikor" po izucheniiu Birobidzhana* (Moscow: Izd. tsentr. pravleniia Ozet, 1930), 3–5.

9. Quoted in Weinberg, *Stalin's Forgotten Zion*, 22.

10. *Otchët ekspertov*, 16–17.

11. David Shneer, *Through Soviet Jewish Eyes: Photography, War, and the Holocaust* (New Brunswick, NJ: Rutgers University Press, 2011), 69–76.

12. For Fink's biography, see Maxim D. Shrayer, ed., *An Anthology of Jewish-Russian Literature: Two Centuries of Dual Identity in Prose and Poetry*, vol. 1 (Armonk, NY: M. E. Sharpe, 2007), 361–362. For Gekht's biography, see S. Gekht, *Izbrannoe: stikhotvoreniia, proza, vospominaniia*, ed. A. L. Iavorskaia (Odessa: Optimum, 2010), 7–32.

13. S. Gekht, "Amerikantsy v Biro-Bidzhane," *Ogonëk*, no. 43 (1929): 13.

14. Viktor Fink, "Birobidzhan: Evreiskaia Avtonomnaia Oblast'," *Ogonëk*, June 5, 1934, 4–5.

15. First edition: Viktor Fink, *Evrei v taige* (Moscow: Federatsiia, 1930); revised edition: Viktor Fink, *Evrei v taige: ocherki* (Moscow: Federatsiia, 1932). Earlier, Fink published a book about the USSR's designs to settle Jews in agricultural colonies in Ukraine and Crimea, which the Far Eastern plan eventually supplanted: Viktor Fink, *Evrei na zemle* (Moscow: Gos. izd-vo, 1929). Two more short books by Fink about Ukrainian and Crimean agricultural colonies came out in large print runs: Viktor Fink, *Na puti iz Egipta* (Moscow: Akts. izd. o-vo "Ogonëk," 1929) and *Evrei v pole* (Moscow: Molodaia gvardiia, 1930). With his *Jews in the Taiga* coming out too early to repudiate his writing on colonies in Ukraine, Fink published his sketch in *Ogonëk* in 1934 right after Birobidzhan was upgraded to the status of an autonomous region. A good deal of this sketch negatively characterized the colonization projects in Ukraine that Fink had described earlier: Fink, "Birobidzhan: Evreiskaia Avtonomnaia Oblast'."

16. As quoted in Boris Kotlerman, "The Image of Birobidzhan in Yiddish Belle Lettres," *Jews in Eastern Europe* 49, no. 3 (2002): 51.

17. Katerina Clark, "Socialist Realism and the Sacralizing of Space," in *The Landscape of Stalinism: The Art and Ideology of Soviet Space*, ed. Evgeny Dobrenko and Eric Naiman (Seattle: University of Washington Press, 2003), 5.

18. Evgeny Dobrenko, *Political Economy of Socialist Realism*, trans. Jesse Savage (New Haven: Yale University Press, 2007), 5.

19. S. Gekht, *Parokhod idët v Iaffu i obratno* (Moscow: Khudozhestvennaia literatura, 1936), 193.

20. *Otchët ekspertov*, 69.

21. Gekht, *Parokhod idët v Iaffu i obratno*, 220.

22. Gekht, 201.

23. Kotlerman, "The Image of Birobidzhan in Yiddish Belle Lettres," 48.

24. As quoted in E. I. Zhurbina, *Iskusstvo ocherka* (Moscow: Sovetskii pisatel', 1957), 17. On the sketch as a Soviet literary genre, see Michael S Gorham, *Speaking in Soviet Tongues: Language Culture and the Politics of Voice in Revolutionary Russia* (DeKalb: Northern Illinois University Press, 2003), 152–159.

25. Fink, *Evrei v taige: ocherki*, 3.

26. Fink, 4.

27. Clark, "Socialist Realism and the Sacralizing of Space," 4–5.

28. Clark, 8–9.

29. Vladimir Paperny, *Architecture in the Age of Stalin: Culture Two,* trans. John Hill and Roann Barris (Cambridge: Cambridge University Press, 2002), 15.

30. Evgeny Dobrenko, "The Art of Social Navigation: The Cultural Topography of the Stalin Era," in *The Landscape of Stalinism: The Art and Ideology of Soviet Space,* ed. Evgeny Dobrenko and Eric Naiman (Seattle: University of Washington Press, 2003), 199.

31. Petre Petrov, "The Industry of Truing: Socialist Realism, Reality, Realization," *Slavic Review* 70, no. 4 (2011): 800.

32. Harriet Murav, "New Jews: David Bergelson and Birobidzhan," in *The Jews of Eastern Europe,* ed. Leonard J. Greenspoon, Ronald A. Simkins, and Brian J. Horowitz, vol. 16, Studies in Jewish Civilization (Lincoln: University of Nebraska Press, 2005), 191–202.

33. I. Sudarskii, *Birobidzhan i Palestina* (Moscow: OZET, 1930); I. Sudarskii, *Biro-Bidzhan un Palestine* (Kharkov: Tsentralfarlag, 1929).

34. On the history of Russian-language writing about Palestine, see Vladimir Khazan, *Osobennyi evreisko-russkii vozdukh: k problematike i poetike russko-evreiskogo literaturnogo dialoga v XX veke* (Moscow: Mosty kul'tury / Gesharim, 2001), 17–47.

35. Of particular relevance is the two-part Russian-language account of the Zionist settlement in Palestine by Mark Egart, published prior to Gekht's novel: Mark Egart, *Opalënnaia zemlia: kniga pervaia* (Moscow: Khudozhestvennaia literatura, 1933) and *Opalënnaia zemlia: kniga vtoraia* (Moscow: Khudozhestvennaia literatura, 1934). A revised edition of the novel came out in 1937, a year after Gekht's novel: Mark Egart, *Opalënnaia zemlia* (Moscow: Sovetskii pisatel', 1937).

36. Lewis H. Siegelbaum and Leslie Page Moch, *Broad Is My Native Land: Repertoires and Regimes of Migration in Russia's Twentieth Century* (Ithaca, NY: Cornell University Press, 2014), 5.

37. John J. Stephan, *The Russian Far East: A History* (Stanford: Stanford University Press, 1994), 47–50.

38. Weinberg, *Stalin's Forgotten Zion,* 21.

39. Yuri Slezkine, "The USSR as a Communal Apartment, or How a Socialist State Promoted Ethnic Particularism," *Slavic Review* 53, no. 2 (Summer 1994): 414–452.

40. Chimen Abramsky, "The Biro-Bidzhan Project, 1927–1959," in *The Jews in Soviet Russia since 1917,* ed. Lionel Kochan (London: Oxford University Press, 1972), 68–69.

41. Chizhuko Takao, "The Birobidzhan Project from the Japanese Perspective," in *Mizrekh: Jewish Studies in the Far East,* ed. Boris Ber Kotlerman (New York: Peter Lang, 2009), 54–57.

42. Fink used the substandard Russian spelling in the original. Fink, *Evrei v taige: ocherki,* 171.

43. Emma Widdis, *Visions of a New Land: Soviet Film from the Revolution to the Second World War* (New Haven: Yale University Press, 2003), 128–130.

44. Fink, *Evrei v taige: ocherki,* 194.

45. Fink, 175.

46. Judith Deutsch Kornblatt, *The Cossack Hero in Russian Literature: A Study in Cultural Mythology* (Madison: University of Wisconsin Press, 1992), 107–125.

47. Israel Bartal, "Hanukkah Cossack Style: Zaporozhian Warriors and Zionist Popular Culture (1904–1918)," in *Stories of Khmelnytsky: Competing Literary Legacies of the 1648 Ukrainian Cossack Uprising,* ed. Amelia M. Glaser (Stanford: Stanford University Press, 2015), 139–152. See also Gennady Estraikh, "Jews as Cossacks: A Symbiosis in Literature and Life," in *Soviet Jews in World War II: Fighting, Witnessing, Remembering,* ed. Harriet Murav and Gennady Estraikh (Boston: Academic Studies Press, 2014), 85–103.

48. Jonathan Dekel-Chen, "'New' Jews of the Agricultural Kind: A Case of Soviet Interwar Propaganda," *Russian Review* 66 (July 2007): 446–448.

49. Harriet Murav, *Music from a Speeding Train: Soviet Yiddish and Russian-Jewish Literature of the Twentieth Century* (Stanford: Stanford University Press, 2011), 67.

50. For example, S. Gekht, "Stariki: evreiskaia bednota na Podolii," *Ogonëk,* no. 25 (September 16, 1923): 13–14.

51. Murav, *Music from a Speeding Train,* 67.

52. Fink, *Evrei v taige: ocherki,* 106.

53. Fink, 124. Fink's calling the subjects of his book "dramatis personae" is notable because he went on to write a play, in which entire pages from *Evrei v taige* were reproduced as lines of its dramatis personae. Viktor Fink, *Novaia rodina: p'esa v 4 deistviiakh* (Moscow: Sovetskaia literatura, 1933).

54. Fink, *Evrei v taige: ocherki,* 47.

55. Fink, 47; I transliterated the spelling in this phrase as it appears in Fink's original.

56. Fink, 48.

57. Fink, 48.

58. Fink, 49; I transliterated the spelling in this phrase as it appears in Fink's original.

59. Fink, 50.

60. Fink, 230–231.

61. Fink, 231.

62. N. Matveev, "Viktor Fink: Evrei v taige (Evrei na zemle. Kniga vtoraia)," *Novyi mir* 12 (1930): 198–199.

63. Fink, *Evrei v taige: ocherki,* 60.

64. "Prochtite etu interesnuiu knigu. Fink V. Evrei v taige," *Literaturnaia gazeta,* no. 10 (1931): 3.

65. Fink, *Evrei v taige: ocherki,* 50.

66. J. B. Schechtman, "The U.S.S.R., Zionism, and Israel," in *The Jews in Soviet Russia since 1917*, ed. Lionel Kochan (Oxford: Oxford University Press, 1978), 106–131. Arab riots in Palestine created a rift among U.S.-based Jewish supporters of the USSR, including supporters of Birobidzhan: Gennady Estraikh, "The Stalinist 'Great Break' in Yiddishland," in *1929: Mapping the Jewish World*, ed. Hasia Diner and Gennady Estraikh (New York: New York University Press, 2013), 46–48.

67. Srebrnik, "Diaspora, Ethnicity and Dreams of Nationhood" 86.

68. "Birobidzhan—strana s bol'shim budushchim," *Tribuna*, no. 20 (October 25, 1929): 5–8.

69. Gekht, *Parokhod idët v Iaffu i obratno*, 90.

70. Gekht, 203.

71. Lukasz Hirsczowicz, "Soviet Perceptions of Zionism," *Soviet Jewish Affairs* 9, no. 1 (1979): 53–65.

72. S. Gekht, *"Prostoi rasskaz o mertvetsakh" i drugie proizvedeniia*, ed. M. Vainsthein (Jerusalem: Seriia Pamiat', 1983), 244.

73. Gekht, "Stariki: evreiskaia bednota na Podolii." Also, the narrator of Gekht's novel described the shtetl Litin similarly to how Jerusalem is described: Gekht, *Parokhod idët v Iaffu i obratno*, 170.

74. Semyon Gekht, Parokhod idët v Iaffu i obratno: rasskazy i povest' (Moscow: Tekst, 2016).

75. Zsuzsa Hetényi, *In a Maelstrom: The History of Russian-Jewish Prose (1860–1940)* (Budapest: Central European University Press, 2008), 206–207.

76. Gekht, *Izbrannoe*, 18. See also A. L. Iavorskaia, "Materialy k biografii Semyona Gekhta," *Dom kniazia Gagarina* 3, no. 2 (2004): 157–257; A. L. Iavorskaia, ed., "Pis'ma Gekhta v fondakh OLM [Odesskogo Literaturnogo Muzeia]," *Dom kniazia Gagarina* 3, no. 2 (2004): 216–257; Alëna Iavorskaia, "Dve zametki k biografiiam (S. Gekht i E. Bagritskii)," *Moriia*, no. 10 (2008): 59–64.

77. Jeffrey Veidlinger, *The Moscow State Yiddish Theater: Jewish Culture on the Soviet Stage* (Bloomington: Indiana University Press, 2000), 154–155.

78. I. Sudarskii, *Biro-Bidzhan un Palestine* (Kharkov: Tsentralfarlag, 1929); the Russian translation of this title was published a year later: I. Sudarskii, *Birobidzhan i Palestina* (Moscow: OZET, 1930). Also see *Far vos gist zikh blut in Palestine?* vol. 9, Ikor-bibliotek (New York: Ikor, 1933); P. Novik, *Palestina on a paroykhes* (Minsk: Melukhe-farlag fun Vaysrusland, 1933).

79. Emphasis in the original. Shrayer, *An Anthology of Jewish-Russian Literature*, 1:399.

80. In addition to Egart's novel, Gekht might have relied on other texts about Palestine: travelogues by Russian Orthodox pilgrims in the nineteenth and twentieth centuries (including Nikolai Gogol's letter to Vasilii Zhukovskii written from a train station in Nazareth in 1848); Russian-language travelogues to Palestine by a number of prominent Jewish thinkers such as, for example, Menachem

Ussishkin's 1894 travelogue: M. M. Usyshkin, *Po Palestine: iz putevykh zametok* (St. Petersburg: Tipo-litografiia Berman i Rabinovich, 1894). The ethnographer Lev Shternberg wrote letters from Palestine in 1908: L. Sh. [Lev Shternberg], *Po Palestine: Pis'ma s dorogi* (Odessa: Tipo-lit. kn-va M.S. Kozmana, 1910). A corpus of verse by Russian-language poets from the first two decades of the twentieth century, such as Konstantin Lipskerov, Evgenii Shkliar, Matvei Roizman, and Grigorii Sorokin, also covers the Palestinian theme in Russian literature; see Khazan, *Osobennyi evreisko-russkii vozdukh*, 17–47.

81. S. Bit-Yukhan, "Sionistskaia ideologiia pod prikrytiem 'kritiki sionizma,'" *Revoliutsionnyi vostok*, no. 5–6 (39–40) (1936): 199–207.

82. Iv. Sergeev, "Parokhod idët v Iaffu i obratno," *Literaturnaia gazeta*, no. 41 (604) (1936).

83. Bit-Yukhan, "Sionistskaia ideologiia pod prikrytiem 'kritiki sionizma,'" 206.

84. Gessen, *Where the Jews Aren't*, 50.

85. Gekht, *Parokhod idët v Iaffu i obratno*, 10.

86. Lion Feuchtwanger and André Gide, *Dva vzgliada iz-za rubezha* (Moscow: Politizdat, 1990), 218.

87. Murav, "New Jews: David Bergelson and Birobidzhan," 200.

88. S. Gekht, "Zhizn' posle smerti," *30 dnei*, no. 6 (1933): 41–47.

89. Todd Samuel Presner, *Muscular Judaism: The Jewish Body and the Politics of Regeneration* (New York: Routledge, 2007).

90. Yisrael Bartal, *Galut ba-arets: Yishuv Eretz-Yisrael be-terem Tsiyonut* (Jerusalem: ha-Sifriyah ha-Tsiyonit, 1994), 15.

91. Yael Zerubavel, *Recovered Roots: Collective Memory and the Making of Israeli National Tradition* (Chicago: University of Chicago Press, 1995), 22–33.

92. Sudarskii, *Birobidzhan i Palestina*, 32.

93. Shneer, *Through Soviet Jewish Eyes*, 78–79.

94. Todd Hasak-Lowy, *Here and Now: History, Nationalism, and Realism in Modern Hebrew Fiction* (Syracuse, NY: Syracuse University Press, 2008), 34–67.

95. Gershon Shaked, *Modern Hebrew Fiction*, ed. E. Miller Budick, trans. Yael Lotan (Bloomington: Indiana University Press, 2000), 171–172.

96. Jean-Christophe Attias and Esther Benbassa, *Israel, the Impossible Land*, trans. Susan Emanuel (Stanford, CA: Stanford University Press, 2002), 167.

97. Shneer, *Through Soviet Jewish Eyes*, 72–83.

98. As quoted in Shneer, 82.

99. Widdis, *Visions of a New Land*, 123.

100. Gekht, *Parokhod idët v Iaffu i obratno*, 127.

101. Gekht, 130.

102. Gekht, 236.

103. Fink, *Evrei v taige: ocherki*, 344–353.

104. Gekht, *Parokhod idët v Iaffu i obratno,* 236.

105. S. Epshtein, *Misha iz evreiskogo posëlka (Pioneram ob OZETe)* (Moscow: Ts[entral'noe] P[ravlenie] OZET, 1929). OZET also published a manual on how to discuss OZET's activities with children: N. Levin and D. Davidovich, *OZET rabota sredi detei* (Moscow: Tsentral'noe pravlenie OZET, 1930). On the participation of Soviet children in agitation and discussions of various societal causes, see Catriona Kelly, *Children's World: Growing up in Russia, 1890–1991* (New Haven: Yale University Press, 2007), 76–77.

106. Aleksandr Isaevich Solzhenitsyn, *Dvesti let vmeste, 1795–1995* (Moscow: Russkii put', 2001), 2: 241.

107. Levin and Davidovich, *OZET rabota sredi detei,* 5.

108. Levin and Davidovich, 5.

109. Jack Zipes, *Fairy Tales and Fables from Weimar Days* (Madison: University of Wisconsin Press, 1997), 20.

110. Marina Balina, "'It's Grand to Be an Orphan!': Crafting Happy Citizens in Soviet Children's Literature of the 1920s," in *Petrified Utopia: Happiness Soviet Style,* ed. Marina Balina and Evgeny Dobrenko (New York: Anthem Press, 2009), 103–104.

111. Lisa A. Kirschenbaum, *Small Comrades: Revolutionizing Childhood in Soviet Russia, 1917–1932* (London: Routledge, 2001), 163.

112. Marina Balina, Helena Goscilo, and Mark Lipovetsky, eds., *Politicizing Magic: An Anthology of Russian and Soviet Fairy Tales* (Evanston, IL: Northwestern University Press, 2005), 106.

113. Felix J. Oinas, "The Political Uses and Themes of Folklore in the Soviet Union," in *Folklore, Nationalism, and Politics,* ed. Felix J. Oinas (Columbus: Slavica, 1978), 77.

114. Quoted in Marina Balina, "Creativity through Restraint: The Beginnings of Soviet Children's Literature," in *Russian Children's Literature and Culture,* ed. Marina Balina and Larissa Rudova (New York: Routledge, 2008), 4.

115. Balina, Goscilo, and Lipovetsky, *Politicizing Magic,* 107. "The renovation of life" is a quote from Maxim Gorky's speech at the First All-Union Congress of Soviet Writers in 1934.

116. Vladimir Propp, *Morphology of the Folktale,* trans. Lawrence Scott (Austin: University of Texas Press, 1968), 26–28.

117. S. Gekht, *Istoriia pereselentsev Budlerov* (Moscow: Gosudarstvennoe izdatel'stvo, 1930), 3.

118. Gekht, 3.

119. Gekht, 6.

120. Cathy Caruth, ed., *Trauma: Explorations in Memory* (Baltimore: Johns Hopkins University Press, 1995), 11.

121. Gekht, *Istoriia pereselentsev Budlerov,* 4.

122. Gekht, 4.

123. Epshtein, *Misha iz evreiskogo posëlka*, 10.

124. Gekht, *Istoriia pereselentsev Budlerov*, 14.

125. On the role of electricity and machines in Socialist Realism, see Katerina Clark, *The Soviet Novel: History as Ritual* (Bloomington: Indiana University Press, 2000), 93–113.

126. Gekht, *Istoriia pereselentsev Budlerov*, 24.

127. Gekht, 30.

128. Gekht, 32.

129. Gekht, 38.

130. Gekht, 39.

131. Gekht, 46.

132. Gekht, 46.

133. Jonathan Goldstein, "Some Theoretical Approaches for Comparing Jewish Life in Singapore, Manila, and Harbin," in *Mizrekh: Jewish Studies in the Far East*, ed. Boris Ber Kotlerman (Frankfurt-am-Mein: Peter Lang, 2009), 42.

134. Robert Weinberg, "Jews into Peasants? Solving the Jewish Question in Biro-bidzhan," in *Jews and Jewish Life in Russia and the Soviet Union*, ed. Yaacov Ro'i (Portland: Frank Cass, 1995), 96.

135. Viktor Fink, "Vi zet oys dos Yidishe lebn in Biro-Bidzhan?" *Haynt*, August 16, 1931, 5. The rest of the series ran in the newspaper on August 17, 1931 (p. 4), August 20, 1931 (p. 3), August 23, 1931 (p. 6), and August 25, 1931 (p. 4).

136. Victor Fink, "The Colonies on the Taiga Steppes," trans. Leon Dennen, *Menorah Journal* XIX, no. 4 (June 1931): 416–433.

4. Back in the USSR

1. Il'ia Il'f and Evgenii Petrov, *Sobranie sochinenii*, vol. 2 (Moscow: Gos. izd-vo khudozh. lit-ry, 1961), 294.

2. For the study of the figure of the Wandering Jew, see George Kumler Anderson, *The Legend of the Wandering Jew* (Providence, RI: Brown University Press, 1965); Galit Hasan-Rokem and Alan Dundes, *The Wandering Jew: Essays in the Interpretation of a Christian Legend* (Bloomington: Indiana University Press, 1986). For the specifics of the Wandering Jew myth as having originated with a figure of a cobbler in ancient Jerusalem, see Shelly Zer-Zion, "The Wanderer's Shoe, the Cobbler's Penalty: The Wandering Jew in Search of Salvation," in *Jews and Shoes*, ed. Edna Nahshon (Oxford: Berg, 2008), 133–148.

3. Il'f and Petrov, *Sobranie sochinenii*, 2:308–309.

4. Karl Kautsky, "Are Jews a Race?," accessed August 25, 2020, http://www.marxists.org/archive/kautsky/1914/jewsrace/ch12.htm.

5. Il'f and Petrov, *Sobranie sochinenii*, 2:307.

6. Evgenii Petrov, "Puteshestvie na Dal'nii Vostok: Evreiskaia Avtonomnaia Oblast'," *Ogonëk*, no. 12 (1938): 18. For more on Il'f and Petrov's trip to the United

States and the book that resulted, *The One-Storey America (Odnoetazhnaia Amerika)*, see Aleksandr Etkind, *Tolkovanie puteshestvii: Rossiia i Amerika v travelogakh i intertekstakh* (Moscow: Novoe literaturnoe obozrenie, 2001), 162–165.

7. For a reading of Ostap Bender as a Wandering Jew, see Alice Nakhimovsky, "How the Soviets Solved the Jewish Question: The Il'f-Petrov Novels and Il'f's Jewish Stories," *Symposium* 53, no. 2 (Summer 1999): 103–107. For a reading of the Wandering Jew anecdote in *The Little Golden Calf* as a kind of meta-summary of Il'f and Petrov's Ostap Bender novels, see Maia Kaganskaia and Zeev Bar-Sella, *Master Gambs i Margarita* (Tel Aviv, 1984), 162–163.

8. Roberta Newman, "Pictures of a Trip to the Old Country," *YIVO Annual* 21 (1993): 223–239.

9. Daniel Soyer, "Back to the Future: American Jews Visit the Soviet Union in the 1920s and 1930s," *Jewish Social Studies* 6, no. 3 (Spring–Summer 2000): 124–159.

10. For the discussion of the image of the "old country" constructed by travelers, see Jack Kugelmass and Jeffrey Shandler, eds., *Going Home: How American Jews Invent the Old World* (New York: YIVO Institute for Jewish Research, 1989). The trend of Jewish travel to the USSR was part of a larger phenomenon of travel of left-leaning Western intellectuals: Paul Hollander, *Political Pilgrims: Travels of Western Intellectuals to the Soviet Union, China, and Cuba, 1928–1978* (New York: Oxford University Press, 1981); Lewis S. Feuer, "American Travelers to the Soviet Union 1917–32: The Formation of a Component of New Deal Ideology," *American Quarterly* 14, no. 2 (Summer 1962): 119–149.

11. M. I. Kosinova, *Distributsiia i kinopokaz v Rossii: istoriia i sovremennost'*, ed. V. I. Fomin (Riazan: Riazanskaia oblastnaia tipografiia, 2008), 110–118, 134–142.

12. Lev Kuleshov's "Americanism [*Amerikanshchina*]," in Richard Taylor and Ian Christie, eds., *The Film Factory: Russian and Soviet Cinema in Documents* (Cambridge, MA: Harvard University Press, 1988), 72–73.

13. N. M. Zorkaia, *Istoriia sovetskogo kino* (Saint Petersburg: Aleteia, 2005), 189–201.

14. Miron Chernenko, *Krasnaia zvezda, zhëltaia zvezda: Kinematograficheskaia istoriia evreistva v Rossii* (Moscow: Tekst, 2006), 63–64.

15. Peretz Markish, *Eyns af eyns* (Kharkov: Melukhe farlag far di natsionale minderhaytn in U.S.R.R., 1934); Perets Markish, *Vozvrashchenie Neitana Bekkera*, trans. M. A. Shambadal (Moscow: Sovetskaia literatura, 1934).

16. For the study of *The Return of Neitan Bekker* that emphasizes the film's reliance on carrying a number of folkloric Jewish types into the Soviet era, see Harriet Murav, "Peretz Markish in the 1930s: Socialist Construction and the Return of the Luftmentsh," in *A Captive of the Dawn: The Life and Work of Peretz Markish (1895–1952)*, ed. Joseph Sherman et al. (Leeds: Legenda, 2011), 114–126.

17. Although the name of the character in the film is Jim, his name in the novel that Markish wrote two years later is Kador Ben-Salim. Ben-Salim was, in fact, the

name of the Senegalese actor who played the role of Jim in the film; by the time Markish rewrote his screenplay as a novel, the real actor's name became the name of the novel's Black protagonist. Ben-Salim had been in the Soviet Union for almost a decade by the time Shpis and Mil'man made their film, playing a number of supporting roles in other early Soviet films—including the role of a Black circus actor in the four-part adventure film *The Red Imps* (*Krasnye diavoliata*) shot in the 1920s.

18. For the history of Blacks in Russian and Soviet discourse and culture, see Allison Blakely, *Russia and the Negro: Blacks in Russian History and Thought* (Washington, DC: Howard University Press, 1986). For a discussion of the role of Black Americans in Soviet discourse, see Joy Gleason Carew, *Blacks, Reds, and Russians: Sojourners in Search of the Soviet Promise* (New Brunswick, NJ: Rutgers University Press, 2008).

19. Plot summaries in some of the scholarship on and in reviews of *The Return of Neitan Bekker* incorrectly situate the location of the construction site in Magnitogorsk; for example, Gennady Estraikh, *In Harness: Yiddish Writers' Romance with Communism* (Syracuse, NY: Syracuse University Press, 2005), 147. However, the details of how Neitan and Tsale travel to the construction site do not compute with the distance they would have covered between Ukraine and the Urals. The confusion likely arose for some viewers because Tsale does mention Magnitogorsk as a kind of byword for a large construction site of the First Five-Year Plan—rather than as a destination for his and Neitan's work. In the novel that Markish published in 1934, the construction site is more precisely located in Kharkov in Ukraine.

20. Soyer, "Back to the Future," 143.

21. On the Central Institute of Labor, see Rolf Hellebust, "Aleksei Gastev and the Metallization of the Revolutionary Body," *Slavic Review* 56, no. 3 (Autumn 1997): 500–518; Julia Vaingurt, "Poetry of Labor and Labor of Poetry: The Universal Language of Alexei Gastev's Biomechanics," *Russian Review* 67, no. 2 (April 2008): 209–229.

22. One review of the film opens with an elaborate scene of a viewer disliking the film while watching it in a movie theater and then feeling embarrassed after learning that the film was directed by someone so esteemed as Lev Kuleshov: Lev Shatov, "O 'Gorizonte,'" *Kino*, March 10, 1933.

23. Quoted in J. Hoberman, *Bridge of Light: Yiddish Film between Two Worlds* (Philadelphia: Temple University Press, 1995), 193.

24. Howard Barnes, "'Horizon'-Europa," *New York Herald Tribune*, May 15, 1933, 8.

25. Yuri Slezkine, *The House of Government: A Saga of the Russian Revolution* (Princeton, NJ: University Press, 2017), 363–364.

26. Sheila Fitzpatrick, *The Cultural Front: Power and Culture in Revolutionary Russia* (Ithaca, NY: Cornell University Press, 1992), 237.

27. P. D. Markish and R. Mil'man, "Puteshestviia Neitana Bekkera: literaturnyi stsenarii" (n.d.), RGALI f. 2307, op. 2, d. 219., l. 15.

28. Rosemarie Garland Thomson, "From Wonder to Error—A Genealogy of Freak Discourse in Modernity," in *Freakery: Cultural Spectacles of the Extraordinary Body,* ed. Rosemary Garland Thomson (New York: New York University Press, 1996), 2.

29. Thomson, 2.

30. Lilya Kaganovsky, *How the Soviet Man Was Unmade: Cultural Fantasy and Male Subjectivity under Stalin* (Pittsburgh: University of Pittsburgh Press, 2008), 3.

31. Markish and Mil'man, "Puteshestviia Neitana Bekkera: literaturnyi stsenarii," 2.

32. Kaganovsky, *How the Soviet Man Was Unmade,* 10.

33. Markish, *Eyns af eyns,* 3–5; Markish, *Vozvrashchenie Neitana Bekkera,* 5–7.

34. Robert Bogdan, *Freak Show: Presenting Human Oddities for Amusement and Profit* (Chicago: University of Chicago Press, 2014), 41–44.

35. Cited in Bernadette Poliwoda, *Feks: Fabrik des Exzentrischen Schauspielers: Vom Exzentrismus zur Poetik des Films in der Frühen Sowjetkultur* (Munich: Verlag Otto Sagner, 1994), 72.

36. Yu. Dmitriev, *Sovetskii tsirk* (Moscow: Iskusstvo, 1963), 95–97. On the technological aesthetics of the Russian avant-garde, see Julia Vaingurt, *Wonderlands of the Avant-Garde: Technology and the Arts in Russia of the 1920s* (Evanston, IL: Northwestern University Press, 2013).

37. O. L. Bulgakova, "Bul'vardizatsiia avangarda—fenomen FEKS," *Kinovedcheskie zapiski,* no. 7 (1990): 28.

38. Kh. Abul-Kasymova and Institut istorii iskusstv (Moscow, Russia), eds., *Istoriia sovetskogo kino 1917–1967: v chetyrëkh tomakh* (Moscow: Iskussktvo, 1969), 332–362.

39. Bulgakova, "Bul'vardizatsiia avangarda—fenomen FEKS," 39.

40. Quoted in Bulgakova, 40. The reference is to Yu. Lotman and Yu. Tsivian, "SVD: Zhanr melodramy i istoriia," in *Pervye tynianovskie chteniia* (Riga, 1984).

41. Such discourse was, in particular, associated with the "shock worker" movement and its rhetoric of completing the industrialization tasks at hand in a shorter time. Stephen Kotkin, *Magnetic Mountain: Stalinism as a Civilization* (Berkeley: University of California Press, 1995), 90–93.

42. Chaplin's act, constructed around mockery of another circus act, is also similar to another staple clown act known as "the broken mirror." In this routine, one clown breaks a mirror and tries to be the other clown's mirror. See Tristan Rémy, *Clown Scenes,* trans. Bernard Sahlins (Chicago: Ivan R. Dee, 1997), 208–212.

43. Helen Stoddart, *Rings of Desire: Circus History and Representation* (Manchester: Manchester University Press, 2000), 4–5.

44. Stoddart, 5.

45. On a range of metaphors involving metal in early Soviet culture, see Rolf Hellebust, *Flesh to Metal: Soviet Literature and the Alchemy of Revolution* (Ithaca, NY: Cornell University Press, 2003).

46. Paul Bouissac, *Circus and Culture: A Semiotic Approach* (Lanham, MD: University Press of America, 1985), 165.

47. The entry for Peretz Markish in the *Lexicon of New Yiddish Literature,* for example, refers to Markish as the author of the screenplay for the "first Yiddish sound film [*der ershter Yidisher klang-film*]." J. Hoberman reminds us that *Neitan Bekker* was an ethnic component in "a cycle of now-forgotten talkies dealing with social conflict and epic industrialization—most of them released to coincide with the fifteenth anniversary of the October Revolution [in 1932]." Hoberman, *Bridge of Light,* 171. See also J. Hoberman, "A Face to the Shtetl: Soviet Yiddish Cinema, 1924–36," in *Inside the Film Factory,* ed. Richard Taylor and Ian Christie (London: Routledge, 1991), 139–145.

48. Jay Leyda includes *Neitan Bekker* among early talkies, in which the recording facility of sound technology ("especially in human speech") was perfected; Leyda points out that one of the goals of these films, all dealing with aspects of early Soviet life, was "to sound as natural as possible." Jay Leyda, *Kino: A History of the Russian and Soviet Film* (Princeton, NJ: Princeton University Press, 1983), 287–288.

49. Sergei Eisenstein, *The Film Sense,* trans. Jay Leyda (New York: Harcourt, Brace & World, 1947), 230–233.

50. Sabina Hangsten, "'Audio-Vision': O teorii i praktike sovetskogo zvukovogo kino na grani 1930-x godov," in *Sovetskaia vlast' i media,* ed. Hans Gunther and Sabina Hangsten (St. Petersburg: Akademicheskii proekt, 2006), 352.

51. Jay Leyda has commented on a parallel between early sound films and the Lumière brothers' first silent film of the arriving train, noting that the early sound films' success "with Soviet audiences depended on the shock of recognition—much as a community looking at the film-train's reflection of their problems or foibles." Leyda, *Kino,* 288.

52. Evgenii Margolit, "Problema mnogoiazychiia v rannem sovetskom kino (1930–1935)," in *Sovetskaia vlast' i media,* ed. Hans Gunther and Sabina Hangsten (St. Petersburg: Akademicheskii proekt, 2006), 379.

53. Lilya Kaganovsky, *The Voice of Technology: Soviet Cinema's Transition to Sound, 1928–1935* (Bloomington: Indiana University Press, 2018), 22.

54. Neya Zorkaya, *The Illustrated History of the Soviet Cinema* (New York: Hippocrene Books, 1981), 108.

55. Neia Zorkaia, "'Odna' na perekrëstkakh," *Kinovedcheskie zapiski,* no. 74 (2005): 147–148.

56. Taylor and Christie, *The Film Factory,* 234.

57. Alan M. Ball, *Imagining America: Influence and Images in Twentieth-Century Russia* (Lanham, MD: Rowman & Littlefield, 2003), 94–95.

58. Denise J. Youngblood, *Soviet Cinema in the Silent Era, 1918–1935* (Ann Arbor: UMI Research Press, 1985), 222.

59. Hangsten, "'Audio-Vision,' 352.

60. Hangsten, 352–353.

61. Ball, *Imagining America,* 106–107.

62. Naum Levin, "Vozvrashchenie Neitana Bekkera," *Kino,* November 12, 1932.

63. In a sense, Bekker can be said to be falsely claiming party affiliation, though he does so in jest. Three years later Ivan Pyr'ev's 1935 film *The Party Membership Card (Partiinyi bilet)* would elevate the fear of the other—this time, a member of an alien class hiding under a false Party membership card—in the popular imagination, in the context of the start of purges in the mid-1930s. Stephen Kotkin, *Stalin: Waiting for Hitler, 1929–1941* (New York: Penguin, 2017), 253, 278, 293–294.

64. Quoted in Hoberman, *Bridge of Light,* 193.

65. Lilya Kaganovsky, "The Voice of Technology and the End of Soviet Silent Film: Grigorii Kozintsev and Leonid Trauberg's Alone," *Studies in Russian and Soviet Cinema* 1, no. 3 (January 2014): 266.

66. Kaganovsky, 266.

67. Kaganovsky, 267.

68. Kaganovsky, 270.

69. Kaganovsky, 270.

70. Markish and Mil'man, "Puteshestviia Neitana Bekkera," 12.

71. Murav, "Peretz Markish in the 1930s," 116.

72. Markish and Mil'man, "Puteshestviia Neitana Bekkera," 13.

73. Hoberman, *Bridge of Light,* 194.

74. E. Brusilovskii, "Evreiskaia bez kavychek," *Kino,* October 30, 1932.

75. Marc Shell, *Stutter* (Cambridge, MA: Harvard University Press, 2005), 30.

76. B. Shpis and R. Mil'man, "Natsional'naia po forme," *Kino,* October 30, 1932.

77. Evg. Kriger, "Granitsa," *Izvestiia,* October 3, 1935, 4.

78. Robert Weinberg, "Demonizing Judaism in the Soviet Union during the 1920s," *Slavic Review* 67, no. 1 (Spring 2008): 120–153.

79. Markish and Mil'man, "Puteshestviia Neitana Bekkera" [unnumbered first page].

80. On the link between the Great Depression and the appeal of the USSR to American Jews, see Mary M. Leder, *My Life in Stalinist Russia: An American Woman Looks Back,* ed. Laurie Bernstein (Bloomington: Indiana University Press, 2002). The Soviet-born American Jewish writer Sana Krasikov explores the story of American Jews' travel to Stalin's Russia during the Great Depression in her novel as well: Sana Krasikov, *The Patriots* (New York: Spiegel & Grau, 2017).

81. Anna Wexler Katsnelson, "Aesopian Tales: The Visual Culture of the Late Russian Avant-Garde" (PhD diss., Harvard University, 2007), 300.

82. Kotkin, *Stalin*, 60–62.

83. On agitation trials in the 1920s, see Elizabeth A. Wood, *Performing Justice: Agitation Trials in Early Soviet Russia* (Ithaca, NY: Cornell University Press, 2005).

84. Julie A. Cassiday, *The Enemy on Trial: Early Soviet Courts on Stage and Screen* (DeKalb: Northern Illinois University Press, 2000), 102–103.

85. Stephen Kotkin, *Stalin: Paradoxes of Power, 1878–1928* (New York: Penguin Books, 2014), 687–697.

86. Cassiday, *The Enemy on Trial*, 100.

87. Cassiday, 6.

88. Cassiday, 7.

89. Cassiday, 111.

90. B. Vaks, "Iskateli schast'ia," *Kino*, June 4, 1936. In her plot summary of the film, Anna Shternshis states that the travel of Pinya and his family is "from Palestine to Birobidzhan." Anna Shternshis, *Soviet and Kosher: Jewish Popular Culture in the Soviet Union, 1923–1939* (Bloomington: Indiana University Press, 2006), 166.

91. V. Botov, "Iskateli schast'ia," *Krasnaia zvezda*, October 8, 1936.

92. Breeding pigs—animals whose meat is not kosher and whose presence on Jewish collective farms highlighted the farm members' distance from Judaism—was a common theme in Soviet Jewish literature and life of the time. Gennady Estraikh, "Pig-Breeding, Shiksas, and Other Goyish Themes in Soviet Yiddish Literature and Life," *Symposium* 57, no. 3 (Fall 2003): 157–174.

93. Vaks, "Iskateli schast'ia."

94. Botov, "Iskateli schast'ia."

95. A. Timofeev, "'Iskateli schast'ia': Noyi fil'm kinostudii 'Sovetskaia Belarus'," *Vecherniaia Moskva*, May 23, 1936.

96. Shternshis, *Soviet and Kosher*, 167.

97. Hoberman, *Bridge of Light*, 233.

98. Shternshis, *Soviet and Kosher*, 168.

99. Chernenko, *Krasnaia zvezda, zhëltaia zvezda*, 86.

100. Kaganovsky, *How the Soviet Man Was Unmade*, 9–10.

101. Harriet Murav, *Music from a Speeding Train: Soviet Yiddish and Russian-Jewish Literature of the Twentieth Century* (Stanford: Stanford University Press, 2011), 102.

102. For a detailed analysis of Isaak Dunaevskii's musical score for *Seekers of Happiness*, see M. Shafer, "V poiskakh evreiskogo schast'ia. K 70-letiiu fil'ma 'Iskateli schast'ia,'" *Kinovedcheskie zapiski*, no. 78 (n.d.): 162–186.

103. Barnes, "'Horizon'-Europa."

104. Karen Grumberg, *Hebrew Gothic: History and the Poetics of Persecution* (Bloomington: Indiana University Press, 2019), 15–18, 54–59.

105. Galit Hasan-Rokem, "Ex oriente fluxus: The Wandering Jew—Oriental Crossings of the Paths of Europe," in *L'Orient dans l'histoire religieuse de l'Europe;*

l'invention des origines, ed. Mohammad Ali Amir-Moezzi and John Scheid (Turnhout: Brepols, 2000), 153.

106. Kaganovsky, *The Voice of Technology,* 161.

5. The Soviet Jew as a Trickster

1. I. Babel', "Shabos-nakhamu (Iz tsikla 'Gershele')," *Vecherniaia zvezda* [Petrograd], March 16, 1918, 2–3. The preferred Yiddish transliteration of the term is *Shabes nakhamu* (different vowel in the first word and no hyphen between the two words). However, to avoid any potential confusion that alternating between Babel's more idiosyncratic spelling and the preferred standard Yiddish spelling would have entailed, I use the hyphen and spell the first word as *Shabos*—a transliteration of Isaac Babel's Russian-language usage—throughout.

2. Gregory Freidin limits the impact of the story to Babel's "growing interest in Jewish folklore, evident among the educated public, both Russian and Jewish, on the eve of and during World War I"; see Isaac Babel, *Isaac Babel's Selected Writings,* ed. Gregory Freidin, trans. Peter Constantine (New York: W. W. Norton, 2010), 26. James Falen has claimed that "the saga of Hershele may have ceased to occupy the forefront of [Babel's] mind"; see James E. Falen, *Isaac Babel, Russian Master of the Short Story* (Knoxville: University of Tennessee Press, 1974), 31–33. Valerii Dymshitz notes the popularity of Hershele among Ashkenazi Jews and cites Babel's short story as an example of this popularity but concludes that the cycle of stories about Hershele that Babel had promised "did not continue"; see Valerii Dymshitz, ed., *Evreiskie narodnye skazki: Predaniia, bylichki, rasskazy, anekdoty sobrannye E. S. Raize* (St. Petersburg: Symposium, 2000), 450.

3. Efraim Sicher has argued that Jewish cultural references in Babel are references to a Jewish cultural and literary memory aimed at readers who are knowledgeable enough to recognize them: Efraim Sicher, "Shabos-nakhamu v Petrograde: Babel' i Sholom-Aleykhem," in *Isaak Babel' v istoricheskom i literaturnom kontekste: XXI vek,* ed. E. I. Pogorel'skaia (Moscow: Knizhniki, 2016), 469.

4. Isaak Babel', *Sobranie sochinenii,* vol. 3 (Moscow: Vremia, 2006), 80.

5. Babel', 3:84.

6. William J. Hynes and William G. Doty, eds., *Mythical Trickster Figures: Contours, Contexts, and Criticisms* (Tuscaloosa: University of Alabama Press, 1993); Lewis Hyde, *Trickster Makes This World: Mischief, Myth and Art* (Edinburgh: Canongate, 2008). Babel's "Shabos-nakhamu" shares characteristics with other tales of folktale type 1540, "A Visitor from Paradise," of the Aarne-Thompson folktale classification system: Antti Aarne, *The Types of the Folktale: A Classification and Bibliography,* trans. Stith Thompson (Helsinki: Finnish Academy of Sciences and Letters, 1961), 444; Hans-Jörg Uther, *The Types of International Folktales: A Classification and Bibliography Based on the System of Antti Aarne and Stith Thompson* (Helsinki: Suomalainen Tiedeakatemia, 2004), 2:277–278.

7. Babel', *Sobranie sochinenii*, 2006, 3:80.

8. James C. Scott, *Domination and the Arts of Resistance: Hidden Transcripts* (New Haven: Yale University Press, 1990), 2–4.

9. Scott, 4–16.

10. Scott, 33.

11. Nathan Ausubel, ed., *A Treasury of Jewish Folklore* (New York: Crown Publishers, 1949), 286. For a structuralist study of Hershele stories, see Toby Blum-Dobkin, *Yiddish Folktales about Jesters: A Problem in Structural Analysis and Genre Definition* (New York: YIVO Institute for Jewish Research, 1977). For additional Hershele narratives see M. Shtern, ed., *Hershele Ostropoler un Motke Habad: zayere anekdoten, vitsen, stsenes un shtukes* (New York: Star Hebrew Book Co., n.d.); Dymshitz, *Evreiskie narodnye skazki*, 229–243. There is a sampling of Hershele stories, collected after 1945 from the descendants of Ashkenazi Jews in Israel, in Dan Ben-Amos, ed., *Folktales of the Jews* (Philadelphia: Jewish Publication Society, 2007), 2:326–333.

12. Benzion Dinur, "The Origins of Hasidism and Its Social and Messianic Foundations," in *Essential Papers on Hasidism: Origins to Present,* ed. Gershon David Hundert (New York: New York University Press, 1991), 86–208.

13. Eliezer Sherman, ed., *Hirsheleh Ostropoler: Emtza'otav ve-ta'alulav, bedihotav ve-halatzotav, toldotav ve-harpatka'otav,* trans. M. Harizman (Tel Aviv: Lema'an ha-sefer, 1930), 10. By another account, Shimshen gathered the town's Jews in a synagogue, where they all died. Zoia Kopel'man, "Evreiskii shut Girsh Ostropoler," in *Anekdoty ot Gershele Ostropolera,* ed. Khaim Beyder (Moscow: Gesharim-Mosty kul'tury, 2000), 13.

14. Ada Rapoport-Albert, "God and the Zaddik as the Two Focal Points of Hasidic Worship," in *Essential Papers on Hasidism: Origins to Present,* ed. Gershon David Hundert (New York: New York University Press, 1991), 299–329.

15. Y. Y. Trunk, *Der freylekhster Yid in der velt: oder Hersheles lern-yorn* (Buenos Aires: Yiddishbukh, 1953), xviii–xix. In the preface to his novel based on Hershele narratives, Trunk notes that Jewish history is marked by disappointment (*antoyshung*) with persistent messianic promises, embodied in the figures of Elijah the Prophet, the thirty-six righteous men (*lamed-vovnikes*), and the Messiah.

16. Sherman, *Hirsheleh Ostropoler,* 11.

17. Sherman, 7.

18. Ruth R. Wisse, *The Modern Jewish Canon: A Journey through Language and Culture* (Chicago: University of Chicago Press, 2000), 103.

19. Sheila Fitzpatrick, *Tear off the Masks! Identity and Imposture in Twentieth-Century Russia* (Princeton, NJ: Princeton University Press, 2005), 268.

20. Fitzpatrick, 271.

21. Fitzpatrick, 281.

22. Mark Lipovetsky, "Trikster i 'zakrytoe' obshchestvo," *Novoe literaturnoe obozrenie* 100 (2009): 239.

23. Victor W. Turner, *The Ritual Process: Structure and Anti-Structure* (Chicago: Aldine, 1969), 95.

24. Lipovetsky, "Trikster i 'zakrytoe' obshchestvo," 229. On Turner's concept of liminality in the study of folkloric tricksters, see Barbara Babcock-Abrahams, "'A Tolerated Margin of Mess': The Trickster and His Tales Reconsidered," *Journal of the Folklore Institute* 11, no. 3 (March 1975): 147–186.

25. Henry Louis Gates Jr., *The Signifying Monkey: A Theory of Afro-American Literary Criticism* (New York: Oxford University Press, 1988), 49.

26. Gates, 58.

27. Gates, 15.

28. Gates, 42.

29. On S. An-sky's ethnographic expeditions, see Gabriella Safran, *Wandering Soul: The Dybbuk's Creator, S. An-sky* (Cambridge, MA: Harvard University Press, 2010), 186–284. On primitivism's role in Soviet culture in the decade and a half after 1917—the time of the development of archaeology and ethnography, particularly in the study of ethnic groups that had been formerly colonized by the Russian Empire, see Michael Kunichika, *"Our Native Antiquity": Archaeology and Aesthetics in the Culture of Russian Modernism* (Boston: Academic Studies Press, 2015).

30. *Dos freylikhe hershele ostropolier* (Odessa: Bletnitsky Brothers [printed in Warsaw], 1890), 4–5; *Dos freylikhe hershele ostropolier* (Odessa: Bletnitsky Brothers [printed in Warsaw], 1895), 4–5. In 1870, Odessa's Bletnitsky brothers established a publishing house and a bookstore in Odessa, for which printing presses elsewhere in the Russian Empire produced books by arrangement; the Bletnitsky brothers set up their own printing operation in Odessa by the beginning of the twentieth century. On the history of the Bletnitsky brothers' publishing business, see V. V. Knorring, "Vosem' knig odnogo izdatel'stva," *Trudy po iudaike: Istoriia i etnografiia*, no. 7 (2013): 90. Similarly titled chapbooks of stories about Hershele were printed for and distributed by and on behalf of the Bletnitsky brothers in Vilna (1895, 1899) and Odessa itself (1908, 1913), but only the two editions printed in Warsaw contained the story "Shabos-nakhamu." A variant of this story in German translation, "Hersch als Engel," appeared in Chajim Bloch, ed., *Hersch Ostropoler, ein jüdischer Till-Eulenspiegel des 18. Jahrhunderts, seine Geschichten und Streiche* (Berlin: Benjamin Harz Verlag, 1921), 25–28.

31. On "My First Fee" as the generative story of Babel's oeuvre, see A. K. Zholkovskii and M. B. Iampolskii, *Babel'/Babel* (Moscow: Carte Blanche, 1994).

32. *Dos freylikhe hershele ostropolier*, 1890, 4.

33. Babel', *Sobranie sochinenii*, 2006, 3:78.

34. Babel', 3:80.

35. *Dos freylikhe hershele ostropolier*, 1895, 5.

36. Modified translation from Isaac Babel, *The Essential Fictions*, trans. Val Vinokur (Evanston, IL: Northwestern University Press, 2018), 13.

37. Michel de Certeau, *The Practice of Everyday Life,* trans. Steven Rendall (Berkeley: University of California Press, 1984), 97–98.

38. de Certeau, 96.

39. The first sketch about Odessa was published in *Vecherniaia zvezda* (Petrograd) no. 36, on March 19, 1918; the second, in the same newspaper, no. 38, on March 21, 1918. Both appeared under the title "Dispatches about Odessa" ("*Listki ob Odesse*"). Isaak Babel', *Sobranie sochinenii,* vol. 1 (Moscow: Vremia, 2006), 536–538.

40. Babel', 1:43–48. "Odessa" was first published in *Journal of Journals* (*Zhurnal zhurnalov*) in December 1916; the author's name appeared as Bab-El.

41. Babel', 1:57.

42. One story involved Hershele making fun of an antisemitic colonel stationed in Medzhibozh. The colonel had a dog named Jew—*zhid,* the offensive Russian term for a Jew. Hearing the colonel giving orders to the dog, "Come here, *zhid!* Go get it, Jew!" etc., Hershele said to the colonel that he pitied the poor dog: "He is such a good dog, but, alas, a Jew! Had the poor thing not been a Jew, he could have achieved a great deal—he would certainly have been promoted to the rank of colonel by now." Khaim Beyder, ed., *Anekdoty ot Gershele Ostropolera: Klassicheskii evreiskii iumor,* trans. Khaim Beyder (Moscow: Gesharim-Mosty kul'tury, 2000), 53–54. In this Hershele story, the trickster challenges not the culture of Hasidism but the hierarchy of the Russian Empire.

43. In his brief—only four paragraphs long—autobiography published in 1924, Babel wrote of his meeting with Gorky at the end of 1916: "And so, I owe everything to that encounter and to this day pronounce [Gorky's] name with love and admiration." Isaak Babel', *Sochineniia,* vol. 1 (Moscow: Khudozhestvennaia literatura, 1991), 31.

44. In July 1918 *Novaia zhizn'* was closed down by the Bolsheviks for its oppositional editorial stance.

45. For a detailed account of life in Petrograd around 1917–1921, including in reflections of Russian writers and foreigners, see V. I. Musaev, "Byt gorozhan," in *Petrograd na perelome epokh: Gorod i ego zhiteli v gody revoliutsii i grazhdanskoi voiny* (St. Petersburg: Rossiiskaia akademiia nauk, 2000), 61–132.

46. Babel', *Sobranie sochinenii,* 2006, 1:274.

47. Babel', 1:237.

48. Isaac Babel, *Collected Stories,* ed. Efraim Sicher, trans. David McDuff (New York: Penguin, 1994), 84. On Halevi's pilgrimage, see Raymond P. Scheindlin, *The Song of The Distant Dove: Judah Halevi's Pilgrimage* (Oxford: Oxford University Press, 2008).

49. Peter Cole, ed., *The Dream of the Poem: Hebrew Poetry from Muslim and Christian Spain, 950–1492,* trans. Peter Cole (Princeton, NJ: Princeton University Press, 2009), 164.

50. Sidra DeKoven Ezrahi, *Booking Passage: Exile and Homecoming in the Modern Jewish Imagination* (Berkeley: University of California Press, 2000), 46.

51. *Midrash Tanhuma Pekude,* Siman Alef, and *Babylonian Talmud,* Ta'anit 5a, respectively. I thank Liora Halperin for her help with these references.

52. Polina Barskova, "Piranesi in Petrograd: Sources, Strategies, and Dilemmas in Modernist Depictions of the Ruins (1918–1921)," *Slavic Review* 65, no. 4 (Winter 2006): 700–701.

53. Viktor Shklovskii, "Peterburg v blokade," in *Khod konia* (Berlin: Gelikon, 1923), 22. Shklovsky draws on biblical sources about Jerusalem under siege: "You shall eat it [the food available in the besieged city] as a barley-cake, baking it in their sight in human dung" (Ezekiel 4:12) followed by God's permission to substitute cow droppings for human excrement in Ezekiel 4:15.

54. Babel', *Sobranie sochinenii,* 2006, 1:244.

55. Babel, *Collected Stories,* 88.

56. Oleg Budnitskii, "The Reds and the Jews, or Comrades in Arms of the Military Reporter Liutov," in *The Enigma of Isaac Babel: Biography, History, Context,* ed. Gregory Freidin (Stanford: Stanford University Press, 2009), 65–81.

57. Michael Gorham, "Writers at the Front: Language of State in the Civil War Narratives of Isaac Babel and Dmitrii Furmanov," in *The Enigma of Isaac Babel,* 101.

58. Gorham, 103.

59. Babel, *Collected Stories,* 87.

60. Modified translation from Babel, 124–125; Isaak Babel', *Sobranie sochinenii,* vol. 2 (Moscow: Vremia, 2006), 80.

61. Babel', *Sobranie sochinenii,* 2006, 3:77.

62. Evgeny Dobrenko sees the events of "My First Goose" as the trial of a person who must relinquish his individuality and submit to "herd consciousness" (*roevoe soznanie*). This trial is the reason why the narrative texture of "Gedali" and "Rebbe" is interrupted by "My First Goose." "Rebbe" becomes "My First Goose" in reverse: it speaks of the difficulty in entering not the new world but the old one, not of succumbing to the "herd consciousness" but rather to the consciousness that is elegiac. E. A. Dobrenko, "Logika tsykla," in *"Konarmiia" Isaaka Babelia,* ed. G. A. Belaia, E. A. Dobrenko, and I. A. Esaulov (Moscow: Rossiiskii universitet, 2004), 55.

63. Isaac Babel, *Red Cavalry,* trans. Boris Dralyuk (London: Pushkin Press, 2014), 51.

64. Babel', *Sobranie sochinenii,* 2006, 2:76.

65. Ausubel, *A Treasury of Jewish Folklore,* 287. A version of this story for children also appears in Eric A. Kimmel, *Hershel of Ostropol* (Philadelphia: Jewish Publication Society, 1981), 8–17.

66. Johan Huizinga, *Homo Ludens: A Study of the Play-Element in Culture* (London: Routledge, 2003), 110.

67. Babel, *Red Cavalry,* 46. Charles Rougle sees "My First Goose" as a rupture between "Gedali" and "Rebbe": "Rebbe" picks up the narrative where "Gedali" left off, with "the abruptness of the break with the intervening narrative serving to

emphasize the duality of the narrator's consciousness." Charles Rougle, "Isaac Babel and His Odyssey of War and Revolution," in *Red Cavalry: A Critical Companion,* ed. Charles Rougle (Evanston, IL: Northwestern University Press, 1996), 41.

68. Babel, *Collected Stories,* 123; Babel', *Sobranie sochinenii,* 2006, 2:78.

69. Scott, *Domination and the Arts of Resistance,* 18.

70. Babel, *Red Cavalry,* 54.

71. Babel, 54; Babel', *Sobranie sochinenii,* 2006, 2:78.

72. Babel', *Sobranie sochinenii,* 2006, 2:224. Peter Constantine misleadingly translates this exchange in Babel, *The Complete Works of Isaac Babel,* 380. The last two lines translated as "People are alive" and "Here it's terrible" leave out the words "there" in reference to Odessa and the conjunction "and," which, in the Russian original ("a") expresses contrast rather than equivalence. Babel's diary entry is clear about the contrast between Zhitomir and Odessa that Babel attributes to the rebbe.

73. Modified translation from Babel, *Collected Stories,* 124–125; Babel', *Sobranie sochinenii,* 2006, 2:80.

74. Modified translation from Babel, *Collected Stories,* 123–124.

75. Babel, 124.

76. Steven J. Zipperstein, *The Jews of Odessa: A Cultural History, 1794–1881* (Stanford: Stanford University Press, 1985), 1.

77. Babel', *Sobranie sochinenii,* 2006, 2: 258. Two English translations of Babel's diary make mistakes in this sentence. Babel is not thinking about how he *should* describe Hershele, as Peter Constantine's translation has it; rather, he invokes Hershele as he thinks about how to describe the collapsing state of Dubno's synagogue and of traditional Jewish life. Constantine's version: "I pray, rather, I almost pray, and think about Hershele, this is how I should describe him." Babel, *The Complete Works of Isaac Babel,* 230. H. T. Willets's translation of the July 23 entry is equally misleading: "I pray, or rather almost pray, thinking of Hershele and how to describe him." Isaac Babel, *1920 Diary,* ed. Carol Avins, trans. H. T Willetts (New Haven: Yale University Press, 1995), 33.

78. Babel, *1920 Diary,* 35.

79. Babel', *Sobranie sochinenii,* 2006, 2:262.

80. Modified translation of Babel, *The Complete Works of Isaac Babel,* 236; Babel', *Sobranie sochinenii,* 2006, 2:82.

81. Victoria Smolkin, *A Sacred Space Is Never Empty: A History of Soviet Atheism* (Princeton, NJ: Princeton University Press, 2018), 21–56.

82. Terry Martin, *The Affirmative Action Empire: Nations and Nationalism in the Soviet Union, 1923–1939* (Ithaca, NY: Cornell University Press, 2001), 432–461.

83. Elissa Bemporad, *Becoming Soviet Jews: The Bolshevik Experiment in Minsk* (Bloomington: Indiana University Press, 2012), 135–143.

84. One story in an atheist periodical focused on competing practices—circumcision and baptism—demanded to be performed on the body of a newborn

by the boy's two grandmothers, one Jewish and the other Russian Orthodox. Kl. Gul'binskaia, "Babushki," *Bezbozhnik u stanka,* no. 5 (1927): 14–15.

85. On public trials of various practices of Judaism, see Zvi Y. Gitelman, *A Century of Ambivalence: The Jews of Russia and the Soviet Union, 1881 to the Present* (Bloomington: Indiana University Press, 2001), 79.

86. Gregory Freidin reads this episode in "Karl-Yankel" in light of Babel's biography, as a reflection on the adoption by the writer Vsevolod Ivanov, a non-Jewish man, of the son Babel had with Tamara Kashirina. Gregory Freidin, "Two Babels— Two Aphrodites: Autobiography in *Maria* and Babel's Petersburg Myth," in *The Enigma of Isaac Babel,* 35–36.

87. Isaak Babel', *Detstvo i drugie rasskazy,* ed. Efraim Sicher (Jerusalem: Biblioteka-Aliia, 1979), 308. This edition follows the first published version of the story: I. Babel', "Karl-Iankel'," *Zvezda,* no. 7 (1931): 55–60. The modified translation is from Babel, *Collected Stories,* 330.

88. Svetlana Boym, *The Off-Modern* (New York: Bloomsbury, 2017), 17.

89. Modified translation from Babel, *Red Cavalry,* 15.

90. Babel also took liberties with geography in this *Red Cavalry* story, "Crossing the Zbrucz," which placed the wrong river—the correct river was the Slucz—into the story's title. Babel, *The Essential Fictions,* 372–373.

91. Em. [sic] Babel, "Karl-Yankl," *Der apikoyres,* no. 3 (1933): 11. Published alongside antireligious propaganda, the journal showcased Babel's story as a specimen of the same genre. Harriet Murav reads the story, especially given its appearance in the Yiddish translation, as harboring traces of the blood libel accusation as far back as the Mendel Beilis case in Kiev in 1913: Harriet Murav, *Music from a Speeding Train: Soviet Yiddish and Russian-Jewish Literature of the Twentieth Century* (Stanford: Stanford University Press, 2011), 92–95.

92. Lawrence Venuti, *The Translator's Invisibility: A History of Translation* (London: Routledge, 1995), 15–16, 18–20.

93. Naomi Seidman, *Faithful Renderings: Jewish-Christian Difference and the Politics of Translation* (Chicago: University of Chicago Press, 2006), 93–94.

94. Babel, *Collected Stories,* 302; Babel', *Sobranie sochinenii,* 2006, 1:143.

95. Venuti, *The Translator's Invisibility,* 1–42.

96. "Red corners" were briefly renamed "Lenin corners" after Lenin's death in 1924. "Some Lenin Corners displayed busts of the leader, others exhibited serialized photographs of his life, and a few even contrived to illuminate Lenin's portrait with concealed electric lamps. These last were secular counterparts to the votive candles that burned before icons in Russian homes." Nina Tumarkin, *Lenin Lives! The Lenin Cult in Soviet Russia* (Cambridge, MA: Harvard University Press, 1997), 221–222.

97. Simon Markish, "The Example of Isaac Babel," in *Isaac Babel,* ed. Harold Bloom (New York: Chelsea House, 1987), 188. Efraim Sicher sees the scene as

reflective of slogans about the "friendship of the Soviet People": Efraim Sicher, *Jews in Russian Literature after the October Revolution: Writers and Artists between Hope and Apostasy* (Cambridge: Cambridge University Press, 1995), 107. Carol J. Avins sees the scene as parodic, but for reasons other than its ethnic display, which she takes at face value: Carol J. Avins, "Jewish Ritual and Soviet Context in Two Stories of Isaac Babel," in *American Contributions to the Twelfth International Congress of Slavists,* ed. Robert A. Maguire and Alan Timberlake (Bloomington: Slavica, 1998), 13.

98. Babel', *Sobranie sochinenii,* 2006, 1:149.

99. Eileen M. Kane, *Russian Hajj: Empire and the Pilgrimage to Mecca* (Ithaca, NY: Cornell University Press, 2015), 47–48, 124.

100. Maya K. Peterson, *Pipe Dreams: Water and Empire in Central Asia's Aral Sea Basin* (Cambridge: Cambridge University Press, 2019), 276–277, 292, 296.

101. Babel', *Sobranie sochinenii,* 2006, 1:141.

102. Babel, *Collected Stories,* 303–304. This translation is based on the text of the first publication of "Karl-Yankel" in *Zvezda* in 1931: Babel', "Karl-Iankel'," 57.

103. Isaak Babel', *Sobranie sochinenii,* 4:289.

104. Coincidentally, adjacent to Babel's "Karl-Yankel" in its first printing in *Zvezda* was a story by a different author titled "Gapa" after its eponymous protagonist, which was set on a collective farm in Ukraine. A. Rakitnikov, "Gapa," *Zvezda,* no. 7 (1931): 61–81.

105. Modified translation of Babel, *The Complete Works of Isaac Babel,* 646.

106. Babel', *Sobranie sochinenii,* 2006, 3:152.

107. George Liber, *Alexander Dovzhenko: A Life in Soviet Film* (London: BFI Publishing, 2002), 102–113.

108. Babel, *Collected Stories,* 126; Babel', *Sobranie sochinenii,* 2006, 2:82.

109. Babel, *The Complete Works of Isaac Babel,* 649; Babel', *Sobranie sochinenii,* 2006, 3:157–158.

110. Modified translation from Babel, *Collected Stories,* 308; Babel', *Sobranie sochinenii,* 2006, 1:150.

111. Efraim Sicher, "Text, Intertext, Context: Babel, Bialik, and Others," in *The Enigma of Isaac Babel,* 212.

112. Babel', *Sobranie sochinenii,* 2006, 1:142.

113. Babel, *Collected Stories,* 308–309.

114. Sicher, "Text, Intertext, Context," 212.

115. Yuri Slezkine, *The Jewish Century* (Princeton, NJ: Princeton University Press, 2004), 124.

116. Slezkine, 136.

117. As quoted in Slezkine, 135; Babel', *Sobranie sochinenii,* 2006, 1:208.

118. Stephanie Sandler, *Commemorating Pushkin: Russia's Myth of a National Poet* (Stanford: Stanford University Press, 2004), 108.

Epilogue

1. Grigorii Polianker, *Uchitel' iz Medzhibozha* (Kiev: Radianskii pis'mennik, 1977), 25. The Russian edition notes that this is a translation from the Yiddish but does not name the translator. For the Yiddish original, which was published five years after the Russian translation, see Hirsh Polyanker, *Der lerer fun Medzhibozh: roman, dertseylungen* (Moscow: Sovetskii pisatel', 1982).

2. Harriet Murav and Gennady Estraikh, eds., *Soviet Jews in World War II: Fighting, Witnessing, Remembering* (Boston: Academic Studies Press, 2014), 7.

3. Polianker, *Uchitel' iz Medzhibozha*, 89–93.

4. Jeffrey Veidlinger, *In the Shadow of the Shtetl: Small-Town Jewish Life in Soviet Ukraine* (Bloomington: Indiana University Press, 2013), xiv.

5. On Soviet Yiddish literature after the war, see Harriet Murav, *Music from a Speeding Train: Soviet Yiddish and Russian-Jewish Literature of the Twentieth Century* (Stanford: Stanford University Press, 2011), 209–284; Gennady Estraikh, *Yiddish in the Cold War* (Leeds: Legenda, 2008). For a recent book-length English translation of short stories by a Yiddish writer from the Soviet Union, see Yenta Mash, *On the Landing,* trans. Ellen Cassedy (DeKalb: Northern Illinois University Press, 2018).

6. Adrien Ivy Smith, "Elements of Yiddish Style: Sensibility in the Late Soviet Union in Comparative Perspective" (Ph.D. diss., Stanford University, 2019), 278.

7. Murav, *Music from a Speeding Train,* 262. On the history of the publication and production of *Berdichev,* see Yuri Veksler, "O Fridrikhe Gorenshteine," *Arzamas,* March 18, 2019, https://arzamas.academy/mag/658-gorenshtein.

8. Evgeny Dobrenko, *Late Stalinism: The Aesthetics of Politics,* trans. Jesse M. Savage (New Haven: Yale University Press, 2021), 1–13.

9. S. Gekht, *Dolgi serdtsa: rasskazy* (Moscow: Sovetskii pisatel', 1963).

10. David Shneer, *Yiddish and the Creation of Soviet Jewish Culture, 1918–1930* (Cambridge: Cambridge University Press, 2004), 2.

11. Margarita Khemlin, *Zhivaia ochered': povesti i rasskazy* (Moscow: Vagrius, 2008), 213.

12. Ostyor figures prominently in Khemlin's novels, including *Klotsvog* (2010) and *The Investigator* (*Doznavatel',* 2013), both of which won major literary prizes in Russia. Both novels are available in English translation: Margarita Khemlin, *The Investigator,* trans. Melanie Moore (London: Glagoslav, 2015), and *Klotsvog,* trans. Lisa C. Hayden (New York: Columbia University Press, 2019).

13. Khemlin, *Zhivaia ochered': povesti i rasskazy,* 215.

14. Khemlin, 231.

15. Khemlin, 255.

Acknowledgments

Long before I had any idea that I would one day write a book, and that the idea for this book would emerge from a single perplexing sentence by Isaac Babel, I was introduced to Babel's work at my mother's knee. My mother tells me that a family acquaintance shared Babel's stories with her as a child, not long after the writer's work—unavailable for nearly two decades after his execution in 1940—was first republished. When in her youth she again came across a rare edition of Babel on someone else's bookshelf, she permanently "borrowed" it—the untranslatable and wonderful Russian verb for this is *zachitala*. It is from this legendary volume, published in 1957, that she read Babel's stories to me when I was a child.

I first rediscovered Babel in Jane Taubman's seminar on twentieth-century Russian literature at Amherst College (a University of Massachusetts student, I was taking the class through the Five College consortium). A 1,000-word paper assigned by Jane, its strict word limit her attempt to teach English writing to this then-fresh-off-the-boat immigrant, was my first attempt to consider what Lyutov might have meant in *Red Cavalry* when he told his interlocutor that he was "putting into verse the adventures of Hershele Ostropoler." A year earlier, when I was an exchange student at Oxford, the late Joseph Sherman introduced me to Moyshe Kulbak's *Zelmenyaner*—in the abridged translation from Yiddish that was the only one then available—and made me realize that Babel was hardly the only mind-blowing writer of his day to write about Jews after the Bolshevik Revolution. During the hours-long tutorials Joseph conducted in a basement cafeteria, I became excited enough about this rich text to return to it years later once I was equipped with the requisite linguistic skills to read the original.

While I was in graduate school at Harvard, William Mills Todd III taught me the importance—and the intellectual excitement—of approaching literature as a set of cultural and political institutions. He furnished me with the skill to, whenever possible, track down the original publications of literary works and to examine the imprint they left on contemporary culture. Ruth R. Wisse encouraged and supported my study of Yiddish literature and the Yiddish language; I was able to begin learning Yiddish thanks to dedicated language teachers, including David Braun and Yuri Vedenyapin at Harvard, and Hanan Bordin, Rivka Margolis, Dov-Ber Kerler, Avrom Lichtenbaum, among several others at various summer programs. The late Svetlana Boym pushed me to think about reading literary texts as an exuberantly creative process during which the rigors of scholarly inquiry can miraculously transform into pleasure. She encouraged me to write this book—at the time, I was somehow trying not to—when we last met, about a year before her untimely passing. I spent the last several years writing at home in front of a rumpled wall hanging with the angelic face of Lenin as a young child and decorated with dozens of Soviet pins that had once belonged to Svetlana and that ended up being her ironic bequest to me.

I owe an intellectual and professional debt to the scholars who helped me begin envisioning this project as a book. At the University of Colorado Boulder, the late David Shneer and Mark Lipovetsky read the early messy drafts, taking on the burden of showing me how to separate the wheat from the chaff while imparting to me their nuanced understanding of Soviet Jewish culture and of Soviet-era literature, respectively. Over the years and, fittingly, across multiple geographies, Galit Hasan-Rokem became an important interlocutor about mobility and the Wandering Jew. Amelia Glaser at the University of California San Diego, Harriet Murav at the University of Illinois Urbana-Champaign, and Gabriella Safran at Stanford invited me to present at their home institutions, some of them more than once, at key moments in the evolution of my thinking; they have also helped me develop my ideas in other ways over the years. The work of these three scholars—comparatists who have dedicated their careers to reading Russian and Yiddish works side by side—has inspired my own. Mikhail Krutikov and Gennady Estraikh answered many questions over the years. Among the numerous people—too many to name—who saw and gave feedback on different aspects of this work, Grisha Freidin graciously read and offered criticism on the Isaac Babel chapter, Alex Moshkin helped me think through the introduction, and the manuscript's two external reviewers supplied insightful criticism that I incorporated into revisions. I am also grateful to have had the opportunity to share parts of this project with audiences at Brandeis University (at a conference organized by ChaeRan Freeze), Columbia University (at Jeremy Dauber's invitation), ETH Zurich (at a conference organized by Andreas Kilcher and Gabriella Safran), Oxford University (at a conference organized by Zehavit Stern), Rutgers (where I was the Aresty Visiting Scholar in Jewish Studies in Spring 2013), and, twice, at the Jewish Community Library in San Francisco.

In one way or another, I worked on this book for a decade. For at least half of this time, I busied myself with literary translation projects that allowed me to procrastinate through writer's block, manage my recurring sense of despair about the place of this book in the world, and weather the stresses and uncertainties of the academic job market. I was lucky to become involved in projects to translate the two

Yiddish novels that would later become the subjects of the first two chapters in this book. The support I received during that period helped me generate insights that I later incorporated into the book. A Mellon Postdoctoral Fellowship at the Center for the Humanities at Tufts University under the directorship of Jonathan Wilson made it possible for me to edit Hillel Halkin's translation of Moyshe Kulbak's novel *Zelmenyaner* and to write the book's introduction. The book was published as *The Zelmenyaners* in 2013 by Yale University Press, in the New Yiddish Library series edited by David G. Roskies. The Yiddish Book Center's Translation Fellowship, then directed by Sebastian Schulman, and the mentorship of Susan Bernofsky allowed me to work collaboratively with Harriet Murav to make David Bergelson's *Mides-hadin* available to the English-language reader. A Faculty Fellowship from the Center for the Humanities and the Arts at the University of Colorado Boulder during the fall 2015 semester made it possible for us to complete this translation, which was published under the title *Judgment* by Northwestern University Press in 2017. Translating Bergelson together with Harriet was easily the most enriching experience of my scholarly career so far, not least because of the joyful collaboration an intellectual partnership of this kind made possible.

I began to write this book in earnest in 2016 while on a fellowship at the Center for Jewish Studies at Harvard. I am thankful to my co-fellows that year—all of us postdocs or junior faculty—for the warm intellectual atmosphere. I am particularly indebted to Rachel Wamsley, a truly brilliant, generous thinker who, in our regular hours-long conversations over multiple Guinness pints that winter and spring, single-handedly reignited my curiosity about some of the key texts at the core of this project.

Since 2017 at the University of Washington in Seattle, I have been lucky to be surrounded by caring colleagues in Slavic Languages and Literatures and the Jackson School of International Studies. I am grateful to Galya Diment, Barbara Henry, Noam Pianko, and Glennys Young for their mentorship. The Stroum Center for Jewish Studies, directed by Noam Pianko and expertly administered by Associate Director Sarah Zaides Rosen, supported my research with funding during one of the summers when I needed to dedicate time to writing, and my Slavic colleagues José Alaniz, Galya Diment, and Katarzyna Dziwirek kindly approved the department's first-ever funding package for the costly business that is image permissions and book indexing. Lee Scheingold, a devoted friend of the department who has become a dear personal friend, generously volunteered her services as a seasoned proofreader.

Over the years, librarians at the Slavic Reference Service at the University of Illinois at Urbana-Champaign, including Jon Adamczyk, Joe Lenkart, and Dmitry Tartakovsky, have fielded my queries about hard-to-find contemporary reviews in the Soviet press of the works I was researching. The riches of Harvard's Widener Library (and especially its Judaica Division) made a lot of my research possible; I am grateful especially to Vardit Samuels for her assistance tracking down various materials over the years. I first came across some of the material in this book in the Jewish National Library in Jerusalem, whose often-packed reading room had the inspiring vibes of something like a sewing factory that might have been represented in a Soviet film. The Odessa Literary Museum's Alyona Yavorskaya generously answered my questions about Semyon Gekht. Anna Misiuk, the guardian of Odessa's literary history, guided me around her native city, emphasizing its geography in ways that allowed me to understand its importance to Isaac Babel's work (and later she tracked down some crucial references I was curious about). Alexander Ivanov helped me procure texts about Birobidzhan. When accessing materials became especially difficult during the lockdowns of the COVID-19 pandemic, Valérie Pozner at the Center for Russian, Central European, and Caucasian Studies (part of the Centre National de le Recherche Scientifique in Paris), saved the day and furnished me with the film stills that I needed. Staff at Saint Petersburg's National Library of Russia and Minsk's Belarusian Archive for Cinema, Photography, and Sound Recordings, as well as David Mazower at the Yiddish Book Center and Richard Pontius at the National Center for Jewish Film, helped me locate the necessary images for this book's illustrations.

Access to several colleagues' book and article manuscripts was pivotal at several stages in my writing process; I thank Elissa Bemporad, Marc Caplan, Amelia Glaser, Adrien Smith, Miriam Udel, and Jeffrey Veidlinger for letting me take a sneak peek at their works prior to their publication. Isabelle Lewis patiently worked with me to create a map for this book, which I hope will be a useful resource to many—and Eugene Avrutin, Eileen Kane, and Matthew Mosca graciously volunteered their time to proofread it. Kathleen McDermott, this book's supportive and generous editor—together with assistant editor Kathi Drummy—at Harvard University Press, saw this project through its development and publication.

Over the past decade, I have been privileged and lucky to teach wonderful students at Tufts University, Lafayette College, Rutgers University, the University of Colorado Boulder, the University of Washington—and, last but certainly not least, the brilliant and bookish high schoolers at the Great Jewish Books summer program at the Yiddish Book Center. I got to test-drive with these student cohorts some of the translations about which I would later write. Class discussions about several other texts that form this book's primary source base became invaluable opportunities for me to sharpen my own thinking about this material. I am especially thankful to the insights of university students enrolled in my courses on the experience of Russian Jews, and especially to Haley Taylor-Manning—an undergraduate student in this course's latest iteration at UW, whose interest in the work of Margarita Khemlin and our many conversations about it sent me down my own Khemlin rabbit hole during the book's final stages.

I am grateful for the unconditional support and love of my family and close friends. The decision of my parents, Marina and Mikhail Senderovich, to immigrate to the United States when I was sixteen made it possible for me to think about the

Soviet Jewish experience from a distance. Once my maternal grandmother, Nella Glinberg, took up writing her recollections about her childhood, she regaled me with some of those Soviet Jewish stories during our phone calls between Boston and wherever I happened to live at the time. My paternal grandparents, Iosif and Dina Senderovich, never left Russia and died long before I began working on this book; I lived with them during my earlier teen years and somehow their stories— stories of the first generation of Jews born not long after the revolution—have long been part of my self-understanding, too. Mihaela Pacurar has been a kind and thoughtful friend for many years, wise in her counsel about life's many twists and turns and always ready with a recipe for me to try to cook. I first met Bella Grigoryan twenty years ago, and we have enjoyed many conversations, over meals and drinks, comparing our very different memories of our late Soviet childhoods and sharing our American experiences. I had the incredible gift of beginning a conversation— and a friendship—with Adriana X. Jacobs over a bottle of retsina on the porch of Emily's B&B in Amherst one July week several years ago, and I have been learning a great deal (about translation, among other things) from her since.

Liora Halperin has been a kind and loving partner through our many moves; we have been lucky to work on building a life together for the last decade and a half in several different places. An insightful scholar, whose wordsmithing talents are legendary among our colleagues and friends near and far, Liora read every word of this book numerous times and guided me in finding the best way to say what I was trying to say. The birth of our child, Rami, has been life's most significant gift so far. Rami's name is an anagram of the name of my great grandmother, Mira Zugman, who was the only family member I got to know who was born in the Pale of Settlement before the revolution. Rami was a year and a half old when the three of us first hunkered down for the months-long lockdown of the pandemic. The opportunity to spend more time together relatively free of distractions from the rest of the wounded, hurting world made it oddly easier to finally finish this book. As I look forward to continuing to build a home with these two, I dedicate this book to Liora, with gratitude, appreciation, and love.

Index

The letter *f* following a page number denotes a figure.

"About Zhenya" (Khemlin), 278–282
Abramovitch, Sh. Y., 14; *Brief Adventures of Benjamin the Third, The,* 92–93
agitation trials of 1920s, 204, 205; transition to show trials, 205–206
agricultural colonies, Jewish: in Palestine, 130, 145, 146, 152, 153; propaganda regarding, 157–158, 171; Soviet attempts to establish, 4, 124, 125, 306n1, 307n15; as weapon against antisemitism, 158. *See also* Birobidzhan
agriculture: in efforts to transform Jewish men, 4, 7, 18; and figure of New Soviet Man, 125; industrialization of, Jewish colonists associated with, 127, 137; Jewish tradition associated with (sukkah), 114–115. *See also* agricultural colonies; collectivization of agriculture
Aleksandrov, Hillel, *Research Your Shtetl!,* 105–106
Alexander II (tsar of Russia), 3
Alexandrov, Grigorii, 187
Alone (film), 191, 196–197
"Among Refugees" (Bergelson), 26
Amur Cossacks, 136; experiences in Far East, 136–143, 156
Amur River, 123, 135–136, 210
analogies. *See* substitution(s)
Anna Karenina (Tolstoy), 89
An-sky, S., 228
antisemitism: agricultural resettlement as weapon against, 158; of Bolshevik hero, in Bergelson's *Judgment,* 62–63, 67, 72; campaigns against "cosmopolitanism" of

late 1940s–early 1950s and, 277; criminalization of Jewish economic activities as, 18, 60–64; "fifth line" in Soviet passport and, 17; myth of Judeo-Bolshevism and, 36; official opposition to, 4, 10–11, 18, 22, 36, 58; in Russian literary history, 9; trickster's (Hershele's) response to, 323n42; tropes of, in *Seekers of Happiness* (film), 208–209. *See also* pogroms
anxiety: cinematic montage encoding, 190; in early Soviet state, 40, 58, 192, 203; and figure of Soviet Jew, 7, 22, 25, 38, 190, 192, 203, 216–217; in Gothic literature, 22–23, 40
Aquila of Sinope, 258
Arrival of the Train, The (film), 190
Ashes out of Hope (Howe and Greenberg), 54
Ashkenazi Jews: Bolshevik Revolution and dispersal of, 1–2, 4; dominant mother tongue of, 14. *See also* Jew(s)
At the Depot (Bergelson), 38
Attias, Jean-Christophe, 153
Austen, J. L., 233
Austria, emancipation of Jews in, 7
avant-garde film: circus associated with, 181, 182; exaggerated gestures associated with, 189, 192; Factory of the Eccentric Actor (FEKS) and, 182–184; influence on *Return of Neitan Bekker, The* (film), 173, 181, 182–184

Baal Shem Tov (Besht), 223, 260
Babel, Isaac, 229f; as army correspondent, 57, 242, 243; arrest and execution of, 271, 277;

Black Hundreds, 71
Bletnitsky brothers, 229, 322n30
Blok, Alexander, "Twelve, The," 68
body, Jewish: circumcised, in Babel's "Karl-Yankel," 253, 259, 260–261; disabled, in *Return of Neitan Bekker, The* (film), 179–181, 186–187, 195; disaggregation of, Bergelson's textual strategy of, 61–62; physical characteristics of, focus on, 7, 64
Boese, Carl, 24
Bolshevik(s) / Bolshevik regime: association of Jews with, myth of, 10, 34, 36–37, 293n64; commitment to internationalism and racial equality, global appeal of, 173; criminalization of economic activity associated with Jews, 18, 58, 60–64; ethnographic research by, 18, 105–106, 118; inclusive rhetoric toward Jews, 168, 170; as messengers, Jewish perspective on, 65; messianic ideology of, Hershele and challenges to, 224; nationalities policy of, 16–17, 124, 306n6; official opposition to antisemitism, 4, 10–11, 18, 22, 36, 58; and Red Terror, 22; vs. Socialist Revolutionaries (SRs), 20–21; succession struggle after Lenin's death, 69; tenuous hold on power by, literary works suggesting, 45–49, 58; and War Communism, 22, 40, 60; writers' role in legitimating regime of, 242–243
Bolshevik hero: antisemitism of, literary depiction of, 62–63, 67, 72; in Bergelson's *Judgment*, 24, 46–51, 53–55, 60, 64, 66–68, 70–71; self-sacrifice of, literary texts on, 48–49, 51, 55–57; in Tarasov-Rodionov's *Chocolate*, 48–49. *See also* Jewish Bolshevik, figure of
Bolshevik-Polish War of 1920, 19; Babel's diary of, 36, 249, 250–251; Babel's fictional stories on, in *Red Cavalry*, 241–252; Babel's reporting on, 57, 242, 243
Bolshevik Revolution, 4; Christological understanding of, 67–69; and dispersal of Jewish communities, 1–2, 4; and economic devastation of Pale of Settlement, 41–42, 58–59, 60; and figure of New Soviet Man, 7–8; as foundational event of Soviet experience, 276; imagined as end of history, 169; indeterminate trajectory of, 8, 45–46, 69, 73, 236; Jewish emigration after, 3, 25–26; Petrograd's demise after, Babel

on, 234–239, 242; strange world brought forth by, 33
border(s): of Birobidzhan with Manchuria, threats along, 136, 164; in Pale of Settlement, smuggling across, 20, 41–42, 58–60; population relocation policies to secure, 136
Border, The (film), 19, 176, 201–202, 202f, 214
Borukhl, Rebbe, 219, 223, 232, 233, 235, 245, 250, 255, 261
Boym, Svetlana, 255
Brief Adventures of Benjamin the Third, The (Abramovitch), 92–93
Bronshteyn, Yasha, 296n122; on Bergelson's *Judgment*, 53, 62, 65; on Kulbak's *Zelmenyaners*, 87, 88, 91, 111–112, 113, 116
"brotherhood of peoples," Soviet narrative of, 138, 253; homage to, in Babel's "Karl-Yankel," 254, 259–261
"Brothers" (Markish), 30
Brown, Benjamin, 130; in Gekht's *Ogonëk* article, 144; protagonist based on, in Gekht's *Ship Sails to Jaffa and Back*, 130–131, 146, 150
Brusilovskii, E., 198
Budler Family's Resettlement, The (Gekht), 128, 157, 159–166; abrupt ending of, 165–166; Birobidzhan as antithesis to shtetl in, 162–163, 164, 165; cover of, 161f; folktale elements in, 159–164; theme of non-arrival in, 158, 166; transitional moment in Soviet children's literature and, 158, 159
Budyonny, Semyon, 242
Bulgakova, Oksana, 182, 183

Cabinet of Dr. Caligari, The (film), 24
Caplan, Marc, 53
Caruth, Cathy, 160
Cassiday, Julie, 204
castle, chronotrope of, in Gothic texts, 23–24, 40
Castle of Otranto, The (Walpole), 40
Chapaev (Furmanov), 243
Chaplin, Charlie, 187, 316n42
Cheka: in Bergelson's *Judgment*, 20, 24–25, 39, 41, 45–46, 49; downfall of agents of, in fiction about early Bolshevik era, 46; head of, in Bergelson's *Judgment*, 24, 46–51, 53–55, 60, 64; mandate of, 20; meaning of term, 45; suicidal inclinations of agents of, literary texts suggesting, 48–49, 51, 55–57; in Tarasov-Rodionov's *Chocolate*, 30, 46, 48–49

Chekhov, Anton, 9
Chernenko, Miron, 211
children's books, Soviet: about Birobidzhan, 157, 159–166; orphan / child who ran away from home in, 159; transitional moment in evolution of, 158, 159
China: acquisition of Birobidzhan from, 135; attempted escape to, in *Seekers of Happiness* (film), 210; Russian emigration to, 165–166; White Russians in, 164–165
Chocolate (Tarasov-Rodionov), 30–31, 46, 48–49
Christ, protagonist in Bergelson's *Judgment* compared to, 67–68, 70–71
Christianity: early, communism compared to, 258; image of Jew in, 6; Jewish conversion to, during Russian civil war, 27, 29
circumcision: Bolshevik position on, 253; compared to translation, 257–258; of heart vs. flesh, 258; as marker of Jewishness, 6, 253, 259, 260–261
circus / circus arena: acrobat vs. clown figure in, 187–188; in avant-garde film, 181, 182; and political show trials of Stalin era, 203–204; in *Return of Neitan Bekker, The* (film), 181, 184, 185f, 187; in Soviet image of America, 183
Circus (silent film), 187
Circus (Socialist Realist film), 187, 203–204
citizenship, Jews and issue of, 6–7
"City, The" (Kulbak), 111–112, 113, 121
civil war. *See* Russian civil war
Clark, Katerina, 88, 90, 129, 132, 133
clown: vs. acrobat, in *Return of Neitan Bekker, The* (film), 187–189. *See also* trickster(s)
Cohen, Shaye J. D., 6
Cold War, figure of Soviet Jew during, 5, 277
collectivization of agriculture: Babel as witness to horrors of, 263; Babel's "Gapa Guzhva" on, 264–265; and internal passports, 17; subtext of, in Babel's "Karl-Yankel," 262–264; trickster figure (Hershele) in descriptions of, 19
commissar (term), 54
construction, Soviet: vs. American, in *Return of Neitan Bekker, The* (film), 174–175, 184–189, 186f, 195; in films about returning Jewish émigrés, 175, 177, 178–179; and Jewish migration, 3, 120; metaphor of, in Socialist Realist descriptions, 132; reporting to global

audiences, 168, 169; socialist *(sotsboyung)*, in Kulbak's *Zelmenyaners*, 86, 110–113
"conversion," to Soviet ideology: in agitation trials of 1920s, 205; in Bergelson's *Judgment*, 44–45, 55–56, 66, 68–69; and loss of speech, in Stalin-era cultural artifacts, 194–195, 200–203, 214; returning Jewish émigrés and, 275; in *Return of Neitan Bekker, The* (film), 175, 194–196, 199–201, 206; in *Seekers of Happiness* (film), 211–212. *See also* Jewish Bolshevik, figure of
Cossacks: in Babel's *Red Cavalry*, 137; in Fink's *Jews in the Taiga*, 136–143, 156; Jewish resettlement compared to relocation of, 138, 139, 142–143; relations with Jewish settlers in Birobidzhan, 137–138, 156; relocation to Birobidzhan, 136, 138; uprisings in 17th century, and anti-Jewish violence, 21, 27–29, 137, 222–223
courtyard, Jewish *(hoyf)*: compared to sukkah, 114–115, 119, 120; compared to Tabernacle *(mishkan)*, 117–118; compared to train station, 114, 115, 120; dismantling of, 115–116, 119–120, 122; ethnography of, 104–105; in Kulbak's *Zelmenyaners*, 74, 75, 76, 79, 80, 97, 103–105, 113–116, 119–120, 122; as microcosm of shtetl, 76, 105, 122; in Minsk, 75f; montage used to create image of, 115; stasis and mobility encompassed in, 117
Crimea, failed Jewish agricultural colony in, 124, 306n1, 307n15
criminality, conflation of Jewish livelihoods with: in Bergelson's *Judgment*, 18, 60–64; demise of Pale of Settlement and, 60–64, 124; in Kulbak's *Zelmenyaners*, 97

Damesek, A., 90, 106–108
"Dead Body of Christ in the Tomb, The" (Holbein the Younger), 68
Deaf Man, The (Bergelson), 100
de Certeau, Michel, 233, 234
Demons (Dostoevsky), 46
Dennen, Leon, 167
de Sade, Marquis, 22, 23
Descent (Bergelson), 38
"Di Grasso" (Babel), 269–270
disabled body: cultural representations in Stalinist era, 180–181; in film portrayal of returning Jewish émigrés, 179–181, 186–187, 195

dispersal / displacement, of Jewish communities: Bolshevik Revolution and, 1–2, 4; in
Fink's *Jews in the Taiga*, 123, 139–142;
in Gekht's *Ship Sails to Jaffa and Back*,
146; and idealized Jewish version of New
Soviet Man, 212; in Kulbak's *Zelmenyaners*,
113–117; in *Seekers of Happiness* (film),
214–216; traditional ways of dealing with
memory of, 114–115; train as symbol of,
75–76, 214–216; World War II and, 5
Dobrenko, Evgeny, 130, 132, 276, 324n62
Dobroliubov, Nikolai, "What is Oblomovism?,"
106
Dostoevsky, Fyodor: antisemitic stereotypes
in works of, 9; *Demons*, 46
Dovzhenko, Oleksandr, 265
Dubnow, Simon, 26
Dubson, Mikhail, *Border, The* (film), 176,
201–202, 214
Dunaevsky, Isaak, 213
Dunets, Khatskl, 89–90
Dymshitz, Valerii, 320n2

Earth (film), 265
Eastern Europe: emigration of Jews from,
3; Haskalah in, and modern Yiddish
literature, 14
economic criminality, conflation of Jews with,
18, 58, 60–64; Birobidzhan settlement touted
as solution to, 124
economic devastation, of Pale of Settlement,
41–42, 58–59, 60
Egart, Mark, *Scorched Earth*, 148–149, 308n35
Ehrenburg, Ilya: *Life and Death of Nikolai
Kurbov*, 46; "Ship Fare, A," 34–37; *Stormy
Life of Lazik Roytshvants, The*, 297n147
Eisenstein, Sergei: international reputation
of, 172; montage associated with films of,
78, 190, 191; *Old and the New, The*, 100; on
sound film and challenges to montage, 191
electrification: in Kulbak's *Zelmenyaners*,
84–86, 114–115; sukkah as simile for, 114–115,
119
emigration: of Eastern European Jews, 3,
25–26; of White Russians, 164–166. *See also*
Jewish émigrés, return to Soviet Union
End of Everything, The (Bergelson), 38
"End of the Almshouse, The" (Babel), 1–2, 8–11,
278; antisemitic stereotypes in, 9–10; dissolution of Jewish community structures

in, 1–2; indeterminate road in, 1–2, 19;
Jewish Bolshevik in, figure of, 9, 10, 11;
old Jew in, figure of, 1–2, 10, 11, 14, 19
Envy (Olesha), 83
Epshtein, S., *Misha from a Jewish Settlement*,
157, 159, 162
Erdman, Nikolai: *Suicide, The*, 305n117
Estonia, Soviet occupation of, 4–5
Esu-Elegbara (trickster), 225
ethnic groups, in Soviet state: defining and
counting, 17; diversity of, and ideological
compliance, 253; and nationalities policy,
124, 136
ethnography: about Jews, 18, 105–106, 118;
local, approaches to, 303n95; parody of,
in Kulbak's *Zelmenyaners*, 108; and
Soviet state building, 105. *See also*
salvage ethnography
Evening Star, The (Vecherniaia zvezda)
(periodical): Babel's literary sketches
about Odessa in, 235; Babel's "Shabos-
nakhamu" in, 218, 235, 236
evolution: Lamarck's theories of, 77, 105, 107;
of Soviet Jew, in Kulbak's *Zelmenyaners*,
76–77, 78, 79–80, 97, 112, 113, 114, 119, 120,
122
expressionism, 24
*Extraordinary Adventures of Mr. West in the
Land of the Bolsheviks, The* (film), 171–172
Ezrahi, Sidra, 237

Factory of the Eccentric Actor (FEKS),
182–184, 189, 192
Fadeev, Alexander, *Last of the Udege, The*, 76
fairy tales. *See* folktales / fairy tales
Falen, James, 320n2
family: conflicts among members of, in
Kulbak's *Zelmenyaners*, 83, 85, 96–98, 108;
postrevolutionary hostility toward, 159
Far East. *See* Birobidzhan
Feuchtwanger, Leon, 150–151
film(s): early sound, 190; Gothic mode in, 24;
influence on Bergelson's literary works,
38–39; influence on Kulbak's *Zelmenyaners*,
77, 78. *See also* avant-garde film; film(s),
Soviet; montage; silent film; sound film;
specific film titles
film(s), Soviet: disabled body in, 180; early
sound, 190–191; figure of Soviet Jew in,
212–213; growth and international reputation

Gorky, Maxim: and Babel, 236, 323n43; and Bolshevik regime, 240; on folklore / folktale, 159; on literary sketch *(ocherk),* 131; on "little men," 86–87; on Socialist Realism, 156

Gorshman, Mendel, illustrations by, 28*f,* 32*f*

GOSET (Moscow State Yiddish Theater), 148

Gothic literature: and Bergelson's *Judgment,* 22, 23, 24–25, 39–41, 47, 67, 69, 71; chrono-trope of castle / monastery in, 23–24; and Gekht's *Shoemaker's Son,* 29; postrevolu-tionary terror in France and, 22–23; uncertain succession in, 40–41; and Wandering Jew, figure of, 27–29, 216

Great Depression, and Jewish émigrés' return to Soviet Union, 4, 18–19, 175, 203

Greenberg, Eliezer, 54

Grinberg, Marat, 288n46

Grossman, Vasily, "In the Town of Berdichev," 37

Grumberg, Karen, 216

Gutman, David, 173, 185*f*

Halevi, Yehuda, 237–238

Harbin (China): Russian emigration to, 165–166; White Russians in, 164–165

Harris, Franklin S., 123, 144

Hasan-Rokem, Galit, 217

Hasidism, 219, 222–223; imaginative geography of, in Babel's work, 255–256, 261; references to, in Babel's "Karl-Yankel," 254–255; trick-ster's role in context of, 219, 222, 223–224, 225, 226. *See also* Hershele Ostropoler; *niggun*

Haskalah: in Berlin, 7; and modern Yiddish literature, 14

Havdalah ceremony, 115

Haynt (periodical), Birobidzhan reportage in, 166–167

Hebrew language, 14–15

Hershele Ostropoler (trickster figure): antisemitism tackled by, 323n42; Babel's identification with, 235, 271–272; Babel's implicit cycle of stories about, 19, 218, 228, 234–235, 240–252, 255, 265, 268, 270–272, 320n2; in Babel's "Shabos-nakhamu," 218–222, 224, 226, 228; chapbooks of stories about, 229, 322n30; as cipher for Soviet Jew, 19, 218, 226, 228, 234–235, 240, 247, 252, 253, 265, 271, 275; in folk narratives, 223, 228–231, 246; as guide to dealing with wartime violence, 242, 243, 249, 251, 270; as historical figure, 222–223; influence on Soviet culture, 273; as jester in Borukhl's court, 219, 223, 232, 233, 235, 245, 249, 250, 255, 261; as model for literary messiah, 239, 242; in Polyanker's *Teacher from Medzhibozh, The,* 273–274; role in context of Hasidism, 223–224, 225; in stories about Soviet experience, 273; Trunk's novel based on narratives of, 321n15; walking associated with, 228, 230–231, 232, 233

Hetényi, Zsuzsa, 147–148, 149

Hoberman, J., 198

Holbein the Younger, Hans, "Dead Body of Christ in the Tomb, The," 68

Holocaust, 22, 273, 278

Holodomor, 263

Howe, Irving, 54

How the Steel Was Tempered (Ostrovsky), 89–90

hoyf. See courtyard, Jewish

Hughes, Langston, 173

Huizinga, Johann, 246

humor: in Bergelson's *Judgment,* 41, 42, 70; Freud's theory of, 227; Hasidic trickster (Hershele) and, 223–224, 274; in Kulbak's *Zelmenyaners,* 70–71, 86, 104, 106, 108, 118–119, 122, 304n114; in *Return of Neitan Bekker, The* (film), 187–189; in *Seekers of Happiness* (film), 211. *See also* merriment

Iavorskaia, Alëna, 148, 149

IKOR. *See* Organization for Jewish Coloniza-tion of Russia

Il'f, Ilya: *Little Golden Calf, The,* 168–171, 216; trickster figure in novels by, 168, 225

imprecision, narrative: in Bergelson's *Judgment,* 45–46; in Birobidzhan texts, 124, 127–129, 133, 144, 149, 151, 154, 157; in Gekht's works, 33–34; in *Seekers of Happiness* (film), 214–216; and strange world of Bolshevik revolution, 33. *See also* omission(s); substitution(s)

industrialization, Soviet: English-language publications about, 169; and figure of Soviet Jew, 114; and Jewish mobility, 3; Jews as leading members of, narrative of, 127, 137, 138; in Minsk, 80; portrayal in Kulbak's *Zelmenyaners,* 80–86, 114–115, 120–121; portrayal in *Return of Neitan Bekker, The* (film), 174–175

Industrial Party, show trial of, 204
Inspector General, The (Gogol), 90
Institute of Belorussian Culture (Inbelkult),
    Jewish Department of, 103–104
"In the Town of Berdichev" (Grossman), 37

Japan, influence in Manchuria, 136
Jazz Singer, The (film), 190
Jerusalem: in Gekht's *Ship Sails to Jaffa and
    Back, A*, 145–146; Halevi's inability to
    reach, 237–238; heavenly vs. earthly, 238;
    Petersburg compared to, 237, 239, 242,
    324n53
Jew(s): association with Bolshevik regime,
    myth of, 10, 34, 36–37, 77, 293n64; citizen-
    ship in Soviet Union, 6–7; male, physical
    characteristics of, 7, 64; and technological
    and industrial progress, Soviet narrative of,
    137, 138. *See also* body, Jewish; Jewish
    Bolshevik; Jewish communities; Jewish
    émigrés; Soviet Jew; Wandering Jew
Jewish Antifascist Committee, 54, 277
Jewish Bolshevik, figure of, 30–33; in Babel's
    "End of the Almshouse, The," 9, 10, 11; in
    Bergelson's *Judgment*, 44–45, 55–56, 66,
    68–69; in Kulbak's *Zelmenyaners*, 83, 93–96;
    in Markish's "Brothers," 30; pogroms
    incorporated into psyche of, 30, 31, 33; in
    Return of Neitan Bekker, The (film), 173–175,
    194–195, 196, 198; in *Seekers of Happiness*
    (film), 209, 210, 211–212; Soviet Jew
    distinguished from, 10; in Tarasov-
    Rodionov's *Chocolate*, 30; as variant
    of New Soviet Man, 10
Jewish communities: criminalization of
    economic activities of, 18, 58, 60–64; in
    Minsk, 76; in Russian Empire, 2–3, 4, 17.
    See also Birobidzhan, Jewish settlement in;
    dispersal / displacement; Pale of Settlement
Jewish émigrés, return to Soviet Union, 4,
    18–19; and "conversion" to Soviet ideology,
    194–196, 199–201, 206, 275; doubly compro-
    mised ("socially crippled") bodies of, 179;
    in Gekht's *Ship Sails to Jaffa and Back,
    A*, 18, 128, 130–131, 134, 143–157; Great
    Depression and, 4, 18–19, 175, 203; in Il'f
    and Petrov's *Little Golden Calf*, 168–171;
    motivations of, 4, 18–19, 171; and New
    Soviet Man, figure of, 177, 178, 187–189,
    212; in *Return of Neitan Bekker, The* (film),

19, 172–175, 174f, 179; in *Seekers of Happiness*
    (film), 207–212; symbolic rehabilitation of,
    209–210; and Wandering Jew, figure of, 178
"Jewish question," 168; Bolshevik claims
    of having resolved, 168, 170; and Soviet
    Jew, figure of, 169
Jewish Section (Evsektsiia), 36
Jews in the Taiga (Fink), 18, 123, 128; on Amur
    Cossacks' experiences in Far East, 136–143;
    clichéd responses by Jewish settlers in,
    141–142; contemporary critics on, 142–143;
    ending of, 156; excerpts from, in *Haynt*,
    167; Fink's previous publications and,
    306n1, 307n15; footnotes in, 132; lack
    of detail on Jewish settlement in, 129;
    narrative of displacement in, 123, 139–142;
    play based on, 309n53; on relationship
    between Cossacks and Jewish settlers,
    137–138; revisions between editions of, 132;
    substitution strategy in, 143, 156; subversive
    interpretive strategies suggested by, 138–139,
    142; time frame in, 131
Joseph II (Holy Roman Emperor), 7
journalism: Babel's work in, 234–236; and
    creative fiction, intermediate genre between,
    131. *See also specific titles of periodicals*
Judeo-Bolshevism, myth of, 10, 34, 293n64;
    and pogroms, 36–37
Judgment (Bergelson), 18, 20–25, 37–72; abrupt
    ending of, 56–58; ambiguity and liminality
    of Russian civil war in, 37–38; anti-Bolshevik
    forces portrayed in, 20–21, 31, 43–44, 70,
    71, 72; antisemitism of Bolshevik hero in,
    62–63, 67, 72; as apparent endorsement of
    Bolshevik regime, 44–45, 51–53; Bolshevik
    hero in, 24, 46–51, 53–55, 60, 64, 66–68,
    70–71; Cheka outpost in, 20, 24–25, 39, 41,
    45–46, 49; Cheka policies targeting shtetl
    Jews in, 60–66; Christian references in,
    67–72; cinematic influences in, 38–39;
    concern about fate of shtetl dwellers in,
    51; contemporary critics on, 53, 62, 65,
    68; cross-border smuggling in, 20, 41–42,
    47–48, 60–61; disaggregation of body
    in, 61–62; Gothic mode in, 22, 23, 24–25,
    39–41, 47, 67, 69, 71; historical context of,
    290n3; Jewish Bolsheviks in, 44–45, 55–56,
    66, 68–69; Jewish speculator in, 63–66;
    publication of, 51, 52f; scholarship on, 53–55;
    shtetl in, 20, 41–42, 59, 73; on "strange"

world after Bolshevik Revolution, 33, 45–46; textual strategies used in, 42–43, 45–46, 61–62; threat of pogroms in, 23, 25, 43, 49–50, 71–72; tribunal / trial in, 63–67; uncertain succession in, 40–41, 45–46, 69

Kaganovsky, Lilya, 180, 190, 217
Kalinin, Mikhail, 125
"Karl-Yankel" (Babel), 252–269; circumcised body in, 259, 260–261; collectivization subtext in, 262–264; ending of, 265, 266; figure of Soviet Jew emerging in, 265–266; imaginative geography in, 255–256, 261; narrator of, 267–268; performance of "brotherhood of peoples" in, 254, 259–261; as story of authorial self-invention, 266–269; traces of blood libel accusation in, 326n91; trial in, 254, 260, 262, 265, 266; women's role in, 254–255, 259–260, 281; Yiddish translation of, 267
Kashnitskaya, Yelena, 173
Katsnelson, Anna Wexler, 204
Katz, Maya Balakirsky, 288n46
Kautsky, Karl, 169
Khemlin, Margarita, 328n12; "About Zhenya," 278–282
Khmelnytsky, Bohdan, Cossack uprisings led by, 21, 137
khurbn, during Russian civil war, 22, 29
"khvostism," accusation of, 94
Kipnis, Itsik, *Months and Days*, 33, 34
Kishinev, pogroms in, 31
Kolas, Jakub, 90
Korn, Rokhl, 54
Korsh-Sablin, Vladimir, 176. *See also Seekers of Happiness* (film)
Kozintsev, Leonid, 182, 183; *Alone* (film), 191, 196–197
Kristeva, Julia, 68
Krupskaia, Nadezhda, 159
Krutikov, Mikhail, 38, 53, 54, 55
Kukulin, Ilia, 77–78
Kulbak, Moyshe, 78f, 300n32; "Belorussia," 121; at Belorussian Academy of Sciences, 103–104, 118, 303n89; in Berlin, 77, 299n7; "City, The," 111–112, 113, 121; execution of, 78, 276–277; influences on, 77; poetics of, 120–122; as translator and literary editor, 90, 113; *Zelmenyaners, The*, 18, 74–122. *See also Zelmenyaners, The*

Kulbak, Raya, 303n94
Kulbak, Zelda, 104, 303n89
Kuleshov, Lev: *Extraordinary Adventures of Mr. West in the Land of the Bolsheviks, The* (film), 171–172; *Gorizont* (film), 175–176, 177, 213–214, 315n22; international reputation of, 172
Kvitko, Leyb, *1919*, 34

Labor Zionism, 153
Lamarck, Jean-Baptiste, 77, 105, 107
language(s): of Belorussian Soviet Socialist Republic (BSSR), 82, 82f; and changes in meaning of trickster tale, 230–231; as tool for establishing Bolsheviks' legitimacy, 242–243; as trickster's tool for creating alternative meanings, 226–227. *See also* Hebrew language; Russian language; Yiddish language
Last of the Udege, The (Fadeev), 76
Latvia, Soviet occupation of, 4–5
Lenin, Vladimir Ilyich: and Cheka, establishment of, 20; death of, and succession struggle, 69; "little light bulbs" of, 85; on older vs. younger generations' role in communist society, 300n21; seizure of power by, 3; spontaneity-consciousness dialectic articulated by, 88; and Trotsky, 293n64; "What Is to Be Done?," 87–88
Lewis, Matthew, *Monk, The*, 22–23
Leyda, Jay, 317n48, 317n51
Libedinskii, Yuri, *Week, A*, 44, 49
"Life after Death" (Gekht), 151
Life and Death of Nikolai Kurbov (Ehrenburg), 46
Lipovetsky, Mark, 225, 226
literacy campaign, in Kulbak's *Zelmenyaners*, 86, 113
literary messiah: Babel's visions of becoming, 235, 237, 268; Hershele as model for, 239, 242
literary sketch *(ocherk)*, 131
Lithuania, Soviet occupation of, 4–5
Little Golden Calf, The (Il'f and Petrov), 168–171, 216
Lotman, Yuri, 184
luftmentsh, figure of, 207, 212
Lumière, Auguste and Louis, 190, 317n51
Lunacharsky, Anatoly, 31
Lysenko, Timofey, 107

male gender: and figure of New Soviet Man, 178; and figure of Soviet Jew, 6–7, 173, 281

Manchuria, 123, 135, 136. *See also* China

Mandelshtam, Osip, 11

Man Who Forgot His Life, The (Gekht), 27–29, 28*f*

Margolit, Evgeny, 190

Markish, Peretz, 317n47; "Brothers," 30; execution of, 277; "Mound, The," 29–30; and *Return of Neitan Bekker, The*, 173, 178, 181, 197

Marr, Wilhelm, 63

maskilim. See modernization

Mayzel, Nakhmen, 87

McGeever, Brendan, 31, 60, 293n64

McKay, Claude, 173

Medzhibozh: in Babel's work, 218, 219, 233, 235, 254–256, 261; in history of Hasidism, 223, 235; in Polyanker's *Teacher from Medzhibozh, The*, 273

Menorah Journal, The (periodical), 167

merriment: in Freud's theory of humor, 227; Hershele as figure of, 222, 225, 235; and horror, uncanny proximity in Babel's work, 226, 241, 243–244, 249, 264; and verse, in Babel's work, 244–245

metaphor(s): in *Circus* (film), 204; construction, in Socialist Realist descriptions, 132; in Kulbak's *Zelmenyaners*, 120–122; in texts about Birobidzhan, 126–129, 153. *See also* substitution(s)

mezuzah, 116

Michaelis, Johann David, 7

Mikhoels, Solomon, 174, 174*f*, 277

Mil'man, Rashel': and avant-garde film, 182, 183; and *Return of Neitan Bekker, The* (film), 173, 178, 199, 214

Minsk: Belorussian State Yiddish Theater in, 100, 101*f*; films shown in, 98–100, 100*f*; identification with former Pale of Settlement, 76, 299n4; industrialization of, 80; Jewish Sector of Belorussian Academy of Sciences in, 103–104; Kulbak in, 77; movie theater in, 98, 99*f*, 102; residential courtyard in, 75*f*; tramway in, 80, 81*f*, 84

Misha from a Jewish Settlement (Epshtein), 157, 159, 162

mishkan. See Tabernacle

Mishnah Sanhedrin (tractate), 65

mobility, Jewish: in Kulbak's *Zelmenyaners*, 113–115; from Pale of Settlement to Far East, 125; of postrevolutionary era, 3–4, 19, 135; Russian civil war and, 3; Soviet industrialization and, 3, 114; Soviet state's program of, in texts about Birobidzhan, 134–135. *See also* dispersal / displacement, of Jewish communities

Moch, Leslie Page, 135

modernization *(maskilim)*: and family dispersal, in Kulbak's *Zelmenyaners*, 80–81, 114; Jewish proponents of, 7; traditional way of life undermined by, in *Nanook of the North* (film), 102. *See also* industrialization, Soviet

Molotov-Ribbentrop Pact, 5

monarchists. *See* Whites

monastery: in Bergelson's *Judgment*, 20, 24, 39; chronotrope of, in Gothic texts, 24

Monk, The (Lewis), 22–23

montage, film technique of, 38; agitation trials compared to, 206; anxieties encoded in, 190; and destabilization of reality, 77–78; in *Earth* (film), 265; Eisenstein's use of, 78, 190, 191; in Kulbak's *Zelmenyaners*, 77, 78, 112, 113, 115, 121, 122; in *Return of Neitan Bekker, The* (film), 192–193; silent film and, 190, 191; sound film and challenges to, 191

Months and Days (Kipnis), 33, 34

Morphology of the Folktale (Propp), 160

Moscow State Yiddish Theater (GOSET), 148

"Mound, The" (Markish), 29–30

movie theater(s): in Kulbak's *Zelmenyaners, The*, 98, 103; in Minsk, 98, 99*f*, 102; Soviet, sound equipment in, 192

Murav, Harriet: on Babel's "Karl-Yankel," 326n91; on Bergelson's *Judgment*, 54–55; on Bergelson's textual strategies, 61, 151; on Bergelson's "Uphill," 151; on chain of calamities in Jewish history, 73; on Gekht's sketch about decaying shtetl, 138; on Gorenshtein's *Berdichev*, 276; on Jewish Bolshevik, figure of, 30; on Jewishness, assumptions about, 13; on Kipnis's *Months and Days*, 33; on *Return of Neitan Bekker, The* (film), 197, 212; on Russian-Yiddish linguistic interaction, 15

Muraviev, Nikolai, 140

Murnau, F. M., 24

music, Jewish, in film, 198–199, 208–209, 212, 213, 214–215. *See also niggun*
"My First Fee" (Babel), 229
"My First Goose" (Babel), 245–248, 324n62, 324n67
Mysteries of Udolpho, The (Radcliffe), 22–23

Naiman, Eric, 40
Nakhimovsky, Alice, 11, 12, 16
Nanook of the North (film), 98–102; Kulbak's *Zelmenyaners* compared to, 102–103
nationalities policy, Soviet, 16–17, 124, 306n6; and Jewish settlement in Birobidzhan, 124–125, 136, 158
"NEP Gothic," 40
neveyle (term), 47
New Economic Policy (NEP), 40, 60
New Homeland, The (Fink), 128
New Life (Novaia zhizn') (periodical), Babel as reporter for, 236, 240, 263
New Soviet Man, figure of, 178; Birobidzhan settlement and, 133; Bolshevik Revolution and, 7–8; in films about Jewish returnees, 177, 178, 212; First All-Union Congress of Soviet Writers on, 93; gender of, 178; Jewish Bolshevik as variant of, 10; scholarship on, 288n39; vs. shtetl Jew, in *Return of Neitan Bekker, The* (film), 177, 178, 187–189; Soviet Jew and, 8, 10, 76, 178; transformation of shtetl Jew into, Birobidzhan settlement and, 125; trickster evolving together with, 225
Niger, Shmuel, 304n114
niggun (Hasidic wordless melody): in *Border, The* (film), 201, 202; in *Return of Neitan Bekker, The* (film), 175, 198, 212; in *Seekers of Happiness* (film), 208–209
1919 (Kvitko), 34
non-arrival, and figure of Soviet Jew, 126, 128, 129, 133, 157, 158, 160, 166, 167, 275
Nordau, Max, 7
Nosferatu (film), 24

Oblomov (Goncharov), 106
ocherk (literary sketch), 131
October (film), 191
Odessa: Babel's literary sketches about, 235, 323n39; Bletnitsky brothers in, 229, 322n30; dissolution of Jewish community structures in, 1–2; Jewish cemetery in, 1, 2, 14; Pushkin's statue in, 269–270; reputation among Jews, 287n34; streets in, Babel on, 266–269
"Odessa" (Babel), 235, 237, 238, 239, 250, 255, 323n40; messianic dreams in, 235, 237, 268
Odessa Tales (Babel), 83, 218
Ogonëk (journal): Babel's "Di Grasso" in, 270; Fink's article in, 127, 307n15; Gekht's article in, 126–127, 144, 145f, 151; Petrov's travel sketch in, 170
Old and the New, The (film), 100
Old Dudino (film), 176. *See also Border, The* (film)
old Jew, figure of, 11; in Babel's "End of the Almshouse, The," 1–2, 10, 11, 19; in Kulbak's *Zelmenyaners, The*, 83–84, 87, 95–97; in *Seekers of Happiness* (film), 209
Olesha, Yuri, *Envy*, 83
Olgin, Moyshe, 193
omission(s): in Birobidzhan texts, 124, 151; in depictions of pogroms, 34–35; and figure of Soviet Jew, emergence of, 13; Hershele's strategy of, 246, 263; "strange" world of Bolshevik Revolution depicted through, 33
Organization for Jewish Colonization of Russia (IKOR): expedition to Birobidzhan (1929), 18, 123–124, 125, 126; study commissioned by, 123–124, 125, 129, 131
Ostap Bender (trickster figure), 168, 225
Ostropoler, Hershele (trickster figure). *See Hershele Ostropoler*
Ostrovsky, Nikolai, *How the Steel Was Tempered*, 89–90
Overcoat, The (film), 182
OZET (Society for the Settlement of Toiling Jews on the Land), 144, 157; children's division of, 157–158

Pale of Settlement, 2–3; Babel's observations on, 250–251; Birobidzhan compared to, 126, 129; criminalization of Jewish livelihoods in, 18, 60–64, 124; cross-border smuggling in, 41–42, 47–48, 58–61; as degenerate space, descriptions of, 7, 138; dispersal of Jewish communities of, 1–2, 4, 158; dissolution of, 3, 4, 59, 80; economic devastation after Bolshevik Revolution, 41–42, 58–59, 60; Gekht's sketches about, 138, 147; Jewish refugees from, in Berlin, 25–26; Minsk's identification with, 76, 299n4; physical destruction of, 29–30, 250–251;

Pale of Settlement (*continued*)
  post-World War I division of, 41–42;
  residence restrictions in, 2–3, 17; scattered
  cultural attributes of, 275, 278; shtetl's
  persistence after destruction of, 274–275;
  simultaneous revulsion and nostalgia
  regarding, 11–12; smell associated with
  Jewish residents of, as symbol of cultural
  preservation in Kulbak's *Zelmenyaners,* 75,
  76–77, 80, 106, 120, 121–122; traces of, in
  figure of Soviet Jew, 11–12, 275. *See also*
  pogroms; shtetl(s)
Palestine: in Gekht's *Ship Sails to Jaffa
  and Back,* 130, 134, 143–147, 151–154, 155;
  immigration of Eastern European Jews
  to, 3; Old Yishuv vs. New Yishuv in, 152;
  Soviet political discourses on, 134; Soviet
  texts about, in 1930s, 148–149; Zionist
  settlers in, appeal of Cossack image to, 137
Panopticon, 233
Paperny, Vladimir, 132
parallel editing, film technique of, 38
parody: in Kulbak's *Zelmenyaners,* 70–71,
  86, 104–105, 106, 108, 118–119, 122, 304n114.
  See also humor
Party Membership Card, The (film), 318n63
passport(s): in Russian Empire, notation of
  ethnoreligious origins in, 17; in Soviet
  Union, "fifth line"/"nationality" declaration
  in, 16, 17
Paul, Apostle, 258
peasants, Russian: after Bolshevik Revolution, 3; restrictions on residence of, 17
Peterson, Dale, 23
Petliura, Symon, 21; in Gekht's *Man Who
  Forgot His Life, The,* 27, 33; and White monarchists, equating in literary texts, 33, 36
Petrograd (Petersburg): Babel's journalistic
  work in, 234–236; demise after Bolshevik
  Revolution, Babel on, 234–239, 242; Jerusalem compared to, 237, 239, 242, 324n53;
  journey to, in Babel's "Road, The," 236–237,
  238
Petrov, Evgeny: on Jewish Autonomous
  Region in Birobidzhan, 170; *Little Golden
  Calf, The,* 168–171, 216; trickster figure in
  novels by, 168, 225
pogroms: accounts of, in 1920s, 25–30;
  allusions to, in early Soviet literature,
  30–33; armed formations responsible for,

equating in literary texts, 33–34; in
  Bergelson's *Judgment,* 20–21; Bergelson's
  Pomegranate essay on, 72–73; children's
  story hinting at, 160–161, 164, 165; Cossack
  17th-century uprisings and, 21, 27–29, 137,
  222–223; in Gekht's *Shoemaker's Son, A,*
  27–29, 28*f,* 32*f;* gendered nature of violence
  in, 281; internalization of violence of, 29;
  Jewish survivors of, in Berlin, 26; Kishinev,
  31; in Markish's "Mound, The," 29–30;
  myth of Judeo-Bolshevism and, 36–37;
  Red Army's role in, 22, 34, 36; during
  Russian civil war, 20–22, 25–30, 34–37;
  strange aspects of, literary texts about,
  33–36; threat of return of, in Bergelson's
  Judgment, 23, 25, 43, 49–50, 71–72; threat
  of return of, in Ehrenburg's "Ship Fare, A,"
  37; trauma of, and figure of Soviet Jew, 18,
  25, 26, 29, 33, 45, 73, 275; tsarist-era, 3, 31, 34
Poland: post-World War I borders and, 41–42;
  Soviet occupation of, 4–5. *See also*
  Bolshevik-Polish War of 1920
Polyanker, Hirsh (Grigorii), *Teacher from
  Medzhibozh, The,* 273–274
Pomegranate (Milgroym) (journal),
  Bergelson's essay in, 72–73
Portnoy's Complaint (Roth), 276
present: avoidance in Socialist Realism,
  129–130; erasure of, in writings about
  Birobidzhan, 129–130, 133
Presner, Todd, 15
Propp, Vladimir, *Morphology of the Folktale,*
  160
proste yidn (simple Jews), 77
Pudovkin, Vsevolod, 190, 191
purges, Stalin's, 276–277; Bergelson as victim
  of, 54; Dunets as victim of, 89; Kulbak as
  victim of, 78
Pushkin, Alexander, 266, 269; High Stalinism
  and status of, 270; statue in Odessa, 269–270
Pyr'iev, Ivan, 318n63

Radcliffe, Anne, *Mysteries of Udolpho,
  The,* 22–23
"Rebbe" (Babel), 244, 245, 248, 251–252,
  324n62, 324n67; implied Yiddish text
  in, 256–257
Red Army: anti-Jewish violence perpetrated
  by, 22, 36; anti-Jewish violence prevented
  by, 34; founder of, 36

Seidman, Naomi, 258
"Shabos-nakhamu" (Babel), 218–222, 224, 226; historical context and audience for, 233, 234, 235–236, 239; *Red Cavalry* stories compared to, 244–245; Russian language used to retell, and changes in meaning, 230–233; subtitle of, 270–272; Yiddish original of, 228–231, 230*f*, 232
Shakhty trial, 204–205, 206
"Shchepka" (Zazubrin), 49
Shell, Marc, 199
Sherman, Joseph, 55
shiluye (term), 87; Kulbak's protagonists as, 87, 88
Shimshen (rabbi of Ostropol), 223
"Ship Fare, A" (Ehrenburg), 34–37
Ship Sails to Jaffa and Back, A (Gekht), 18, 128, 130–131, 143–157; abrupt ending of, 155–156, 165; Birobidzhan plot in, 144, 146–147, 150, 151; as covert attempt to discuss Zionism, criticism of, 147–148, 149; hilltop conversation in, 150, 155; Palestine plot in, 147, 151, 152; protagonist of, 145–146, 151, 156–157; scholarship on, 147–149; Socialist Realism and, 145; substitution of Palestine for Birobidzhan in, 134, 143–147, 151–154, 155–157; time frame in, 131
Shklovsky, Viktor, 236, 239, 324n53
Shneer, David, 154, 277, 288n46
Shoemaker's Son, The (Gekht), 27–29, 28*f*, 32*f*
Sholem Aleichem, 83–84
show trial(s): Industrial Party, 204; Shakhty, 204–205, 206; shift from agitation trials to, 205–206; of Stalin era, circus arena associated with, 203–204; traces of, in *Return of Neitan Bekker, The* (film), 204, 205, 206
Shpis, Boris: and avant-garde film, 182, 183; and *Return of Neitan Bekker, The* (film), 173, 199, 214
Shrayer, Maxim D., 12, 13, 148
Shtern (journal), Kulbak's publications in, 82, 90–93
Shternshis, Anna, 211, 212, 289n51
shtetl(s), 4, 76; in Bergelson's *Judgment*, 20, 41–42, 59, 73; Birobidzhan as antithesis to, 162–163, 164, 165; collapse of, sketches about, 138; courtyard *(hoyf)* as microcosm of, 76, 105, 122; economic devastation of,

after Bolshevik Revolution, 41–42, 58–59, 60; ethnographic research on, 18, 105–106, 118; films depicting, 173–174, 176; in Gekht's *Shoemaker's Son, A*, 27; Gekht's sketches of, 138, 147; Old Yishuv compared to, 152; persistence after Pale's destruction, 274–275; physical destruction after Bolshevik Revolution, 29–30, 250–251; Sovietization of, 76, 118; and Soviet Jew, figure of, 178; storytelling and dissemination of culture of, 275
Siberia, Jewish settlement in, 4. *See also* Birobidzhan
Sicher, Efraim, 16, 266–267, 268, 269, 270, 320n3
Siegelbaum, Lewis, 135
Signifying Monkey, in Black American folklore, 226, 227–228, 248
silent film: circus associated with, 181; exaggerated gestures associated with, 189–190; montage used in, 190, 191; Soviet film industry's transition from, 189; transition to sound film from, 192, 196, 206; vestiges of, in *Return of Neitan Bekker, The*, 183, 192
Slezkine, Yuri, 3, 11, 77, 177, 269–270
Sloin, Andrew, 60
Slotnick, Susan, 53
smell, as symbol of persistent cultural characteristics, 75, 76–77, 80, 106, 120, 121–122
Smith, Adrien, 276
Smola, Klavdia, 288n46
Smugglers (Varshavsky), 59–60
smuggling: in Bergelson's *Judgment*, 20, 41–42, 47–48, 60–61; criminalization of trade as, 60; new state borders in former Pale of Settlement and, 20, 41–42, 58–60
Snyder, Timothy, 5
Sobol, Valeria, 23
Socialist Realism, 90, 144–145; future-oriented project of, 129–130, 132, 134; and Gekht's *Ship Sails to Jaffa and Back,* 145; Gorky's dictum about, 156; and Kulbak's *Zelmenyaners,* 91–96, 118–119; notion of "reality" in, 133; and *Return of Neitan Bekker, The* (film), 173, 183; and sacralizing space, 132, 133; and sound film, 191–192; and spontaneity-consciousness dialectic, 88, 107, 112; Zionist art and literature compared to, 153–154
Socialist Revolutionaries (SRs), 20; in Bergelson's *Judgment*, 20–21, 31, 43–44, 70, 71, 72; and violence against Jews, 20, 31

Society for the Settlement of Toiling Jews on the Land (OZET), 144, 157–158

Solzhenitsyn, Alexander, 158

Someone Else's Coat (film), 183

sound film: and challenges to montage technique, 191; early, 190–191, 196–197, 317n51; first Soviet, 196–197; and ideological messaging, 191, 192, 196–197, 206; preference for character-based plots, 192; *Return of Neitan Bekker* as early representative of, 189, 192–193, 195–196, 197, 199, 317n47; Socialist Realism and, 191–192; transition from silent film to, 192, 196, 206

Soviet Jew: doubt about Jewishness of, Western and Israeli Jews' expression of, 6; stories of, true inheritors of, 282; use of term, 5

Soviet Jew, figure of, 2; ambivalence associated with, 8, 172; anxieties shaping, 7, 22, 25, 38, 190, 192, 203, 216–217; Babel's Karl-Yankel as prototype of, 265–266; Cold War and, 5, 277; as collector of ethnographic and linguistic tidbits, 275; complexities of culture after Bolshevik Revolution and, 270; cultural prehistory of, 5–6; as cultural type, 11; defined by limits and possibilities of Soviet culture, 18; displaced cultural elements of Pale and, 275; evolution in Kulbak's *Zelmenyaners*, 76–77, 78, 79–80, 97, 112, 113, 114, 119, 120, 122; features revealed through contemporary texts, 18–19; "fifth line" in Soviet passport and, 16, 17; in film, 212–213; gender of, 6–7, 173, 281; indeterminacy of Soviet project and, 8, 17, 19, 192, 203; industrialization and, 114; vs. Jewish Bolshevik, 10; vs. Jewish elites in Soviet system, 77; "Jewish question" and, 169; vs. Judaic heritage, 12; marked by hidden difference, 6, 253, 259; marked by shtetl origin and foreign travel, 169, 211, 213; mobility of postrevolutionary era and, 3–4, 19, 135; as mockery of normative culture, 189; modernizing and preservationist tendencies in, 79–80, 102, 217; vs. New Soviet Man, 8, 10, 178; non-arrival as defining feature of, 126, 128, 129, 133, 157, 158, 160, 166, 167, 275; omission and emergence of, 13; as partially transformed figure, 217; rootlessness and migration defining, 132; Russian-Yiddish linguistic interaction and, 15–16; suspension of assumptions

about, 12–13; symbolic Christian prototypes and, 6; traces of Pale of Settlement in, 11–12, 275; traces of Wandering Jew in, 170–171, 178, 217; tragic history of, 277–282; trauma of pogrom violence and, 18, 25, 26, 29, 33, 45, 73, 275; trickster (Hershele) as cipher for, 19, 218, 226, 228, 234–235, 240, 247, 252, 253, 265, 271, 275; in Western imagination, 5, 6; World War II and growing suspicion of, 277

Soviet Union: "brotherhood of peoples" narrative in, 138, 253, 254, 259–261; enfranchisement of Jewish population in, 6–7; indeterminacy during early years of, 8, 17, 19, 192, 203; Jewish émigrés returning to, 4, 18–19; Jewish mobility within, 3–4, 19, 125, 135; nationalities policy of, 16–17, 124, 306n6; and Nazi Germany, secret nonaggression agreement between, 5; official opposition to antisemitism in, 4, 10–11, 18, 22, 36, 58. *See also* Bolshevik(s) / Bolshevik regime; construction; industrialization

speculation *(spekuliatsiia)*, crime of, 60; in Bergelson's *Judgment*, 64, 65

speech: progressive loss of, in Stalin-era cultural production, 194–196, 200–201, 203, 207, 210, 214; walking compared to, 233–234

spontaneity-consciousness dialectic, Socialist Realism and, 88, 107, 112

"Squadron Commander Trunov" (Babel), 57

Stalin, Joseph: consolidation of power by, 203; on cultural differences, 108; and disabled body, cultural representations of, 180–181; literature of era of, 86–87, 89; and Pushkin, status of, 270; speech on Soviet industrialization, 80. *See also* purges

Stormy Life of Lazik Roytshvants, The (Ehrenburg), 297n147

substitution(s): in Babel's imaginative geography, 255–256, 261; of less transgressive acts for violence, 245–246; of "merriment" for "horror," in Babel's work, 226, 241, 243–244, 249, 264; in texts about Birobidzhan settlement, 126–129, 133, 134–135, 143–147, 151–157; in world of Soviet utopia, 132–133. *See also* metaphor(s)

suicide: in Kulbak's *Zelmenyaners*, 108, 109–110; revolutionary hero and, literary texts on, 48–49, 51, 55–57; as societal concern in Soviet Union of 1930s, 109

urbanization, and Soviet Jews, 3, 4
USSR in Construction (publication), 169
Utkin, Iosif, "Tale of Red-Headed Motele, Mr. Inspector, Rabbi Isaiah, and Commissar Blokh, The," 31–33

Vainshtein, Mikhail, 147, 149
Varshavsky, Oyzer, 297n147; *Smugglers*, 59–60
Veidlinger, Jeffrey, 274
Venuti, Lawrence, 257, 259
Vertov, Dziga, 172, 190
Vilna: Jewish community in, 2; Kulbak in, 77; YIVO Institute in, 103
violence: antisemitic campaigns of late 1940s–early 1950s and, 277; substitution of less transgressive acts for, 245–246. *See also* pogroms

Wailing Wall, The (play), 148
walking: compared to speech, 233–234; trickster figure and, 228, 230–231, 232, 233
Walpole, Horace, *Castle of Otranto, The*, 40
wandering(s), Jewish: Birobidzhan as metaphor for end of, 126; in Gekht's *Ship Sails to Jaffa and Back, A*, 146; trickster figure and, 228, 230–231, 232, 233
Wandering Jew, figure of: in films about returning Jews, 178; in Gekht's *Shoemaker's Son*, 27–29; gender of, 6; in Gothic literature, 27–29, 216; in Il'f and Petrov's *Little Golden Calf*, 169, 170; instability of modernity reflected in, 216–217; legend about, 169; in *Seekers of Happiness* (film), 213, 215f, 216, 217; and Soviet Jew, 170–171, 178, 217
War Communism, 22, 40; charges of speculation during, 60
Week, A (Libedinskii), 44, 49
"What is Oblomovism?" (Dobroliubov), 106
"What Is to Be Done?" (Lenin), 87–88
Whites (monarchists): in Bergelson's *Judgment*, 70; as folkloric villain in children's books, 162; in Gekht's *Budler Family's Resettlement*, 160–162, 164–165; and Petliura's troops, equating in literary texts, 33, 36; refugees in Berlin, 26; and threat along Amur River border, 136, 164
Wiene, Robert, 24

Wilson, Woodrow, 171
Wisse, Ruth R., 15, 111, 112, 223
women: in Babel's "Karl-Yankel," 254–255, 259–260, 281; as co-creators of trickster's stories, 220, 231, 281; and "conversion" to Soviet ideology, in *Seekers of Happiness* (film), 211–212, 281; in Kulbak's *Zelmenyaners, The*, 83, 97–98, 108–110, 113, 281; as narrator in Khemlin's "About Zhenya," 281–282; role in literature about Soviet Jew, 281
Worker, The (Rabochii) (periodical): celebration of tramway in, 80; film listings and reviews in, 98, 100; Kulbak's article on translation of Yiddish literature in, 90
World War I, division of Pale of Settlement after, 41–42
World War II: Bolshevik Revolution replaced by, as foundational event of Soviet experience, 276; and displacement of Jews into Soviet interior, 5; growing suspicion of Soviet Jew after, 277; Soviet Jews during, novel about, 273–274
writers: role in legitimating Bolshevik regime, 242–243. *See also* First All-Union Congress of Soviet Writers; *specific writers*

Yiddish language: Babel's "Karl-Yankel" translated in, 267; dialectical variants of Russian shaped by, 276; as diasporic language, 15; and figure of Soviet Jew, 15–16; first Soviet sound film in, 189, 192–193; folktale in, Russian language used to retell and changes in meaning of, 230–233; implied text in, in Babel's writings, 256–257; persistence of, 275–276; Russian-Jewish literature in, 12, 13–14; in Shabos-nakhamu folktale, 230–231; in Soviet Belorussia, 82; Sovietizing Russian vocabulary and syntax and, 275; Soviet Jews and, 4; Soviet literature in, scholarship on, 15; state-level support for, in early Soviet era, 14; translation of Ostrovsky's *How the Steel Was Tempered* into, 89–90; as vernacular of Ashkenazi Jews, 14
YIVO Institute, 103
Youngblood, Denise, 191

Zamiatin, Evgeny, 236
Zazubrin, Vladimir, "Shchepka," 49